Principles of Equity

You are holding a reproduction of an original work that is in the public domain in the United States of America, and possibly other countries. You may freely copy and distribute this work as no entity (individual or corporate) has a copyright on the body of the work. This book may contain prior copyright references, and library stamps (as most of these works were scanned from library copies). These have been scanned and retained as part of the historical artifact.

This book may have occasional imperfections such as missing or blurred pages, poor pictures, errant marks, etc. that were either part of the original artifact, or were introduced by the scanning process. We believe this work is culturally important, and despite the imperfections, have elected to bring it back into print as part of our continuing commitment to the preservation of printed works worldwide. We appreciate your understanding of the imperfections in the preservation process, and hope you enjoy this valuable book.

PRINTED BY ALEX. LAWRIE & CO.

LETTER

TO

LORD MANSFIELD.

An author, not more illustrious by birth than by genius, says, in a letter concerning enthusiasm, " That he had so. much need of some considerable " presence or company to raise his thoughts on any " occasion, that, when alone, he endeavoured to sup- " ply that want, by fancying some great man of su- " perior genius, whose imagined presence might in- " spire him with more than what he felt at ordinary " hours." To judge from his Lordship's writings, this receipt must be a good one. It naturally ought to be so ; and I imagine that I have more than once felt its enlivening influence., With respect to the first edition of this Treatise, in particular, I can affirm with great truth, that *a great man of superior genius* was never out of my view ; will Lord. Mansfield relish this passage ?—How would he have expressed it ?— were my constant questions.

But though by this means I commanded more vi- gour of mind, and a keener exertion of thought, than I am capable of *at ordinary hours ;* yet I had not courage to mention this to his Lordship, nor to the world. The subject I had undertaken was new : I could not hope to avoid errors, perhaps gross ones; and the absurdity appeared glaring, of acknowledging a sort of inspiration in a performance that might not exhibit the least spark of it.

No trouble has been declined upon the present edition; and yet that the work, even in its improved state, deserves his Lordship's patronage, I am far from being confident. But however that be, it is no longer in my power to conceal, that the ambition of gaining Lord Mansfield's approbation, has been my chief support in this work. Never to reveal that secret, would be to border on ingratitude.

Will your Lordship permit me to subscribe myself, with heart-satisfaction,

Your zealous friend,

HENRY HOME.

August 1765.

PREFACE

TO THE SECOND EDITION.

An author who exerts his talents and industry upon a new subject, without hope of assistance from others, is apt to flatter himself; because he finds no other work of the kind to humble him by comparison. The attempt to digest equity into a regular system, was not only new, but difficult; and for these reasons, the author hopes he may be excused for not discovering more early several imperfections in the first edition of this book. These imperfections he the more regretted, because they concerned chiefly the arrangement, in which every mistake must be attended with some degree of obscurity. No labour has been spared to improve the present edition: and yet, after all his endeavours, the author dare not hope that every imperfection is cured: that the arrangement is considerably improved, is all that with assurance he can take upon him to say.

For an interim gratification of the reader's curiosity before entering upon the work, a few particulars shall here be mentioned. The defects of common law seemed to the author so distinct from its excesses, that he thought it proper to handle these articles separately. But almost as soon as the printing was finished, the author observed, that he had been obliged to handle the same subject in different parts of the book, or at least to refer from one part to another; which he holds to be an infallible mark of an unskilful distribution. This led him to reflect, that these defects and excesses proceed both of them equally from the very constitution of a court of common law, too limited in its power of doing justice; whence it appeared evident, that they ought to be handled promiscuously as so many examples of imperfection in common law,

vi PREFACE.

which ought to be supplied by a court of equity. This is so evident, that even in the same case we find common law sometimes defective, sometimes excessive, according to occasional or accidental circumstances, without any fundamental difference.* For example, many claims, good at common law, are reprobated in equity, because of some incidental wrong that comes not under the cognisance of common law. A claim of this kind must be sustained by a court of common law, which cannot regard the incidental wrong; and in such instances, common law is excessive, by transgressing the bounds of justice: On the other hand, where a claim for reparation is brought by the person who suffered the wrong, a court of common law can give no redress; and in such instances, common law is defective. And yet the *ratio decidendi* is precisely the same in both cases, namely, the limited power of a court of common law.

The transgression of a deed or covenant is a wrong that ought to be distinguished from a wrong that misleads a man to make a covenant or to grant a deed. The former only belongs to the chapter *Of Covenants;* the latter, to the chapter *Of the powers of a court of equity to protect individuals from injuries.* For example, a man is fraudulently induced to enter into a contract: the reparation of this wrong, which is antecedent to the contract, cannot arise from the contract; and for that reason, it is put under the chapter last mentioned.

PREFACE

TO THE THIRD EDITION.

An useful book ought not to be a costly book. To bring this edition within a moderate price, not only the size is smaller, but the preliminary discourse on the principles of morality is left out, being published more complete in *Sketches of the History of Man.* *

To mould the principles of equity into a regular system, was a bold undertaking. The pleasure of novelty gave it a lustre, and made every article appear to be in its proper place. The subject becoming more familiar in labouring upon a second edition, the many errors I discovered produced an arrangement differing considerably from the former. My satisfaction, however, in the new arrangement, was not entire: the errors I had fallen into produced a degree of diffidence, and a suspicion of more. And now, after an interval of no fewer than ten years, I find the suspicion but too well founded, chiefly with respect to the extensive chapter *Of Deeds and Covenants.* The many divisions and subdivisions of that chapter, I judged at the time to be necessary; but after pondering long and frequently upon them, I became sensible that they tend to darken rather than to enlighten the subject. That chapter is now divided into fewer and more distinct heads; which I expect will be found a considerable improvement. In an institute of law, or of any other science, the analysing it into its constituent parts, and the arranging every article properly, is of supreme importance. One could not conceive, without experience, how greatly accurate distribution contributes to clear conception. Before I was far advanced in the present edition, the many errors I found in the distribution surprised and vexed me. I have be-

---

* This new edition, in *one* volume, is printed verbatim from the third edition in two volumes.

viii   PREFACE.

stowed much pains in correcting these errors; and yet I will not
answer that there are none left. Many escaped me before; and
some may again escape me. No work of man is perfect: it is
good, however, to be on the mending hand; and in every new
attempt, to approach nearer and nearer to perfection. To compile
a body of law, the parts intimately connected and every link hang-
ing on a former, requires the utmost effort of the human genius.
Have I not reason to think so, considering how imperfect in that
respect the far greater part of law-books are; witness in particular
the famous body of Roman law compiled under the auspices of
the emperor Justinian, remarkable even among law-books for defective arrangement? Let the candid reader keep this in view,
and he will be indulgent to the errors of arrangement in this edition, if, after my utmost application, any remain.

But imperfect arrangement in the former editions, is not the
only thing that requires an apology. Frequent and serious reflection on a favourite subject, have unfolded to me several errors,
still more material, as they concern the reasoning branch of my
subject. These I blush for; and yet, to acknowledge an erroneous opinion, sits lighter on my mind than to persevere in it.

CONTENTS.

	Page.
INTRODUCTION, - - -	1

BOOK I.

Powers of a court of equity derived from the principle of justice, — 27

PART I. Powers of a court of equity to remedy the imperfections of common law with respect to pecuniary interest, by supplying what is defective, and correcting what is wrong, - - - 28

CHAP. I. Powers of a court of equity to remedy what is imperfect in common law with respect to the protecting individuals from harm, - - ib.

SECT.

1. Harm done by a man in exercising a right or privilege, - - - . 29

2. Harm done by one who has it not in view to exercise any right or privilege, - - - 39

3. A man tempted or overawed by undue influence to act knowingly against his interest, - - 43

Art.

1. Where a man, yielding to a temptation, acts knowingly against his interest, - - ib.

CONTENTS.

Page.

2. Where a man is overawed to act knowingly against
his interest,   45

4. A man moved to act unknowingly against his interest, by fraud, deceit, or other artificial means,   56

5. What remedy is applied by a court of equity against
the wrongs above stated,   62

CHAP. II. Powers of a court of equity to remedy what
is imperfect in common law, with respect to protecting the weak of mind from harming themselves
by unequal bargains and irrational deeds,   66

CHAP. III. Powers of a court of equity to remedy what
is imperfect in common law, with respect to the
natural duty of benevolence,   70

SECT.

1. Connections that make benevolence a duty when not
prejudicial to our interest,   74

2. Connections that make benevolence a duty even against
our interest,   89

Art.

1. Connections that entitle a man to have his loss made
up out of my gain,   ib.

2. Connections that entitle a man who is not a loser to
partake of my gain,   109

3. Connections that entitle one who is a loser to be indemnified by one who is not a gainer,   117

CHAP. IV. Powers of a court of equity to remedy what
is imperfect in common law with respect to deeds
and covenants,   126

SECT.

1. Where will is imperfectly expressed in the writing, 132

Art.

1. Where the words leave us uncertain about will,   133
2. Where the words are short of will,   139
3. Where the words go beyond will,   144
2. Implied will,   154

CONTENTS. xi

	Page
3. Whether an omission in a deed or covenant can be supplied, - - -	158
4. A deed or covenant that tends not to bring about the end for which it was made, - -	168
5. Equity with respect to a deed providing for an event that now can never happen, -	177
6. Errors in deeds and covenants, - -	179
7. A deed or covenant being void at common law as *ultra vires,* can a court of equity afford any relief?	201
8. Where there is a failure in performance, -	208
9. Indirect means employed to evade performance,	219

CHAP. V. Powers of a court of equity to remedy what is imperfect in common law with respect to statutes, 220

SECT.

1. Where the will of the legislature is not justly expressed in the statute, - -	235

Art.

1. Where the words are ambiguous, -	236
2. Where the words fall short of will, -	237
3. Where the words go beyond will, -	ib.

SECT.

2. Where the means enacted fall short of the end purposed by the legislature, - - -	239
3. Where the means enacted reach unwarily beyond the end purposed by the legislature, -	250

CHAP. VI. Powers of a court of equity to remedy what is imperfect in common law with respect to matters between debtor and creditor, - - 257

SECT.

1. Injustice of common law with respect to compensation,	ib.
2. Injustice of common law with respect to indefinite payment, - - - - -	265
3. Injustice of common law with respect to rent levied indefinitely, - - - -	272

CHAP. VII. Powers of a court of equity to remedy what

CONTENTS.

	Page
is defective in common law with respect to a process, - - - - -	277

Chap. VIII. Powers of a court of equity to remedy what is imperfect in common law with respect to legal execution, - - - - - 280

Sect.
1. Where the common law is defective, ib.
    Art.
    1. Subjects that cannot be attached by the executions of common law, - - - 281
    2. Circumstances where even common subjects are withdrawn from these executions, - 282
    3. These executions are in some cases imperfect, 286
    4. They serve only to make debts effectual, and give no aid to other claims, - - 287

Sect.
2. Where the common law with respect to execution is oppressive or unjust, - - - 289
    Appendix to Chapter VIII. - - 296

Chap. IX. Powers of a court of equity to inflict punishment, and to mitigate it, - - 302

PART II. Powers of a court of equity to remedy the imperfection of common law with respect to matters of justice that are not pecuniary, 315

Chap. I. How far a covenant or promise in favour of an absent person, is effectual, - - 316

Chap. II. Powers of a court of equity to repress immoral acts that are not pecuniary, - 331

BOOK II.

Powers of a court of equity founded on the principle of utility, - 333

CONTENTS. xiii

Page

CHAP. I. Acts in themselves lawful reprobated in equity as having a tendency to corrupt morals, - 334

CHAP. II. Acts and covenants in themselves innocent prohibited in equity, because of their tendency to disturb society, and to distress its members, 336

CHAP. III. Regulations of commerce and of other public concerns, rectified where wrong, - 341

CHAP. IV. Forms of the common law dispensed with in order to abridge law-suits, - - 344

CHAP. V. *Bona fides* as far as regulated by utility, 347

CHAP. VI. Interposition of a court of equity in favour even of a single person, to prevent mischief, 353

CHAP. VII. Statutes preventive of wrong or mischief, extended by a court of equity, - - 354

CONCLUSION of BOOK II. Justice and Utility compared, 361

BOOK III.

Application of the principles of equity and utility to several important subjects, - - - 367

CHAP. I. What equity rules with respect to rents levied upon an erroneous title of property, - 368

CHAP. II. Powers of a court of equity with respect to a conventional penalty, - ; 378

CHAP. III. What obligations and legacies transmit to heirs, - - - 384

CHAP. IV. Arrestment and process of forthcoming, 389

CHAP. V. Powers of a court of equity with relation to bankrupts, - - - 405

CHAP. VI. Powers and faculties, - - 451

xiv

CONTENTS.

Page.

CHAP. VII. Of the power which officers of the law have to act *extra territorium*, - - 473

CHAP. VIII. Jurisdiction of the Court of Session with respect to foreign matters, - - 480

SECT.

1. Personal actions founded on foreign covenants, deeds, or facts, - - - 487
2. Foreign covenants and deeds respecting land, - 492
3. Moveables, domestic and foreign, and their legal effects, 495
4. Debts, whether regulated by the law of the creditor's country, or that of the debtor, - - 501
5. Foreign evidence, - - · 505
6. Effect of a statute, of a decree, of a judicial conveyance, or legal execution, *extra territorium*, - 508

EXPLANATION of some SCOTCH LAW TERMS
used in this Work.

Adjudication, is a judicial conveyance of the debtor's
land for the creditor's security and payment. It
corresponds to the English *Elegit*.

Arrestment, defined, book 3, chap. 4.

Cautioner, a surety for a debt.

Cedent, assignor.

Contravention. An act of contravention signifies the
breaking through any restraint imposed by deed,
by covenant, or by a court.

Decree of forthcoming, defined, book 3, chap. 4.

Fiar, he that has the fee or feu; and the proprietor
is termed *fiar*, in contradistinction to the liferenter.

Gratuitous, *see* Voluntary.

Heritor, a proprietor of land.

Inhibition, defined, book 3, chap. 4.

Lesion, loss, damage.

Pursuer, plaintiff.

Propone. To propone a defence, is to state or move
a defence.

Reduction, is a process for voiding or setting aside
any consensual or judicial right.

Tercer, a widow that possesses the third part of her
husband's land as her legal jointure.

xvi EXPLANATION OF SCOTCH LAW TERMS.

Voluntary, in the law of Scotland bears its proper sense as opposed to involuntary. A deed in the English law is said to be voluntary when it is granted without a valuable consideration. In this sense it is the same with *gratuitous* in our law.

Wadset, answers to a mortgage in the English law. A proper wadset is where the creditor in possession of the land takes the rents in place of the interest of the sum lent. An improper wadset is where the rents are applied for payment, first of the interest, and next of the capital.

Writer, scrivener.

PRINCIPLES

FOUNDED ON IN THIS WORK.

A man who is innocent is not liable to repair any hurt done by him.

Where there is a right, some court must be empowered to make it effectual.

For every wrong there ought to be a remedy.

No interest of mine, not even the preservation of life itself, authorises me to do any mischief to an innocent person.

Every man may prosecute his own right, without regarding any indirect or consequential damage that another may suffer.

Justice will not permit a man to exercise his right where his intention is solely to hurt another.

An action at law will not be sustained if the plaintiff cannot show that it will benefit him.

It is an immoral act, to strip people of their property by throwing a strong temptation in their way.

He that demands equity must give equity.

Equity holds a deed to be granted where it ought to be granted.

One is permitted to take advantage of another's error *in damno evitando*, not *in lucro captando*.

No man is entitled to the aid of a court of equity when that aid becomes necessary by his own fault.

No person, however innocent, ought to take advantage of a tortious act by which another is hurt.

A man ought not to take advantage of an improvement or reparation made upon a common subject, without refunding part of the expence, in proportion to the benefit he has received.

A thought retained within the mind cannot have the effect to qualify an obligation more than to create it.

PRINCIPLES.

To bind a man by words beyond consent, is repugnant to justice.

He who wills the end is understood to will the means proper for accomplishing the end.

A person honoured in a deed can take no benefit by it, if he counteract the declared will of the granter.

A man who has committed no fault, cannot be deprived of his property.

No person is bound to fulfil an obligation that answers not the end purposed by it.

Cujus commodum ejus debet esse incommodum.

Every crime against the law of nature may be punished at the discretion of the judge, where the legislature has not appointed a particular punishment.

A case out of the mischief, is out of the meaning, of the law, though it be within the letter.

No man is permitted to take advantage of a defect in evidence when that defect is occasioned by his fraud.

Potior debet esse conditio ejus qui certat de damno evitando, quam ejus qui certat de lucro captando.

It is unjust to demand from the debtor privately, or even by legal execution, any subject that he is bound to convey to another.

No man is suffered to take benefit by his own fraud or wrong.

No person is suffered to make a defence contrary to conscience, more than to make a claim.

Frustra petis quod mox es restituturus.

The motive of preventing loss will not justify an unjust act, or the being accessory to it.

PRINTED BY ALEX. LAWRIE & CO.

INTRODUCTION.

EQUITY, scarce known to our forefathers, makes at present a great figure. It has, like a plant, been tending to maturity, slowly indeed, but constantly; and at what distance of time it shall arrive at perfection, is perhaps not easy to foretell. Courts of equity have already acquired such an extent of jurisdiction, as to obscure, in a great measure, courts of law. A revolution so signal, will move every curious enquirer to attempt, or to wish at least, a discovery of the cause. But vain will be the attempt, till first a clear idea be formed of the difference between a court of law and a court of equity. The former, we know, follows precise rules: but does the latter act by conscience solely, without any rule? This would be unsafe while men are the judges, liable no less to partiality than to error: nor could a court without rules ever have attained that height of favour, and extent of jurisdiction, which courts of equity enjoy. But if a court of equity be governed by rules, why are not these brought to light in a system? One would imagine, that such a system should not be useful only, but necessary; and yet writers, far from aiming at a system, have not even defined with any accuracy what equity is, nor what are its limits and extent. One operation of equity, universally acknowledged, is, to remedy imperfections in the common law, which sometimes is

2 INTRODUCTION.

defective, and sometimes exceeds just bounds; and as equity is constantly opposed to common law, a just idea of the latter may probably lead to the former. In order to ascertain what is meant by common law, a historical deduction is necessary; which I the more chearfully undertake, because the subject seems not to be put in a clear light by any writer.

After states were formed, and government established, courts of law were invented, to compel individuals to do their duty. This innovation, as commonly happens, was at first confined within narrow bounds. To these courts power was given to enforce duties essential to the existence of society; such as that of forbearing to do harm or mischief. Power was also given, to enforce duties derived from covenants and promises, such of them at least as tend more peculiarly to the well-being of society: which was an improvement so great, as to leave no thought of proceeding farther; for to extend the authority of a court to natural duties of every sort, would, in a new experiment, have been reckoned too bold. Thus, among the Romans, many pactions were left upon conscience, without receiving any aid from courts of law: buying and selling only, with a few other covenants essential to commercial dealing, were regarded. Our courts of law in Britain were originally confined within still narrower bounds: no covenant whatever was by our forefathers countenanced with an action: a contract of buying and selling was not *; and as buying and selling is of all covenants the most useful in ordinary life, we are not at liberty to suppose that any other was more privileged †.

* Reg. Mag. lib. 3, cap. 10. Fleta, lib. 2, cap. 58, § 3, and 5.
† See Historical Law-tracts, tract 2.

INTRODUCTION.

But when the great advantages of a court of law were experienced, its jurisdiction was gradually extended, with universal approbation: it was extended, with very few exceptions, to every covenant and every promise: it was extended also to other matters, till it embraced every obvious duty arising in ordinary dealings between man and man. But it was extended no farther; experience having discovered limits, beyond which it was deemed hazardous to stretch this jurisdiction. Causes of an extraordinary nature, requiring some singular remedy, could not be safely trusted with the ordinary courts, because no rules were established to direct their proceedings in such matters; and, upon that account, such causes were appropriated to the king and council, being the paramount court (a). Of this nature were actions for proving the tenor or contents of a lost writ; extraordinary removings against tenants possessing by lease; the causes of pupils, orphans, and foreigners; complaints against judges and officers of law*, and the more atrocious crimes, termed, *Pleas of the Crown.* Such extraordinary causes, multiplying greatly by complex and intricate connections among individuals, became a burden too great for the king and council. In order, therefore, to relieve this court, extraordinary causes of a civil nature were, in England, devolved upon the court of chancery; a measure the

(a) We find the same regulation among the Jews: " And " Moses chose able men out of all Israel, and made them heads " over the people, rulers of thousands, rulers of hundreds, rulers " of fifties, and rulers of tens. And they judged the people at all " seasons: the hard causes they brought unto Moses, but every " small matter they judged themselves." *Exodus,* xviii, 25, 26.

* See act 105, parl. 1487.

A 2

INTRODUCTION.

more necessary, that the king, occupied with the momentous affairs of government, and with foreign as well as domestic transactions, had not leisure for private causes. In Scotland, more remote, and therefore less interested in foreign affairs, there was not the same necessity for this innovation: our kings, however, addicted to action more than to contemplation, neglected, in a great measure, their privilege of being judges, and suffered causes peculiar to the king and council to be gradually assumed by other sovereign courts. The establishment of the court of chancery in England, made it necessary to give a name to the more ordinary branch of law, that is, the province of the common or ordinary courts; it is termed, *the Common Law:* and in opposition to it, the extraordinary branch devolved on the court of chancery is termed *Equity;* the name being derived from the nature of the jurisdiction, directed less by precise rules, than *secundum æquum et bonum*, or according to what the judge in conscience thinks right (*a*). Thus equity, in its proper sense, comprehends every matter of law that, by the common law, is left without remedy; and supposing the boundaries of the common law to be ascertained, there can no longer remain any difficulty about the powers of a court of equity. But as these boundaries are not ascertained by any natural rule, the jurisdiction of common law must depend in a great measure upon accident and

(*a*) At curiæ sunto et jurisdictiones, quæ statuant ex arbitrio boni viri et discretione sana, ubi legis norma deficit. Lex enim non sufficit casibus, sed ad ea quæ plerumque accidunt aptatur: sapientissima autem res tempus, (ut ab antiquis dictum est), et novorum casuum quotidie author et inventor. *Bacon de Aug. Scien. lib.* 8, *cap.* 3, *aphor.* 32.

INTRODUCTION. 5

arbitrary practice; and, accordingly, the boundaries of common law and equity vary in different countries, and at different times in the same country. We have seen, that the common law of Britain was originally not so extensive as at present; and instances will be mentioned afterward, which evince, that the common law is in Scotland farther extended than in England. Its limits are perhaps not accurately ascertained in any country; which is to be regretted, because of the uncertainty that must follow in the practice of law. It is lucky, however, that the disease is not incurable: a good understanding between the judges of the different courts, with just notions of law, may, in time, ascertain these limits with sufficient accuracy.

Among a plain people, strangers to refinement and subtilities, law-suits may be frequent, but never are intricate. Regulations to restrain individuals from doing mischief, and to enforce performance of covenants, composed originally the bulk of the common law; and these two branches, among our rude ancestors, seemed to comprehend every subject of law. The more refined duties of morality were, in that early period, little felt, and less regarded. But law, in this simple form, cannot long continue stationary: for, in the social state, under regular discipline, law ripens gradually with the human faculties; and by ripeness of discernment, and delicacy of sentiment, many duties, formerly neglected, are found to be binding in conscience. Such duties can no longer be neglected by courts of justice; and as they made no part of the common law, they come naturally under the jurisdiction of a court of equity.

The chief objects of benevolence, considered as a

INTRODUCTION.

duty, are our relations, our benefactors, our masters, our servants, &c. ; and these duties, or the most obvious of them, come under the cognisance of common law. But there are other connections, which, though more transitory, produce a sense of duty. Two persons shut up in the same prison, though no way connected but by contiguity and resemblance of condition, are sensible, however, that to aid and comfort each other is a duty incumbent on them. Two persons, shipwrecked upon the same desert island, are sensible of the like mutual duty. And there is even some sense of this kind, among a number of persons in the same ship, or under the same military command.

Thus mutual duties among individuals multiply by variety of connections ; and in the progress of society, benevolence becomes a matter of conscience in a thousand instances, formerly disregarded. The duties that arise from connections so slender, are taken under the jurisdiction of a court of equity ; which, at first, exercises its jurisdiction with great reserve, interposing in remarkable cases only, where the duty is palpable. But, gathering courage from success, it ventures to enforce this duty in more delicate circumstances : one case throws light upon another : men, by the reasoning of the judges, become gradually more acute in discerning their duty : the judges become more and more acute in distinguishing cases ; and this branch of law is imperceptibly moulded into a system. (a) In rude ages, acts of benevolence, however

(a) At curiæ illæ uni viro ne committantur, sed ex pluribus constent. Nec decreta exeant cum silentio : sed judices sententiæ suæ rationes adducant, idque palam, atque adstante corona ; ut

INTRODUCTION.

peculiar the connection may be, are but faintly perceived to be our duty : such perceptions become gradually more firm and clear by custom and reflection ; and when men are so far enlightened, it is the duty as well as honour of judges to interpose*.

This branch of equitable jurisdiction shall be illustrated by various examples. When goods by labour, and perhaps with danger, are recovered from the sea after a shipwreck, every one perceives it to be the duty of the proprietor to pay salvage. A man ventures his life to save a house from fire, and is successful ; no mortal can doubt that he is entitled to a recompence from the proprietor, who is benefited. If a man's affairs by his absence be in disorder, ought not the friend who undertakes the management to be kept *indemnis*, though the subject upon which his money was usefully bestowed, may have afterward perished casually ? Who can doubt of the following proposition, That I am in the wrong to demand money from my debtor, while I withhold the sum I owe him, which, perhaps, may be his only resource for doing me justice ? Such a proceeding must, in the common sense of mankind, appear partial and oppressive. By the common law, however, no remedy is afforded in this case, nor in the others mentioned. But equity affords a remedy, by enforcing what in such circumstances every man perceives to be his duty. I shall add but one example more : in a violent storm, the heaviest goods are thrown overboard, in order to disburden the ship : the proprietors of

quod ipsa potestate sit liberum, fama tamen et existimatione sit circumscriptum. *Bacon de Aug. Scient. lib. 8, cap. 3, aphor. 38.*

* See Essays on Morality and Natural Religion, Second Edition, p. 106.

8 INTRODUCTION.

the goods, preserved by this means from the sea, must be sensible that it is their duty to repair the loss ; for the man who has thus abandoned his goods for the common safety, ought to be in no worse condition than themselves. Equity dictates this to be their duty; and if they be refractory, a court of equity will interpose in behalf of the sufferer.

It appears now clearly, that a court of equity commences at the limits of the common law, and enforces benevolence where the law of nature makes it our duty. And thus, a court of equity, accompanying the law of nature in its gradual refinements, enforces every natural duty that is not provided for at common law.

The duties hitherto mentioned, arise from connections independent altogether of consent. Covenants and promises also, are the source of various duties. The most obvious of these duties, being commonly declared in words, belong to common law. But every incident that can possibly occur in fulfilling a covenant, is seldom foreseen ; and yet a court of common law, in giving judgment upon covenants, considers nothing but declared will, neglecting incidents that would have been provided for, had they been foreseen, Further, the inductive motive for making a covenant, and its ultimate purpose and intendment, are circumstances disregarded at common law : these, however, are capital circumstances ; and justice, where they are neglected, cannot be fulfilled. Hence the powers of a court of equity, with respect to engagements. It supplies imperfections in common law, by taking under consideration every material circumstance, in order that justice may be distributed in the most perfect manner. It supplies a de-

.INTRODUCTION. 9

.fect in words, where will is evidently more extensive: it rejects words that unwarily go beyond will ; and it gives aid to will where it happens to be obscurely or imperfectly expressed. By taking such liberty, a covenant is made effectual, according to the aim and purpose of the contractors ; and without such liberty, seldom it happens that justice can be accurately distributed.

In handling this branch of the subject, it is not easy to suppress a thought that comes cross the mind. The jurisdiction of a court of common law, with respect to covenants, appears to me odd and unaccountable. To find the jurisdiction of this court limited, as above mentioned, to certain duties of the law of nature, without comprehending the whole, is not singular nor anomalous. But with respect to the circumstances that occur in the same cause, it cannot fail to appear singular, that a court should be confined to a few of these circumstances, neglecting others no less material in point of justice. This reflection will be set in a clear light by a single example. Every one knows, that an English double bond was a contrivance to evade the old law of this island, which prohibited the taking interest for money ; the professed purpose of this bond is, to provide for interest and costs, beyond which the penal part ought not to be exacted ; and yet a court of common law, confined strictly to the words or declared will, is necessitated knowingly to commit injustice. The moment the term of payment is past, when there cannot be either costs or interest, this court, instead of pronouncing sentence for what is really due, namely, the sum borrowed, must follow the words of the bond, and give judgment for the double. This defect in the consti-

INTRODUCTION.

tution of a court, is too remarkable to have been overlooked: a remedy, accordingly, is provided, though far from being of the most perfect kind; and that is, a privilege to apply to the court of equity for redress. Far better had it been, either to withdraw covenants altogether from the common law, or to empower the judges of that law to determine according to the principles of justice. (a) I need scarce observe, that the present reflection regards England only, where equity and common law are appropriated to different courts. In Scotland, and other countries where both belong to the same court, the inconvenience mentioned cannot happen.——But to return to the gradual extension of equity, which is our present theme:

A court of equity, by long and various practice, finding its own strength and utility, and impelled by the principle of justice, boldly undertakes a matter still more arduous; and that is, to correct or mitigate the rigour, and what even in a proper sense may be termed, the *injustice* of common law. It is not in human foresight to establish any general rule, that, however salutary in the main, may not be oppressive and unjust in its application to some singular cases. Every work of man must partake of the imperfection of its author; sometimes falling short of its purpose, and sometimes going beyond it. If, with respect to the former, a court of equity be useful, it may be pronounced necessary with respect to the latter; for, in society, it is certainly a greater object to prevent legal oppression, which alarms every individual, than to supply legal defects, scarce regarded but

(a) And accordingly, by 4° Annæ, cap. 16, sect. 13, the defendant, pending action on a double bond, offering payment of principal, interest, and costs, shall be discharged by the court.

INTRODUCTION. 11

by those immediately concerned. The illustrious Bacon, upon this subject, expresses himself with great propriety:—" Habeant curiæ prætoriæ potestatem " tam subveniendi contra rigorem legis, quam sup-" plendi defectum legis. Si enim porregi debet re-" medium ei quem lex præteriit, multo magis ei -" quem vulneravit." *

All the variety of matter hitherto mentioned is regulated by the principle of justice solely. It may, at first view, be thought, that this takes in the whole compass of law, and that there is no remaining field to be occupied by a court of equity. But, upon more narrow inspection, we find a number of law-cases into which justice enters not, but only utility. Expediency requires that these be brought under the cognisance of a court; and the court of equity, gaining daily more weight and authority, takes naturally such matters under its jurisdiction. I shall give a few examples. A lavish man submits to have his son made his interdictor: this agreement is not unjust; but, tending to the corruption of manners, by reversing the order of nature, it is reprobated by a court of equity, as *contra bonos mores*. This court goes farther: it discountenances many things in themselves indifferent, merely because of their bad tendency. A *pactum de quota litis* is in itself innocent, and may be beneficial to the client as well as to the advocate: but to remove the temptation that advocates are under to take advantage of their clients instead of serving them faithfully, this court declares against such pactions. A court of equity goes still farther, by consulting the public interest with relation

* De Aug. Scient. lib. 8, cap. 3, aphor. 45.

INTRODUCTION.

to matters not otherwise bad, but by occasioning unnecessary trouble and vexation to individuals. Hence the origin of regulations tending to abridge lawsuits.

A mischief that affects the whole community, figures in the imagination, and naturally moves judges to stretch out a preventive hand. But what shall we say of a mischief that affects one person only, or but a few ? An estate, for example, real or personal, is left entirely without management, by the infancy of the proprietor, or by his absence in a remote country : he has no friends, or they are unwilling to interpose. It is natural, in this case, to apply for public authority. A court of common law, confined within certain precise limits, can give no aid ; and, therefore, it is necessary that a court of equity should undertake cases of this kind ; and the preventive remedy is easy, by naming an administrator, or, as termed in the Roman law, *curator bonorum*. A similar example is, where a court of equity gives authority to sell the land of one under age, where the sale is necessary for payment of debt : to decline interposing, would be ruinous to the proprietor ; for, without authority of the court, no man will venture to purchase from one under age. Here the motive is humanity to a single individual ; but it would be an imperfection in law, to abandon an innocent person to ruin, when the remedy is so easy. In the cases governed by the motive of public utility, a court of equity interposes as a court properly, giving or denying action, in order to answer the end purposed ; but in the cases now mentioned, and in others similar, there is seldom occasion for a process ; the court acts by magisterial powers.

The powers above set forth assumed by our courts

INTRODUCTION. 13

of equity, are, in effect, the same that were assumed by the Roman Prætor, from necessity, without any express authority.—" Jus prætorium est quod prae-" tores introduxerunt, adjuvandi vel supplendi vel " corrigendi juris Civilis gratia, propter utilitatem " publicam."*

Having given a historical view of a court of equity, from its origin to its present extent of power and jurisdiction, I proceed to some other matters, which must be premised before entering into particulars. The first I shall insist on, is of the greatest moment, namely, Whether a court of equity be, or ought to be, governed by any general rules? To determine every particular case, according to what is just, equal, and salutary, taking in all circumstances, is undoubtedly the idea of a court of equity in its perfection ; and had we angels for judges, such would be their method of proceeding, without regarding any rules,—but men are liable to prejudice and error, and for that reason, cannot safely be trusted with unlimited powers. Hence, the necessity of establishing rules, to preserve uniformity of judgment in matters of equity as well as of common law,—the necessity is perhaps greater in the former, because of the variety and intricacy of equitable circumstances. Thus, though a particular case may require the interposition of equity to correct a wrong or supply a defect ; yet the judge ought not to interpose, unless he can found his decree upon some rule that is equally applicable to all cases of the kind. If he be under no limitation, his decrees will appear arbitrary, though substantially just,—and, which is worse, will often be arbitrary, and substantially unjust ; for such, too frequently, are human

* L. 7, § 1, De justitia et jure.

INTRODUCTION.

proceedings when subjected to no control. General rules, it is true, must often produce decrees that are materially unjust; for no rule can be equally just in its application to a whole class of cases that are far from being the same in every circumstance,—but this inconvenience must be tolerated, to avoid a greater, that of making judges arbitrary. A court of equity is a happy invention, to remedy the errors of common law,—but this remedy must stop somewhere; for courts cannot be established without end, to be checks one upon another. And hence it is, that, in the nature of things, there cannot be any other check upon a court of equity but general rules. Bacon expresses himself upon this subject with his usual elegance and perspicuity.—" Non sine causa in usum venerat apud " Romanos album prætoris, in quo præscripsit et " publicavit quomodo ipse jus dicturus esset. Quo " exemplo judices in curiis prætoriis, regulas sibi " certas (quantum fieri potest) proponere, easque " publice affigere, debent. Etenim optima est lex, " quæ minimum relinquit arbitrio judicis, optimus " judex qui minimum sibi."*

In perusing the following treatise, it will be discovered, that the connections regarded by a court of equity seldom arise from personal circumstances, such as birth, resemblance of condition, or even blood, but generally from subjects that in common language are denominated *goods*. Why should a court, actuated by the spirit of refined justice, overlook more substantial ties, to apply itself solely to the grosser connections of interest? doth any connection founded on property make an impression equally strong with that of friendship, or blood-relation, or of country? doth

* De aug. scient. 1. 8. cap. 8. aph. 46.

INTRODUCTION. 15

not the law of nature form duties on the latter, more binding in conscience than on the former? Yet the more conscientious duties are left commonly to shift for themselves, while the duties founded on interest are supported and enforced by courts of equity. This, at first view, looks like a prevailing attachment to riches; but it is not so in reality. The duties arising from the connection last mentioned, are commonly ascertained and circumscribed, so as to be susceptible of a general rule to govern all cases of the kind. This is seldom the case of the other natural duties; which, for that reason, must be left upon conscience, without receiving any aid from a court of equity. There are, for example, not many duties more firmly rooted in our nature than that of charity; and, upon that account, a court of equity will naturally be tempted to interpose in its behalf. But the extent of this duty depends on such a variety of circumstances, that the wisest heads would in vain labour to bring it under general rules: to trust, therefore, with any court, a power to direct the charity of individuals, is a remedy which to society would be more hurtful than the disease; for, instead of enforcing this duty in any regular manner, it would open a wide door to legal tyranny and oppression. Viewing the matter in this light, it will appear, that such duties are left upon conscience, not from neglect or insensibility, but from the difficulty of a proper remedy. And when such duties can be brought under a general rule, I except not even gratitude, though in the main little susceptible of circumscription, we shall see afterward, that a court of equity declines not to interpose.

In this work will be found several instances where equity and utility are in opposition; and when that

16 INTRODUCTION.

happens, the question is, Which of them ought to prevail? Equity, when it regards the interest of a few individuals only, ought to yield to utility when it regards the whole society. It is for that very reason, that a court of equity is bound to form its decrees upon general rules; for this measure regards the whole society, by preventing arbitrary proceedings.

It is commonly observed, that equitable rights are less steady and permanent than those of common law: the reason will appear from what follows. A right is permanent or fluctuating, according to the circumstances upon which it is founded. The circumstances that found a right at common law, being always few and weighty, are not variable: a bond of borrowed money, for example, must subsist till it be paid. A claim in equity, on the contrary, seldom arises without a multiplicity of circumstances; which make it less permanent, for if but a single circumstance be withdrawn, the claim is gone. Suppose, for example, that an infeftment of annualrent is assigned to a creditor for his security: the creditor ought to draw his payment out of the interest before touching the capital; which is an equitable rule, because it is favourable to the assignor or cedent, without hurting the assignee. But if the cedent have another creditor who arrests the interest, the equitable rule now mentioned ceases, and gives place to another; which is, that the assignee ought to draw his payment out of the capital, leaving the interest to be drawn by the arrester. Let us next suppose, that the cedent hath a third creditor, who after the arrestment adjudges the capital. This new circumstance varies again the rule of equity: for though the cedent's interest weighs not in opposition to that of his creditor arresting, the

INTRODUCTION.

adjudging creditor and the arrester are upon a level as to every equitable consideration; and, upon that account, the assignee, who is the preferable creditor, ought to deal impartially between them: if he be not willing to take payment out of both subjects proportionally, but only out of the capital, or out of the interest; he ought to make an assignment to the postponed creditor, in order to redress the inequality; and if he refuse to do this act of justice, a court of equity will interpose.

This example shows the mutability of equitable claims: but there is a cause which makes them appear still more mutable than they are in reality. The strongest notion is entertained of the stability of a right of property; because no man can be deprived of his property but by his own deed. A claim of debt is understood to be stable, but in an inferior degree; because payment puts an end to it without the will of the creditor. But equitable rights, which commonly accrue to a man without any deed of his, are often lost in the same manner: and they will naturally be deemed transitory and fluctuating, when they depend so little on the will of the persons who are possessed of them.

In England, where the courts of equity and common law are different, the boundary between equity and common law, where the legislature doth not interpose, will remain always the same. But, in Scotland, and other countries where equity and common law are united in one court, the boundary varies imperceptibly; for what originally is a rule in equity, loses its character when it is fully established in practice; and then it is considered as common law: thus the *actio negotiorum gestorum*, retention, salvage,

B

INTRODUCTION.

&c. are in Scotland scarce now considered as depending on principles of equity. But by cultivation of society, and practice of law, nicer and nicer cases in equity being daily unfolded, our notions of equity are preserved alive; and the additions made to that fund, supply what is withdrawn from it by common law.

What is now said, suggests a question, no less intricate than important, Whether common law and equity ought to be committed to the same or to different courts. The profound Bacon gives his opinion in the following words.—" Apud nonnullos re-" ceptum est, ut jurisdictio, quæ decernit secundum" æquum et bonum, atque illa altera, quæ procedit" secundum jus strictum, iisdem curiis deputentur:" apud alios autem, ut diversæ: omnino placet curi-" arum separatio. Neque enim servabitur distinctio" casuum, si fiat commixtio jurisdictionum: sed ar-" bitrium legem tandem trahet." * Of all questions those which concern the constitution of a state, and its political interest, being the most involved in circumstances, are the most difficult to be brought under precise rules. I pretend not to deliver any opinion; and feeling in myself a bias against the great authority mentioned, I scarce venture to form an opinion. It may be not improper, however, to hazard a few observations, preparatory to a more accurate discussion. I feel the weight of the argument urged in the passage above quoted. In the science of jurisprudence, it is undoubtedly of great importance, that the boundary between equity and common law be clearly ascertained; without which we shall in vain hope for just decisions: a judge, who is uncertain whether the case belong to equity or to common

* De aug. scient. l. 8, cap. 3, aph. 45.

INTRODUCTION.

law, cannot have a clear conception what judgment ought to be pronounced. But a court that judges of both, being relieved from determining this preliminary point, will be apt to lose sight altogether of the distinction between common law and equity. On the other hand, may it not be urged, that the dividing among different courts things intimately connected, bears hard upon every one who has a claim to prosecute? Before bringing his action, he must at his peril determine an extreme nice point, Whether the case be governed by common law, or by equity. An error in that preliminary point, though not fatal to the cause, because a remedy is provided, is, however, productive of much trouble and expence. Nor is the most profound knowledge of law sufficient always to prevent this evil; because it cannot always be foreseen what plea will be put in for the defendant, whether a plea in equity or at common law. In the next place, to us in Scotland it appears extremely uncouth, that a court should be so constituted, as to be tied down in many instances to pronounce an iniquitous judgment. This not only happens frequently with respect to covenants, as above mentioned, but will always happen where a claim founded on common law, which must be brought before a court of common law, is opposed by an equitable defence, which cannot be regarded by such a court. Weighing these different arguments with some attention, the preponderancy seems to be on the side of an united jurisdiction; so far, at least, as that the court before which a claim is regularly brought, should be empowered to judge of every defence that is laid against it. The sole inconvenience of an united jurisdiction, that it tends to blend common law with equity, may admit a remedy,

B 2

INTRODUCTION.

by an institute distinguishing with accuracy their boundaries : but the inconvenience of a divided jurisdiction admits not any effectual remedy. These hints are suggested with the greatest diffidence; for I cannot be ignorant of the bias that naturally is produced by custom and established practice.

In Scotland, as well as in other civilised countries, the King's council was originally the only court that had power to remedy defects or redress injustice in common law. To this extraordinary power the Court of Session naturally succeeded, as being the supreme court in civil matters ; for in every well-regulated society, some one court must be trusted with this power, and no court more properly than that which is supreme. It may at first sight appear surprising, that no mention is made of this extraordinary power in any of the regulations concerning the Court of Session. It is probable, that this power was not intended, nor early thought of; and that it was introduced by necessity. That the court itself had at first no notion of being possessed of this power, is evident from the act of sederunt, November 27, 1592, declaring, " That in time coming they will judge and " decide upon clauses irritant contained in contracts, " tacks, infeftments, bonds and obligations, precisely " according to the words and meaning of the same ;" which in effect was declaring themselves a court of common law, not of equity. But the mistake was discovered : the act of sederunt wore out of use ; and now, for more than a century, the Court of Session hath acted as a court of equity, as well as of common law. Nor is it rare to find powers unfolded in practice, that were not in view at the institution of a court. When the Roman Pretor was created to be

INTRODUCTION.

the supreme judge, in place of the Consuls, there is no appearance that any instructions were given him concerning matters of equity. And even as to the English Court of Chancery, though originally a court of equity, there was not at first the least notion entertained of that extensive jurisdiction to which in latter times it hath justly arrived.

In Scotland, the union of common law with equity in the supreme court, appears to have had an influence upon inferior courts, and to have regulated their powers with respect to equity. The rule in general is, That inferior courts are confined to common law: and hence it is that an action founded merely upon equity, such as a reduction upon minority and lesion, upon fraud, &c. is not competent before an inferior court. But if against a process founded on common law an equitable defence be stated, it is the practice of inferior courts to judge of such defence. Imitation of the supreme court, which judges both of law and equity, and the inconvenience of removing to another court a process that has perhaps long depended, paved the way to this enlargement of power. Another thing already taken notice of, tends to enlarge the powers of our inferior courts more and more; which is, that many actions, founded originally on equity, have, by long practice, obtained an establishment so firm as to be reckoned branches of the common law. This is the case of the *actio negotiorum gestorum*, of recompence, and many others, which, for that reason, are now commonly sustained in inferior courts.

Our courts of equity have advanced far in seconding the laws of nature, but have not perfected their course. Every clear and palpable duty is countenanced with an action; but many of the more re-fixed duties, as will be seen afterward, are left still without remedy. Until men, thoroughly humanized, be generally agreed about these more refined duties, it is perhaps the more prudent measure for a court of equity to leave them upon conscience. Neither doth this court profess to take under its protection every covenant and agreement. Many engagements of various sorts, the fruits of idleness, are too trifling, or too ludicrous, to merit the countenance of law: a court, whether of common law or of equity, cannot preserve its dignity if it descend to such matters. Wagers of all sorts, whether upon horses, cocks, or accidental events, are of this sort. People may amuse themselves, and men of easy fortunes may pass their whole time in that manner, because there is no law against it; but pastime, contrary to its nature, ought not to be converted into a serious matter, by bringing the fruits of it into a court of justice. This doctrine seems not to have been thoroughly understood, when the Court of Session, in a case reported by Dirleton, sustained action upon what is called there a *sponsio ludicra*. A man having taken a piece of gold, under condition to pay back a greater sum, in case he should be ever married, was after his marriage sued for performance. The Court sustained process; though several of the judges were of opinion, that *sponsiones ludicræ* ought not to be authorised*. But, in the following remarkable case, the Court judged better. In the year 1698, a bond was executed of the following tenor. " I, Mr. William " Cochran of Kilmarnock, for a certain sum of money " delivered to me by Mr. John Stewart, younger, of " Blackhall, bind and oblige me, my heirs and suc-

* February 9, 1676.

INTRODUCTION.

" cessors, to deliver to the said Mr. John Stewart,
" his heirs, executors, and assignees, the sum of
" one hundred guineas in gold, and that so soon as
" I, or the heirs descending of my body, shall suc-
" ceed to the dignity and estate of Dundonald."
This sum being claimed from the heir of the obliger,
now Earl of Dundonald, it was objected, That this
being a *sponsio ludicra* ought not to be countenanced
with an action. It was answered, That bargains
like the present are not against law; for if purchasing the hope of succession from a remote heir be lawful*, it cannot be unlawful to give him a sum, on
condition of receiving a greater when he shall succeed. If an heir pinched for money procure it upon
disadvantageous terms, equity will relieve him: but,
in the present case, there is no evidence, nor indeed
suspicion, of inequality. It was replied, That it
tends not to the good of society to sustain action upon
such bargains: they do not advance commerce, nor
contribute in any degree to the comforts of life; why
then should a court be bound to support them? It
is sufficient that they are not reprobated, but left
upon conscience and private faith. The Court refused to sustain action; reserving it to be considered,
whether the pursuer, upon proving the extent of the
sum given by him, be not entitled to demand it back†.

The multiplied combinations of individuals in society, suggest rules of equity so numerous and various, that in vain would any writer think of collect-
ing all of them. From an undertaking which is in
a good measure new, all that can be expected is a

* See Fountainhall, July 29, 1708, Rag *contra* Brown.

† Feb. 7, 1753, Sir Michael Stewart of Blackhall *contra* Earl
of Dundonald.

INTRODUCTION.

collection of some of the capital cases that occur the most frequent in law-proceedings. This collection will comprehend many rules of equity, some of them probably of the most extensive application. Nor will it be without profit, even as to subjects omitted; for by diligently observing the application of equitable principles to a number of leading cases, a habit is gradually formed of reasoning correctly upon matters of equity, which will enable us to apply the same principles to new ca es as they occur.

- Having thus given a general view of my subject, I shall finish with giving my motive for appearing in print. Practising lawyers, to whom the subject must already be familiar, require no instruction. This treatise is dedicated to the studious in general, such as are fond to improve their minds by every exercise of the rational faculties. Writers upon law are too much confined in their views : their works, calculated for lawyers only, are involved in a cloud of obscure words and terms of art, a language perfectly unknown, except to those of the profession. Thus it happens, that the knowledge of law, like the hidden mysteries of some Pagan Deity, is confined to its votaries; as if others were in duty bound to blind and implicit submission. But such superstition, whatever unhappy progress it may have made in religion, never can prevail in law : men who have life or fortune at stake, take the liberty to think for themselves; and are no less ready to accuse judges for legal oppression, than others for private violence or wrong. Ignorance of law hath in this respect a most unhappy effect: we all regard with partiality our own interest; and it requires knowledge no less than candour, to resist the thought of being treated unjustly when a court pro-

INTRODUCTION.   25

nounceth against us. Thus peevishness and discontent arise, and are vented against the judges of the land. This, in a free government, is a dangerous and infectious spirit, to remedy which, we cannot be too solicitous. Knowledge of those rational principles upon which law is founded, I venture to suggest, as a remedy no less efficacious than palatable. Were such knowledge universally spread, judges who adhere to rational principles, and who, with superior understanding, can reconcile law to common sense, would be revered by the whole society. The fame of their integrity, supported by men of parts and reading, would descend to the lowest of the people; a thing devoutly to be wished! Nothing tends more to sweeten the temper, than a conviction of impartiality in judges, by which we hold ourselves secure against every insult or wrong. By that means, peace and concord in society are promoted, and individuals are finely disciplined to submit with the like deference, to all other acts of legal authority. Integrity is not the only duty required in a judge; to behave so as to make every one rely upon his integrity, is a duty no less essential. Deeply impressed with these notions, I dedicate my work to every lover of science; having endeavoured to explain the subject in a manner that requires in the reader no particular knowledge of municipal law. In that view I have avoided terms of art; not indeed with a scrupulous nicety, which might look like affectation; but so as that, with the help of a law-dictionary, what I say may be easily apprehended.

ORDER, a beauty in every composition, is essential in a treatise of equity, which comprehends an endless

INTRODUCTION.

variety of matter. To avoid obscurity and confusion, we must, with the strictest accuracy, bring under one view, things intimately connected, and handle separately things unconnected, or but slightly connected. Two great principles, Justice and Utility, govern the proceedings of a court of equity; and every matter that belongs to that court, is regulated by one or other of these principles. Hence a division of the present work into two books, the first appropriated to justice, the second to utility; in which I have endeavoured to ascertain all the principles of equity that occurred to me. I thought it would benefit the reader to have these principles illustrated in a third book, where certain important subjects are selected, to be regularly discussed from beginning to end; such as furnish the most frequent opportunities for applying the principles ascertained in the former part of the work.

PRINCIPLES

OF

EQUITY.

BOOK I.

Powers of a Court of Equity, derived from the Principle of Justice.

In the Introduction, occasion was taken to show, that a court of equity is necessary, first, to supply the defects of common law, and, next, to correct its rigour or injustice. The necessity in the former case arises from a principle, That where there is a right, it ought to be made effectual; in the latter, from another principle, That for every wrong there ought to be a remedy. In both, the object commonly is pecuniary interest. But there is a legal interest which is not pecuniary; and which, for the sake of perspicuity, ought to be handled separately. In that view, the present book is divided into two parts. In the first are treated, the powers of a court of equity to supply defects, and to correct injustice in the common law, with respect to pecuniary interest; and in the second, the powers of a court of equity with respect to matters of justice that are not pecuniary.

PART I.

Powers of a Court of Equity to remedy the imperfections of common law with respect to pecuniary interest, by supplying what is defective, and correcting what is wrong.

THE imperfections of common law are so many and so various, that it will be difficult to bring them into any perfect order. The following arrangement, if not the best, seems at least to be natural and easy. 1. Imperfections of common law in protecting men from being harmed by others. 2. In protecting the weak of mind from harming themselves. 3. Imperfections of common law with respect to the natural duty of benevolence. 4. Imperfections with respect to deeds and covenants. 5. With respect to statutes. 6. With respect to transactions between debtor and creditor. 7. With respect to actions at law. 8. With respect to legal execution. 9. Power of a court of equity to inflict punishment.

CHAPTER I.

Powers of a Court of Equity to remedy what is imperfect in common law, with respect to the protecting individuals from harm.

THE social state, however desirable, could never have taken place among men, were they not restrained from injuring those of their own species. To abstain from injuring others is, accordingly, the primary law of society, enforced by the most vigorous sanctions; every culpable transgression of that law subjects the wrong-doer to reparation ; and every intentional transgression subjects him also to punishment.

The moral principle of abstaining from injuring others, naturally takes the lead in every institute of law ; and as the enforcing that principle was a capital object in establishing courts of justice, it is proper to commence a treatise of equity, with examining in what cases the interposition of a court of equity is required to make it effectual ; which can only be where no remedy is provided at common law.

With respect to harm done intentionally, there is no imperfection in common law, and, consequently, no necessity for a court of equity. But that court may be necessary in the following cases. First, Harm done by one in exercising a right or privilege. Second, Harm done by one who has it not in view to exercise any right or privilege. Third, A man tempted or overawed by undue influence to act knowingly against his interest. Fourth, A man moved to act unknowingly against his interest, by fraud, deceit, or other artificial means. I close the chapter with the remedies that are applied by a court of equity against the wrongs above stated. Of these in their order.

SECTION I.

Harm done by a man in exercising a right or privilege.

THE social state, which, on the one hand, is highly beneficial, by affording mutual aid and support, is, on the other, attended with some inconveniences, as where a man cannot have the free exercise of a right or privilege without harming others. How far such

PROTECTING FROM HARM. B. i.

exercise is authorised by the law of our nature, is a question of nice discussion. That men are born in a state of freedom and independence is an established truth ; but whether that freedom and independence may not admit of some limitation from the collision of opposite rights and privileges, deserves to be examined. If the free exercise of my right be indulged me without regarding the harm that may ensue to another, that other is so far under my power, and his interest so far subjected to mine. On the other side, if I be restrained from the exercise of my right in every case where harm may ensue to another, I am so far dependent upon that other, and my interest so far subjected to his. Here is a threatening appearance for civil society, that seems to admit no resource but force and violence. Cases there certainly are that admit no other resource ; as where in a shipwreck two persons lay hold of the same plank, one of whom must be thrust off, otherwise both will go to the bottom. But upon the present supposition, we are not reduced to that deplorable dilemma; for nature has tempered these opposite interests by a rule no less beautiful than salutary. This rule consists of two branches : the first is, That the exercising my right will not justify me in doing any action that directly harms another ; and so far my interest yields to his : the second is, That in exercising my right I am not answerable for any indirect or consequential damage that another may suffer; and so far the interest of others yields to mine : I am sorry if my neighbour happen thus to suffer ; but I feel no check of conscience on that account. The first branch resolves into a principle of morality, That no interest of mine, not even the preservation of life itself, au-

P. 1. 1.   PROTECTING FROM HARM.

thorises me to do any mischief to an innocent person *. The other branch is founded on expediency in opposition to justice; for if the possibility of harming others, whether foreseen or not foreseen, were sufficient to restrain me from prosecuting my own rights and privileges, men would be too much cramped in action, or rather would be reduced to a state of absolute inactivity †.

This rule, which is far from being easy in its application, requires much illustration. I begin with the first branch. However profitable it may be to purge my field of water, yet it is universally admitted, that I cannot legally open a new passage for it into my neighbour's ground; because this is a direct damage to him: " Sic enim debere quem meliorem " agrum suum facere, ne vicini deteriorem faciat‡." Where a river is interjected between my property and that of my neighbour, it is not lawful for me to alter its natural course, whether by throwing it upon my neighbour's ground, or by depriving him of it; because these acts, both of them, are direct encroachments upon his property. Neratius puts the case of a lake which in a rainy season overflows the neighbouring fields, to prevent which on one side, a bulwark is erected. He is of opinion, that if this bulwark have the effect, in a rainy season, to throw a greater quantity of water than usual upon the opposite fields, it ought to be demolished§. As the damage here is only occasional or accidental, this opinion is not well founded. It has not even a plausi-

* Sketches of the History of Man, vol. 4. p. 31, 32.
† Eod. p. 64, 65.
‡ De aqua, et aquæ pluv. l. 1. § 4.
§ De aqua, et aquæ pluv. l. 1. § 2.

PROTECTING FROM HARM B. I.

ble appearance. Is it not natural and common for a proprietor to fence his bank, in order to prevent the encroachments of a river or of a lake? The course of the river is not altered; and the proprietor on the opposite side may fence his bank, if he be afraid of encroachments.

The foregoing examples, being all of the same kind, are governed by a practical rule, That we must not throw any thing into our neighbour's ground; *ne immittas in alienum* as expressed in the Roman law. But the principle of abstaining to hurt others, regards persons as well as property. " It seems the " better opinion, that a brew-house, glass-house, " chandler's shop, or stie for swine, set up in such " inconvenient parts of a town that they cannot but " greatly incommode the neighbourhood, are com- " mon nuisances *." Neighbours in a town must submit to inconveniences from each other; but they must be protected from extraordinary disturbances, that render life uncomfortable. Upon the same ground, the Court of Session was of opinion, that the working in the upper storey of a large tenement, with weighty hammers upon an anvil, is a nuisance; and it was decreed that the blacksmith should remove at the next term †.

As to the second branch of the rule, it is agreed by all, as above mentioned, that where a river gradually encroaches on my property, I may fence my bank in order to prevent further encroachments; for this work does not tend to produce even indirect or consequential damage: all the effect it can have is,

* A new abridgement of the law, vol. 3, p. 686.
† Kinloch of Gilmerton against Robertson, Dec. 9, 1756.

P. I. 1.   PROTECTING FROM HARM.   39

to prevent my neighbour from gaining ground on his side.

In matters of common property, the application of this second branch is sometimes more intricate. A river or any running stream directs its course through the land of many proprietors; who are thereby connected by a common interest, being equally entitled to the water for useful purposes. Whence it follows, that the course of the river or running stream cannot be diverted by any one of the proprietors, so as to deprive others of it. Where there is plenty for all, there can be no interference; but many streams are so scanty, as to be exhausted by using the water too freely, leaving little or none to others. In such a case, there ought to be rule for using it with discretion; though, hitherto, no rule has been laid down. To supply the defect in some measure, I venture to suggest the following particulars, which practice may in time ripen to a precise rule. It will be granted me, that if there be not a sufficiency of water for every purpose, those purposes ought to be preferred that are the most essential to the well-being of the adjacent proprietors. The most essential use is drink for man and beast; because they cannot subsist without it. What is next essential, is water for washing; because cleanness contributes greatly to health. The third is water for a corn-mill, which saves labour, and cheapens bread. The fourth is watering land, for enriching it. The fifth is water for a bleachfield. And the lowest I shall mention, is water for machinery, necessary for cheapening the productions of several arts. There may be more divisions; but these are sufficient in a general view. From this arrangement it follows, that one may use the water of a rivulet for

C

PROTECTING FROM HARM.

drink, and for brewing and baking, however little be left to the inferior heritors. But a proprietor cannot be deprived of that essential use by one above him, who wants to divert the water for a mill, for a bleach-field, or for watering his land. Nor can a proprietor divert the water for a bleachfield, or for watering his land, unless he leave sufficient for a mill below. According to this doctrine, I may lawfully dig a pit in my own field for gathering water to my cattle, though it happens to intercept a spring that run under ground into my neighbour's field, and furnished him with water.*

Under this head comes a question that may be resolved by the principles above laid down, which is, How far the free use of a river in carrying goods can be prevented or impeded by a cruive for catching salmon. It is admitted, that a navigable river fit for sailing ought to be free to all for the purposes of commerce; and that the navigation ought not to be hurt, or rendered difficult, by any work erected in the channel of the river. But supposing a river that can only admit the floating of timber, is it lawful to erect there a cruive with a dam-dike, so as to prevent that operation? A cruive for catching salmon is an extraordinary privilege granted to a single proprietor, prejudicial to all above who have right to fish salmon. The floating of timber, on the contrary, is profitable to the proprietor, and to every person who stands in need of that commodity. A cruive, therefore, ought to yield to the floating of timber, as far as these rights are incompatible. But will positive prescription give no aid to the proprietor of a cruive in this case? This prescription regulates the competition

* L. 1. § 12. De aqua.

among those who pretend right to the same subject; but protects not the possessor from burdens naturally affecting his property. Now it is a rule, That property, which is a private right, must yield to what is essential for the good of the nation. In order to defend a town besieged, a house standing in the way ought to be demolished. The right of property will not avail in this case, even admitting the proprietor and his predecessors to have been in possession for a century. Or suppose, that to repel a foreign enemy, my field is found to be an advantageous situation for the national troops, it is lawful to encamp upon it, though the consequence be to destroy the trees, and all it produces. Or, to come nearer the present case, a manufacturing village is erected on the brink of a rivulet, which is used for a mill below that has been in constant exercise forty years and upward. The manufactures succeed, and the village becomes so populous as nearly to exhaust the water in drink for man and beast, in brewing, and in other purposes preferable to that of a mill. Yet I take it for granted, that positive prescription will not protect the proprietor of the mill; because here there is no competition, but only property subjected to the burdens that naturally attend it. The transition from this example to the case in hand is direct. The possession of a cruive for a hundred years, will not bar a superior heritor from planting trees, nor, consequently, from floating them down the river for sale; for, evidently, positive prescription can have no operation in this case. It can have no effect, but to bestow upon the possessor the property of the cruive, which otherwise might have been doubtful. But such property must, like all other property, be subjected to its natural burdens;

c 2

and cannot stand in the way of a right of greater importance to the public.

It is lawful for me to build a house upon my march, though it intercept the light from a neighbouring house; for this is consequential damage only: beside, that if my neighbour choose to build on his march, he must see that I am equally entitled.

With regard to this section in general, there is a limitation founded entirely upon equity; which is, That though a man may lawfully exercise his right for his own benefit, where the harm that ensues is only consequential; yet, that the exercise is unlawful if done intentionally to distress others, without any view of benefiting himself. Rights and privileges are bestowed on us for our own good, not for hurting others. Malevolence is condemned by all laws, natural and municipal: a malevolent act of the kind mentioned, is condemned by the actor himself in his sedate moments; and he finds himself in conscience bound to repair the mischief he has thus done. The common law, it is true, overlooks intention, considering the act in no other view but as legal exercise of a right. But equity holds intention to be the capital part, being that which determines an action to be right or wrong; and affords reparation accordingly. Hence, a general rule in equity, That justice will not permit a man to exercise his right where his intention is solely to hurt another; which, in law-language, is termed the acting *in æmulationem vicini*. In all cases of this nature, a court of equity will give redress by voiding the act, if that can be done; otherwise, by awarding a sum in name of damages. We proceed to examples.

A man may lawfully dig a pit in his own field, in

P. I. 1.   PROTECTING FROM HARM.   37

order to intercept a vein of water that runs below the surface into his neighbour's property, provided his purpose be to have water for his own use; but if his purpose be to hurt his neighbour, without any view to benefit himself, the act is unlawful, as proceeding from a malevolent intention; and a court of equity will restrain him from this operation.[*]

Upon the same principle is founded the noted practice in a court of equity, of refusing to sustain an action at law, unless the plaintiff can show an interest; for, if he can take no benefit by the action, the presumption must be, that it is calculated to distress the defendant, and done *in æmulationem vicini.*

In order to establish the *jus crediti* in an assignee, and totally to divest the cedent or assignor, the law of Scotland requires, that notification of the assignment be made to the debtor, verified by an instrument under the hand of a notary, termed *an intimation.* Before intimation, the legal right is in the cedent, and the assignee has a claim in equity only. In this case, payment made to the cedent by the debtor ignorant of the assignment, is, in all respects, the same as if there were no assignment: it is payment made to the creditor, which, in law, must extinguish the debt. But what if the debtor, when he makes payment to the cedent before intimation, be in the knowledge of the assignment? The common law knows no creditor but him who is legally vested in the right; and, therefore, disregarding the debtor's knowledge of the assignment, it will sustain the payment made to the cedent as made to the legal creditor. But equity teaches a different doctrine. It was wrong in the cedent to take payment after he conveyed his

[*] De aqua, et aquæ pluv. l. 1, § 12.

right to the assignee: and though the debtor was only exercising his own right in making payment to the cedent, who is still the creditor ; yet being in the knowledge of the assignment, the payment must have been made intentionally to distress the assignee, without benefiting himself. A court of equity, therefore, correcting what is imperfect in common law, will oblige the debtor to make payment over again to the assignee, as reparation of the wrong done him.

: With respect to this matter, there is a wide difference between the solemnities that may be requisite for vesting in an assignee a complete right to the subject, and what are sufficient to bar the debtor from making payment to the cedent. In the former view, a regular intimation is necessary, or some solemn act equivalent to a regular intimation, a process for example. In the latter view, the private knowledge of the debtor is sufficient; and hence it is, that a promise of payment made to the assignee, though not equivalent to a regular intimation, is however sufficient to bar the debtor from making payment to the cedent. The court went farther: they were of opinion, that the assignee having shewn his assignment to the debtor, though without intimating the same by a notary, the debtor could not make payment to the cedent.* But historical knowledge of an assignment, where it falls short of ocular evidence, will scarce be sustained to put the debtor *in mala fide*. And this rule is founded on utility : a debtor ought not to be furnished with pretexts against payment ; and if private conviction of an assignment, without certain knowledge, were sufficient, private

* Fountainhall, February 16, 1703, Leith *contra* Garden.

SECT. II.

Harm done by one who has it not in view to exercise any right or privilege.

In tracing the history of courts of law with respect to this branch, one beforehand would conjecture, that common law should regard no acts injuring others in their rights and privileges, but where mischief is intended; neglecting acts that are culpable only, as having a foundation too slight for that law. But upon examination we discover a very different plan; so different as that damage occasioned even by the slightest fault is, and always was, repaired in courts of common law. In the criminal law, very little distinction was originally made between a criminal and a culpable act, even with respect to punishment,* not to talk of reparation: the passion of resentment; in a fierce and lawless people, is roused by the slightest harm; and is too violent for any deliberate distinction between intentional and culpable wrong. In fact, both were equally subjected to punishment, even after the power of punishment was transferred to the magistrate. Of this we have a notable example in the *lex Aquilia* among the Romans :—" Qui servum " alienum, quadrupedem vel pecudem, injuria occi- " derit; quanti id in eo anno plurimi fuit, tantum " æs dare domino damnas esto."† Here the word *injuria* is interpreted, " quod non jure factum est;

---

* Historical law-tracts, tract 1.   † L. 2, p. ad leg. Aquil.

" i. e. si culpa quis occiderit."* The retrospect here may happen to be a great punishment; for the obliging a man who kills a lame horse not worth fifty shillings, to pay fifty pounds because the horse was of that value some months before, is evidently a punishment. And as even a *culpâ levissima* subjects a man to the *lex Aquilia*,† it is clear, that the slightest fault by which damage ensues is punishable by that law. The *lex Aquilia* was accordingly held by all to be penal; and for that reason no action upon it was sustained against the heir.‡ The only thing surprising is, to find this law continuing in force, without alteration or improvement, down to the reign of the Emperor Justinian. The Roman law was cultivated by men of great talents, and was celebrated all the world over for its equitable decisions: is it not amazing, that in an enlightened age such gross injustice should prevail, as to make even the slightest fault a ground for punishment?

When such was the common law of the Romans with regard to punishment, there can be no difficulty to assign a reason, why that law was extended to reparation even for the slightest fault; and as little, to assign a reason why the same obtains in the common law of most European nations, the principles of which are borrowed from the Roman law. The penal branch, it is true, of wrongs that are culpable only, not criminal, has been long abolished; having given way to the gradual improvement of the moral sense, which dictates, that where there is no intention to do mischief, there ought to be no punishment; and that the person who is hurt by a fault only, not by a crime,

---

* L. 5, § 1, ad leg. Aquil.   † L. 44, eod.

‡ L. 23, § 8, ad leg. Aquil.

P. I. 1.   PROTECTING FROM HARM.   41

cannot justly demand more than reparation. And as this is the present practice of all civilized nations, it is clear, that the reparation of damage occasioned by acts of violence comes under courts of common law, which consequently is so far a bar to a court of equity.

And considering, that regulations restraining individuals from injuring others, and compelling them to perform their engagements, composed originally the bulk of common law,* it will not be surprising, that courts of common law took early under their cognisance every culpable act that occasions mischief; which was the more necessary, in respect that punishment being laid aside, reparation is the only mean left for repressing a culpable act. Thus, we find ample provision made by common law, not only against intentional mischief, but also against mischief that is only foreseen, not intended. And so far there is no occasion for a court of equity.

But for the security of individuals in society, it is not sufficient that a man himself be prohibited from doing mischief; he ought over and above to be careful and vigilant, that persons, animals, and things, under his power, do no mischief; and if he neglect this branch of his duty, he is liable to repair the mischief that ensues, equally as if it had proceeded from his own act. With respect to servants, it is the master's business to make a right choice, and to keep them under proper discipline; and, therefore, if they do any mischief that might have been foreseen and prevented, he is liable. Thus, if a passenger be hurt by my servant's throwing a stone out of a window in my house, or have his clothes sullied by dirty water pour-

---

* See Introduction.

PROTECTING FROM HARM. B. I.

ed down upon him, the damage must be repaired by me at the first instance ; reserving to me relief against my servant. But if a man be killed or wounded by my servant in a scuffle, I am not liable ; unless it can be specified, that I knew him to be quarrelsome, and, consequently, might have foreseen the mischief. With respect to animals, it is the proprietor's duty to keep them from doing harm ; and if harm ensue that might have been foreseen, he is bound to repair it ; as, for example, where he suffers his cattle to pasture in his neighbour's field ; or where the mischief is done by a beast of a vicious kind ; or even by an ox or a horse, which, contrary to its nature, he knows to be mischievous.* As to things, it is also the duty of the proprietor to keep them from doing harm. Thus, both fiar and liferenter were made liable to repair the hurt occasioned to a neighbouring tenement by the fall of their house.† It is the duty of a man who carries stones in a waggon along the highway, to pack them so as to prevent harm ; and if by careless package a stone drop out and bruise a passenger, the man is liable. But as to cases of this kind, it is a good defence against a claim of reparation, that the claimant suffered by his own fault :—" Si quis aliquem e- " vitans, magistratum forte, in taberna proxima se " immisisset, ibique a cane feroce læsus esset, non " posse agi canis nomine quidam putant : at si so- " lutus fuisset, contra." ‡ If a fierce bull of mine get loose, and wound a person, I am liable ; but if a man break down my fence, and is hurt by the bull in my inclosure, I am not liable ; for, by an unlawful act,

* Exodus, chap. xxi, 29, 36.
† Stair, 16th February 1666, Kay contra Littlejohn.
‡ L. 2, § 1. Si quadrupes pauperiem fecisse dicatur.

P. I. 1. PROTECTING FROM HARM. 43

he himself was the occasion of the hurt he suffered. Thus, with respect to matters falling under the present section, it appears, that faults come under common law as well as crimes, and omissions as well as commissions; and, therefore, so far the common law appears complete, leaving no gleanings to a court of equity.

SECT. III.

A man tempted or overawed by undue influence to act knowingly against his interest.

THE imperfections of man are not confined to his corporeal part: he has weaknesses of mind as well as of body; and if the taking advantage of the latter to distress a person by acts of violence, be a moral wrong, entitling the sufferer to reparation, it is no less so to take advantage of the former. Society could not subsist without such prohibition; and happy it is for man, as a social being, that the prohibition with respect to both articles makes a branch of his nature.

For the sake of perspicuity, this section shall be split into two parts: the first, where a man, yielding to a temptation, acts knowingly against his interest: the next, where he is overawed to act knowingly against his interest.

ARTICLE I. *Where a man, yielding to a temptation, acts knowingly against his interest.*

JEAN MACKIE, heiress of Maidland, having disponed several parcels of land, lying about the town of Wigton, to persons who were mostly innkeepers there, a reduction was brought upon the head of fraud and circumvention by her sister, next heir, in virtue of a settlement. It came out upon proof, 1st, That Jean Mackie was a habitual drunkard; that she sold her very clothes to purchase drink, scarce leaving herself a rag to cover her nakedness; and that, by tempting her with a few shillings, it was in the power of any one to make her accept a bill for a large sum, or to make her dispone any part of her land. 2dly, That the dispositions challenged were granted for no adequate cause. The court accordingly voided these dispositions.* Upon this case it ought to be observed, that though fraud and circumvention were specified as the foundation of this reduction, which is a common but slovenly practice in processes of that sort; yet there was not the least evidence, that Jean was imposed upon or circumvented in any manner. Nor was there any necessity for recurring to such artifice: a little drink, or a few shillings to purchase it, would have tempted her at any time, drunk or sober, to give away any of her subjects. And she herself, being called as a witness, deponed, that she granted these dispositions freely, knowing well what she did. Where then lies the ground of reduction? Plainly here: It is undoubtedly an immoral act, to take advantage of weak persons who are incapable to resist certain temptations, thereby to strip them of their goods. To justify such an act, the consent of the person injured is of no avail, more than the consent of a child. With respect to the end, it is no less pernicious than theft or robbery.

* November 24, 1752, Mackie contra Maxwell, &c.

Art. II. *Where a man is overawed to act knowingly against his interest.*

If it be a moral wrong to tempt a weak man to act against his interest, extortion is a wrong still more flagrant, by its nearer approach to open violence. What therefore only remains upon this article, is to illustrate it by examples.

Every benefit taken indirectly by a creditor, for the granting of which no impulsive cause appears but the money lent, will be voided as extorted. Thus an assignment to a lease was voided, being granted of the same date with a bond of borrowed money, and acknowledged to have had no other cause.* At the time of granting an heritable bond of corroboration, the debtor engaged, by a separate writing, That in case he should have occasion to sell the land, the creditor should have it for a price named. The price appeared to be equal; and yet the paction was voided, as obtained by extortion.† Upon the same ground, a bond for a sum taken from the principal debtor by his cautioner, as a reward for lending his credit, was voided.‡

Rigorous creditors go sometimes differently to work. If they dare not venture upon greater profit directly than is permitted by law, they aim at it indirectly, by stipulating severe irritancies upon failure of payment. One stipulation of that sort, which makes a great figure in our law, is, That if the sum lent upon a wadset or pledge be not repaid at the term convenanted, the property of the wadset or

---

* Fount. June 20, 1696, Sutherland *contra* Sinclair.

† Nov. 30, 1736, Brown *contra* Muir.

‡ Forbes 24. Fount. 27. January 1711, King *contra* Ker.

46   PROTECTING FROM HARM.   B. I.

pledge shall *ipso facto* be transferred to the creditor. in satisfaction of the debt. This paction is, in the Roman law, named *lex commissoria in pignoribus*, and in that law seems to be absolutely reprobated.* With us it must be effectual at common law, because there is no statute against it. But then, as it is a hard and rigorous condition, extorted from a necessitous debtor, a court of equity will interpose to give relief. And this can be done by following a general rule applicable to all cases of the kind; which is, to admit the debtor to redeem his pledge by payment, at any time, till the creditor in a declaratory process signify his will to hold the pledge in place of his money. This process affords the debtor an opportunity to purge his failure by payment; which is all that in fair dealing can be demanded by the creditor. And thus, the declarator serves a double purpose: it relieves the debtor from the hardship of a penal irritancy, by furnishing him an opportunity to pay the debt; and if he be silent, the extracted decree operates a transference of the property to the creditor, which extinguishes the debt.

Hence it follows, that the debtor can redeem the wadset or pledge, whether the bargain be lucrative or no. A declarator being necessary, the property is not transferred to the creditor, if the debtor be willing to redeem his pledge: and this option he must have, whether the creditor have made profit or no by possession of the pledge. Supposing a proper wadset granted, by which the creditor makes more than the interest of his money; justice requires, that the debtor have an option to redeem even after the term limit-

---

* L. ult. C. De pactis pignorum.

ed, until the equity of redemption be foreclosed by a declarator; and if a declarator be necessary, as is proved, the debtor must have his option, even where the creditor has drawn less than his interest.

In equity, however, there is a material difference between a proper wadset with a *pactum legis commissoriæ*, and a proper wadset, where the term of redemption is not limited. In the latter case, the parties stand upon an equal footing: the creditor may demand his money when he pleases; and he has no claim for interest, because of his agreement to accept the rents instead of interest: the debtor, on the other hand, may redeem his land when he pleases, upon repayment of the sum borrowed. But the matter turns out differently in equity, where the power of redemption is by paction limited to a certain term. There being no limitation upon the creditor, he may demand his money when he pleases; and he has no claim for interest, even though the rents have fallen short of the interest. But if the debtor insist upon the equity of redemption after the term to which the redemption is limited, he must, beside repaying the sum borrowed, make good the interest, as far as the rent of the land has proved deficient. For impartiality is essential to a court of equity: if the one party be relieved against the rigour of a covenant, the other has the same claim: after taking the land from the creditor contrary to paction, it would be gross injustice to hold the paction good against him, by limiting him to less interest than he is entitled to by law upon an ordinary loan.*

* To this case is applicable an English maxim of equity, " That " he that demands equity must give equity."

48   PROTECTING FROM HARM.   B. t.

From what is said it will be clear, that a power of redeeming within a limited time annexed to a proper sale for an adequate price, cannot be exercised after the term limited for the redemption. The purchaser, to whom the property was transferred from the beginning, has no occasion for a declarator; nor doth equity require the time for redemption to be enlarged contrary to paction, in a case where an adequate price is given for the subject.

Many other hard and oppressive conditions in bonds of borrowed money, invented by rigorous creditors for their own conveniency, without the least regard to humanity or equity, were repressed by the act 140, parl. 1592. And, by the authority of that statute, such pactions may be brought under challenge in courts of common law, against which otherwise no remedy was competent except in a court of equity.

It was, perhaps, the statute now mentioned, that misled the Court of Session into an opinion, that it belongs to the legislature solely to repress such rigorous conditions in agreements as are stated above. One thing is certain, that immediately after the statute there is an act of sederunt, November 27, 1592, in which the court declares, " That in time coming, " they will judge and decide upon clauses irritant " contained in contracts, tacks, infeftments, bonds, " and obligations, precisely according to the words " and meaning of the same." Such a resolution, proper for a court of common law, is inconsistent with the nature of a court of equity. The mistake was soon discovered: the act of sederunt wore out of observance; and now, for a long time, the Court of Session has acted as a court of equity in this as well as in other matters.

It is usury by statute to bargain with a debtor for more than the legal interest; but it is not usury to take a proper wadset, even where the rent of the land exceeds the interest of the money. For the creditor who accepts the rent instead of interest, takes upon himself the insolvency of the tenants; and the hazard of this insolvency, however small, saves from usury, which consists in stipulating a yearly sum certain above the legal interest. But though such a bargain, where the rent exceeds the legal interest, is not, strictly speaking, usury, it is rigorous and oppressive, and plainly speaks out the want of credit in the person who submits to it; upon which account, it might be thought a proper subject for equity, did we not reflect that all wadsets are not lucrative. When such is the case, what shall be the judge's conduct? Must he give an opinion upon every wadset, according to its peculiar circumstances? or ought he to follow some rule that is applicable to all cases of the kind? The former opens a door to arbitrary proceedings: the latter, fettering a judge, forces him often to do what is materially unjust. Here equity, regarding individuals, weighs against utility, regarding the whole society. The latter being by far the more weighty consideration, must preponderate: and for that reason only are wadsets tolerated, even the most lucrative; for it is not safe to give any redress in equity.

This doctrine may be illustrated by a different case. A debtor standing personally bound for payment of the legal interest, is compelled to give an additional real security, by infefting the creditor in certain lands, the rent of which is paid in corn, with this proviso, " That the creditor, if he levy the rents for

D

"his payment, shall not be subjected to an account,
"but shall hold the rents in lieu of his interest."
This, from what is observed above, is not usury;
because the value of the corn, however much above
the interest in common years, may possibly fall below it. But as the creditor is in all events secure of
his interest, by having his debtor bound personally,
and may often draw more than his interest by levying the rent when corn sells high, equity will relieve
against the inequality of this bargain. For here the
court may follow a general rule, applicable to all cases
of the kind, affording a remedy equally complete, in
every case; which is, to oblige the creditor to account for what he receives more than his interest,
and to impute the same into his capital. In the case
of a proper wadset this rule would be unjust, because
the creditor has a chance of getting less than his interest, which ought to be compensated with some benefit beyond the ordinary profit of money : and if the
door be once opened to an extraordinary benefit, a
precise boundary cannot be ascertained between more
and less. But the covenant now mentioned is in its
very conception oppressive; and the creditor may
justly be deprived of the extraordinary benefit he
draws from it, when he runs no chance of getting
less than the legal interest.

Pactra contra fidem tabularum nuptialium belong
to this article. Such private pactions between the
bridegroom and his father, contrary to the marriage-
articles, openly agreed on, are hurtful to the wife
and children: who will therefore be relieved upon
the head of fraud. But the husband cannot be so
relieved; because as to him there is no fraud : he is
relieved upon the head of extortion. Every such

P. I. 1.   PROTECTING FROM HARM.   51

private paction is, by construction of law, extorted
from him : and the construction is just, considering
his dependent situation ; for the fear of losing his
bride, leaves him not at liberty to refuse any hard
terms that may be imposed by his father, who settles
the estate upon him.   The relief granted to the wife
and children upon the head of fraud, comes properly
under the following section ; but for the sake of connection is introduced here.   In a contract of marriage the estate was settled upon the bridegroom by
his father ; and the bride's portion was taken payable to the father, which he accepted for satisfaction
of the debts he owed, and for provisions to his younger children.   The son afterward, having privately
before the marriage granted bond for a certain sum
to his father, it was voided at the wife's instance, as
contra fidem tabularum nuptialium.[*]   Hugh Campbell of Calder, in the marriage-articles of his son
Sir Alexander, became bound to provide the family-
estate to him and the heirs-male of the marriage,
" free of all charge and burden."   He at the same
time privately obtained from his son a promise to
grant him a faculty of burdening the estate with
£2,000 sterling to his younger children ; which promise Sir Alexander fulfilled after the marriage, by
granting the faculty upon a narrative " of the pro-
" mise, and that the marriage-articles were in com-
" pliance with the bride's friends, that there might
" be no stop to the marriage."   In a suit against the
heirs of the marriage for payment of the said sum,
at the instance of Hugh's younger children, in whose
favour the faculty was exercised, the defendants were
assoilzied, the deed granting the faculty being *in frau-*

[*] Stair, July 21, 1668, Paton *contra* Paton.

dam pactorum nuptialium. [*] The following cases relate to the other branch, namely oppression, entitling
the husband to reduce deeds granted by himself. A
man, after settling his estate upon his eldest son, in
that son's contract of marriage, warranting it to be
worth 8,000 merks of yearly rent, did, before the
marriage, take a discharge from his son of the said
warrandice. The estate settled on the son falling
short of the rent warranted, he insisted in a process
against his father's other representatives for voiding
the discharge; and the same, accordingly, was voided, as *contra fidem.* [†] A discharge of part of the portion before solemnisation of the marriage, was voided as *contra fidem*, at the instance of the granter himself, because it was taken from him privately, without the concurrence of the friends whom he had engaged to assist him in the marriage-treaty. [‡] In England the same rule of equity obtains. It is held, that
where the son, without privity of the father or parent,
treating the match, gives a bond to refund any part
of the portion, it is voidable. [§] Thus the bridegroom's
mother surrenders part of her jointure, to enable her
son to make a settlement upon the bride, and the
bride's father agrees to give £3,000 portion. The
bridegroom, without privity of his mother, gives a
bond to the bride's father, to pay back £1,000 of the
portion, at the end of seven years. Decreed, That
the bond shall be delivered up, as obtained in fraud

[*] Feb. 8, 1718, Pollock *contra* Campbell of Calder.

[†] Forbes, Jan. 28, 1709, M'Guffock *contra* Blairs.

[‡] Home, Nov. 22, 1716, Viscount of Arbuthnot *contra* Morison of Prestongrange.

[§] Abridg. cases in equity, chap. 13, sect. E, § 1.

P. I. 1. PROTECTING FROM HARM. 55

of the marriage-agreement.* On the marriage of
Sir Henry Chancey's son with Sir Richard Butler's
daughter, it was agreed, that the young couple should
have so much for present maintenance. The son privately agrees with his father to release part. The
agreement was set aside, though the son, as was
urged, gave nothing but his own, and might dispose
of his present maintenance as he thought fit.† ‡

I promise a man a sum not to rob me. Equity
will relieve me, by denying action for payment, and
by affording me an action for recalling the money, if
paid. The latter action is, in the Roman law, styled,
Condictio ob injustam causam. To take money for
doing what I am bound to do without it, must be
extortion: I hold the money *sine justa causa*, and
ought, in conscience, to restore it. Thus it is extortion for a tutor to take a sum from his pupil's mother
for granting a factory to her.‡ And it was found
extortion in a man to take a bond from one whose
curator he had been, before he would deliver up the
family-writings.§

A bargain of hazard with a young heir, to have
double or treble the sum lent, after the death of his
father, or other contingency, is not always set aside
in equity; for, at that rate, it would be difficult to
deal with an heir during the life of his ancestor.
But if such bargain appear very unequal, it is set
aside, upon payment of what was really lent, with

---

* Abridg. cases in equity, chap. 13, sect. E, § 2.

† Absid. cases in equity, chap. 13, sect. E, § 3.

‡ Durie, penult. Feb. 1639, Mushet *contra* Dog.

§ Nicolson, (*turpis causa*), July 24, 1634, Rossie *contra* her
curators.

54 PROTECTING FROM HARM. B. I.

interest.* One entitled to an estate after the death
of two tenants for life, takes £350 to pay £700 when
the lives should fall, and mortgages the estate as a
security. Though both the tenants for life died within two years, yet the bargain being equal, no relief
was given against it.† A young man, presumptive
heir to an estate-tail of £800 yearly, being cast off
by his father, and destitute of all means of livelihood,
made an absolute conveyance of his remainder in tail
to I. S. and his heirs, upon consideration of £30
paid him in money, and a security for £20 yearly
during the joint lives of him and his father.
Though the father lived ten years after this transaction, and though I. S. would have lost his money
had the heir died during his father's life, yet the
heir was relieved against the conveyance.‡ The
plaintiff, a young man, who had a narrow allowance from his father, on whose death a great
estate was to descend to him in tail, having, in the
year 1675, borrowed £1,000 from the defendant, became bound, in case he survived his father, to pay
the defendant £5,000 within a month after his father's death, with interest; but that, if he did not
outlive his father, the money should not be repaid.
After the father's death, which happened *anno* 1679,
the plaintiff brought his bill upon the head of fraud
and extortion, to be relieved of this bargain, upon repayment of the sum borrowed, with interest. The
cause came first before the Lord Nottinghame, who
decreed the bargain to be effectual. But, upon a re-
hearing before Lord Chancellor Jeffreys, it was in-

* Abridg. cases in equity, chap. 13, sect. G, § 1. note.
† Abridg. cases in equity, chap. 32, sect. 1. § 2.
‡ Ibid. § 1.

sisted, that the clause freeing the the plaintiff from the debt, if he died before his father, made no difference; for in all such cases, the debt is lost of course, upon predecease of the heir of entail; and, therefore, that this clause, evidently contrived to colour a bargain, which, to the defendant himself, must have appeared unconscionable, was in reality a circumstance against him. Though in this case there was no proof of fraud, nor of any practice used to draw the plaintiff into the bargain; yet, because of the unconscionableness of the bargain, the plaintiff was relieved against it.* In the year 1730, the Earl of Peterborough, then Lord Mordaunt, granted bond at London, after the English form, to Dr. William Abercromby, bearing, " That £210 was then advanced to " his lordship; and that, if he should happen to sur- " vive the Earl of Peterborough, his grandfather, he " was to pay £840 to the doctor, two months after " the Earl's death; and if he, the Lord Mordaunt, " died in the lifetime of the Earl, the obligation was " to be void." Upon the death of the Earl of Peterborough, which happened about five years after the date of the bond, an action was brought in the Court of Session against the Lord Mordaunt, now Earl of Peterborough, for payment; and the court, upon authority of the case immediately foregoing, unanimously judged, that the bond should only subsist for the sum actually borrowed, with the interest.†

* 2. Vernon 14, Berny *contra* Pitt.
† July 13, 1745, Dr. William Abercromby, *contra* Earl of Peterborough.

SECT. IV.

A man moved to act unknowingly against his interest by fraud, deceit, or other artificial means.

It is thought, that a court of common law, seldom interposes in any of the cases that come under the section immediately foregoing; and the reason is, that whether a man be led against his own interest by a violent temptation, or by extortion, there is still left to him in appearance a free choice. But with respect to the matters that belong to the present section, a man is led blindly against his own interest, and has no choice. This species of wrong, therefore, being more flagrant, is not neglected by courts of common law. It is accordingly laid down as a general rule in the English law, " That without the " express provision of an act of parliament, all de- " ceitful practices in defrauding another of his known " right, by means of some artful device, contrary to " the plain rules of common honesty, are condemned " by the common law, and punished according to the " heinousness of the offence."* Thus the causing an illiterate person to execute a deed to his prejudice, by reading it to him in words different from those in the deed, is a fraud, which a court of common law will redress, by setting the deed aside. The same where a woman is deceived to subscribe a warrant of attorney for confessing a judgment, understanding the writing to be of a different import.† In selling

---

* New Abridgment of the Law, vol. 2, p. 594.

† 1. Sid. 431.

a house, it being a lie to affirm that the rent is £30, instead of £20, by which the purchaser is moved to give a greater price than the house is worth; this loss will be repaired by a court of common law, though the purchaser, by being more circumspect, might have prevented the loss.

In general, every covenant procured by fraud, will be set aside in a court of common law. But with regard to covenants or agreements disregarded at common law, there can be no relief but in a court of equity. Thus a policy of insurance was set aside upon fraud, by a bill in chancery.*

We next proceed to enquire, whether every deceitful practice to impose upon others comes under common law. Fraud consists in my persuading a man who has confidence in me, to do an act as for his own interest, which I know will have the contrary effect. But in whatever manner a man may be deceived or misled, yet if he was not deceived by relying upon the friendship and integrity of another, it is not a fraud. Fraud, therefore, implies treachery, without which no artifice nor double dealing can be termed *fraud* in a proper sense. But there are double-faced circumstances without number, and other artful means, calculated to deceive, which do not involve any degree of treachery. Where a man is deceived by such artifice, it must in some measure be his own fault; and bystanders are more apt to make him the object of their ridicule than of their sorrow: for which reason, frauds of this inferior nature have been overlooked by common law. But as every attempt to deceive another to his prejudice is criminal in conscience, it is the duty of a court of equity to repress such deceit, by

* 2. Vernon, 206.

awarding reparation to the person who suffers. Utility pleads for reparation as well as equity; for if law were not attentive to repress deceit in its bud, corruption would gain ground, and even the grossest frauds would become too stubborn for law. It is this species of deceit, excluding treachery, that Lord Coke probably had in his eye,[*] when he lays down the following doctrine, That all covins, frauds, and deceits, for which there is no remedy at common law, are and were always redressed in the court of chancery.

It is mentioned above, that a covenant procured by fraud will be set aside in a court of common law; and I now give instances where a covenant procured by deceit that amounts not to fraud, is set aside in a court of equity. A man having failed in his trade, compounded with his creditors at so much per pound, to be paid at a time certain. Some of the creditors refusing to fulfil the agreement, a bill was brought by the bankrupt to compel a specific performance. But it appearing, that he had underhand agreed with some of his creditors to pay their whole debts, in order that they might draw in the rest to a composition, the court would not decree the agreement, but dismissed the bill.[†] A purchase made by a merchant in the course of commerce will be effectual, however soon his bankruptcy follow, provided it was his intention, by continuing in trade, to pay the price. But if he had bankruptcy in view, and no prospect to pay the price, the bargain brought about by a palpable cheat, will be reduced in a court of equity, and the subject be restored to the vender. The only thorny point is, to detect the *animus* of the purchaser to de-

[*] 4, Inst. 81,

[†] 2. Vernon. 71. Child *contra* Danbridge.

P. I. 1.   PROTECTING FROM HARM.   59

fraud the vender. In the case of *Joseph Cave*,* the presumptive fraud was confined to three days before the *cessio bonorum*; but in that case Cave the purchaser was in good credit, till he demanded a meeting of his creditors in order to surrender his effects to them. Other circumstances may concur with insolvency to enlarge that period. Gilbert Barclay, merchant in Cromarty, was in labouring circumstances, and owed much more than he was worth, when he made a purchase of salmon from Mackay of Bighouse; and before delivery, several of his creditors proceeded to execution against him. A few days after delivery, he made over the salmon to William Forsyth, another merchant of the same town, in part payment of a debt due to Forsyth; who was in the knowledge that Barclay was in labouring circumstances, and that the price of the salmon was not paid. Execution thickened more and more upon him, and he broke in ten days or a fortnight after the salmon were delivered to Forsyth. From these circumstances, the court presumed an intention in Barclay to defraud Bighouse: and considering that Forsyth's purchase was not made *bona fide*, they found him liable to pay to Bighouse the value of the salmon.†

Next of other transactions brought about by deceitful means. By a marriage-settlement *A* is tenant for life of certain mills, remainder to his first son in tail. The son, knowing of the settlement, encourages a person, after taking a thirty years lease of these mills, to lay out a considerable sum in new buildings, and other improvements, intending to take the benefit af-

* Dict. tit. Fraud.

† Mackay of Bighouse *contra* William Forsyth, merchant in Cromarty, January 20, 1758,

PROTECTING FROM HARM. B. I.

ter his father's death. This is a deceit which justice
discountenances; and, therefore, it was decreed, that
the lessee should enjoy for the residue of the term
that was current at the father's death.[*] The defendant, on a treaty of marriage for his daughter with
the plaintiff, signed a writing comprising the terms
of the agreement. Designing afterward to get loose
from the agreement, he ordered his daughter to en-
tice the plaintiff to deliver up the writing, and then
to marry him. She obeyed; and the defendant stood
at the corner of the street to see them go along to be
married. The plaintiff was relieved on the point of
deceit. A man having agreed to be bound for certain provisions in his son's contract of marriage, upon a promise from the son to discharge the same,
which, accordingly, was done before the marriage;
and, after the marriage, money having been lent to
the son upon the faith of the said provisions in his
contract, the discharge was set aside at the instance
of the creditors, as being a deceitful contrivance between father and son to entrap them.[†] In a suit
by the indorsee of a note or ticket, the debtor pleaded compensation upon a note for the equivalent sum,
granted him by the indorser, bearing the same date
with that upon which the process was founded. The
court deemed this a deceitful contrivance to furnish
the indorser credit; and, therefore, refused to sustain the compensation[‡].

A having an encumbrance upon an estate, is witness to a subsequent mortgage, but conceals his own
incumbrance. For this wrong his incumbrance shall

[*] Abridgment cases in equity, cap. 47, sect. B. par. 10.
[†] Stair, January 21, 1680, Caddel *contra* Raith.
[‡] Fount. Forbes, June 11, 1708, Bundy *contra* Kennedy.

P. I. 1.   PROTECTING FROM HARM.   61

be postponed.* To mortgage land as free, when there is an incumbrance upon it, is a cheat in the borrower; to which cheat the incumbrancer is accessory by countenancing the mortgage, and subscribing it as a witness. The hurt thus done to the lender, by putting him off with a lame security, was properly repaired by preferring him before the incumbrancer. The following cases are of the same kind. A man lends his mortgage-deed to the mortgager, to enable him to borrow more money. The mortgagee being thus in combination with the mortgager to deceive the lender, is accessory to the fraud. And the hurt thereby done was properly repaired by postponing his mortgage to the incumbrance, which the lender got for his money.† A counsel having a statute from *A* which he conceals, advises *B* to lend *A* £1,000 on a mortgage, and draws the mortgage with a covenant against incumbrances. The statute was postponed to the mortgage.‡ *A* being about to lend money to *B* on a mortgage, sends to inquire of *D*, who had a prior mortgage, whether he had any incumbrance on *B*'s estate. If it be proved that *D* denied he had any incumbrance, his mortgage will be postponed.§ An estate being settled by marriage-articles upon the children of the marriage, which estate did not belong to the husband, but to his mother; yet she was compelled in equity to make good the settlement; because she was present when the son declared that the estate was to come to him after

* 2. Vern. 151, Clare *contra* Earl of Bedford.
† Ibid. 726, Peter *contra* Russel.
‡ New abridgment of the law, vol. 2, p. 598, Draper *contra* Borlace.
§ 2. Vern. 554, Ibbotson *contra* Rhodes.

PROTECTING FROM HARM. B. I.

her death, and because she was also one of the instrumentary witnesses. *

SECT. V.

What remedy is applied by a Court of Equity against the wrongs above stated.

It is proper to be premised, that regulations for preventing harm cannot be other but prohibitory; and, consequently, cannot afford opportunity for the interposition of any court of law till the wrong be committed. To restore the party injured to his former situation, where that method is practicable, will be preferred as the most complete remedy. Thus goods stolen are restored to the owner; and a disposition of land procured by fear, or undue influence, is voided, in order that the disponer may be restored to his property. But it seldom happens, that there is place for a remedy so complete: it holds commonly, as expressed in the Roman law, that *factum infectum fieri nequit*; and when that is the case, the person injured, who cannot be restored to his former situation, must be contented with reparation in money.

The first question that occurs here is, Whether in money-reparation, consequential damage can be stated? Consequential damage is sometimes certain, sometimes uncertain. A house of mine rented by a tenant, is unlawfully demolished: the direct damage is the loss of the house: the consequential damage is the loss of the rent; which in this case is certain, because

* 2. Vern. 150, Hunsdens *contra* Cheiney.

the unlawful act necessarily relieves the tenant from paying rent. Again, a man robs me of my horse: the direct damage is the horse lost to me: the consequential damage is the being prevented from making profit by him; which is not certain, because the opportunity of making profit might have failed me, and possibly might have been neglected though it had offered. In the case first mentioned, the loss of the rent, being certain, comes properly under the estimation of actual damage; and consequently will not be excluded by a court of common law. But consequential damage that is uncertain, is not always taken into the account. And the reason follows. It is regularly incumbent on the man who claims reparation, to prove the extent of the damage he has sustained, which cannot be done with respect to consequential damage, as far as uncertain. But as it is undoubtedly a prejudice to be deprived of profit that probably might have been made, the claimant is in equity relieved from this proof, where the direct damage is the effect of a criminal act: every presumption is turned against the delinquent; and he is charged with every probable article of profit, unless he can give convincing evidence that the profit claimed could not have been made. And this is conformable to the rules of equity; for as the profits are rendered uncertain by a criminal act, the consequences of this uncertainty ought to affect the delinquent, not his party, who is innocent. Here is a fair opportunity for the interposition of equity. A court of common law cannot listen to any proof but what is complete; and cannot award damages except as far as rendered certain by evidence. A court of equity, with respect to criminal acts, turns the uncertainty against the

PROTECTING FROM HARM. B. I.

delinquent; and by that means affords complete reparation to the person injured. Thus, in a spuilzie, which is a claim for damages in a civil court founded on the violent abstraction of moveable goods, the profit that might have been made by the horses carried off termed *violent profits*, makes always an article in the estimation of damage. The rule is different, where the damage is occasioned by a culpable act only.; for as there is nothing here to vary the rule of law, *Quod affirmanti incumbit probatio*, no article of profit will be sustained but what can be rendered certain by evidence. This, it is true, may possibly be prejudicial to the person who is hurt by the culpable act; but *humanum est errare*; and it is more expedient that he suffer some prejudice than that men should be terrified from industry and activity, by a rigorous and vague claim. *(a)* This doctrine is espoused by Ulpian: * " Item Labeo scribit, si cum " vi ventorum navis impulsa esset in funes anchora- " rum alterius, et nautæ funes præcidissent, si nullo " alio modo, nisi præcisis funibus explicare se potuit, " nullam actionem dandam. Idemque Labeo, et Pro- " culus, et circa retia piscatorum, in quæ navis inci- " derat, æstimârunt. Plane, si culpa nautarum id " factum esset, lege Aquilia agendum. Sed ubi danmi " injuria agitur, ob retia, non piscium, qui capti non " sunt, fieri æstimationem ; cum incertum fuerit, an " caperentur. Idemque et in venatoribus, et in au-

. (*a*) In the English courts of common law there is no accurate distinction made between damage certain and uncertain. Damages are taxed by the jury, who give such damages as in conscience they think sufficient to make up the loss, without having any precise rule.

* L. 29. § 3. ad leg. Aquil.

P. I. 1. PROTECTING FROM HARM. 65

" cupibus probandum." The following instance is
an apt illustration of this doctrine. The Duke of
Argyle's right of admiralty reaches over the western
islands : on the coast of which a wrecked ship, floating without a living creature in it, was laid hold of
and sold by authority of the Duke's depute to one
Robertson, who refitted the ship at a considerable
charge, and provided a crew to carry her to Clyde.
Sir Ludovick Grant, who had a deputation from the
Admiral of Scotland, misapprehending the bounds of
his jurisdiction, gave orders for seizing the ship as
his property ; and these orders were put in execution
after the ship was refitted by Robertson. As soon
as the mistake was discovered, the ship was redeliver-
ed. But Robertson, who lost considerably by the delay, brought a process against Sir Ludovick for damages, and obtained a decree* for a large sum, to
which the direct damage amounted. It was considered, that the defendant's error was culpable in acting
rashly without duly examining the limits of his jurisdiction, which might have been ascertained by in-
specting the Duke's title on record. But as to the
consequential damage, namely, the profits Robertson
could have made by the ship had he not been unjustly deprived of the possession, which must be uncertain, the court unanimously rejected that branch of
the claim.

The next question is, Whether in estimating damage there be ground in any case for admitting the
pretium affectionis. Paulus answers, That there is
not : " Si servum meum occidisti, non affectiones
" aestimandas esse puto, (velnti si filium tuum natura-

---

* December 21, 1756.

E.

66 PROTECTING FROM HARM. B. L.

" lem quis occiderit, quem tu magno emptum velles),
" sed quanti omnibus valeret. Sextus quoque Pedius
" ait pretia rerum, non ex affectione, nec utilitate sin-
" gulorum, sed communiter fungi. Itaque eum, qui
" filium naturalem possidet, non eo locupletiorem
" esse, quod eum plurimo, si alius possideret, re-
" dempturus fuit: nec illum, qui filium alienum pos-
" sideat, tantum habere, quanti eum patri vendere
" posset: in lege enim Aquilia (damnum) consequi-
" mur, et amisisse dicemur, quod aut consequi po-
" tuimus, aut erogare cogimur."* As this response
is given in general terms, without distinction of cases,
it must be considered as declaratory of the common
law. The same rule must obtain in equity where the
wrong is culpable only. But in repairing mischief
done intentionally, the *pretium affectionis* ought in
equity to be admitted; because otherwise the person
who suffers obtains no adequate reparation; and also
because that otherwise there is no proper distinction
made between a crime and a fault.

CHAPTER II.

*Powers of a Court of Equity to remedy what is im-
perfect in common law, with respect to protecting
the weak of mind from harming themselves by unequal bargains and irrational deeds.*

THE weakness and imbecility of some men make
them a fit prey for the crafty and designing. But as
every deed, covenant, or transaction, procured by un-

* L. 33, ad legem Aquiliam.

P. I. 2.   PROTECTING FROM HARM.   67

due influence, comes under the foregoing chapter, the present chapter is confined to cases where equity protects individuals, who are not misled by undue influence, from hurting themselves by their own weakness and imbecility. And here, though for the sake of commerce, utility will not listen to a complaint of inequality among *majores, scientes, et prudentes;* yet the weak of mind ought to be excepted; because such persons ought to be removed from commerce, and their transactions be confined to what is strictly necessary for their subsistence and well-being. And this is justly confining to the weak of mind a rule against inequality in bargains, which the Romans, ignorant of commerce, made general in respect to every person.

I begin with deeds granted by persons under age, who cannot be supposed mature in judgment. A reduction upon the head of minority and lesion, unknown in the common law, is an action sustained by a court of equity for setting aside any unequal transaction done during nonage. But inequality ought not to be regarded in a deed that proceeds from a virtuous and rational motive, which would be a laudable deed in one of full age. I give the following examples. A young man under age, having no means of his own, is alimented and educated by a near relation, till he happens to succeed to an opulent fortune. Full of gratitude, he grants to his benefactor a remuneratory bond for a moderate sum, and dies without arriving to full age. A court of equity will never give countenance to the heir attempting to reduce this bond; for gratitude is a moral duty, and the young man was in conscience bound to make a grateful return. A court of equity, it is true, has not many opportunities to enforce the duty of gratitude, because it can seldom be brought under a general rule ; but here the court may safely interpose to support a grateful return, the extent of which is ascertained by the young man himself. I put another case. A man of an opulent fortune dies suddenly without making provisions for his younger children. His eldest son and heir supplies this omission by giving suitable provisions, and dies under age. I put a third case. A man of an opulent fortune dies suddenly, leaving a numerous family of children, all of the female sex, without making provisions for them. A collateral heir-male succeeds, who supplies this omission by giving suitable provisions, but dies under age. A court of equity would deviate from the spirit of its institution, if it should authorize a reduction of such provisions by the granter's heir, upon the head of minority and lesion. For a rational and laudable deed never can be lesion in any proper sense.

The same doctrine is applicable to those who have a natural imbecility which continues for life. A transaction made by such a person is not voided by a court of equity, unless it appear irrational, and the effect of imbecility. Where this is the case, it becomes indeed necessary that the court interpose, though there can be no general rule for direction.

The protection afforded by equity to the weak in mind, is extended to save them from hurting themselves by irrational settlements. The opinions of men with respect to the management of affairs, and the exercising acts of property, are no less various than their faces : and as the world is seldom agreed about what is rational and irrational in such matters, there can be no rule for restraining the settlements

PROTECTING FROM HARM.

of those who are not remarkably weak, unless such settlements be not only irrational but absurd. But as the weak and facile are protected against unequal bargains, there is the same reason for their being protected against absurd settlements. Take the following example. In a process at the instance of a brother next of kin, for voiding a testament made by his deceased sister, in favour of a stranger: it came out upon proof, that, some time before making the testament, the testatrix, being seized with madness, was locked up; and that, not long after making the testament, her madness recurred, and continued till her death; that at the time of the testament she was in a wavering state, sometimes better, sometimes worse; in some instances rational, in others little better than delirious, never perfectly sound in mind. In particular, it appeared from the proof, that when in better health, she expressed much affection for her brother the pursuer; but that, when the disease was more upon her, she appeared to have some grudge or resentment at him without any cause. The testament was holograph; and the scroll she copied was furnished by the defendant, in whose favour the testament was made, who had ready access to her at all times, while her brother lived at a distance. In reasoning, it was yielded, that the woman was capable of making a testament, and that the testament challenged might be effectual at common law. But then, it was urged, That though a testament made in the condition of mind above described, preferring one relation before another, a son before a father, or a sister before a brother, might be supported in equity as well as at common law; yet that the testament in question, proceeding not from rational views, but from a

70 DUTY OF B. I.

diseased mind, occasioning a causeless resentment against the pursuer, ought not to be supported in equity, being a deed which the testatrix herself must have been ashamed of had she recovered health. Weight also was laid upon the following circumstance, That the testament was made *remotis arbitris*, and kept secret; which showed the defendant's consciousness, that the testatrix would have been easily diverted by her friends from making so irrational a settlement. In this view, it was considered as a wrong in him to take from her, in these circumstances, an irrational deed; and consequently, that he ought to be restrained in equity from taking any benefit by it. The testament was voided.*

A temporary weakness ought, for the time of its endurance, to have the same effect in law with one that is perpetual; for which reason a discharge obtained from a woman during the pains of childbirth, was reduced; *Fountainhall, 7th December* 1686.

CHAPTER III.

Powers of a court of equity to remedy what is imperfect in common law, with respect to the natural duty of benevolence.

IN the Introduction there was occasion to observe, that the virtue of benevolence is, by various connections, converted into a duty; and that duties of this kind, being neglected by the common law, are enforced by a court of equity. This opens a wide field

* Jan. 26. 1759, Tulloch *contra* Visc. of Arbuthnott.

BENEVOLENCE.

of equity, boundless in appearance, and which would be so in reality as well as in appearance, were it not for one circumstance, That the duty of benevolence is much more limited than the virtue. The virtue of benevolence may be exercised in a great variety of good offices : it tends often to make additions to the positive happiness of others, as well as to relieve them from distress or want. But abstracting from positive engagement, the duty of benevolence is, with respect to pecuniary interest, confined to the latter. No connection, no situation, nor circumstance, makes it my duty to enlarge the estate of any person who has already a sufficiency, or to make him *locupletior*, as termed in the Roman law. For even in the strictest of all connections, that of parent and child, I feel not that I am in conscience or in duty bound, to do more than to make my children independent, so as to preserve them from want : *(a)* all beyond is left

(*a*) This proposition is illustrated in the following case. Mary Scot, daughter of Scot of Highchester, having, by unlucky circumstances, been reduced to indigence, was alimented by her mother, Lady Mary Drummond, at the rate of £20 yearly. Lady Mary, at the approach of death, settled all her effects upon Mary Sharp, her daughter of another marriage, taking no other notice of her daughter, Mary Scot, but the recommending her to the charity of Mary Sharp. After the mother's death, Mary Scot brought a process for aliment against her sister, Mary Sharp, founded chiefly on the said recommendation. A proof was taken of the extent of the effects contained in the settlement to the defendant, which amounted to about £300 sterling. No action, either in law or equity, could be founded on the recommendation, very different in its nature from an obligation or a burden. But it was stated, that the pursuer, being very young when her father died, was educated by her mother to no business by which she could gain a livelihood ; and it occurred to the court, that though the *patria potestas* is such, that a peer may breed his son a cobler,

upon parental affection. Neither doth gratitude make it my duty to enrich my benefactor, but only to aid and support him, when any sort of distress or want calls for help. A favour is, indeed, scarce felt to be such, but when it prevents or relieves from harm; and a favour naturally is returned in kind.

Here is a clear circumscription of equity, as far as concerns the present chapter. A court of equity cannot force one man, whether by his labour or money, to add to the riches of another; because, abstracting from a promise, no connection makes this a duty. What then is left for a court of equity, is, in certain circumstances, to compel persons to save from mischief those they are connected with, or to relieve them from want or distress. Benevolence, in this case is a strong impulse to afford relief; and in this case, benevolence, assuming the name of *pity* or *compassion*, is, by a law in our nature, made a positive duty. In all other cases, benevolence is a virtue only, not a duty: the exercise is left to our own choice; and the neglect is not punished, though the practice is highly rewarded by the satisfaction it af-

and after settling him in business with a competent stock, is relieved from all further aliment; yet if a son be bred as a gentleman, without being instructed in any art that can gain him a farthing, he is entitled to be alimented for life; for otherwise a palpable absurdity will follow, that a man may starve his son, or leave him to want or beggary. Thus, Lady Mary Drummond, breeding her daughter to no business, was, by the law of nature, bound to aliment her for life, or at least till she should be otherwise provided; and the pursuer, therefore, being a creditor for this aliment, has a good action against her mother's representatives. The court, accordingly, found the pursuer entitled to an aliment of £12 sterling yearly, and decerned against the defendant for the same.—*8th March* 1759, *Mary Scot* contra *Mary Sharp.*

fords. In this branch of our nature, a beautiful final cause is visible : the benevolence of man, by want of ability, is confined within narrow bounds ; and in order to make the most of that slender power he has of doing good, it is wisely directed where it is the most useful, namely, to relieve others from distress.

It appears then, that equity, with respect to the duty of serving others, is not extended beyond pity or compassion. But it is circumscribed within still narrower bounds ; for compassion, though a natural duty, is not adopted in its utmost extent by courts of equity. In many cases, this duty is too vague and undetermined to be reached by human laws ; and a court of equity pretends not to interpose, but where the duty, being clear and precise, can be brought under general rules.* Some of the connections that occasion duty so precise I shall proceed to handle, confining myself to those that are in some measure involved in circumstances ; for the more simple connections, such as that of parent and child, require little or no elucidation. Though all the duties of this kind that are enforced by a court of equity, belong to the principle of justice ; they may, however, be divided into different classes. The present chapter is, accordingly, divided into two sections. In the first are handled connections that make benevolence a duty, when not prejudicial to our interest. In the second are handled connections that make benevolence a duty even against our interest. These connections are distinguishable from each other so clearly, as to prevent any confusion of ideas ; and the foregoing order is chosen, that we may pass gradually from the slighter to the more intimate connections.

* See the Introduction.

74 DUTY OF B. I.

To prompt a man to serve those with whom he is connected, requires not any extraordinary motive, when the good office thwarts not his own interest: any slight connection is sufficient to make this a duty, and, therefore, such connections are first discussed. It requires a more intimate connection, to make it our duty to bestow upon another any part of our substance. Self-interest is not to be overcome but by connections of the most intimate kind, which, therefore, are placed last in order.

SECT. I.

Connections that make benevolence a duty when not prejudicial to our interest.

THE connection I shall first take under consideration, is that which subsists between a creditor and a cautioner. The nature of this engagement demands benevolence on the part of the creditor. The cautioner, when he pays the debt, suffers loss by the act of the creditor, though not by his fault; and the creditor will find himself bound in humanity, as far as consistent with his own interest, to assist the cautioner in operating his relief against the principal debtor. He ought, in particular, to convey to the cautioner, the bond with the execution done upon it, in order that the cautioner may the more speedily obtain relief from the principal. The law, favouring this moral act, considers the money delivered to the creditor not as payment, but as a valuable consideration for assigning his debt and execution to the cautioner. I cannot explain this better than in the words

P. I. 3.   BENEVOLENCE.   75

of Papinian, the most eminent of all the writers on the Roman law : " Cum possessor unus, expediendi " negotii causa, tributorum jure conveniretur ; ad- " versus cæteros, quorum æque prædia tenentur, ei, " qui conventus est, actiones a fisco præstantur : sci- " licet ut omnes pro modo prædiorum pecuniam tri- " buti conferant : nec inutiliter actiones præstantur " tametsi fiscus pecuniam suam reciperaverit, quia " nominum venditorum pretium acceptum videtur."* From which consideration it follows, that this assignment may be demanded and granted *ex post facto*, if the precaution be omitted when the money is paid.

From this connection it also follows, that the creditor is bound to convey to the cautioner every separate security he has for the debt ; and, consequently, that if the creditor discharge or pass from his separate security, the cautioner, as far as he suffers thereby, hath an exception in equity against payment.

I must observe historically, that there are many decisions of the Court of Session, declaring the creditor not bound to grant the assignment first mentioned. These decisions, remote in point of time, will not be much regarded ; because the rules of equity lay formerly in greater obscurity than at present. And there is an additional reason for disregarding them, that they are not consistent with others relating to the same subject. If it be laid down as a rule, that the creditor is not bound to assign his bond and execution, it ought to follow, that neither is he bound to assign any separate security ; if it be not his duty to serve the cautioner in the one case, it cannot be his duty to serve him in the other. And yet, it is a rule established in this court, that the caution-

* L. 5, De censibus.

er, making payment of the debt, is entitled to every separate security of which the creditor is possessed. One is at no loss to discover the cause of this discrepancy : when the question is about a separate security, upon which the cautioner's relief may wholly depend, the principle of equity makes a strong impression : its impression is slighter when the question is only about assigning the bond, which has no other effect but to save a process.

It is of the greater consequence to settle with precision the equitable rule that governs questions between the creditor and cautioner, because upon it depends, in my apprehension, the mutual relief between co-cautioners. Of two cautioners bound for the same debt at different times, and in different deeds, one pays the debt upon a discharge, without an assignment : where is the legal foundation that entitles this man to claim the half from his fellow-cautioner? The being bound in different deeds, affords no place for supposing an implied stipulation of mutual relief : nay, supposing them bound in the same deed, we are not, from that single circumstance, to imply a mutual consent for relief, but rather the contrary, when the clause of mutual relief is omitted ; for, in general, when an obvious clause is left out of a deed, it is natural to ascribe the omission to design rather than to forgetfulness. The principal debtor is *ex mandato* bound to relieve all his cautioners : but there is no medium at common law, by which one cautioner can demand relief from another. And with respect to equity, the connection of being bound for payment of the same debt, is too slight to entitle that cautioner who pays the whole debt, to be indemnified in part out of the goods of his fellow. It ap-

BENEVOLENCE.

pears, then, that the claim of mutual relief among co-cautioners can have no foundation, other than the obligation upon the creditor to assign upon payment. This assignment in the case of a single cautioner must be total; in the case of several must be *pro rata;* because the creditor is equally connected with each of them. The only difficulty is, that, at this rate, there is no mutual relief unless an assignment be actually given. But this difficulty is easily surmounted. We have seen above, that such assignment may be granted *ex post facto:* hence, it is the duty of the creditor to grant the assignment at whatever time demanded; and if the creditor prove refractory, the law will interpose to hold an assignment as granted, because it ought to be granted. And this suppletory or implied legal assignment, is the true foundation of the mutual relief among co-cautioners, which obtains both in Scotland and England.

Utility concurs to support this equitable claim: no situation with regard to law would be attended with more pernicious consequences, than to permit a creditor to oppress one cautioner and relieve others: judges ought to be jealous of such arbitrary powers, which will generally be directed by bad motives; often by resentment, and, which is still worse, more often by avarice. It is happy, therefore, for mankind, that two different principles coincide in matters of this kind, to put them upon a just and salutary footing.

The creditor, as has been said; being bound to all the cautioners equally, cannot legally give an assignment to one of them in such terms as to entitle him to claim the whole from the other cautioners. In what terms, then, ought the assignment to be granted? or, when granted without limitation, what effect ought it to have in equity? This is a question of some subtilty. To permit the assignee to demand the whole from any single cautioner, deducting only his own part of the debt, is unequal; because it evidently gives the assignee an advantage over his co-cautioners. On the other hand, the assignee is in a worse situation than any other of them, if he must submit to take from each of them separately his proportion of the debt: upon this plan, the cautioner who pays the debt is forced to run the circuit of all his co-cautioners; and if one or two prove insolvent, he must renew the suit against the rest, to make up the proportions of those who are deficient. To preserve, therefore, a real equality among the cautioners, every one of them against whom relief is claimed, ought to bear an equal proportion with the assignee. To explain this rule, I suppose six cautioners bound in a bond for six hundred pounds. The first paying the debt is entitled to claim the half from the second, who ought to be equally burdened with the first. When the first and second again attack the third, they have a claim against him each for a hundred pounds; which resolves in laying the burden of two hundred pounds upon each;—and so on till the whole cautioners be discussed. This method not only preserves equality, but avoids after-reckonings in cases of insolvency.

So far clear when relief can be directly obtained. But what if the assignee be put to the trouble of adjudging for his relief? In that case, the assignment is a legal title to lead an adjudication for the whole debt. Equity is satisfied, if no more be actually

BENEVOLENCE.

drawn out of the estate of the co-cautioners, than what that co-cautioner is bound to contribute, as above. And in leading the adjudication, not even the adjudger's own proportion of the debt ought to be deducted: it is a benefit to the other cautioners that the security be as extensive as possible; for it entitles the adjudger to a greater proportion of the subject or price, in competition with extraneous creditors.

The same principles and conclusions are equally applicable to *correi debendi*, where a number of debtors are bound conjunctly and severally to one creditor. Equity requires the utmost impartiality in him to his debtors: if, for his own ease, he take the whole from one, he is bound to grant an assignment precisely as in the case of co-cautioners. Utility joins with equity to enforce this impartiality. And it makes no difference whether the *correi debendi* be bound for a civil debt, or be bound *ex delicto*; for in both causes equally it is the duty of the creditor to act impartially, and in both cases equally utility requires impartiality.

Another connection, of the same nature with the former, is that between one creditor who is infeft in two different tenements for his security, and another creditor, who hath an infeftment on one of the tenements, of a later date. Here the two creditors are connected, by having the same debtor, and a security upon the same subject. Hence it follows, as in the former case, that if it be the will of the preferable creditor to draw his whole payment out of that subject in which the other creditor is infeft, the latter for his relief is entitled to have the preferable security assigned to him: which can be done upon the con-.

straction above mentioned; for the sum recovered by the preferable creditor out of the subject on which the other creditor is also infeft, is justly understood to be advanced by the latter, being a sum which he was entitled to, and must have drawn had not the preferable creditor intervened; and this sum is held to be the purchase-money of the conveyance. This construction, preserving the preferable debt entire in the person of the second creditor, entitles him to draw payment of that debt out of the other tenement. By this equitable construction, matters are restored to the same state as if the first creditor had drawn his payment out of the separate subject, leaving the other entire for payment of the second creditor. Utility also concurs to support this equitable claim.

It is scarce necessary here to observe, that a supposed conveyance, sufficient, as above mentioned, to found a claim of relief among co-cautioners, will not answer in the present case. In order to found an execution against land, there must be an infeftment; and this infeftment must be conveyed to the person who demands execution. Any just or equitable consideration may be sufficient to found a personal action; but even personal execution cannot proceed without a formal warrant, and still less real execution.

But now, admitting it to be the duty of the preferable creditor to assign, the question is, To what extent. Whether ought the assignment to have a total effect, or only to put the disappointed creditor in the same situation as if the preferable creditor had drawn his payment proportionally out of both subjects? It will be made appear by and by, that the assignment must be confined to the latter effect in the

BENEVOLENCE.

case of two secondary creditors. But there is no equity to limit the assignment in this manner, where there is no interest in opposition but that of the debtor. He has no equitable interest to oppose a total assignment; and the second creditor has an equitable claim to all the aid the first creditor can afford him.

The rules of equity must be the same in every country where law is cultivated. By the practice in England,[*] if the creditor sweep away the personal estate, the real estate will be charged for payment of the legacies. In this case, the legatees need no assignment to found their equitable claim against the heir who succeeds to the real estate.

We proceed to another connection, which is that between the preferable creditor infeft in both tenements, and two secondary creditors, one infeft in one of the tenements, and one in the other. The duty of the preferable or catholic creditor, with relation to these secondary creditors, cannot be doubtful, considering what is said above. Equity, as well as expediency, bars him from arbitrary measures. He is equally connected with his two fellow-creditors, and he must act impartially between them. The equitable measure is, to draw his payment proportionally out of both tenements; but if, for his own ease or conveniency, he chuse to draw the whole out of one, the postponed creditor is entitled to an assignment; not indeed total, which would be an arbitrary act, but proportional, so as to entitle him to draw out of the other subject, what he would have drawn out of his own, had the preferable creditor drawn proportionally out of both subjects. I need scarce mention, that the same rule which obtains in the case of se-

[*] 2. Chancery Cases, 4.

condary creditors, must equally obtain among purchasers of different parcels of land, which, before the purchase, were all *in cumulo* burdened with an infeftment of annualrent. A man grants a rent-charge out of all his lands, and afterwards sells them by parcels to divers persons : the grantee of the rent-charge levies his whole rent from one of these purchasers : this purchaser shall be eased in equity by a contribution from the rest of the purchasers.*

A case connected with that last handled, will throw light upon the present subject. Let it be supposed that the catholic or preferable creditor purchases one of the secondary debts : will this vary the rule of equity ? This purchase, in itself lawful, is not prohibited by any statute, and, therefore, must have its effect. The connection here between the creditors is by no means so intimate, as to oblige any one of them, at the expence of his own interest, to serve the others. There is no rule in equity to bar the catholic creditor from drawing full payment of the secondary debt out of the tenement which it burdens, reserving his catholic debt to be made effectual out of the other tenement ; though of consequence the secondary creditor upon that tenement is totally disappointed. This secondary creditor has no claim for an assignment, total or partial, when the interest of the catholic creditor stands in opposition. But here the connection among the parties must, in my apprehension, have the following equitable operation, that the catholic creditor, by virtue of his purchase, cannot draw more than the sum he paid for it. Equity in this case will not allow the one to profit by the

---

* Abridg. cases in equity, chap. 18, sect. A, § 1.

other's loss. But a hint here must suffice; because the point belongs more properly to another head.*

The following case proceeds upon the principle above laid down. The husband, on the marriage, charged the lands with a rent-charge for a jointure to his wife, and afterward devised part of these lands to the wife. After the husband's death, the heir prayed that the lands devised to the wife, might bear their proportion of the rent-charge : the bill was dismissed, because the grantee of the rent-charge may distrain in all or any part of the lands for her rent ; and there is no equity to abridge her remedy.†

If the catholic creditor, after the existence of both secondary debts, renounce his infeftment with respect to one of the tenements, which makes a clear fund for the secondary creditor secured upon that tenement ; such renunciation ought to have no effect in equity against the other secondary creditor, because it is an arbitrary deed, and a direct breach of that impartiality which the catholic creditor is bound to observe with relation to the secondary creditors. It is in effect the same with granting a total assignment to one of the secondary creditors against the other.

In every one of the cases mentioned, the catholic creditor is equally connected with each of the secondary creditors, and, upon that account, is bound to act impartially between them. But this rule of equity cannot take place where the connections are unequal. It holds here as among blood-relations : those who are nearest to me, are entitled to a preference in my favour. The following case will be a sufficient illus-

* Immediately below, sect 2, art. 1.
† 1. Vern. 347.

tration. A man takes a bond of borrowed money with a cautioner; obtains afterward an infeftment from the principal debtor as an additional security; and last of all, another creditor for his security obtains infeftment upon the same subject. Here the first mentioned creditor has two different means for obtaining payment: he may apply to the cautioner, or he may apply to the land in which he is infeft. He proceeds to execution against the land, by which he cuts out the second creditor. Is he bound to grant an assignment to the second creditor against the cautioner, total or partial? The second creditor is in this case not entitled to demand an assignment: on the contrary, the preferable creditor, taking payment from the cautioner, is bound to give him a total assignment; because he is more intimately connected with the cautioner than with the second creditor. A cautionary engagement is an act of pure benevolence; and when a creditor lays hold of this engagement to oblige one man to pay another's debt, this connection makes it evidently the duty of the creditor to aid the cautioner with an assignment, in order to repair his loss; and it proceeds from the same intimacy of connection, that, as above mentioned, he is obliged to include in this assignment every separate security he has for the debt. It is his duty accordingly to convey to the cautioner the real security he got from the principal debtor. Nor is the interest of the second creditor regarded in opposition; for he is no other way connected with the preferable creditor, but by being both of them creditors to the same person, and both of them infeft on the same subject for security.

A question of great importance, that has frequently

P. I. 3.   BENEVOLENCE.   85.

been debated in the Court of Session, appears to depend upon the principles above set forth. The question is, Whether a tenant in tail be bound to extinguish the annual burdens arising during his possession, so as to transmit to the heirs of entail the estate in as good condition as when he received it? To treat this question accurately, we must begin with considering how the common law stands. With respect to feu-duties, cess, and teind, these are *debita fructuum*, and at common law afford an action for payment against every person who levies the rents, and against a tenant in tail in particular. But this is not the case of the entailer's personal debts, which burden the heirs of entail personally, but not the fruits. Let us consider what that difference will produce. An heir in a fee-simple is liable to the debts of his predecessor, and every heir is so liable successively. But this obligation respects the creditors only; and affords no relief to one heir against another, either for principal or interest. Does an entail make a difference at common law? A tenant in tail possesses the rents: but these rents are his property, just as much if the estate were a fee-simple; and the consuming rents belonging to himself, cannot subject him as tenant in tail more than if his estate were a fee-simple. Hence it appears clear, that at common law a tenant in tail is not bound to relieve the heirs of entail of any growing burdens, unless what is a *debitum fructuum*.

A court of equity, less confined than a court of common law, finds this case resolvable into one above determined, namely, that of *correi debendi*, where several debtors are conjunctly bound for payment of one debt. There is no difference between *correi de-*

86 DUTY OF B. I.

bendi and heirs of entail, but that the former are all of them liable at the same time, the latter only successively ; which makes no difference either in equity or in expediency, the same impartiality being required of the creditor with respect to both. While the debt subsists, the creditor is bound to lay the burden of his interest upon each heir equally ; consequently each heir is bound to pay the interest that arises during his time. And if the principal be demanded, the heir who pays is only entitled to an assignment of the principal sum, and of the interest that shall arise after his own death. This rule accordingly obtains in England, as where a proprietor of land, after charging it with a sum of money, devises it to one for life, remainder to another in fee. Equity will compel the tenant for life to pay the arrears due on the rent-charge, that all may not fall upon the remainder-man. *

A tenant by courtesy is, like a tenant in tail, bound to extinguish the current burdens. The courtesy is established by customary law ; and a court of equity is entitled to supply any defect in law, whether written or customary, in order to make the law rational. The law, authorising the husband to possess the wife's estate, intends no more but to give him the enjoyment of it for life, without waste, confining him to act like a *bonus paterfamilias.*†

The following case seems to require the interposition of a court of equity ; and yet, whether its powers reach so far is doubtful. A man assigns to a relation of his £500 contained in a bond specified, without power of revocation, reserving only his own life-

* 1. Chancery Cases 223.
† Home, Jan. 3, 1717, Anna Monteith.

P. I. 3.   BENEVOLENCE.   87

rent. Many years after, forgetting the assignment, he makes a will, naming this same relation his exe-cutor and residuary legatee, bequeathing in the testament the foresaid bond of £500 to another relation. The testator's effects, abstracting from the bond, not exceeding in value £500, it becomes to the executor-nominate a matter indifferent, whether he accept the testament, or betake himself to his own bond. But it is not indifferent to others ; for if he undertake the office of executor, he must convey the bond to the special legatee ; if he cling to the bond, rejecting the office, the testament falls to the ground, and the next of kin will take the effects, leaving nothing to the special legatee. The interest of others ought not to depend on the arbitrary will of the executor-nomin-ate ; and yet, as far as appears, there is no place here for the interposition of equity. The privilege of accepting or rejecting a right, no man can be deprived of ; and, admitting this privilege, the consequences that follow seem to be out of the reach of equity.

Land-estates that are conterminous, form such a connection between the proprietors, as to make certain acts of benevolence their duty, which belong to the present subject. To save my ground from water flowing upon it from a neighbouring field, a court of equity will entitle me to repair a bulwark within that field, provided the reparation do not hurt the proprietor.* The following is a similar case. The course of a rivulet which serves my mill, happens to be diverted, a torrent having filled with stones or mud the channel in my neighbour's ground above. I will be permitted to remove the obstruction though in my neighbour's property, in order to restore the

* L. 2, § 5, in fine, De aquæ et pluviæ arcen.

88 DUTY OF B. I.

rivulet to its natural channel. My neighbour is bound to suffer this operation, because it relieves me from damage without harming his property.

But in order to procure any actual profit, or to make myself *locupletior*, equity will not interpose or entitle me to make any alteration in my neighbour's property, even where he cannot specify any prejudice by the alteration. The reason is given above, That equity never obliges any man, whether by acting or suffering, to increase the estate of another. Thus, the Earl of Eglinton having built a mill upon the river of Irvine, and stretched a dam-dike cross the channel, which occasioned a restagnation to the prejudice of a superior mill; Fairly, the proprietor of this mill, brought a process, complaining that his mill was hurt by the back-water, and concluding, that the Earl's dam-dike be demolished, or so altered as to give a free course to the river. The restagnation being acknowledged, the Earl proposed to raise the pursuer's mill-wheel ten inches, which would make the mill go as well as formerly; offering security against all future damage: and urged, that to refuse submitting to this alteration would be acting *in æmulationem vicini*, which the law doth not indulge. The court judged the defendant's dam-dike to be an encroachment on the pursuer's property, and ordained the same to be removed or taken down as far as it occasioned the restagnation.*

* Jan. 27, 1744, Fairly *contra* Earl of Eglinton.

SECT. II.

Connections that make benevolence a duty even against our interest.

THESE connections must be very intimate; for, as observed in the beginning of the present chapter, it requires a much stronger connection to oblige me to bestow upon another any portion of my substance, than merely to do a good office which takes nothing from me. The bulk of these connections, though extremely various, may be brought under the following heads. 1st, Connections that entitle a man to have his loss made up out of my gain. 2d, Connections that entitle a man who is not, properly speaking, a loser, to partake of my gain. 3d, Connections that entitle one who is a loser to a recompence from one who is not a gainer.

ART. I. *Connections that entitle a man to have his loss made up out of my gain.*

No personal connection, supposing the most intimate, that of parent and child, can make it an act of justice, that one who is a gainer, should repair the loss sustained by another, unless there be also some connection between the loss and gain; and that connection is a capital circumstance in the present speculation. The connections hitherto mentioned relate to persons; this relates to things. If, for example, I lay out my money for ameliorating a subject that I consider to be my own, but which is afterward disco-

90   DUTY OF   B. I.

vered to be the property of another; my loss in this case is intimately connected with his gain, because in effect my money goes into his pocket.

The connection between the loss and gain may be more or less intimate : and its different degrees of intimacy ought to be carefully noted. When this connection is found in the highest degree, there is scarce requisite any other circumstance to oblige one to apply his gain for making up another's loss : in its lower degrees no duty arises, unless the persons be otherwise strongly connected. Proceeding then to trace these degrees, the lowest I have occasion to mention, is where the loss and gain are connected by their relation to the same subject. For example, a man purchases at a low rate one of the preferable debts upon a bankrupt estate ; and, upon a sale of the estate, draws more than the transacted sum : he gains while his fellow-creditors lose considerably. The next degree going upward, is where my gain is the occasion of another's loss. For example, a merchant foreseeing a scarcity, purchases all the corn he can find in the neighbourhood, with a view to make great profit ; before he opens his granaries, I import a large cargo from abroad, retailing it at a moderate price, under what my brother-merchant paid for his cargo ; by which means he loses considerably. The third, pretty much upon a level with the former, is where another's loss is the occasion of my gain. For example, my ship loaded with corn proceeds, in company with another, to a port where there is a scarcity : the other ship being foundered in a storm, and the cargo lost, my cargo by that means draws a better price. The fourth connection is more intimate, the loss and the gain proceeding from the same cause. In the case last mentioned, suppose the weaker vessel, dashed against the other in a storm, is sunk : here the same cause by which the one proprietor loses, proves beneficial to the other. The last connection I shall mention, and the completest, is where that which is lost by the one is gained by the other ; or, in other words, where the money of which the one is deprived benefits the other. This is the case first mentioned, of money laid out by a *bona fide possessor*, in meliorating a subject that is afterward claimed by the proprietor. The money that the former loses is gained by the latter.

A famous maxim of the Roman law, *Nemo debet locupletari aliena jactura*, is applicable to this acticle : and in order to ascertain, if it can be done, what are the connections that make it the duty of one man to part with his gain for repairing another's loss, I shall begin with a commentary upon that maxim. I observe first, That it is expressed abstractly, as holding true in general, without distinction of persons ; and, therefore, that the duty it establishes must be founded upon a real connection, independent altogether of personal connections ; which leads us to examine what that real connection must be. *Nemo debet locupletari aliena jactura*, or, No person ought to profit *by* another's loss, implies a connection between the loss and the gain : it implies that the gain arises *by* the loss, or *by means* of the loss. Taking, therefore, the maxim literally, it ought to take place wherever the gain is occasioned by the loss, or, perhaps, occasions the loss : which certainly is not good law. In the second and third cases above mentioned, the same cause that destroys the one merchant is profitable to the other : yet no man who in such

circumstances makes profit, finds himself bound in
conscience to make up the other's loss. It appears,
then, that this maxim, like most general maxims, is
apt to mislead, by being too comprehensive. Upon
serious reflection, we find, that what a man acquires
by his own industry, or by accident, however connected with the loss sustained by another, will not
be taken from him to make up that loss, if there be
no personal connection. The only real connection
that of itself binds him, is where another's money is
converted to his use. This circumstance, though
without any intention to benefit him, will bind him
in conscience to make up the other's loss as far as he
himself is a gainer. Here the maxim, *Nemo debet
locupletari aliena jactura*, taken in its most extensive
sense, is applicable; and the single case, as far as I
understand, where it is applicable. The most noted
case of this kind is, where the possessor of a subject
which he *bona fide* considers to be his own, bestows
his money on reparations and meliorations, intending
nothing but his own benefit; the proprietor claims
the subject in a process, and prevails: he profits by
the meliorations; and the money bestowed on these
meliorations is converted to his use. Every one
must be sensible of a hardship that requires a remedy; and it must be the wish of every disinterested
person, that the *bona fide possessor* be relieved from
the hardship. That the common law affords no relief, will be evident at first sight: the labour and
money of the *bona fide possessor* is sunk in the subject, and has no separate existence upon which to
found a *rei vindicatio:* the proprietor, in claiming
the subject, does no more but exercise his own right;
which cannot subject him personally to any demand.

P. I. 3. BENEVOLENCE. 93

If, then, there be a remedy, it can have no other foundation but equity; and that there is a remedy in equity, will appear from the following considerations. Man being a fallible creature, society would be uncomfortable were individuals disposed in every case to take advantage of the mistakes and errors of others. But the author of our nature has more harmoniously adjusted its different branches to each other. To make it a law in our nature, never to take advantage of error in any case, would be giving too much indulgence to indolence and remission of mind, tending to make us neglect the improvement of our rational faculties. On the other hand, to make it lawful to take advantage of error in every case, would be too rigorous, considering how difficult it is for a man to be always upon his guard. The author of our nature has happily moulded it so as to avoid these extremes. No man is conscious of wrong, when, to save himself from loss, he takes advantage of an error committed by another: if there must be a loss, the moral sense dictates, that it ought to rest upon the person who has committed an error, however innocently, rather than upon him who has been careful to avoid all error. But *in lucro captando*, the moral sense teaches a different lesson: every one is conscious of wrong, when an error is laid hold of to make gain by it. The consciousness of injustice, when such advantage is taken, is indeed inferior in degree, but the same in kind with the injustice of robbing an innocent person of his goods or of his reputation. This doctrine is supported by utility as well as by justice. Industry ought to be encouraged; and chance as much as possible ought to be excluded from all dealings, in order that individuals may promise to themselves the fruits of their own industry. This affords a fresh instance of that beautiful harmony which subsists between the internal and external constitution of man. A regular chain of causes and effects, leaving little or nothing to accident, is advantageous externally by promoting industry, and internally by the delight it affords the human mind. No scene is more disgustful than that of things depending on chance, without order or connection. When a court of equity therefore preserves to every man, as much as possible, the fruits of his own industry; such proceeding, by rectifying the disorders of chance, is authorised by utility as well as by justice, And hence it is a principle of morality, founded both on the nature of man and on the interests of society, That we ought not to make gain by another's error.

This principal is clearly applicable to the case above mentioned. The titles of land property being intricate, and often uncertain, instances are frequent, where a man in possession of land, the property of another, is led by unavoidable error to consider it as belonging to himself: his money is bestowed without hesitation on repairing and meliorating the subject. Equity will not permit the owner to profit by such a mistake, and in effect to pocket the money of the innocent possessor: he will be compelled by a court of equity to make up the loss, as far as he is *locupletior*. Thus the possessor of a tenement, having, on the faith and belief of its being his own, made considerable meliorations, was found entitled to claim from the proprietor the expence of such meliorations

BENEVOLENCE.

as were profitable to him by raising the rent of his tenement.* In all cases of this kind, what is lost to the one accrues to the other. The maxim then must be understood in this limited sense ; for no connection between the loss and gain inferior in degree to this, will, independent of personal connections, be a sufficient foundation for a claim in equity against the person who gains, to make up the other's loss.

. But supposing the subject meliorated to have perished before bringing the action, is the proprietor notwithstanding liable ? I answer, That where equity makes benevolence a duty to those who benefit us without intending it, it is not sufficient that there has been gain one time or other : it is implied in the nature of the claim, that there must be gain at the time of the demand ; for if there be no gain at present, there is no subject out of which the loss can be made up.

It will not be thought an unnecessary digression to observe a peculiarity in the Roman law with respect to this matter. As that law stood originally, the *bona fide possessor* had no claim for his expences. This did not proceed from ignorance of equity, but from want of a *formula* to authorise the action ; for at first, when brieves or forms of action were invented,† this claim was not thought of. But an exception was soon thought of to entitle the *bona fide possessor* to retain the subject, till he got payment of his expence ; and this exception the judges could have no difficulty to sustain, because exceptions were not subjected to any *formula.* The inconvenient restraint of these *formulæ* was in time broken through, and

* Stair, January 18, 1676, Binning *contra* Brotherstanes.
† See Historical law-tracts, tract 3.

actiones in factum, or *upon the case*, were introduced, which are not confined to any *formula*. After this innovation, the same equity that gave an exception, produced also an *actio in factum*; and the *bona fide possessor* was made secure as to his expences in all cases, namely, by an exception while he remained in possession, and by an action if he happened to lose the possession.

Another case, differing nothing from the former in effect, though considerably in its circumstances, is where, upon a fictitious mandate, one purchases my goods, or borrows my money, for the use of another. That other is not liable *ex mandato*, because he gave no mandate; but if I can prove that the money or goods were actually applied for his use, equity affords me a claim against him, as far as he is a gainer. Thus, in an action for payment of merchant-goods purchased in name of the defendant, and applied to his use, the defendant insisted, that he gave no commission; and that if his name was used without his authority, he could not be liable. " It was decreed, " That the goods being applied to the defendant's " use, he was liable, unless he could prove that he " paid the price to the person who bespoke the " goods." * This case, like the former, rests entirely upon the real connection between the loss and gain, independent of which there was no connection between the parties. And in it, perhaps more clearly than in the former, every one must be sensible, that the man who reaps the benefit is in duty bound to make up the other's loss. Hence the action *de in rem verso*, the name of which we borrowed from the Romans. In a case precisely similar, the court inclined

* Stair, Feb. 20, 1669, Bruce *contra* Stanhope.

to sustain it relevant to assoilzie or acquit the defendant, that the goods were gifted to him by the person who purchased them in his name. But as donation is not presumed, he was found liable, because he could not bring evidence of the alleged donation.[*] Upon the supposition of a gift, it could not well be specified that the defendant was *locupletior* : a man will spend liberally what he considers as a present, though he would not lay out his money upon the purchase.

Having endeavoured to ascertain, with all possible accuracy, that degree of connection between the loss and gain, which is requisite to afford a relief in equity, by obliging the person who gains to make up the other's loss, I proceed to ascertain the precise meaning of loss and gain as understood in the maxim. And the first doubt that occurs is, Whether the term *locupletior* comprehends every real benefit, prevention of loss as well as a positive increase of fortune; or whether it be confined to the latter. I explain myself by examples. When a *bona fide possessor* rears a new edifice upon another man's land, this is a positive accession to the subject, which makes the proprietor *locupletior* in the strictest sense of the word. But it may happen that the money laid out by the *bona fide possessor* is directed to prevent loss; as, where he fortifies the bank of a river against its encroachments, where he supports a tottering edifice, or where he transacts a claim that threatened to carry off the property. Is the maxim applicable to cases of this kind, where loss is only prevented, without any positive increase of wealth or fortune? When a work is done that prevents loss, the subject is thereby im-

* July 1726, Hawthorn *contra* Urquhart.

98   DUTY OF   B. 1.

proved and made of greater value. A bulwark, that prevents the encroachments of a river, makes the land sell at a higher price; and a real accession, such as a house built, or land inclosed, will not do more. The only difference is, that a positive accession makes a man richer than he formerly was; a work done to prevent loss, makes him only richer than he would have been had the work been left undone. This difference is too slight to have any effect in equity. The proprietor gains by both equally; and in both cases equally he will feel himself bound in justice to make up the loss out of his gain. A *bona fide possessor* who claims money laid out by him to support a tottering edifice, is *certans de damno evitando*, as well as where he claims money laid out upon meliorations; and the proprietor claiming the subject, is *certans de lucro captando* in the one case, as well as in the other. Here equity supports the claim of him who is *certans de damno evitando*; for, as observed above, there is in human nature a perception of wrong, where a man avails himself of an error to make profit at another's expence. Nor does the principle of utility make any distinction. It is a great object in society, to rectify the disorders of chance, and to preserve to every man, as much as possible, the fruits of his own industry; which is the same whether it has been applied to prevent loss, or to make a real accession to a man's fortune. In the cases, accordingly, that have occurred, I find no distinction made; and in those which follow, there was no benefit but what arose from preventing loss. A ship being ransomed from a privateer, every person benefited must contribute a proportion of the ransom.* A written testament being voided for in-

* Fount. June 29, 1710. Ritchie *contra* Lord Salton.

formality, the executor-nominate was allowed the expences of confirming the testament, because to the executrix *qua* next in kind, pursuer of the reduction, it was profitable by saving her the expence of a confirmation.*

From what is said, it may possibly be thought that the foregoing rule of equity is applicable wherever it can be subsumed, that the loss sustained by one proves beneficial to another. But this will be found a rash thought, when it is considered, that one may be benefited without being in any proper sense *locupletior* or a gainer upon the whole. I give an example. A man erecting a large tenement in a borough, becomes bankrupt by overstretching his credit. This new tenement, being the chief part of his substance, is adjudged by his creditors for sums beyond the value. In the meantime the tradesmen and the furnishers of materials for the building, trusting to a claim in equity, forbear to adjudge. They are losers to the extent of their work and furnishings; and the adjudgers are in one sense *locupletiores*, as, by means of the tenement, they will draw perhaps ten shillings in the pound instead of five. Are the adjudgers then, in terms of the maxim, bound to yield this profit, in order to pay the workmen and furnishers? By no means. For here the benefit is partial only, and produceth not upon the whole actual profit: on the contrary, the adjudgers, even after this benefit, are equally with their competitors *certantes de damno evitando*. The Court of Session accordingly refused to sustain the claim of the tradesmen and furnishers.†
Hence appears a remarkable difference between pro-

* Fount. Feb. 26, 1712, Moncrieff *contra* Monypenny.
† Dec. 4, 1735, Burns *contra* creditors of Maclellan.

perty and obligation. Money laid out upon a subject by the *bona fide possessor*, whether for melioration or to preserve it from damage, makes the proprietor *locupletior*, and a *captator lucri ex aliena jactura*. But though a creditor be benefited by another's loss, so as by that means to draw a greater proportion of his debt ; he is not, however, a gainer upon the whole, but is still *certans de damno evitando*. And when the parties are thus *in pari casu*, a court of equity cannot interpose, but must leave them to the common law.

I add another limitation, which is not peculiar to the maxim under consideration, but arises from the very constitution of a court of equity. It is not sufficient that there be gain, even in the strictest sense : it is necessary that the gain be clear and certain ; for otherwise a court of equity must not undertake to make up the loss out of that gain. The principle of utility, in order to prevent arbitrary proceedings, prohibits a court of equity to take under consideration a conjectural loss or a conjectural gain ; because such loss or gain can never be brought under a general rule. I give the following illustrations. Two heritors having each of them a salmon-fishing in the same part of a river, are in use to exercise their rights alternately. One is interrupted for some time by a suit at the instance of a third party : the other by this means has more capture than usual, though he varies not his mode of fishing. What the one loses by the interruption, is probably gained by the other, at least in some measure. But as what is here transferred from the one to the other cannot be ascertained with any degree of certainty, a court of equity must not interpose. Again, a tenant, upon the faith of a long lease, lays out considerable sums upon improving his land, and reaps the benefit a few years. But the landlord, who holds the land by a military tenure, dies suddenly in the flower of his age, leaving an infant heir; the land by this means comes into the superior's hand, and the lease is superseded during the ward. Here a great part of the extraordinary meliorations which the lessee intended for his own benefit, are converted to the use of the superior. Yet equity cannot interpose, because no general rule can be laid down for ascertaining the gain made by the superior. The following case confirms this doctrine. In an action at a tercer's instance for a third of the rents levied by the fiar, the court refused to sustain a deduction claimed by the defendant, namely, a third of the factor-fee paid by him for levying the rents; though it was urged, that the pursuer could not have levied her third at less expence.* The loss here was not ascertained, and was scarce capable of being ascertained; for no one could say what less the factor would have accepted for levying two-thirds of the rent than for levying the whole. Neither was the profit capable to be ascertained: the lady herself might have levied her share, or have got a friend to serve her *gratis*.

I shall close with one further limitation, which regards not only the present subject, but every claim that can be founded on equity. Courts of equity are introduced in every country to enforce natural justice, and by no means to encourage any wrong. Whence it follows, that no man is entitled to the aid of a court of equity, where he suffers by his own fault. For this reason the proprietor is not made li-

* Durie, March 27, 1634, Lady Dunfermline *contra* her son.

able for the expence of profitable meliorations, but where the meliorations were made *bona fide* by a person intending his own profit, and not suspecting any hazard. It is laid down, however, in the Roman law, That the necessary expence laid out in upholding the subject, may be claimed by the *mala fide possessor*.* If such reparations be made while the proprietor is ignorant of his right, and the ruin of the edifice be thereby prevented, there possibly may be a foundation in utility for the claim : but I deny there can be any foundation in justice. And, therefore, if a tenant, after being ejected by legal execution, shall obstinately persist to plough and sow, he ought to have no claim for his seed nor his labour. The claim, in these circumstances, hath no foundation either in justice or utility : yet the claim was sustained. †

But there are many personal connections joined with a much slighter real connection than that above mentioned, which entitle a man to have his loss made up out of my gain. Of which take the following examples.

There are three creditors connected by their relation to the same debtor who is a bankrupt, and by their relation to two land-estates, *A* and *B* belonging to the debtor, the first creditor being preferably secured on both estates, one of the secondary creditors being secured upon *A*, the other upon *B*. The catholic creditor purchases one of the secondary debts under its value, by which he is a gainer ; for by his preferable debt he cuts out the other secondary cre-

---

* L. 5, C. De rei vindic.
† Stair, February 22, 1671, Gordon *contra* Macculloch.

ditor, and by that means draws the whole price of the two subjects. The question is, Whether equity will suffer him to retain his gain against the other secondary creditor, who is thus cut out of his security. It cannot indeed be specified here, as in the case of the *bonæ fidei possessor rei alienæ*, that money given out by the one is converted to the use of the other: but then the loss and gain are necessarily connected by having a common cause, namely, the purchase made by the catholic creditor. This connection between loss and gain, joined with the personal connections above mentioned, make it the duty of the catholic creditor to communicate his profit, in order to make up the loss that the other creditor sustains. And one with confidence may deliver this opinion, when the following circumstance is added, that the loss was occasioned by the catholic creditor, in making a purchase that he was sensible would ruin his fellow-creditor.

The next case in order is of two assignees to the same bond, ignorant of each other. The cedent or assignor contrives to draw the purchase-money from both, and walks off in a state of bankruptcy. The latter assignment, being first intimated, will be preferred. But to what extent? Will it be preferred for the whole sum in the bond, or only for the price paid for it? The circumstances here favour the postponed assignee, though they have not the same weight with those in the former: the material difference is, that the assignee preferred made his purchase without knowing of his competitor, and consequently without any thought of distressing him. The personal connection, however, joined with the necessary connection between the loss and gain, ap-

104   DUTY OF   B. I.

pears sufficient to deprive the last assignee of his gain, in order to make up the loss sustained by the first. The case would be more doubtful, had the first assignment been first completed; because it may appear hard, that the intervention of a second purchaser should deprive the first of a profitable bargain. I leave this point to be ripened by time and mature deliberation. The progress of equity is slow, though constant, toward the more delicate articles of natural justice. If there appear any difficulty about extending equity to this case, the difficulty probably will vanish in course of time.

One thing is certain, that in the English court of Chancery there would be no hesitation to apply equity to this case. That court extends its power a great way farther; farther indeed than seems just. A stranger, for example, who purchases a prior incumbrance, can draw no more from the other incumbrancers than the sum he really paid:* and to justify this extraordinary opinion, it is said, " That the " taking away one man's gain to make up another's " loss, is making them both equal." This argument, if it prove any thing, proves too much, being applicable to any two persons indifferently, who have not the smallest connection, supposing only the one to have made a profitable, the other a losing bargain. There ought to be some connection to found such a demand : the persons ought to be connected by a common concern ; and the loss and gain ought to be connected, so at least as that the one be occasioned by the other. The first connection only is found in this case : a stranger who purchases a prior incumbrance is indeed, by a common subject, connected with the

* 1. Vernon 476.

other incumbrancers : but this purchase does not harm the other incumbrancers ; for when the purchaser claims the debt in its utmost extent, it is no more than what his author could do. The rule of chancery, in this view, appears a little whimsical : it deprives me of a lucrative bargain, the fruit of my own industry, to bestow it, not upon any person who is hurt by the bargain, but upon those who are in no worse condition than before the bargain was made. Neither am I clear, that this rule can be supported upon a principal of utility : for though it is preventive of hard and unequal bargains, yet as no prudent man will purchase an incumbrance on such a condition, it is in effect a prohibition of such purchases, which would prove a great inconveniency to many whose funds are locked up by the bankruptcy of their debtors.

That an heir acquiring an incumbrance should be allowed no more but what he really paid, or, which comes to the same, that he should be bound to communicate eases, is a proposition more agreeable to the principles of equity. This is the law of England,[*] and it is the law of Scotland with regard to heirs who take the benefit of inventory. But the case of an heir is very different from that of a stranger. He hath in his hand the fund for payment of the creditors, which he ought faithfully to account for ; and, therefore, he is not permitted to state any article for exhausting that fund beyond what he hath actually expended : if a creditor accept less than his proportion, the fund for the other creditors is so much the larger.

[*] 1. Salkeld, 155.

A cautioner upon making payment obtaining an ease, must communicate the same to the principal debtor, upon a plain ground in common law, that being secure of his relief from the principal debtor, he has no claim but to be kept *indemnis*. But supposing the principal debtor bankrupt, I discover no ground other than paction, that can bind one cautioner to communicate eases to another: and yet it is the prevailing, I may say the established, opinion, that a cautioner who obtains an ease, must communicate the benefit to his co-cautioner. I am aware of the reason commonly assigned, that cautioners for the same debt are to be considered as in a society, obliged to bear the loss equally. But this, I doubt, is arguing in a circle: they resemble a society, because the loss must be equal; and the loss must be equal, because they resemble a society. We must, therefore, go more accurately to work. In the first place, let us examine whether an obligation for mutual relief ought to be implied. This implication, at best doubtful, supposes the cautioners to have subscribed in a body. And, therefore, to leave no room for an implied obligation, we need but suppose, that two persons, ignorant of each other, become cautioners at different times, and in different deeds. It appears, then, that common law affords not an obligation for mutual relief. The matter is still more clear with regard to equity: for the connection between two cautioners can never be so intimate, as to oblige the one who is not a gainer, to make up the other's loss; which is the case of the cautioner who obtains an ease, supposing that ease to be less than that proportion of the debt which he stands bound to pay. Upon the whole, my notion is, that if a cautioner, upon account of objections against the debt, or upon account of any circumstance that regards the principal debtor, obtain an ease, he is bound to communicate that ease to his fellow-cautioner, upon the following rational principle, that both cautioners ought equally to partake of an ease, the motive to which respects them equally. This appears to be the *ratio decidendi* in the case reported by Stair, July 27, 1672, Brodie *contra* Keith. But if, upon prompt payment by one cautioner after the failure of others, or upon any consideration personal to the cautioner, an ease be given ; equity, I think, obliges not the cautioner to communicate the benefit to his fellow-cautioners. And this was decreed, Stair, July 8, 1664, Nisbet *contra* Leslie.

There is one circumstance, that, without much connection real or personal, extends to many cases the maxim, *Nemo debet locupletari aliena jactura* ; and that is fraud, deceit, or any sort of wrong. If, by means of a third person's fraud, one gains and another loses, a court of equity will interpose to make up the loss out of the gain. And this resolves into a general rule, " That no man, however innocent, " ought to take advantage of a tortious act by which " another is hurt." Take the following example.— A second disposition of land, though gratuitous, with the first infeftment, is preferred at common law before the first disposition without infeftment, though for a valuable consideration. But as the gratuitous disponee is thus benefited by a moral wrong done by his author, he ought not, however innocent, to take advantage of that moral wrong to hurt the first disponee. This circumstance makes the rule applicable, *Non debet locupletari aliena jactura* ; and, therefore,

108 DUTY OF **B. I.**

a court of equity will compel him, either to give up his right to the land, or to repair the loss the first disponee has suffered by being deprived of his purchase.

The following cases rest upon the same principle. A disposition by a merchant of his whole estate to his infant-son, without a reserved liferent or power to burden, was deemed fraudulent, in order to cheat his correspondents, foreign merchants, who had traded with him before the alienation, and continued their dealings with him upon the belief that he was still proprietor; and their claims, though posterior to the disposition, were admitted to affect the estate.*

Where a tutor, acting to the best of his skill for the good of his pupil, happens, in the ordinary course of administration, to convert a moveable debt into one that is heritable, or an heritable debt into one that is moveable; such an act, after the pupil's death, will have its effect with respect to the pupil's succession, by preferring his heir or executor, as if the act had been done by a proprietor of full age. But where the tutor acts in this manner unnecessarily, with the sole intention to prefer the heir or the executor, this is a tortious act, contrary to the duty he owes his pupil, which will affect the heir or executor, though they had no accession to the wrong. In common law, the succession will take place according to the tutor's act, whether done with a right or a wrong intention; but this will be corrected in equity, upon the principle, That no person ought to take advantage of a tortious act that harms another.

A donation *inter virum et uxorem* is revocable; but not a donation to the husband or wife's children,

* Stair, July 2, 1673, Street *contra* Mason.

or to any other relation. A wife makes a donation of her land-estate to her husband; who afterward, in order to bar revocation, gives up the disposition granted to him, and instead of it, takes a disposition to his eldest son. Will this disposition be revocable? Where a wife, out of affection to her husband's eldest son, makes a deed in his favour, it is not revocable, because it is not a *donatio inter virum et uxorem*. But in this case it is clear, that the donation was intended for the husband, and that the sole purpose of the disposition to the son was to bar revocation; which was an unlawful contrivance to elude the law. It would be wrong, therefore, in the son, however innocent, to take advantage of his father's tortious act, calculated to deprive the woman of her privilege; and, therefore, the disposition to him will be revocable in equity, as that to the father was at common law.

ART. II. *Connections that entitle a man who is not a loser, to partake of my gain.*

FOR the sake of perspicuity, this article shall be divided into two branches:—1*st*, Where the gain is the operation of the man who claims to partake of it.—2*d*, Where he has not contributed to the gain.

I introduce the first branch with a case which will be a key to the several matters that come under it. Two heirs-portioners, or in general two proprietors of a land-estate *pro indiviso*, get for a farm a rent of eighty pounds yearly; and an offer of ten pounds additional rent if they will drain a lake in it. John is willing; but James refuses, judging it impracticable,

110 DUTY OF B. Y.

or at least too expensive. John proceeds at his own risk; and for the sum of £100 drains the lake. He cannot specify any loss by this undertaking; because the sum he laid out is fully compensated by the five pound additional rent accruing to him; and, therefore, the maxim, *Nemo debet locupletari aliena jactura*, is not applicable to his case. But James is a profiter, not only by John's advancing the money, but at his risk; for if the undertaking had proved abortive, John would have lost both his labour and money. Is it just that James should be permitted to lay hold of an additional rent of £5, without defraying any part of the expence? He cannot justify this to his own conscience, nor to the world. The moral sense dictates, that where expence is laid out in improving or repairing a common subject, no one ought to take the benefit, without refunding a part of the expence in proportion to the benefit received.

This leads to a general rule, That expence laid out upon a common subject, ought to be a burden upon the benefit procured. And this rule will hold even against the dissent of any of the parties concerned; for they cannot in conscience take the benefit without the burden. A dissent cannot have any effect in equity, but only to free the person dissenting from any risk.

The following cases come clearly under the same general rule. One of three joint proprietors of a mill, having raised a declarator of thirlage, and, notwithstanding a disclamation by the others, having insisted in the process till he obtained a decree; the others, who reaped the profit equally with him, were made liable for their share of the expence.* And one of

* Stair, January 6, 1676, Forbes *contra* Ross.

.P. i. 3.   BENEVOLENCE.   111

many co-creditors having obtained a judgment against the debtor's relict, finding her liable to pay her husband's debts; the other creditors who shared the benefit were decreed to contribute to the expence.* For the same reason, where a tenement destroyed by fire was rebuilt by a liferenter, the proprietor, after the liferenter's death, was made liable for the expence of rebuilding, as far as he was *lucratus* thereby.† And if rebuilt by the proprietor, the liferenter will be liable for the interest of the sum expended, as far as he is *lucratus*.‡ Action was sustained at the instance of a wadsetter for declaring that his intended reparation of a harbour in the wadset-lands, would be profitable to the reverser; and that the reverser, upon redemption, should be bound to repay the expence thereof.‖ Upon the same principle, if a lessee erect any buildings by which the proprietor is evidently *lucratus* at the end of the lease, there is a claim in equity for the expence of the meliorations. But reparations, though extensive, will scarce be allowed, where the lessee is bound to uphold the houses; because a lessee who bestows such reparation without his landlord's consent, is understood to lay out his money in order to fulfil his obligation, without any prospect of retribution.§ The present minister was not found liable for the meliorations of the glebe made by his predecessor.¶ But what if meliorations be made, inclosing,

* Bruce, July 30, 1715, Creditors of Calderwood *contra* Borthwick.

† Forbes, Feb. 20, 1706, Halliday *contra* Garden.

‡ Stair, Jan. 24, 1672, Hacket *contra* Watt.

‖ Durle, July 22, 1626, Morison *contra* Earl of Lothian.

§ Gilmour, Feb. 1664, Hodge *contra* Brown.

¶ Nicolson, (Kirkman), June 14, 1623, Dunbar *contra* Hay.

draining, stoning, &c. which are clearly profitable to all future possessors? If the expence of these, in proportion to the benefit, be not in some way refunded, glebes will rest in their original state forever. I do not say, that the minister immediately succeeding ought to be liable for the whole of this expence: for as the benefit is supposed to be perpetual, the burden ought to be equally so; which suggests the following opinion, That the sum total of the expence ought to be converted into a perpetual annuity, to be paid by the ministers of this parish; for the only equitable method is, to make each contribute in proportion to the benefit he receives.

The following case belongs undoubtedly to the maxim of equity under consideration; and yet was judged by common law, neglecting the equitable remedy. In a shipwreck, part of the cargo being saved, was delivered to the owners for payment of the salvage. The proprietor of the ship claiming the freight of the goods saved *pro rata itineris*, the freighters admitted the claim; but insisted, that as the salvage was beneficial to him on account of his freight, as well as to them on account of their goods, he ought to contribute a share. His answer was sustained to free him from any part, That the expence was wholly laid out on recovering the freighter's goods; and therefore that they only ought to be liable. * The answer here sustained resolves into the following proposition, That he only is liable whose benefit is intended: which holds not in equity; for at that rate, the *bona fide possessor*, who in meliorating the subject intends his own benefit solely, has no claim

* January 18, 1735, Lutwich *contra* Gray.

against the proprietor. Here the freighters and the proprietor of the ship were connected by a common interest: the recovering the goods from shipwreck was beneficial to both; to the freighters, because it put them again in possession of their goods; and to the proprietor of the ship, because it gave him a claim for freight. The salvage accordingly was truly *in rem versum* of both; and for that reason ought to be paid by both in proportion to the benefit received. This case may be considered in a different light that will scarce admit a dispute. Suppose that the owners of the cargo, in recovering their goods to the extent of £1,000, have laid out £100 upon salvage: they have in effect saved or recovered but £900; and beyond that sum they cannot be liable for the freight: which in numbers will bring out a greater sum than what results from the rule above mentioned.

It will not escape the reader, that equity is further extended in this branch than in the former; and he will also discover a solid reason for the difference. With respect to matters contained in the former branch, the real connection is only, that what is lost by the one is gained by the other; as in the case of a *bona fide possessor rei alienæ*. But the real connection in the present branch is so far more intimate, that every acquisition must benefit all equally, and every loss burden all equally.

It appears, that a benefit accruing to another by my labour, occasionally only, not necessarily, will not entitle me to a claim where I am not a loser. To make the truth of this observation evident, a few examples will be sufficient. A drain made by me in my own ground for my own behoof, happens to discharge a quantity of water that stagnated in a supe-

114 DUTY OF B. 1.

rior field belonging to a neighbour. Justice does not entitle me to claim from this neighbour any share of the expence laid out upon the drain. The drain has answered my intention, and overpays the sum bestowed upon it; therefore my case comes not under the maxim, *Nemo debet locupletari aliena jactura.* Neither can I have any claim upon the rule, That expence laid out upon a common subject ought to be a burden upon the benefit procured; for here there is no common subject, but only another person accidentally or occasionally benefited by an operation intended solely for my own benefit. And Providence has wisely ordered that such a claim should have no support from the moral sense; for as there can be no precise rule for estimating the benefit that each of us receives from the drain, the subjecting my neighbour to a claim would tend to create endless disputes between us. For the same reason, if my neighbour, in making an inclosure, take advantage of a march-fence built by me, he will not be liable to any part of the expence bestowed by me upon it; because the benefit, as in the former case, is occasional only or consequential.

From the nature of the claim handled in the present branch, it follows, that if the party against whom the claim is laid, renounce the benefit, he cannot be subjected to the burden.

With respect to the branch now handled, the circumstance that the benefit accruing to another was occasioned by my means, is the connection that entitles me to a proportion of the sum I laid out in procuring that benefit. But with respect to the second branch, which we are next to enter upon, it must require some personal relation, extremely intimate, to

BENEVOLENCE.

entitle me to partake of another man's profit when I have not contributed to it. And this will be made evident by the following examples.

When land is held ward, and the superior is under age, a gift of his ward is effectual against his vassal as well as against himself. But where the gift of ward was taken for behoof of the superior, it was the opinion of the court, that the vassal also had the benefit thereof upon paying his proportion of the composition.* Against this opinion it was urged, That a vassal must reckon upon being liable to all casualties arising from the nature of his right; and that there is no reason for limiting the superior's claim, more than that of any other donator. But it was answered, That the relation between superior and vassal is such, as that the superior cannot *bona fide* take advantage against his vassal of a casualty occasioned by his own minority. The same rule was applied to a gift of marriage taken for behoof of the superior.† And it appearing that the superior had obtained this gift for alleged good services, without paying any composition, the benefit was communicated to the vassal, without obliging him to pay any sum.‡

If a purchaser of land, discovering a defect in the progress, secure himself by acquiring the preferable title, common law will not permit him to use this title as a ground of eviction, and to make his author, bound in absolute warrandice, liable for the value of the subject: for the purchaser is not entitled to the

* Dirleton, December 1, 1676, Grierson *contra* Ragg.
† Harcase, (Ward and Marriage), Jan. 1686, Drummelzier *contra* Murray of Stanhope.
‡ Ibid.

value unless the land be evicted from him : and therefore he cannot have any claim upon the warrandice beyond the sum he paid for the title. This point is still more clear upon the principle of equity above mentioned. The connection is so intimate between a purchaser, and a vender bound in absolute warrandice, that every transaction made by either, with relation to the subject purchased, is deemed to be for behoof of both.

But now supposing several parcels of land to be comprehended under one title-deed. One parcel is sold with absolute warrandice ; and the purchaser, discovering the title-deed to be imperfect, acquires from a third party a preferable title to the whole parcels. He is no doubt bound to communicate the benefit of this acquisition to the vender, as far as regards the parcel he purchased. But there is nothing at common law to bar him from evicting the other parcels from the vender. Whether a relief can be afforded in equity, is doubtful. The connection between the parties is pretty intimate : the purchaser is bound to communicate to the vender the benefit of his acquisition with respect to one parcel, and it is natural to extend the same benefit to the whole. One case of this nature occurred in the Court of Session. A man having right to several subjects contained in an adjudication, sold one of them with absolute warrandice ; and the purchaser having acquired a title preferable to his author's adjudication, claimed the subjects that were not disponed to him. The court restricted the claim to the sum paid for the preferable title.* It is not certain whether this decree was

* February 21, 1741, James Drummond contra Brown and Miln.

laid upon the principle above mentioned : for what moved some of the judges was the danger of permitting a purchaser acquainted with the title-deeds of his author, to take advantage of his knowledge by picking up preferable titles'; and that this, as an unfair practice, ought to be prohibited.

Art. III. *Connections that entitle one who is a loser to be indemnified by one who is not a gainer.*

Cases daily occur, where, by absence, infancy, inadvertence, or other circumstances, effects real or personal are left without proper management, and where ruin must ensue, if no person of benevolence be moved to interpose. Here friendship and good-will have a favourable opportunity to exert themselves, and to do much good, perhaps without any extraordinary labour or great expence; and when a proprietor is benefited by such acts of friendship or benevolence, justice and gratitude claim from him a retribution, to the extent at least of the benefit received. Here the maxim, *Nemo debet locupletari aliena jactura*, is applicable in the strictest sense. Hence the *actio negotiorum gestorum* in the Roman law, which, for the reason given, is adopted by all civilized nations.

But what if this friendly man, after bestowing his money and labour with the utmost precaution, happen to be unsuccessful? What if, after laying out his money profitably upon repairing houses, or purchasing cattle for my use, the benefit be lost to me by the casual destruction of the subject; would it be just that this friend, who had no view but for my interest, should run the risk? As there was no contract

118 DUTY OF B. 1.

between us, a claim will not be sustained at common law for the money expended. But equity pierces deeper, in order to fulfil the rules of justice. Service undertaken by a friend upon an urgent occasion, advances gratitude from a virtue to be a duty; and binds me to *recompense* my friend as far as he has laid out his own money in order to do me service. The moral sense teaches this lesson; and no person, however partial in his own concern, but must perceive this to be the duty of others. Utility also joins with justice to support this claim of recompense. Men ought to be invited to serve a friend in time of need: but instead of invitation, it would be a great discouragement, if the money advanced upon such service were upon their own risk, even when laid out with the greatest prudence. *(a)* This doctrine is laid down

(a) The Roman writers found this duty upon their *quasi*-contracts, of which *negotiorum gestio* is said to be one. And to understand this foundation, the nature of *quasi*-contracts must be explained. In human affairs certain circumstances and situations frequently happen that require a covenant, which nothing can prevent but want of opportunity. The present case affords a good illustration. A sudden call forces me abroad, without having time to regulate my affairs; disorder ensues, and a friend undertakes the management. Here nothing prevents a mandate but want of opportunity; and it is presumed that the mandate would not have been wanting, had I known the good intentions of my friend. Equity accordingly holds the mandate as granted, and gives the same actions to both that the common law gives in pursuance of a mandate. Though this serves to explain the Roman *quasi*-contracts, yet it seems a wide stretch in equity to give to a supposition the effects of a real contract; especially without any evidence that the person who undertakes the management would have been my choice. But I have endeavoured to make out in the text, that this claim for recompence has a solid foundation in justice, and in human nature, without necessity of recurring to the strained supposition of a contract.

BENEVOLENCE.

by Ulpian in clear terms:—"Is autem, qui negotio-
" rum gestorum agit, non solum si effectum habuit
" negotium quod gessit, actione ita utetur; sed suf-
" ficit, si utiliter gessit, etsi effectum non habuit ne-
" gotium. Et ideo, si insulam fulsit, vel servum
" ægrum curavit, etiamsi insula exusta est, vel ser-
" vus obiit, aget negotiorum gestorum. Idque et
" Labeo probat." *

From what is said above it is evident, that the man
who undertakes my affairs, not to serve me, but to
serve himself, is not entitled to the *actio negotiorum
gestorum*. Nor, even supposing me to be benefited
by his management, is he entitled to have his loss repaired out of my gain: for wrong can never found
any claim in equity. Yet Julianus, the most acute
of the Roman writers, answers the question in the
affirmative. Treating of one who *mala fide* meddles
in my affairs, he gives the following opinion : " Ipse
" tamen, si circa res meas aliquid impenderit, non in
" id quod ei abest, quia improbe ad negotia mea ac-
" cessit, sed in quod ego locupletior factus sum, habet
" contra me actionem."† It appears at the same time,
from *L. ult. C. De negot. gest.* that this author was
of a different opinion, where the management of a
man's affairs was continued against his will; for
there no action was given. This, in my apprehension, is establishing a distinction without a difference : for no man can hope for my consent to continue the management of my affairs, when he began
that management, not to serve me, but with a view
to his own interst. A prohibition involved in the
nature of the thing, is equivalent to an express prohibition.

* L. 10, § 1, Negot. gest.   † L. 6, § 3, De Negot. gest.

The master of a ship, or any other, who ransoms the cargo from a privateer, is, according to the doctrine above laid down, entitled to claim from the owners of the cargo the sum laid out upon their account: they profit by the transaction, and they ought to indemnify him. But what if the cargo be afterward lost in a storm at sea, or by robbery at land? The owners are not now profiters by the ransom, and, therefore, they cannot be made liable upon the maxim, *Nemo debet locupletari aliena jactura.* They are, however, liable upon the principle here explained. The moment the transaction was finished, they became debtors to the ransomer for the sum he laid out profitably upon their account. He did not undertake the risk of the cargo ransomed; and, therefore, the casual loss of the cargo cannot have the effect to deprive him of his claim.

The *lex Rhodia de jactu*, a celebrated maritime regulation, has prevailed among all civilized nations, ancient and modern. Where in a storm weighty goods of little value are thrown over board to disburden the ship, the owners of the remaining cargo must contribute to make up the loss. This case, as to the obligation of retribution, is of the same nature with that now mentioned, and depends on the same principle. The throwing over board weighty goods, of little value, is beneficial to the owners of the more precious goods, which by that means are preserved; and, according to the foregoing doctrine, these owners ought to contribute for making up the loss of the goods thrown into the sea, precisely as if there had been a formal covenant to that effect. But what if the whole cargo be afterward lost, by which eventually there is no benefit? If lost at sea in the same

BENEVOLENCE.

voyage, the owner of the goods thrown overboard has certainly no claim; because, at any rate, he would have lost his goods along with the rest of the cargo. But as soon as the cargo is laid upon land, the obligation for retribution is purified; the value of the goods abandoned to the sea is, or ought to be, in the pocket of the owner; and the delay of payment will not afford a defence against him, whatever becomes of the cargo after it is landed.

It is a question of greater intricacy, Whether the goods saved from the sea ought to contribute according to their weight, or according to their value. The latter rule is espoused in the Roman law: " Cum in " eadem nave varia mercium genera complures merca- " tores coegissent, praetereaque multi vectores, servi, " liberique in ea navigarent, tempestate gravi orta, ne- " cessario jactura facta erat. Quaesita deinde sunt " haec: An omnes jacturam praestare oporteat, et si " qui tales merces imposuissent, quibus navis non " oneraretur, velut gemmas, margaritas? et quae " portio praestanda est? Et an etiam pro liberis ca- " pitibus dari oporteat? Et qua actione ea res expe- " diri possit? Placuit, omnes, quorum interfuisset " jacturam fieri, conferre oportere, quia id tributum " observatae res deberent: itaque dominum etiam " navis pro portione obligatum esse. Jacturae sum- " mam pro rerum pretio distribui oportet. Corporum " liberorm aestimationem nullam fieri posse." * This rule is adopted by all the commercial nations in Europe, without a single exception, as far as I can learn. And in pursuance of the rule, it is also adopted, That the owner of the ship ought to contribute, because the shipwreck being prevented by throwing over-

* L. 2, § 2, De lege Rhodia de jactu.

board part of the cargo, his claim for freight is preserved to him. "Thus, if, in stress of weather, or "in danger and just fear of an enemy, goods be "thrown overboard, in order to save the ship and "the rest of the cargo, that which is saved shall "contribute to repair that which is lost, and the "owners of the ship shall contribute in proportion." *

These authorities notwithstanding, to which great regard is justly due, it is not in my power to banish an impression, that the rule of contribution ought to be weight, not value. In every case where a man gives away his money or his goods, for behoof of a plurality connected by a common interest, two things are evident : first, That his equitable claim for a recompence cannot exceed the loss he has sustained ; and next, That each individual is liable to make up the loss of that part which was given away on his account. When a ransom is paid to a privateer for the ship and cargo, a share of the money is understood to be advanced for each proprietor, in proportion to the value of his goods; and that share each must contribute, being laid out on his account, or for his service. That the same rule is applicable where a ship is saved by abandoning part of its cargo, is far from being clear. Let us proceed warily, step by step. The cargo, in a violent storm, is found too weighty for the ship, which must be disburdened of part, let us suppose the one half. In what manner is this to be done ? The answer would be easy, were there leisure and opportunity for a regular operation : each person who has the weight of a pound aboard, ought to throw the half into the sea ; for one person

* Shower's Cases in Parliament, 19.

BENEVOLENCE.

is not bound to abandon a greater proportion than another. This method, however, is seldom or never practicable; because in a hurry the goods at hand must be heaved over: and were it practicable, it would not be for the common interest to abandon goods of little weight and great value, along with goods of great weight and little value. Hence it comes to be the common interest, and, without asking questions, the common practice, to abandon goods, the value of which bears no proportion to their weight. This, as being done for the common interest, entitles the proprietors of these goods to a recompence from those for whose service the goods were abandoned. Now, the service done to each proprietor is, instead of his valuable goods, to have others thrown overboard of a meaner quality; and for such service, all the recompence that can be justly claimed, is the value of the goods thrown overboard. Let us suppose with respect to any owner in particular, that regularly he was bound to throw overboard twenty ounces of his goods: all that he is bound to contribute, is the value of twenty ounces of the goods that in place of his own were actually thrown overboard. In a word, this short-hand way of throwing into the sea the least valuable goods, appears to me in the same light, as if the several owners of the more valuable part of the cargo, had each of them purchased a quantity of the mean goods to be thrown into the sea instead of their own.

I must observe, at the same time, that the doctrine of the Roman law appears very uncouth in some of its consequences. Jewels, and I may add bank-bills, are made to contribute to make up the loss, though they contribute not in any degree to the distress;

nor is a single ounce thrown overboard upon their account; nay, the ship itself is made to contribute, though the *jactura* is made necessary, not by the weight of the ship, but by that of the cargo. On the other hand, passengers are exempted altogether from contributing, for a very whimsical reason, that the value of a free man cannot be estimated in money: and yet passengers frequently make a great part of the load. If they contribute to the necessity of disburdening the ship, for what good reason ought they to be exempted from contributing to make up the loss of the goods thrown into the sea upon their account?

Under this article comes a case that appears to be *in apicibus juris*. A bond extinguished by payment is assigned for a valuable consideration, and the assignee, ignorant of the payment, obtains payment a second time from the debtor's heir. After several years the error is discovered, but the cedent by this time has become bankrupt. The heir is at common law entitled to demand from the assignee the sum he paid; as twice payment can have no support in law. The assignee paying this sum is barred by the insolvency of the cedent from any relief against him. What does equity rule in this intricate case, where there is a real connection between the parties by their concern in the same subject? A strong circumstance for the assignee is, that the payment he received from the heir *bona fide*, was to him invincible evidence that he could have no claim against the cedent. He was led into that mistake by the heir's remissness or rather rashness in paying without examining his father's writings. They are equally *certantes de damno vitando*; and yet the heir's claim at common

P. I. 3. BENEVOLENCE. 125

law must be sustained, if there be nothing in equity to balance it. The balance in equity is, that the loss ought to rest on the heir, by whose remissness it was occasioned, and not on the assignee, who had it not in his power to prevent it. But as the assignee's loss is only the price he paid to the cedent, his equitable defence against the heir can go no further. This principle of equity is acknowledged by the Court of Session, and has been frequently applied. Thus an heir having ignorantly paid a debt to an assignee, and several years after having discovered that his ancestor had paid the debt to the cedent, he insisted in a *condictio indebiti*. The defendant was assoilzied, because the cedent had become insolvent after the erroneous payment. * In this case it seems to have been overlooked, that the assignee was not entitled to withhold from the heir more than what he himself had paid to the cedent. So far he was *certans de damno vitando* : to demand more was *captare lucrum ex aliena jactura*. A creditor, after receiving a partial payment, assigned the whole sum for security of a debt due by him to the assignee, who, having got payment of the whole sum from the debtor, ignorant of the partial payment, was, on discovery of the fact, sued for restitution *condictione indebiti*. His defence was sustained, That he was not bound to restore what he received in payment of a just debt. † This judgment is founded on a mistake in fact. The debt due to the assignee by the cedent was a just debt : but the sum paid by the debtor to the assignee was

---

* 24th July 1723, Duke of Argyle *contra* Representatives of Lord Halcraig.

† Stair, 23d Feb. 1681, Earl Mar *contra* Earl Callender.

DEEDS AND COVENANTS. B. I.

not in payment of that debt, but of the debt due by him to the cedent, which was not wholly just, as part had been formerly paid. The debtor, therefore, was well entitled to demand the overplus from the assignee, because a second payment can have no support from law. But probably the cedent had become insolvent after the erroneous payment, which brings this case under the rule of equity handled above.

CHAPTER IV.

Powers of a court of equity to remedy what is imperfect in common law with respect to deeds and covenants.

W E have seen above, that, abstracting from positive engagements, the affording relief to a fellow-creature in distress, is the only case that exalts our benevolence to be an indispensable duty. A man, however, is singly the most helpless of all animals; and, unless he could rely upon assistance from others, he would in vain attempt any work that requires more than two hands. To secure aid and assistance in time of need, the moral sense makes the performance of promises and convenants a duty; and to these, accordingly, may justly be attributed, the progress at least, if not the commencement, of every art.

Among the various principles that qualify men for society, that by which one man can bind himself to another by an act of will, is eminent. By that act, a new relation arises between them : the person bound is termed *obligor*, the other *obligee*. But a man may exert an act of will in favour of another without

P. I. 4.   DEEDS AND COVENANTS.   127

binding himself, which is the case of a testament or latter-will: during the testator's life, his will expressed in his testament, differs not from a resolution, as he is bound by neither; but after death it differs widely, for death puts an end to the power of alteration. A testament, therefore, must be effectual by the testator's death, or it never can be effectual.

Where two persons bind themselves to each other by mutual acts of will, this is termed a *contract* or *covenant.* Where one binds himself to another without any reciprocal obligation, that act of will is termed a *promise.* I promise to pay to John £100. An *offer* is a different act of will: it binds not unless it be accepted; and acceptance is an act of will of a fourth kind. Where one by an act of will conveys a subject to another, that is a fifth kind; and that act expressed in writing is termed a *deed.*

Nature, independent of will, bars absolutely men from harming each other. It binds them positively to afford relief to the distressed as far as they are able. But in no case is a man bound to add to the estate of another, or to make him *locupletior*, as termed in the Roman law, otherwise than by voluntary engagement. This distinguishes the obligation of a voluntary engagement from the other duties mentioned. The latter cannot be transgressed without making others suffer in person, in goods, or in reputation: but in relieving from the obligation of a promise or covenant, the person in whose favour it is made is indeed deprived of any benefit from it, but suffers no positive loss or damage: to him it is *lucrum cessans* only, not *damnum datum.* Hence it is, that the moral sense is less rigid as to voluntary engagements, than as to duties that arise without consent. To fulfil a rational promise or covenant, is a duty no less inflexible, than to fulfil the duties that arise without consent. But as man is a fallible being, liable to fraud and deceit, and apt to be misled by ignorance and error, the moral sense would be ill-suited to his nature, did it compel him to fulfil every engagement, however irrational, however rashly or ignorantly made. Deplorable indeed would be our condition, were we so strictly bound by the moral sense: the innocent would be a prey to the designing, the ignorant would be overreached by the crafty, and society be an uncomfortable state. But the Author of our nature leaves none of his works imperfect: the moral sense, corresponding to the fallibility of our nature, binds us by no engagement but what is fairly entered into with every consequence in view, and what in particular answers the end for which it was made.

Few persons pass much of their time without having purposes to fulfil, and plans to execute; for accomplishing which, means are employed. Among these means, deeds and covenants make a capital figure; no man binds himself or others for the sake merely of binding, but in order to bring about a desired event. Every deed and covenant may accordingly be considered to be a mean employed to bring about some end or event.

Sometimes the desired event is mentioned in the deed or covenant, and expressly agreed on to be performed; in which case performance concludes the transaction, being all that was intended. A bond for borrowed money is a proper example; what is stipulated in the bond to be performed, is repayment of the money, beyond which the parties have no view;

DEEDS AND COVENANTS.

and that end is accomplished when the money is repaid. A legacy bequeathed in a testament is another example: payment of the legacy is the only end in view; and that end is accomplished when the legatee receives the money. But in many deeds and contracts, the fact appointed to be done, is not ultimate, but intended to bring about a further end. Thus, when I buy a stone-horse for propagation, the contract is performed upon delivery of the horse to me. But this performance does not fulfil my promise: I have a further end in view, which is to breed horses; and unless the horse be fit for that end, my purpose in contracting is frustrated. I purchase a hogshead of flax-seed for raising a crop of flax. It is not enough that the seed be delivered to me: if it be rotten, the end I have in view is disappointed.

This suggests a division of voluntary engagements into two kinds: the first, where the performance mentioned is ultimate, by fulfilling all that was intended; the other, where the performance mentioned is not ultimate, but intended as a mean to a further end, not mentioned. In this kind, a contract is a mean to bring about the immediate end, namely, the performance of what was mentioned and agreed on; and this immediate end is a mean to bring about the ultimate end.

In contracts of this kind, there is place for judging how far the means are proportioned to the end: they may be insufficient to bring about the end; they may be more than sufficient; and they may have no tendency to bring about the end. Here equity may interpose, to vary these means in some cases, and to proportion them more accurately to the ultimate end: in other cases, to set aside the contract altogether, as

130   DEEDS AND COVENANTS.   B. I.

insufficient to bring about the ultimate end. Hence it is, that such contracts are termed *contracts bonæ fidei*; that is, contracts in which equity may interpose to correct inequalities, and to adjust all matters according to the plain intention of the parties. With respect to contracts where the performance stipulated is the ultimate end, there is evidently no place for the interposition of equity; for what defence can a man have, either in law or in equity, against performing his engagement, when it fulfils all that he had in view in contracting? Contracts accordingly of that kind, are termed *contracts stricti juris*.

To the distinction between contracts *bonæ fidei* and *stricti juris*, great attention is given in the Roman law. We are told, that equity may interpose in the former, and that the latter are left to common law. But as to what contracts are *bonæ fidei*, what *stricti juris*, we are left in the dark by Roman writers. Some of their commentators give us lists or catalogues; but they pretend not to lay down any precise rule by which the one kind may be distinguished from the other. I have endeavoured to supply that defect: whether satisfactorily or not, is the province of others to judge.

Have we in Scotland any action similar to what in the Roman law is termed *Condictio ex pœnitentia*? Voet, upon the title *Condictio causa data*, &c. says, that the *condictio ex pœnitentia* is not admitted in modern practice, because every paction is now obligatory. I admit that every paction is obligatory so far as to produce an action; but that does not bar an equitable defence. And it appears to me, that there are contracts where repentance may be sustained in equity as a good defence; as where the

P. I. 4. DEEDS AND COVENANTS. 181

contract is of a deep concern to one of the parties, and of very little to the other. For example, I bargain with an undertaker to build me a dwelling-house for a certain sum, according to a plan concerted. Before the work is begun, the plan is discovered to be faulty in many capital articles. Am I bound notwithstanding to fulfil my covenant with the undertaker? Will not ignorance here relieve me, as error would do, where it is *lucrum cessans* only to the undertaker, and a very deep loss to me? Suppose again, that upon a more narrow inspection into my finances, the sum agreed on for building is found to be more than I ought to afford. Or what if, *rebus integris*, I succeed to an estate with a good house upon it, or am invited by an employment to settle elsewhere? If I be relieved, the undertaker is at liberty to accept of employment from others; and perhaps of more beneficial employment than mine: if I be kept bound, a great interest on my side is sacrificed to a trifling interest on his. Covenants, intended for the support of society, ought not rashly to be converted to the ruin of an individual. It is a delicate point to determine in what cases a court of equity ought to interpose. All arbitrary questions are dangerous, and this is one of them. The Court of Session, however, must not decline such questions, where it is to relieve from deep inequality and distress. In the cases above mentioned, they certainly would not refuse to interpose.

Great interest on the one side, and very little on the other, is not the only instance where a court of equity will admit of repentance. Of all articles of commerce, that of land is of the highest importance. For that reason, repentance is permitted in a verbal

I 2

DEEDS AND COVENANTS. B. I.

bargain of land, however fair and equal the bargain may be. It requires writing to fix the bargain. Marriage is a contract still more important, as the happiness of one's whole life may depend on it. Hence it is that nothing but a contract *de præsenti* can bind. Repentance is permitted of every agreement that can be made about a future marriage. Thus a bond granted by a woman to marry the obligee under a penalty, will not be effectual even for the penalty.*

This chapter, consisting of many parts, requires many divisions: and in the divisions that follow, a proper arrangement is studied, which ought to be a capital object in every didactic subject.

SECT. I.

Where will is imperfectly expressed in the writing.

In applying the rules of equity to deeds and covenants, what comes first under consideration is, whether the will be fully or fairly taken down in the writing. A man expressing his thoughts to others, is not always accurate in his terms, neither is the writer always accurate in expressing the will of his employer: and between the two, errors are often multiplied. Thus, clauses in writings are sometimes ambiguous or obscure, sometimes too limited, sometimes too extensive. As in common law, the words are strictly adhered to, such imperfections are remedied by a court of equity. It admits words and writing to be the proper evidence of will; but excludes not other evidence. Sensible that words and writing

* 2. Vernon, 102.

P. L 4. DEEDS AND COVENANTS. 133

are not always accurate, it endeavours to reach will, which is the substantial part; and if, from the end and purpose of, the engagement, from collateral circumstances, or from other satisfying evidence, will can be ascertained, it is justly made the rule, however it may differ from the words. The sole purpose of the writing is to bear testimony of will; and if that testimony prove erroneous, it can avail nothing against the truth. This branch of equitable jurisdiction, which comprehends both deeds and covenants, is founded on the principle of justice, which declares for will against every erroneous evidence of it.

This section may be divided into three articles. First, Where the words leave us uncertain about will. Second, Where they are short of will. Third, Where they go beyond it.

ART. I. *Where the words leave us uncertain about will.*

This imperfection may be occasioned by the fault of the writer, mistaking the meaning of his employer; or by the fault of the employer, exerting an act of will imperfectly, or expressing his will obscurely. But I purposely neglect these distinctions; because in most of the cases that occur, it is extremely doubtful upon whom the inaccuracy is to be charged. Nor will this breed any confusion; for from whatever cause the doubt about will arises, the method of solving it is the same, namely, to form the best conjecture we can, after considering every relative circumstance.

Contracts shall furnish the first examples. In a

bargain of sale, the price is referred to a third person: the referee dies suddenly without naming the price; and there is no performance on either side. There being no remedy here at common law, because the price is not ascertained, can a court of equity supply the defect in order to validate the bargain? This question depends on what the parties intended by the reference. If they intended not to be bound but by the opinion of the referee, it is in effect a conditional bargain, never purified, which no court will make effectual. But if it was intended, that the sale should in all events stand good, leaving only the price to be determined by the referee; the unexpected accident of his death cannot resolve the bargain; upon which account, it belongs to a court of equity, in place of the referee, to name a price *secundum arbitrium boni viri.* A man having purchased land, obliged himself in a back-bond to redispone, upon receiving back the price from the vender within a time specified. The vender having died within the time, it was questioned, Whether his heir was privileged to redeem the land. If it was the meaning of the contract to confine the privilege of redemption to the vender personally, his heir could have no right. But if it was understood sufficient that the price should be repaid within the time specified, the heir was entitled to redeem, as the predecessor was. This construction, as the more equal and rational, was adopted by the Court of Session. And, accordingly, the land was found legally redeemed, upon the heir's offering the price before the term was elapsed.* A gentleman having given a bond of provision to his sister for 3,000 merks, took from her a back-bond, importing,

* Stair, 9th Jan. 1662, Earl of Moray *contra* Grant.

P. 1. 4.   DEEDS AND COVENANTS.   155

" That the sum being rather too great for his circum-
" stances, she consented that the same should be mi-
" tigated by friends to be mutually chosen, their mo-
" ther being one." After the mother's decease without mitigation, the brother's creditors insisting for a
mitigation *secundum arbitrium boni viri*, the defence
was, That the condition of the mitigation had failed
by the mother's death ; and, therefore, that the bond
must subsist *in totum*. The defence was sustained.*
Supposing the back-bond to be conditional, the judgment is right. But as it seems the more natural
construction, that there should be a mitigation if the
brother's circumstances required it, the unexpected
death of the mother ought not to have prevented the
mitigation.

The next examples shall be of deeds. The minister of Weem settled his funds upon five trustees, and
their successors, for the use of the schoolmasters of
that parish, declaring the major part to be a quorum.
Two only of the trustees having accepted and intermeddled with the funds, a process was brought
against them by the representatives of the minister
claiming the funds, upon the following ground, that
the deed of mortification was conditional, requiring
the acceptance of a quorum at least of the trustees ;
and therefore void, the condition not having been
purified. The defence was, that the deed of mortification was pure, vesting a right in the schoolmasters
of Weem ; that the nomination of trustees was only
intended, like the nomination of an executor, to make
the funds effectual ; and that it was not intended to
make the deed depend on their acceptance or non-
acceptance. The deed was sustained ; the court being

* 19th February 1734, Corsan *contra* Maxwell of Barncleuch.

136 DEEDS AND COVENANTS. B. I.

of opinion, that it would have been effectual though all the trustees had declined acceptance.* I illustrate this by an opposite case, where it was understood that no right was created by the deed. Lady Prestonfield made a settlement of considerable funds to Sir John Cuninghame her eldest son, and Anne Cunninghame her eldest daughter, as trustees for the ends and purposes following. First, the yearly interest to be applied for the education and support of such of her descendants as should happen to be in want, or stand in need thereof, and that at the discretion of the trustees. Second, failing descendants, the capital to return to her heirs. The trustees declining to accept this whimsical settlement, a process for voiding it was brought by the heir-at-law, in which were called all the existing descendants of the maker. As here it appeared to be the maker's will to leave all to the discretion of the trustees, without the least hint of giving any right to her descendants, independent of the trustees, the deed was declared void by their non-acceptance.†

Colonel Campbell being bound in his contract of marriage to secure the sum of 40,000 merks, and the conquest during the marriage, to himself and spouse in conjunct fee and liferent, and to the children to be procreated of the marriage in fee, did, by a death-bed deed, settle all upon his eldest son, burdened with the sum of 30,000 merks to his younger children, to take place, if their mother could be prevailed on to give up her claim to the liferent of the con-

* December 1752, Campbell *contra* Campbell of Monzie and Campbell of Achallader.

† 22d January 1758, Sir Alexander Dick *contra* Mrs. Fergusson and her children.

DEEDS AND COVENANTS. 187

quest, and restrict herself to a less jointure: otherwise, the provision to the younger children to be void; in which event, it was left upon the Duke of Argyle, and Earl of Ilay, to name such provisions to the children as they should see convenient. The referees having declined to accept, the question occurred between the heir and the younger children, what was the Colonel's intention, whether to make a provision for his younger children, referring the quantum only to the Duke and Earl; or to make the provision conditional, that it should not be effectual unless the referees named a sum. The court adopted the latter construction; and refused to interpose in place of the referees to name a sum.* The judgment probably would have been different, had no provision been made for the children in the contract of marriage.

A married woman gives a security on her estate to her husband's creditors; but with what intention it is not said. If a donation was intended, she has no claim for relief against her husband: but *in dubio,* a cautionary engagement will be presumed; which affords her a claim.† A court of common law would hardly be brought to sustain a claim of this nature, where there is no clause in the deed on which it can be founded.

Where a man provides a sum to his creditor, without declaring it to be in satisfaction, it will be sustained as a separate claim at common law. But as the granter probably intended that sum to be in sa-

* 22d December 1739, Campbell *contra* Campbells.

† Stair, 11th January 1679, Bowie *contra* Corbet; Fountainhall, 16th July 1696, Leishman *contra* Nicols; 29th November 1728, Trail of Sabae *contra* Moodie.

138   **DEEDS AND COVENANTS.**   **B. 1.**

tisfaction, according to the maxim, *Quod debitor non præsumitur donare*, a court of equity, supplying a defect in words, decrees the sum to be in satisfaction. Thus, a man being bound for £10 yearly to his daughter, gave her at her marriage a portion of £200. Decreed, That the annuity was included in the portion.* But where a man leaves a legacy to his creditor, this cannot be constructed as satisfaction; for in that case it would not be a legacy or donation.

Anthony Murray, *anno* 1738, made a settlement of his estate upon John and Thomas Belsches, taking them bound, among other legacies, to pay £300 sterling to their sister Emilia, at her marriage. Anthony altered this settlement, *anno* 1740, in favour of his heir-at-law; obliging him, however, to pay the legacies contained in the former settlement. In the year 1744, Anthony executed a bond to Emilia upon the narrative of love and favour, binding himself to pay to her in liferent, and to her children *nati et nascituri* in fee, at the first term after his decease, the sum of £1,200 sterling. The doubt was, whether both sums were due to Emilia, or only the latter. It was admitted, that both sums would be due at common law, which looks no farther than the words. But that this was not the intention of the granter, was urged, from the following circumstance, That in the bond for the £1,200, there is no mention of the former legacy, nor of any legacy; which clearly shews, that Anthony had forgot the first legacy, and consequently, that he intended no more for Emilia but £1,200 in whole. Which was accordingly decreed.†

---

* Tothill's Reports, 78.

† 22d December 1752, Emilia Belsches and her husband *contra* Sir Patrick Murray.

Art. II. *Where the words are short of will.*

BETWEEN this article and a following section, intitled, *Implied will*, there is much affinity; but as the blending together things really distinct, tends to confusion of ideas, I have brought under the present article, acts of will that are indeed expressed, but so imperfectly as to leave room for doubt, whether the will does not go farther than is spoken out; leaving to the section *Implied will*, articles essential to the deed or covenant, that must have made a part of the maker's will, and yet are totally omitted to be expressed.

In England, where estates are settled by will, it is the practice to make up any defect in the words, in order to support the will of the devisor. But here it is essential that the will be clearly ascertained, in order that the court may run no hazard of overturning the will, instead of supporting it. An executor being named with the usual power of managing the whole money and effects of the deceased, the following clause subjoined, " And I hereby debar and se- " clude all others from any right or interest in my " said executry," was held by the court to import an universal legacy in favour of the executor.* A man having two nephews who were his heirs-at-law, made a settlement in their favour, dividing his farms between them, intending probably an equal division. A farm was left out by the omission of the clerk, which the scrivener swore was intended for the plaintiff. The

---

* 1st Feb. 1789, John Beisly *contra* Gabriel Napier

DEEDS AND COVENANTS.

court refused to amend the mistake, leaving the farm to descend as *ab intestato*.[*] For here it was not clear, that the maker of the deed intended an equal division.

There being an entail of the estate of Cromarty to heirs-male, the Earl, in his contract of marriage, *anno* 1724, became bound, in case of children of the marriage who should succeed to and enjoy the estate, to infeft his lady in a liferent locality of forty chalders victual; and in case of no children to succeed to and enjoy the estate, he became bound to make the said locality fifty chalders. The following clause is added : " That if, at the dissolution of the mar- " riage, there should be children succeeding to and " enjoying the estate, but who should afterward de- " cease during the life of his said spouse, she, from " that period, should be entitled to fifty chalders, as " if the said children had not existed." The Earl being forfeited in the year 1745, having issue both male and female, a claim was entered by his lady for the jointure of fifty chalders, to take effect after her husband's death. Objected by his Majesty's Advocate, That she is entitled to forty chalders only, there being sons of the marriage, who, but for the forfeiture, would have succeeded to the estate. Here evidently the words fall short of intention; for as the claimant would have had a jointure of fifty chalders if the Earl's brother or nephew had succeeded to the estate, there can be no doubt that had the event of forfeiture been foreseen, the Earl would have given her at least fifty chalders. The claim accordingly was sustained. [†]

[*] 1. Vernon, 37.

[†] 26th January 1764, Countess of Cromarty *contra* the Crown.

P. I. 4. · DEEDS AND COVENANTS. 141

Walter Riddel, in his contract of marriage 1694, became bound to settle his whole land-estate on the heir-male of the marriage.' In the year 1727, purposing to fulfil that obligation, he disponed to his eldest son the lands therein specified, burdened with his debts, reserving to himself' an annuity of 2000 merks only. The lands of Stewarton, which came under the said obligation, were left out of the disposition 1727. But that they were omitted by oversight, without intention, was made evident from the following circumstances: first, That the title-deeds of that farm were delivered to the son along with the other title-deeds; second, That he took possession of the whole; third, That a subsequent deed by the father *anno* 1733, proceeds upon this narrative, "That " the whole lands belonging to him were conveyed " to his son by the disposition 1727." Many years after, the father, having discovered that Stewarton was not mentioned in the said disposition, ventured to convey that farm to his second son, who was otherwise competently provided. It was not pretended, that Stewarton was actually conveyed to the eldest son, which could not be but in a formal disposition; but as there was clear evidence of the father's obligation to convey it with the rest of the estate, which obligation he was still bound to fulfil, the court judged this a sufficient foundation for voiding the gratuitous disposition to the second son.*

In the cases mentioned, writing is necessary as evidence only: it is of no consequence what words be used in the nomination of an heir or of an executor, provided the will of the maker be ascertained. But in several transactions, writing, beside the evidence

* January 4, 1766, Riddel *contra* Riddel of Glenriddel.

DEEDS AND COVENANTS. B. I.

it affords, is an indispensable solemnity. Land cannot be conveyed without a procuratory or a precept, which must be in a set form of words. A man may lend his money upon a verbal paction, but he cannot proceed directly to execution, unless he have a formal bond containing a clause of registration, authorising execution. Neither can such a bond be conveyed to a purchaser, otherwise than by a formal assignment in writing. Here a new speculation arises, What power a court of equity hath over a writing of this kind? In this writing, no less than in others, the words may happen erroneously to be more extensive than the will of the granter; or they may happen to be more limited. Must the words in all cases be the sovereign rule? Far from it. Though in certain transactions writ is an essential solemnity, it follows not, that the words solely must be regarded, without relation to will; for to bind a man by words where he hath not interposed his will, is contrary to the most obvious principles of justice. Hence it necessarily follows, that a deed of this kind may, by a court of equity, be limited to a narrower effect than the words naturally import; and that this ought to be done, where, from the context, from the intendment of the granter, or from other convincing circumstances, it can be certainly gathered, that the words, by mistake, go beyond the will. But though in ordinary cases, such as those above mentioned, the defect of words may be supplied, and force given to will, supposing it clearly ascertained; yet this cannot be done in a deed to which writ is essential. The reason is, that to make writ an essential solemnity, is, in other words, to declare, that action must not be sustained, except as far as authorised by writ. How-

P. I. 4. DEEDS AND COVENANTS. 143

ever clear, therefore, will may be, a court of equity
hath not authority to sustain action upon it, independent of the words where these are made essential;
for this, in effect, would be to overturn law, which is
beyond the power of equity. A case that really happened, is a notable illustration of this doctrine. A
bond of corroboration granted by the debtor with a
cautioner, was of the following tenor:—" And seeing
". the foresaid principal sum of 1000 merks, and in-
" terest since Martinmas 1742, are resting unpaid;
" and that *A* the creditor is willing to supersede pay-
" ment till the term after mentioned, upon *B* the
" debtor's granting the present corroborative securi-
" ty with *C* his cautioner; therefore *B* and *C* bind
" and oblige them, conjunctly and severally, &c. to
" content and pay to *A* in liferent, and to her child-
" ren in fee, equally among them, and failing any of
" them by decease, to the survivors, their heirs or
" assignees, in fee, and that at Whitsunday 1744,
" with 200 merks of penalty, together with the due
" and ordinary annualrent of the said principal sum
" from the said term of Martinmas 1742," &c. Here
the obligatory clause is imperfect, as it omits the
principal sum corroborated, namely, the 1000 merks,
a pure oversight of the writer. In a suit upon this
bond of corroboration against the heir of the cautioner, it was objected, That upon this bond no action
could lie against him for payment of the principal
sum. It was obvious to the court, that the bond,
though defective in the most essential part, afforded
clear evidence of *C's* consent to be bound as cautioner. But then it occurred, that a cautionary engagement is one of those deeds that require writing in
point of solemnity. A defective bond, like the pre-

144 DEEDS AND COVENANTS. B. I.

sent, whatever evidence it may afford, is still less formal than if it wanted the requisites of the act 1681. Action, accordingly, was denied; for action cannot be sustained upon consent alone, where a formal deed is essential.* The following case concerning a registrable bond, or, as termed in England, *a bond in judgment*, is another instance of refusing to supply a defect in words. A bond for a sum of money bore the following clause, *with interest and penalty*, without specifying any sum in name of penalty. The creditor moved the court to supply the omission, by naming the fifth part of the principal sum, being the constant rule as to consensual penalties. There could be no doubt of the granter's intention; and yet the court justly thought that they had not power to supply the defect.†

But though a defect in a writ that is essential in point of solemnity, cannot be supplied so as to give it the full effect that law gives to such a deed, it will, however, be regarded by a court of equity in point of evidence. A bond of borrowed money, for example, null by the act 1681, because the writer's name was neglected, may, in conjunction with other evidence, be produced in an action for payment; in order to prove delivery of the money as a loan, and, consequently, to found a decree for repayment.

ART. III. *Where the words go beyond will.*

It is a rule in daily practice, That however express the words may be, a court of equity gives no force to a deed beyond the will of the granter. This

* 2d June 1749, Colt *contra* Angus.
† Fount. 6th January 1705, Leslie *contra* Ogilvie.

P. I. 4.   DEEDS AND COVENANTS.   145

rule is finely illustrated in the following case. John Campbell, provost of Edinburgh, did, in July 1734, make a settlement of the whole effects that should belong to him at the time of his death, to William, his eldest son, with the burden of provisions to his other children, Matthew, Daniel, and Margaret. Daniel being at sea, in a voyage from the East Indies, made his will, May 1739, in which he " gives and " bequeaths all his goods, money, and effects, to " John Campbell, his father; and in case of John's " decease, to his beloved sister, Margaret." The testator died at sea in the same month of May; and, in June following, John, the father, also died, without hearing of Daniel's death, or of the will made by him. William brought an action against his sister, Margaret, and her husband, concluding, That Daniel's effects, being vested in the father, were conveyed to him, the pursuer, by the father's settlement; and that the substitution in favour of Margaret, contained in Daniel's will, was thereby altered. It was answered, That nothing could be intended by the Provost, but to settle his proper estate upon his eldest son, without any intention to alter the substitution in his son Daniel's testament, of which he was ignorant: That words are not alone, without intention, sufficient to found a claim; and, therefore, that the present action ought not to be sustained. " The court " judged, That the general disposition 1734, granted " by John Campbell to his son, the pursuer, several " years before Daniel's will had a being, does not e- " vacuate the substitution in the said will."† Charles Farquharson, writer, being in a sickly condition, and apprehensive of death, did, *anno* 1721, settle all the

† 13th June 1740, Campbell *contra* his Sister.

K

effects, real and personal, that should belong to him at his death, upon his eldest brother, Patrick Farquarson of Inverey, and his heirs; reserving a power to alter, and dispensing with the delivery. Charles was at that time a bachelor, and died so. Being restored to health, he not only survived his brother Patrick, but also Patrick's two sons, who successively inherited the estate of Inverey. Patrick left daughters; but as the investitures were to heirs-male, Charles was infeft as heir-male, died in possession; and left the estate open to the next heir-male. Against him a process is raised by the daughters of Patrick, claiming the estate of Inverey upon the settlement 1721, as belonging to Charles at the time of his death, and, consequently, now to them as heirs of line to Patrick. The defence was, That here the words of the settlement are more extensive than the will of the granter, which was only to augment the family-estate, by settling his own funds on Patrick, the heir of the family; that this purpose was fulfilled by the coalition of both estates in the defendant, the present head of the family; whereas the claim made by the pursuers, the purpose of which is to take from the representative of the family the family-estate itself, is not only destitute of any foundation in the maker's will, but is in direct opposition to it. The court judged, That the pursuers had no action on the deed 1721, to oblige the defendant to denude of the estate of Inverey.* A contract of marriage providing the estate to the heirs-male of the marriage, whom failing, to the husband's other heirs-male, contained the following clause,

* 10th February 1756, Heirs of line of Patrick Farquharson *contra* his Heir-male.

P. I. 4.   DEEDS AND COVENANTS.   147

" And seeing the earldom of Perth is tailzied to
" heirs-male, so that if there be daughters of the
" marriage, they will be excluded from the succes-
" sion ; therefore, the said James, Lord Drummond,
" and his heirs, become bound to pay to the said daugh-
" ters, at their age of eighteen, or marriage, the sums
" following ; to an only daughter, 40,000 merks," &c.
The estate being forfeited for treason, committed by
the eldest son of the marriage, the only daughter of
the marriage claimed the 40,000 merks, as being excluded from the succession by the existence of an
heir-male. Objected by the King's Advocate, That
the provision not being to younger children in general, but to daughters only, upon consideration that
the estate was entailed to heirs-male, was obviously
intended to be conditional, and only to take effect
failing sons of the marriage ; and that here, inadvertently, the words are more extensive than the will.
It carried, however, by a narrow plurality, to sustain
the claim.* But the judgment was reversed in the
House of Lords.

The same rule obtains with respect to general
clauses in discharges, submissions, assignments, and
such like, which are limited by equity where the
words are more extensive than the will. Thus, a
general submission of all matters debateable, is not
understood to comprehend land or other heritable
right.† Nor was a general clause in a submission
extended to matters of greater importance than those
expressed.‡ A had a judgment of £6,000 against B.

* 10th July 1752, Lady Mary Drummond *contra* the King's
Advocate.

† Hope, (Arbiter), 4th March 1612, Paterson *contra* Forret.

‡ Haddington, 4th March 1607, Inchaffray *contra* Oliphant.

K 2

148   DEEDS AND COVENANTS.   B. I.

B gave *A* a legacy of £5, and died. *A*, on receipt of this £5, gave the executor of *B* a release in the following words. " I acknowledge to have received " of *C* £5, left me as a legacy by *B*, and do release " to him all demands which I against him, as execu- " tor to *B*, can have for any matter whatever." It was adjudged, That the generality of the words *all demands* should be restrained by the particular occasion mentioned in the former part, namely, the receipt of the £5, and should not be a discharge of the judgment.*

. A variety of irritancies contrived to secure an entail against acts and deeds of the proprietor, furnish proper examples of this doctrine. Where such irritancies are so expressed as to declare the proprietor's right voidable only, not *ipso facto* void, an act of contravention may be purged before challenge, and even at any time before sentence in a process of declarator. But what shall be said upon clauses declaring the proprietor to fall from his right *ipso facto* upon the first act of contravention ? Supposing the entailer by this clause to have only intended to keep his heirs of entail to their duty, which *in dubio* will always be presumed, his purpose is fulfilled if the estate be relieved from the debts and deeds of the tenant in tail. The words indeed are clear ; but words unsupported by will have no effect in law. The act 1685 concerning tailzies declares, " That if the provisions and irritant clauses are not repeated in the " rights and conveyances by which the heirs of tail- " zie bruik or enjoy the estate, the omission shall " import a contravention of the irritant and resolu-

* Abridgment Cases in equity, chap. 25, sect. C, note at the end.

DEEDS AND COVENANTS.

" tive clauses against the person and his heirs who " shall omit to insert the same, whereby the estate " shall *ipso facto* fall, accresce, and be devolved upon " the next heir of tailzie ; but shall not militate " against creditors," &c. Here the words go inadvertently beyond will. It cannot be the will of any entailer, to forfeit his heir for an omission that the heir supplies *rebus integris.* Nor could it be the intendment of the legislature to be more severe than entailers themselves commonly are. This irritancy, according to order, ought to come in afterward in treating of equity with respect to statutes ; but by the intimacy of its connection with the irritancies mentioned, it appears in a better light here.

The foregoing irritancies relate to grants and single deeds. The following is an example of a conventional irritancy, an irritancy *ob non solutum cano-nem* in a lease or feu-right. Such a clause, expressed so as to make the right voidable only upon failure of payment, is just and equal ; because, by a declarator of irritancy, it secures to the superior or landlord payment of what is due to him, and at the same time affords to the vassal or tenant an opportunity to purge the irritancy by payment. And even supposing the clause so expressed as to make failure of payment an *ipso facto* forfeiture, it will be held by a court of equity, that the words go inadvertently beyond the will ; and a declarator of irritancy will still be necessary, in order to afford an opportunity for purging the irritancy.

Conditional bonds and grants afford proper examples of the same kind. These are of two sorts. One is where the condition is ultimate ; as for example, a bond for money granted to a young woman upon con-

150   DEEDS AND COVENANTS.   B. I.

dition of her being married to a man named, or a bond for money to a young man upon condition of his entering into holy orders. The other is, where the condition is a means to a certain end; as, for example, a bond for a sum of money to a young woman, upon condition of her marrying with consent of certain friends named, the intendment of which is to prevent an unsuitable match. Conditions of the first sort are taken strictly, and the sum is not due unless the condition be purified. This is requisite at common law; and no less so in equity, because justice requires that a man's will be obeyed. To judge aright of the other sort, we ought to lay the chief weight upon the ultimate purpose of the granter; which, in the case last mentioned, is to confine the young woman to a suitable match. If she, therefore, marry suitably, though without consulting the friends named, I pronounce that the bond ought to be effectual in equity, though not at common law. The reason is given above, that the ultimate will or purpose ought to prevail in opposition to the words. I am aware, that in Scotland we are taught a different lesson. In bonds of the sort under consideration, a distinction is made between a suspensive condition, and one that is resolutive. If the bond to the young woman contain a resolutive condition only, namely, *if she marry without consent she shall forfeit the bond*, it is admitted, that the forfeiture will not take effect unless she marry unsuitably. But it is held by every one, that if the condition be suspensive, as where a bond for money is granted to a young woman, *on condition that if she marry it be with consent of certain friends named*, it must be performed in the precise terms of the clause; because, say they, the will

DEEDS AND COVENANTS.

of the granter must be the rule; and no court has power to vary a conditional grant, or to transform it into one that is pure and simple. This argument is conclusive where a condition is ultimate, whether suspensive or resolutive; but not where the condition is a means to an end. The granter's will, it is true, ought to be obeyed; but whether his will with regard to the means, or his will with regard to the end? The means are of no significancy, but as productive of the end; and, if the end be accomplished without them, they can have no weight in equity or in common sense. Let us try the force of this reasoning by bringing it down to common apprehension. Why is a resolutive condition disregarded, where the obligee marries suitably? For what reason, but that it is considered as a mean to an end; and that if the end be accomplished, the granter's purpose is fulfilled? Is not this reasoning applicable equally to a suspensive condition? No man of plain understanding, unacquainted with law, will discover any difference. And, accordingly, in the latter practice of the English Court of Chancery, this difference seems to be disregarded. A portion of £8,000 is given to a woman, provided she marry with consent of *A*; and if she marry without his consent, she shall have but £100 yearly. She was relieved, though she married without consent; for the proviso is *in terrorem* only.[*]

One having three daughters, devises lands to his eldest, upon condition, that within six months after his death she pay certain sums to her two sisters; and if she fail, he devises the land to his second daughter on the like condition. The court may en-

[*] Abridg. Cases in equity, chap. 17, sect. C, § 1.

152 DEEDS AND COVENANTS. B. I.

large the time for payment, though the premises are devised over. And in all cases where compensation can be made for the delay, the court may dispense with the time, though even in the case of a condition precedent.* This practical rule is evidently derived from the reasoning above stated.

Take another example that comes under the same rule of equity. A claim is transacted, and a less sum accepted, upon condition that the same be paid at a day certain, otherwise the transaction to be void. It is the general opinion, that where the clause is resolutive, equity will relieve against it after the stipulated term is elapsed, provided the transacted sum be paid before process be raised; but that this will not hold where the clause is suspensive. In my apprehension, there is an equitable ground for relief in both equally. The form may be different, but the intention is the same in both, namely, to compel payment of the transacted sum; and, therefore, if payment be offered at any time before a declarator of irritancy, with damages for the delay, the conditional irritancy has had the full effect that was intended. Equity, therefore, requires a declarator of irritancy, whether the clause be suspensive or resolutive; and the defendant ought to be admitted to purge the failure by offering payment of the transacted sum. The case, I acknowledge, is different where the transacted sum is to be paid in parcels, and at different periods; as, for example, where an annuity is transacted for a less yearly sum. A court of equity will scarce interpose in this case, but leave the irritancy to take place *ipso facto*, by the rules of common law; for if the irritant clause be not in this case permitted

* Abridg. Cases in equity, chap. 17, sect. B, § 5.

DEEDS AND COVENANTS. 158

to operate *ipso facto*, it will be altogether ineffectual, and be no compulsion to make payment. If a declarator be necessary, the defendant must be admitted to purge before sentence; and if it be at all necessary, it must be renewed every term where there is a failure of payment. This would be unjust, because it reduces the creditor to the same difficulty of recovering the transacted sum, that he had with respect to his original sum; which, in effect, is to forfeit the creditor for his moderation, instead of forfeiting the debtor for his ingratitude.

The examples above given coincide in the following particular, that the acts of contravention can be purged, so as to restore matters to the same state as if there had been no contravention. But there are acts incapable of being purged, such as the cutting down trees by a tenant. Now, suppose a lease be granted with a clause of forfeiture, in case of felling trees, will equity relieve against this forfeiture in any case? If the act of contravention was done knowingly, and consequently criminally, there can be no equity in giving relief; but if it was done ignorantly and innocently, a court of equity ought to interpose against the forfeiture, upon making up full damages to the landlord. Take the following instance. The plaintiff, tenant for life of a copyhold-estate, felled trees, which, at a court-baron, was found a waste, and consequently a forfeiture. The bill was to be relieved against the forfeiture, offering satisfaction if it appeared to be a waste. The court decreed an issue, to try whether the primary intention in felling the trees was to do waste; declaring, that, in case of a wilful forfeiture, it would not relieve.*

* 1. Chancery Cases, 95.

154 DEEDS AND COVENANTS. **B. I.**

A power granted to distribute a sum or a subject among children, or others, is limited in equity to be exercised *secundum arbitrium boni viri*, unless an absolute power be clearly expressed. A man devised to his wife his personal estate, upon trust and confidence,—" That she should not dispose thereof, but " for the benefit of her children." She, by will, gave to one but five shillings, and all the rest to another. The court set aside so unequal a distribution.* A man, by will, directed that his land should descend to his daughters, " in such shares as his wife, by a " deed in writing, should appoint." The wife makes an unequal distribution. The court at first declared, the circumstances must be very strong, as bribery, for instance, or corruption, that could take from the wife a power given her by the will : but afterward declared the case was proper for equity, and that the plaintiff might be relieved. Here the plaintiff was allowed but a small proportion ; and for any causeless displeasure she might have been put off with a single barren acre; that the court, in the latter case, would have a jurisdiction ; and, therefore, in the case that really happened.†

SECT. II.

Implied will.

IN framing a deed, it belongs to the granter to declare his will and purpose : the proper clauses for expressing these are left to the writer. But seldom it happens that every particular is expressed : nor is it

* 1. Vernon, 66.   † 1. Vernon, 355, 414.

P. 1 4.   DEEDS AND COVENANTS.   155

necessary; for, where a man declares his will, with respect to a certain event, he undoubtedly wills every necessary mean; which is only saying, that he is not a changeling. I grant, for example, to a neighbour, liberty of my coal-pit for the use of his family. It follows necessarily, that he have a coal-road through my land, if he have not otherwise access to the pit. The same holds in covenants. A clause in a lease entitling the lessee to take possession at a time specified, implies necessarily authority from the landlord to remove the tenant in possession.

Tacit will, where made clear from circumstances, ought to have the same authority with expressed will: the only use of words is to signify will or intention; and from the very nature of the thing, will or intention cannot have greater authority when expressed in words, than when ascertained with equal clearness by any other signs or means. A court of common law rarely ventures to dive into tacit will. But it is one of the valuable powers of a court of equity, to imply will where it is not expressed; without which deeds and covenants would often fall short of their purposed end. But a judge ought to be extremely cautious in the exercise of this power, to avoid counteracting will, instead of supporting it; an error that seems to have been committed in the following case. The sum of £120 was given with an apprentice; and as the master was sick when the articles were drawn, it was provided, that if he died within a year, £60 should be returned. He having died within three weeks, a bill was brought in chancery to have a greater sum returned. And notwithstanding the express provision, it was decreed that a hundred guineas should be returned.*

* Vernon, 460.

156 DEEDS AND COVENANTS. B. I.

As tacit will is to be gathered from various circumstances, particularly from the nature and intendment of the deed or covenant, general rules are not
to be expected. All I can venture on, is to give examples of various kinds, which may enure the student of law to judge, in what cases will ought to be
implied, in what not. For the sake of perspicuity,
these examples shall be put in different classes. And
first, of *accessories*. Where a subject is conveyed,
every one of its accessories are understood to be conveyed with it, unless the contrary be expressed. An
assignment, for example, of a bond of borrowed money, implies a conveyance of what execution have
passed upon it : these may be of use to the assignee ;
but can avail nothing to the cedent after he is denuded. Thus, an assignment to a bond was understood to comprehend an inhibition that followed upon it ; though there was no general clause that could
comprehend the inhibition.* In an infeftment of annualrent, a personal obligation for payment is now
common. In the conveyance of an infeftment containing that obligation, no mention was made of it.
It was, however, implied by the Court of Session ;
as there appeared no intention to relieve the debtor.†
Tenants, taken bound by lease to carry their corn-
rent to the place of sale, were decerned to perform
that service to the proprietor's widow, infeft in a
liferent-locality.‡ Such implication is not made with
respect to penal accessories : these will not go to the

* Harcarse, (Assignation), January 1682, Williamson *contra*
Threapland.
† Dury, 23d November 1627, Dunbar *contra* Williamson.
‡ Fountainhall, 29th July 1680, Countess Dowager of Errol
contra the Earl.

P. I. 4.   DEEDS AND COVENANTS.   157

assignee, unless expressly conveyed. The superior of a feu-right dispones the same for a valuable consideration; but, antecedently, the feuar had incurred an irritancy upon failing to pay his feu-duty. Is the purchaser entitled to reduce the feu upon that head? The irritancy is indeed an accessory to the superiority; but loosely connected, and easily separated. The punishment is what few superiors are so hard-hearted as to inflict; and a superior who declines the taking advantage of it for himself, will not readily bestow the power on another. If intended, therefore, to be conveyed, it must be expressed; for it will not be implied by a court of equity.

A discharge of the principal debt includes accessories by implied will. An agent, for example, employed to carry on a process, states an account without any article for pains. He receives payment of the sum in the account, and gives a discharge. The article for pains is understood to be also discharged Implied will is extended still farther. The extract of a decree implies the passing from any claim for costs of suit; because no rational person who purposes to claim such costs will reserve them for a new process, when, by delaying extract, it is so much more easy to claim them in the same process.

So much for accessories. Next, of *consequents*. A commission being given to execute any work, every power necessary to carry it on is implied. Example: A man commissioned to navigate a ship, termed the *master*, can bind his owners to pay what money he has borrowed in a foreign country for repairing the ship.

I shall add but one class more, which is, where, in a settlement upon one person, a benefit is understood

158   DEEDS AND COVENANTS.   B. I.

to be conferred on another. Thus, where a man devises land to his heir after the death of his wife, this,
by necessary implication, is a good device to the wife
for life : by the words of the will, the heir is not to
have it during her life ; and none else can have it, as
the executors cannot intermeddle.* But if a man
devises land to a stranger after the death of his wife,
this does not necessarily infer, that the wife should
have the estate for her life : it is but declaring at
what time the stranger's estate shall commence ; and
in the meantime the heir shall have the land.†(a)

I close this head with the following reflection, that
the power of implying will can only be of use where
tacit will is authoritative : it can avail nothing where
writing, and consequently words, are essential. To
make a valid entail, for example, words are essential :
tacit will avails nothing.

SECT. III.

*Whether an omission in a deed or covenant can be
supplied.*

WITH regard to the former section, a court has no
occasion to extend its equitable power farther than
to dive into tacit will, and to bring it into day-light.
With respect to the present section, the court is called on to extend its power a great way farther, in
order to do justice. In framing a deed or covenant,
every necessary circumstance is not always in view :

---

* New Abridgment of the Law, vol. ii, p. 66.

† Ibid.

(a) This is a proper example of a maxim in the Roman Law,
Positus in conditione non censetur positus in institutione.

DEEDS AND COVENANTS. 159

articles are sometimes omitted essential to the deed or covenant; which, therefore, ought to be supplied, in order to do justice to the parties concerned. It is a bold step in a court to supply will in any particular, which, so far, is making a will for a man who omitted to make one for himself; but where will is declared with respect to capital articles, so as to create a right to one or to both of the parties, it is the duty of a court of equity to supply omissions, in order to make the rights created effectual: a right is created by what is actually agreed on; the court is bound to give force to that right, according to the maxim, that right ought never to be left without remedy.

This extraordinary power ought never to be exercised but where it clearly follows, from the nature of the writing, from the intendment of parties, or from other pregnant circumstances, that there really is an omission of some clause that would have been expressed, had it occurred to the parties. If a court should venture to interpose, without being certain that the clause was not purposely left out, they would be in hazard of making a will for a man, and overturning that which he himself made. But where they are satisfied that there is really an omission, their supplying the omission is not making a will for a man, but, on the contrary, is completing his will.

This doctrine will be illustrated by the following examples. In a wadset, the naming a consignator is omitted; which could not be done purposely, a consignator being an essential person in following out an order of redemption. From the nature of the contract, the granter is entitled to redeem; and to make his right effectual, the court will name a consignator. Upon a wadset granted to be held of the superior, an

160   DEEDS AND COVENANTS.   B. I.

infeftment passed ; but it was omitted to provide, that the wadsetter, on redemption, should surrender the subject to the superior for new infeftment to the reverser. The Court of Session, considering that this is a proper clause, and that the wadsetter could not have objected to it, had it occurred in framing the wadset, decreed him to grant a procuratory of resignation.*

. A man lent a sum on bond, payable to himself and to his children *nominatim* in fee, with the following provision, " That in case of the decease of any of " the said children, the share of that child shall be " equally divided among the survivors." One of the children, a son, having predeceased his father, leaving issue, it was questioned, whether his share of the bond descended to his issue, or accresced to the survivors. Here was evidently an omission ; as the granter could not intend to exheredate the issue of any of his children. And, accordingly, the issue of the son were preferred.† Papinian, the greatest of the Roman lawyers, delivers the same opinion in a similar case : " Cum avus filium ac nepotem ex al- " terio filio heredes instituisset, a nepote petiit, ut " *si intra annum trigesimum moriretur, hereditatem* " *patruo suo restitueret* : nepos, liberis relictis, intra " ætatem suprascriptam vita decessit : fideicommissi " conditionem, conjectura pietatis, respondi defecisse, " quod minus scriptum quam dictum fuerat inveni- " retur."† Our author supposes, that the testator

* Dury, 9th February 1628, Simson *contra* Boswell ; Gosford, 25th June 1625, Duke Lauderdale *contra* Lord and Lady Yester.

† 21st November 1738, Magistrates of Montrose *contra* Robertson.

‡ L. 102, De cond. demonst. et causis.

P. I. 4.   DEEDS AND COVENANTS.   161

had provided for the issue of his grandchildren, but that the provision had been casually omitted by the writer. This is cutting the Gordian knot, instead of untying it; for what if the writer had not received any such instruction? There is no occasion for Papinian's conjecture: it was obviously an omission, which a court of equity ought to supply, in order to do justice, and to fulfil the intendment of the creditor.

A man believing his wife to be pregnant, left a legacy to a friend, in the following terms, " That if a " male child was brought forth, the sum should be " 4,000 merks; if a female, 5,000 merks." The wife produced no child. As a legacy was intended even in case of a child, it cannot be thought that the friend should have no legacy if no children were born. The clause, therefore, is evidently imperfect, a member being wanting, that of the testator's dying without children. The want of that member was a pure omission, which the testator would have supplied, had the event occurred to him; and which a court of equity may supply, in order fully to accomplish the intendment of those who are no longer in being to speak for themselves. The Court of Session, accordingly found the highest sum due, *ex præsumpta voluntate testatoris.** They could go no farther without exerting an act of power altogether arbitrary; as they had no *data* for determining what greater length the testator himself would have gone. Here it is proper to be observed, that in the former cases mentioned, a right was created, to make which effectual, a court of equity ought to lend their aid. In the present case, there was no right created; and a court

* Dirleton, 18th July 1666, Wedderburn *contra* Scrimzeor.

L

162 DEEDS AND COVENANTS. B. I.

of equity had no call to interpose, but in order to give the most liberal effect to deeds made by persons deceased. The present case, then, is much more delicate than any formerly mentioned.

But now, what if the wife had brought forth twins? Though the testator gave a legacy in the event of a single child, it follows not necessarily that he would have given a legacy had he foreseen the birth of two children. Therefore, as it is not certain that in the case here figured there is any omission, a court cannot interpose, without hazarding the making a will for a man that he himself would not have made. I venture this opinion even against the authority of Julianus, the most acute of all the writers on the Roman law. " Si ita scriptum sit, ' Si filius mihi " natus fuerit, ex besse heres esto, ex reliqua parte " uxor mea heres esto ; si vero filia mihi nata fuerit, " ex triente heres esto, ex reliqua parte uxor heres " esto :' et filius et filia nati essent : dicendum est, " assem distribuendum esse in septem partes, ut " ex his filius quatuor, uxor duas, filia unam partem " habeat : ita enim secundum voluntatem testantis, " filius altero tanto amplius habebit quam uxor, item " uxor altero tanto amplius quam filia. Licet enim " subtili juris regulæ conveniebat, ruptum fieri tes- " tamentum, attamen, quum ex utroque nato testator " voluerit uxorem aliquid habere, ideo ad hujusmodi " sententiam humanitate suggerente decursum est ; " quod etiam Juventio Celso appertissime placuit." *

In a contract of marriage there was the following clause : " And in case there shall happen to be only " one daughter, he obliges him to pay the sum " of 18,000 merks ; if there be two daughters, the " sum of 20,000 merks, 11,000 to the eldest, and

* L. 13. pr. De liberis et posthumis heredibus instituendis.

P. I. 4.　DEEDS AND COVENANTS.　163

" 9,000 to the other; and if there be three daughters,
" the sum of 30,000 merks, 12,000 to the eldest,
" 10,000 to the second, and 8,000 to the youngest."
There the contract stops, because probably a greater
number was not expected. The existence of a fourth
daughter brought on the question, Whether she could
have any share of the 30,000 merks, or be left to insist for her legal provision *ab intestato*. As it appeared to be the father's intention to provide for all
the children of the marriage, and as he certainly
would have provided for the fourth daughter, it belonged to a court of equity to supply the omission, by
naming to her such a sum as he himself would have
done. The court decreed 4,500 merks to the fourth
daughter, as her proportion of the 30,000 merks; and
and restricted the eldest daughter to 10,500, the second to 8,500, and the third to 6,500.* The following case stands on the same foundation. " Clemens
" Patronus testamento caverat, ' Ut si sibi filius na-
." tus fuisset, heres esset: si duo filii, ex æquis par-
." tibus heredes essent: si duæ filiæ similiter: si fi-
" lius et filia, filio duas partes, filiæ tertiam dederat.'
" Duobus filiis et filia natis, quærebatur quemadmo-
" dem in proposita specie partes faciemus: cum filii
" debeant pares, vel etiam singuli duplo plus quam
" soror accipere. Quinque igitur partes fieri oportet,
" ut ex his binas masculi, unam fœmina accipiat."†

No article concerning law ought to be more relish-
ed, than the authority a court of equity is endued
with to make effectual deeds and covenants, not only
according to the actual will of the parties, but according to their honest wishes. With respect to fa-

* 18th July 1729, Anderson *contra* Anderson.
† L. 81. pr. De heredibus instituendis.

L 2

164   DEEDS AND COVENANTS.   B. I.

mily-settlements in particular, a man in his last moments has entire satisfaction in reflecting, that his settlement will be made effectual after his death, candidly and fairly, as if he himself were at hand to explain his views. So great stress is laid upon will as the fundamental part of every engagement, that where it is clear, defects in form are little regarded by a court of equity. Take the following instances. A man settles his estate on his eldest son in tail, with a power, by deed or will under seal, to charge the land with any sum not exceeding £500. A deed is prepared and ingrossed, by which he appoints the £500 to his younger children; but dies without its being signed and sealed. Yet this in equity shall amount to a good execution of his power, the substance being performed.* Here there could be no doubt about the man's will creating a right to his younger children. The power he reserved of charging the estate by deed or will under seal, was not intended to make their right conditional, but to give them the highest security that is known in law. This security was indeed disappointed by the man's sudden death; but he had sufficiently declared his purpose to give them £500, which afforded them a good claim in equity for that sum. Provost Aberdeen wishing to have a country-seat near the town of Aberdeen, purchased the lands of Crabstone from Farquharson of Invercauld, for £3,900 sterling; and missive-letters were exchanged, agreeing that the lands should be disponed to the Provost in liferent, and in fee to any of his children he should name. The title-deeds were delivered to a writer, who, by the Provost's order, made out a scroll of the disposition, to the Provost in life-

---

* Abridg. Cases in equity, ch. 44, sect. B, § 14.

P. I. 4.   DEEDS AND COVENANTS.   165

rent, and to Alexander, the only son of his second marriage, in fee. A disposition was extended 12th June 1756, and dispatched to Invercauld, inclosed in the following letter, subscribed by the Provost: " This will come along with the amended disposi-" tion; and upon its being delivered to me duly sign-" ed, I am to put the bond for the price in the hands " of your doer." Invercauld not being at home, the packet was delivered to his lady. As soon as he came home, which was on the 21st of the said month, he subscribed the disposition, and sent it with a trusty hand, to be delivered to the Provost at Aberdeen. But he, having been taken suddenly ill, died on the 24th of June, a few hours before the express arrived; whereby it happened, that the disposition was not delivered to him, nor the bond for the price subscrib-ed by him. This unforeseen accident gave rise to a question between Robert, the Provost's eldest son and heir, and the said Alexander, son of the second mar-riage. For Robert it was pleaded, That the dispo-sition remained an undelivered evident under the power of the granter; nor could it bind the Provost, since it was not accepted by him; and laying aside that incompleted deed, nothing remained binding but the mutual missives; the benefit of which must de-scend to the Provost's heir-at-law, seeing none of his children is named in these missives. It was answer-ed for Alexander, That his father's will being clear-ly for him, it is the duty of the Court of Session to make it effectual. And he accordingly was prefer-red.* A settlement being made on a young woman, proviso that she marry with consent of certain per-

* 13th December 1757, Alexander Aberdeen *contra* Robert Aberdeen.

166   DEEDS AND COVENANTS.   B. I.

sons named, the consent to be declared in writting; a consent by parole was deemed sufficient. * For it was not understood to be the will of the maker to forfeit the young woman merely for the want of form, when the sustance was preserved. Land cannot be charged but by a formal deed ; for such is the common law. But a court of equity may supply a defective deed, considered as a satisfactory evidence of will, by subjecting the heir personally. In one case, the Court of Session made a wide step. In a disposition the granter reserved power to burden the land with a sum to particular persons named. The disponee was made liable for the sum, though the disponer had made no step toward exercising the power.† This, indeed, was a favourable case, the power reserved being to provide younger children. And yet, were this extension of equity to be justified, I cannot discover any bounds to equitable powers. What better evidence can be required of the disponer's resolution not to exert his reserved power, than his forbearing to exert it ?

I must observe upon this section in general, that to ascertain what was a man's will, to make it effectual, and to supply omissions, afford a spacious field in equity for supporting deeds and covenants, upon which the prosperity of society and many of its comforts greatly depend. But as far as I discover, equity, which has a free course in supporting will, never is exerted against it. It ventures not to alter a man's will, far less to void it : it cannot even supply will where totally wanting. Where a deed or cove-

---

* 1. Modern Reports, 310.

† Gosford, 15th Feb. 1673, Graham *contra* Morphey.

DEEDS AND COVENANTS.

nant is fairly made without any reserved power to alter, what before was voluntary, becomes now obligatory; and it must have its course, whatever be the consequence. However clear it may be, that it would not have been made had the event been foreseen, yet no court of law is empowered to void the writing or to alter it; for this would be to make a settlement for a man who himself made none. Power so extensive would be dangerous in the hands of even the most upright judges. I dare not except a British Parliament.

Were a court of law endued with a power to alter will, or to supply its total absence, the following cases would be a strong temptation to exercise power. A gratuitous bond by a minor being voided at the instance of his heir, because a minor cannot bind himself without a valuable consideration; the obligee insisted for an equivalent out of the moveables left by the minor, on the following ground, That he could have left the same sum to his friend by way of legacy. It was admitted, that if the heir's challenge had been foreseen, the minor probably would have given a legacy instead of a bond: but that in fact the minor gave no legacy; and no court can make a testament for a man, who himself made none; which accordingly was found.* The bond here was complete in all its parts, and no article omitted that a court of equity could supply. There was, indeed, a defect of foresight, with respect to what might happen; but a court of equity does not assume a power to supply defects of that kind. The like was found with respect to a gratuitous disposition of an heritable subject, which was voided as being granted on deathbed. The dis-

* Fountainhall, 15th Dec. 1698, Straiton *contra* Wight.

168　　DEEDS AND COVENANTS.　　B. I.

ponee claimed the value from the executor, presuming that the deceased, had the event been foreseen, would have given an equivalent out of his moveables. But as, in fact, the deceased signified no will nor intention to burden his executor, the judges refused to make him liable.* The Roman law concerning a *legatim rei alienæ* adheres to the same principle. Where a testator legates a subject as his property, which, after his death, is discovered to be the property of another, the heir is not bound to give an equivalent, because *deficit voluntas testatoris*. But if the testator knew that the subject was not his, it must have been his will, if he did not mean to be jocular, that it should be purchased by his heir for the legatee; and this implied will was accordingly made effectual by the Pretor, as a judge of equity.

SECT. IV.

A deed or covenant that tends not to bring about the end for which it was made.

WHERE a man exerts an external act, however inconsiderately, he cannot be relieved, *quia factum infectum fieri nequit.* But a man making a deed or covenant may be relieved by a sentence of the judge; and will be relieved if a good cause be shown. With respect, particularly, to the subject of the present section, a deed or covenant, as laid down in the beginning of this chapter, is a mean employed to bring

* Dirleton, 12th November, Stair, 26th November, 1674, Paton *contra* Stirling; Fountainhall, 22d November 1698, Cumming *contra* Cumming.

P. I. 4. DEEDS AND COVENANTS. 169

about a certain end or event: whence it follows, that it ought to be voided where it fails to be a mean, or, in other words, where it tends not to bring about the end or event desired. To think otherwise, is to convert a mean into an end, or to adhere to the mean without regard to the end. Common law, regarding the words only, may give force to such a deed or covenant; but equity pierces deeper into the nature of things. Adverting to the fallibility of our nature, it will not suffer one to be bound by such an engagement; and considers, that when he is freed from it, it is only *lucrum cessans* to the party who insists on its performance, not *damnum datum*.

To prevent mistakes in the application of the foregoing doctrine, it is necessary to be observed, that the end here understood is not that which may be secretly in view of the one or the other party, but that which is spoken out, or understood by both; for a thought retained within the mind, cannot have the effect to qualify an obligation more than to create it. The overlooking this distinction has led Puffendorff into a gross error: who puts the case,* That a man, upon a false report of all his horses being destroyed, makes a contract for a new set; and his opinion is, that in equity the purchaser is not bound. This opinion is of a man unacquainted with the world and its commerce; Were mistakes of that kind indulged with a remedy, there would be no end of lawsuits. At this rate, if I purchase a quantity of body or table-linen, ignorant at the time of a legacy left me of a large quantity, I ought to be relieved in equity, having now no occasion for the goods purchased. And for the same reason, if I purchase a horse by commission

* Lib. 3, cap. 6, § 7.

170   DEEDS AND COVENANTS.   B. I.

for a friend, who happens to be dead at the time of the purchase, there must be a relief in equity, though I made the purchase in my own name. But there is no foundation for this opinion in equity, more than at common law. If a subject answer the purpose for which it is purchased, the vender has no farther concern: he is entitled upon delivery to demand the price, without regarding any private or extrinsic motive that might have led his party to make the purchase. In general, a man who exposes his goods to sale must answer for their sufficiency; because there is no obligation in equity to pay a price for goods that answer not the purpose for which they are sold by the one, and bought by the other: but if a purchaser be led into an error or mistake that regards not the subject nor the vender, the consequences must rest upon himself.

I shall only add upon this general head, that the end purposed to be brought about by a deed or covenant ought to be lawful; for to make effectual an unlawful act is inconsistent with the very nature of a court of law. Thus a bond granted by a woman, binding her to pay a sum if she should marry, is unlawful, as tending to bar population; and, therefore, will be rejected even by a court of common law. And the same fate will attend every obligation granted *ob turpem causam*; a bond, for example, granted to a woman as a bribe to commit adultery or fornication. So far there is no occasion for a court of equity.

The first example shall be from deeds. Upon a young man living abroad under sentence of forfeiture, his father settled an annuity for life, ignorant that it would fall to the crown. This deed will not bind

P. I. 4. DEEDS AND COVENANTS. 171

the granter; for it does not produce the end or effect intended. To sustain it, would be to give force to the mean without regarding the end.

Here a subtile question casts up, What in the view of law is to be held the end upon which the fate of the deed or covenant depends? is a court of equity confined to the immediate end, or may it look forward to consequences? An example will explain the question. In a contract of marriage, the estate is settled on heirs-male of the marriage. The eldest son, being forfeited for high treason, is forced to abandon his native country. The father makes a settlement, excluding him from the succession, in order to prevent his estate from falling to the crown. Can this settlement be supported by a court of equity? I doubt. The contract of marriage was a proper mean for the end in view, namely, that the estate should descend to the heirs-male of the marriage. The contractors had no farther view; and if a court were to be swayed by unforeseen consequences, deeds and covenants could not be much relied on. Suppose that after the father's death a pardon is procured for the son, must not this have the effect to void the last settlement, and to restore the son to his right as heir of the marriage? Yet in a case still more delicate, the Court of Session gave judgment for the father, influenced probably by an overflow of compassion and humanity. James Thomson, in his marriage-contract, provided his estate and conquest to the heirs of the marriage. The heir, a son, idle and profligate, became a notour bankrupt; which induced the old man to settle his estate on his grand-children by that son, burdened with the liferent of the whole to him. A reduction being brought of this settlement as in

172   DEEDS AND COVENANTS.   B. I.

defraud of the marriage contract, the Court of Session repelled the reason of reduction, and sustained the settlement.* Beside setting the father free from a rational and solemn contract, there was a very material point in equity against sustaining the settlement, which seems to have been overlooked. What if the whole debts, or the bulk of them, were contracted by the son for necessaries before his bankruptcy? On that supposition, the creditors were *certantes de damno vitando :* the children, on the other hand, were *certantes de lucro acquirendo.* Take a different view of the case : What if the bankrupt, by some fortunate adventure, a lottery-ticket for example, had been enabled to pay all his debts : would he not have been entitled as a free man to claim the benefit of the contract of marriage, seeing the only cause for disinheriting him was now removed? If so, a contract of marriage is but an unstable security, as it may depend on future contingencies whether it will be effectual or no.

In questions between husband and wife, a contract of marriage is a contract in the strictest sense ; but in questions with the heirs, it is rather to be considered as a deed ; in which light it is viewed above. I proceed now to give examples relative to what are properly contracts. In a contract of sale, the circumstance regarded at common law, is the agreement of the parties, the one to sell, the other to purchase the same subject. What are its qualities, whether the price be adequate, and whether it will answer the end for which it is purchased, are left to the regulation of equity. The last belongs to the present sec-

* 11th February 1762, Thomson and his Creditors *contra* his Children.

DEEDS AND COVENANTS.

tion; one instance of which makes a figure in practice, to wit, where goods sold are by some latent insufficiency unfit for the purchaser's use. A horse is bought for a stallion that happens to be gelt, or a hogshead of wine for drinking that happens to be sour. If the purchaser be notwithstanding bound, he is compelled to accept goods that are of no use to him, and over and above to pay a full price for what is of little or no value. It would, on the other hand, be to act against conscience, for the vender to take a full price in such a case. Supposing the goods to be sufficient at the time of the bargain, but insufficient at the time of delivery, the loss naturally falls on the vender, who continues proprietor till the subject be delivered. If insufficient at the time of the bargain, there is an additional reason for setting it aside, namely error; for error relieves the person who is *certans de damno vitando* against the person who is *certans de damno captando*, which will be more fully explained afterward. (*a.*)

A large cargo of strong ale was purchased from a brewer in Glasgow, in order to be exported to New York. In a suit for the price, the following defence was sustained, That having been not properly prepared for the heat of that climate, it had bursted the bottles and was lost. It was not supposed, that the brewer had been guilty of any wilful wrong; but the defence was sustained upon the following rule of equity, That a man who purchases goods for a cer-

(*a*) The laws of Hindostan go a great way farther against the vender of insufficient goods, farther indeed than either equity or utility will justify. " If a man have sold rice or wheat for sow-" ing, and they do not spring up, the vender shall make good " the crop."

174   DEEDS AND COVENANTS.   B. I.

tain purpose, is not bound to receive them unless they answer that purpose; which holds *a fortiori* where the vender is himself the manufacturer. And where the insufficiency cannot be known to the purchaser but upon trial, the rule holds even where the goods are delivered to him. It was also in view, that if the brewer be not answerable for the sufficiency of ale sold by him for the American market, that branch of commerce cannot be carried on.*

An insolvent debtor makes a trust-right in favour of his creditors; and, among his other subjects, dispones to the trustees his interest in a company-stock. A creditor of the company, who was clearly preferable upon the company-stock before the bankrupt's private creditors, being ignorant of his preference, accedes to the trust-right, and consents to an equal distribution of the bankrupt's effects. Being afterward informed of his preference, he retracts while matters are yet entire. *Quær.* Is he bound by his agreement? He undoubtedly draws by it all the benefit he had a prospect of; and considering the agreement singly, without relation to the end, he is bound; and so says common law. But equity considers the end and purpose of the agreement; which is, that this man shall draw such proportion of the bankrupt's effects as he is entitled to by law. The means concerted, that he shall draw an equal proportion, contribute not to this end, but to one very different, namely, that he shall draw less than what is just, and the other creditors more. Equity relieves from an engagement where such is the unexpected result; there being no authority from the intendment of par-

* 13th December 1765, Baird *contra* Pagan.

P. I. 4.   DEEDS AND COVENANTS.   175

ties to make it obligatory where it answers not the purposed end.

Having laid open the foundation in equity for giving relief against a covenant where performance answers not the end purposed by it, I proceed to examine whether there be any relief in equity after the covenant is fulfilled. I buy, for example, a lame horse unfit for work; but this defect is not discovered till the horse is delivered, and the price paid. If the vender hath engaged to warrant the horse as sufficient, he is liable at common law to fulfil his covenant. But supposing this paction not to have been interposed, it appears to me not at all clear, that there is any foundation in equity for voiding the sale thus completed. The horse is now my property by the purchase, and the price is equally the vender's property. If he knew that the horse was lame, he is guilty of a wrong that ought to subject him to the highest damages :* but supposing him *in bona fide*, I see no ground for any claim against him. The ground of equity that relieves me from paying for a horse that can be of no use, turns now against me in favour of the vender; for why should he be bound to take my horse, of no use to him? The Roman law indeed gave an *actio redhibitoria* in this case, obliging the vender to take back the horse, and to return the price. But I discover a reason for this practice in a principle of the Roman law, that squares not with our practice, nor with that of any other commercial nation. The principle is, That such contracts as are intended to be equal, ought to answer the intention: and, therefore, in such contracts the Roman Pretor never permitted any considerable inequality. Hence

* L. 13, pr. Actionibus empt.

176 DEEDS AND COVENANTS. B. I.

the *actio quanti minoris,* which was given to a purchaser who by ignorance or error paid more for a subject than it is intrinsically worth : and it follows upon the same plan of equity, that if a subject be purchased which is good for nothing, the *actio quanti minoris* must resolve into an *actio redhibitoria.* But equity may be carried so far as to be prejudicial to commerce by encouraging law-suits : and, for that reason, we admit not the *actio quanti minoris :* the principle of utility rejects it, experience having demonstrated that it is a great interruption to the free course of commerce. The same principle of utility rejects the *actio redhibitoria,* as far as founded on inequality ; and after a sale is completed by delivery, I have endeavoured to show, that if inequality be laid aside, there is no foundation for the *actio redhibitoria.* In Scotland, however, though the *actio quanti minoris* is rejected, the *actio redhibitoria* is admitted where a latent insufficiency unqualifies the subject for the end, with a view to which it was purchased. This practice, as appears to me, is out of all rule. If we adhere strictly to equity, without regarding utility, we ought to sustain the *actio quanti minoris,* as well as the *actio redhibitoria.* But if we adhere to utility, the great law in commercial dealings, we ought to sustain neither. To indulge debate about the true value of every commercial subject, would destroy commerce ; and, for that reason, equity, which has nothing in view but the interest of a single person, must yield to utility, which regards the whole society.

SECT. V.

Equity with respect to a deed providing for an event that now can never happen.

THIS section chiefly concerns settlements *intra familiam*, and such like, which, on the part of the maker, are gratuitous. I cannot easily figure a case relative to a covenant where it can obtain.

A bachelor in a deadly disease, daily expecting death, settles his estate on a near relation, without reserving a power to alter, which he had no prospect of needing. He recovers, as by a miracle, and lives many years. The deed, being in its tenor pure, is effectual at common law. But as death was the event provided for, which did not happen, and as he had no intention to give away his estate from himself, it will not be sustained in equity. And, indeed, it would be hard to forfeit the poor man for a mistake in thinking himself past recovery. In this example, the failure of the event is accidental, independent of the granter's will. But equity affords relief, even where the failure is owing to the granter himself. An old man, on a preamble that he was resolved to die a bachelor, settles his estate on a near relation, re-serving his liferent and power to alter. In dotage, he takes a conceit for a young woman, marries her, but dies suddenly without altering his settlement. Seven or eight months after, a male child is born, who claims the estate. The deed cannot stand in equity, being made for an event that has not fallen out, to wit, the granter's dying without children. Take another example, which depends on the same

178   DEEDS AND COVENANTS.   B. I.

principle. In the year 1688, the Duchess of Buccleugh obtained from the crown a gift of her husband the Duke of Monmouth's personal estate, which fell under his forfeiture. As, by this means, their younger son, the Earl of Deloraine, was left unprovided, she gave him a bond for £20,000. The Duke's forfeiture being afterward rescinded, the Earl of Deloraine, executor decerned to him, claimed from his mother the Duke's personal estate. The Duchess was willing to account; but insisted that payment of the bond should be held as part-payment of the personal estate. Which was accordingly found.[*] Here the event provided for, which was the Earl's being deprived of his legal right by his father's forfeiture, had failed; and, consequently, the bond could not be effectual in equity. There was, beside, a still stronger objection against it, namely, that the pursuer had now right to the very subject out of which the bond was intended to be paid.

Cases of this nature are resolved by lawyers into a conditional grant, implied, they say, though not expressed. A condition may be implied in the case last mentioned; but the circumstances of the two former will not admit such implication. In the first, the granter is described as having lost all hope of recovery; in which he would not readily think of making his death a condition of the grant. Neither in the other is there any foundation for implying a condition *si sine liberis*, as the granter declared his firm intention to die a bachelor. In cases of this nature, there is no necessity of cutting the Gordian knot by

[*] 7th December 1723, Earl Deloraine *contra* Duchess of Buccleugh.

P. I. 4.   DEEDS AND COVENANTS.   179

a supposed condition. It is loosed with great facility, by applying to it a maxim, That a deed providing for an event that has failed, cannot in equity be
effectual.

SECT. VI.

Errors in deeds and covenants.

In the beginning of this chapter it is laid down,
that the moral sense, respecting the fallibility of our
nature, binds us by no engagement but what is fairly done with every circumstance in view; and, consequently, that equity will afford relief against rashness, ignorance, and error. In handling the circumstance last mentioned, it will contribute to perspicuity, that we distinguish errors that move a person to
enter into a deed or covenant, from errors that are
found in the deed or covenant itself. Errors of the
former kind happen more frequently with respect to
deeds: of the latter kind, seldom but in contracts.
I begin with the first kind, of which the following is
an example. My brother having died in the East
Indies, leaving children, a boy is presented to me as
my nephew, with credentials in appearance sufficient.
After executing a bond in his favour for a moderate
sum, the cheat is discovered. The moral sense would
be little concordant with the fallibility of our nature,
did it leave me bound in this case. And supposing
the cheat not to be discovered till after my death, a
court of equity, directed by the moral sense, will relieve my heir. Here the relief is founded on error
solely; for the boy is not said to have been privy to
the cheat, or to have understood what was transact-

M 2

180   DEEDS AND COVENANTS.   B. I.

ing for his behoof. To the same purpose Papinian,
" Falsam causam legato non obesse, verius est ; quia
" ratio legandi legato non cohæret. Sed plerumque
" doli exceptio locum habebit, si probetur alias lega-
" turus non fuisse."*   The circumstances of the following case make it evident, that the error was the
sole motive, bringing it under the exception mentioned by Papinian. " Pactumeius Androsthenes Pactu-
" meiam Magnam filiam Pactumeii Magni ex asse
" heredem instituerat; eique patrem ejus substitu-
" erat. Pactumeio Magno occiso, et rumore perlato
" quasi filia quoque ejus mortua, mutavit testamen-
" tum, Noviumque Rufum heredem instituit, hac
" præfatione : ' Quia heredes quos volui habere mihi,
" continere non potui, Novius Rufus heres esto.'
" Pactumeia Magna supplicavit Imperatores nostros ;
" et, cognitione suscepta, licet modus institutione
" contineretur, quia falsus non solet obesse, tamen ex
" voluntate testantis putavit Imperator ei subvenien-
" dum : igitur pronunciavit, ' Hereditatem ad Mag-
" nam pertinere, sed legata ex posteriore testamento
" eam præstare debere, proinde atque si in posteriori-
" bus tabulis ipsa fuisset heres scripta."†   The testament could not stand in equity, proceeding from
an erroneous motive.   To sustain such a testament,
would be to disinherit the favourite heir, contrary to
the will of the maker.   As to the legacies contained
in the latter testament, they were justly sustained, as
there appeared no evidence nor presumption that the
testator was moved by an error to grant them.

In many cases it may be doubted, whether error

* L. 72, § 6. De condition et demonstr.
† L. ult. De hered. instit.

DEEDS AND COVENANTS.

was the sole motive, or one of them only. To solve that doubt, the nature of the deed will have great influence. A rich man executes a bond for a small sum in favour of an indigent relation, upon the narrative, that he had behaved gallantly in a battle, where he was not even present. Equity will not relieve the granter against this bond, because charity of itself was a good cause for granting. The following texts of the *Corpus Juris* belong to the same head. " Longe magis legato falsa causa adjecta, non " nocet : veluti cum quis ita dixerit, ' Titio, quia me " absente negotia mea curavit, stichum do, lego.' " Vel ita : ' Titio, quia patrocina ejus capitali crimine " liberatus sum, stichum do lego.' Licet enim neque " negotia testatoris unquham gesserit Titius, neque " patrocinio ejus liberatus sit, legatum tamen valet. " Sed si conditionaliter enunciata fuerit causa, aliud " juris est : veluti hoc modo, ' Titio si negotia mea " curaverit, fundum meum do, lego." * Again ; " Quod autem juris est in falsa demonstratione, hoc " vel magis est in falsa causa : veluti ita ' Titio fun- " dum do, quia negotia mea curavit.' Item, ' Fun- " dum Titius filius meus præcipito, quia frater ejus " ex arca tot aureos sumpsit : ' licet enim frater hu- " jus pecuniam ex arca non sumpsit, utile legatum " est." †

With respect to a deed entirely gratuitous to a person unconnected with the granter, and above taking charity, an error like what is mentioned above, will be held more readily the sole motive ; and consequently a ground in equity for voiding the deed.

* § 31. Instit. de legatis.
† L. 17. § 2. De condit. et demonst.

DEEDS AND COVENANTS. B. I.

Where there is any foundation of controversy, a transaction putting an end to it must be effectual; for where there is a rational motive for making a deed, the making of it will never be held to proceed from error. But where a man is moved to make a transaction on supposition of a claim that has no foundation, as in the case of a forged deed, he will be relieved from the transaction in equity, the motive being erroneous.* An unequal transaction may be occasioned by error; but here utility forbids relief; for to extinguish lawsuits, the great source of idleness and discord, is beneficial to every member of society.

We proceed now to errors found in a deed or covenant after it is made. These are of two kinds: one prevents consent altogether; as where the purchaser has one subject in view, the vender another. And as no obligation can arise where there is no agreement, such a covenant, if it can bear that name, is void at common law, and there is no occasion for equity. The other kind is where the error is in the qualities of a subject, not in the subject itself; a purchase, for example, of a horse, understood to be an Arabian of true blood, but discovered after to be a mere Plebeian. The bargain is effectual at common law; and the question is, Whether or how far there ought to be a relief in equity.

We begin with errors that regard the subject itself. If, in the sale of a horse, the vender intended to sell the horse *A*, the purchaser to buy the horse *B*, there is no agreement: the one did not agree to sell the horse *B*, nor the other to buy the horse *A*.

---

* L. 42. Cod. De transact.

The same must hold in every bargain of sale, whatever the subject be.

Next, where an error respects not the subject, but its qualities. I purchase, for example, a telescope, believing it to be mounted with silver, though the mounting is only a mixed metal. Or, I purchase a watch, the case of which I take to be gold, though only silver gilt. Equity will not relieve me from the bargain, as the instrument equally answers its end, whether more or less ornamented. The most that can result from such an error, is to abate the price, in order to make the bargain equal; and this was done in the Roman law. But a claim of that nature, impeding the free course of commerce, is rejected by commercial nations.

It is a very different case, where the error is such as would have prevented the purchase had it been discovered in time, termed in the Roman law, *Error in substantialibus*. Example: A horse is purchased as a stallion for breed; but unknown to both, he happened to be gelt before the bargain. It may be doubted, whether such a bargain be not effectual at common law, as the error is only in the quality of the horse; but undoubtedly it may be set aside in equity, upon a principle mentioned more than once above, That the vender *certans de lucro captando*, ought not to take advantage of the purchaser's error, who is *certans de damno vitando*. Another principle concurs, handled sect. 4 of the present chapter, that one is not bound to fulfil a contract which answers not the purposed end.

We proceed to errors that respect the property of the subject sold. As here the Roman law affords not much light, we have the greater need to proceed wari-

184   DEEDS AND COVENANTS.   B. I.

ly. I sell to John a horse, understood by both of us
to be my property. After all is agreed on, it is discovered to be his property. The bargain is void even
at common law, as it is incapable of being fulfilled on
either side. I cannot convey the property to him, nor
can he receive the property from me. It was not my
intention to sell a horse that did not belong to me;
nor was it his intention to pay for his own horse.
The case where the horse belongs to a third person,
is in effect the same. I did not intend to sell a horse
that belongs not to me; nor did John intend to purchase a horse from me that belongs to a third person.
If the mistake be discovered before delivery to John,
I am bound in justice to deliver the horse to the proprietor, not to John; and John is under no obligation
to pay the price. If the discovery be not made till
after John has received the horse and paid the price,
there is no obligation on either side, but that I restore the price, as the bargain was void from the beginning.

That the same doctrine ought to obtain in the sale
of land, is extremely evident. And as, in a sale of
land, writing is essential, the warrandice contained in
the disposition, or in the minute of sale, ought not to
go further than to oblige the vender to repeat the
price in case of eviction; unless the circumstances of
the bargain be such as to justify a more extensive
warrandice. Hence it follows, that the clause of warrandice in a disposition or minute of sale of land, even
what is termed absolute warrandice, ought to be confined to a repetition of the price upon eviction, unless
the vender be further bound in express terms. Yet
absolute warrandice, here, is, by the generality of lawyers, understood as binding the vender to make up to

the purchaser all the loss he sustains by eviction, which, in effect, is the value of the subject at that time. Whether this be a just conception, deserves the most serious consideration, being of capital importance in the commerce of land.

That the eviction of land ought not to subject the vender to harder terms than the eviction of a moveable, is a doctrine that at least has a plausible appearance. A plausible appearance, however, is not sufficient: let us enter into particulars, in order to try whether some lurking objection may not be detected that will overturn it. If none can be detected, we may rest secure, that the doctrine is solidly founded in principles. In communing about a sale of land, the title-deeds are produced for the inspection of the purchaser: there is a search of the records; and the bargain is not concluded till the purchaser have full satisfaction that the vender is proprietor. If there happen, after the strictest examination, to be a latent defect in the progress, it is not to be charged on the vender more than on the purchaser. For what good reason, then, ought he to be made liable for the value of the land as at the time of eviction? The land was understood by both parties to belong to the vender: he wanted to have money for his land; the purchaser to have the land for his money; neither of which purposes can be fulfilled. The purchaser is not bound, because he cannot have the land he bargained for: the vender is not bound, because he agreed to sell his own land, not that of another. Suppose the eviction has taken place while the subject remains with the vender, the minute of sale is void, no less than in the case first mentioned, where the one has it in view to purchase the horse *A*, the other

186   DEEDS AND COVENANTS.   B. I.

to sell the horse *B*. Nor can it make any difference that the purchaser is infeft before eviction. The infeftment is void, as taken without consent of the proprietor : and after restoring the price, both parties are free as before they entered into the contract. Upon the whole, the vender must restore the price, because he cannot perform the mutual cause. And as for the purchaser, he can have no claim for the value of the subject evicted ; because there can be no claim, either for a subject or its value, at the instance of a person who has no right to the subject. Add another argument no less conclusive. From a contract binding on no person, no claim can arise to any person ; not even the claim against the vender for restoring the price, which arises not from the contract, but from being in his hand *sine causa*. Hitherto every particular is the same as in the sale of a moveable. The only difference that can found an argument of favour, is on the side of a vender of land. As in the sale of a moveable, all rests on the information of the vender ; it might be thought, that more is incumbent on him than on a vender of land, whose affirmation is not relied on, but the progress.

So much for common law. Let us now examine, whether there be any ground in equity for subjecting the vender of land to all the loss that the purchaser may suffer by eviction. A bargain of sale is intended to be fair and equal. The purchaser gets the land, the vender the price, and both are equally accommodated. By eviction, the vender is the only sufferer. Land is seldom alienated but to pay debt. The vender is deprived of the price : his debts remain unpaid ; and he is reduced to poverty. But what does the purchaser suffer ? He is indeed deprived of what he

P. I 4. DEEDS AND COVENANTS. 187

probably reckons a good bargain; but the price, which is restored to him, will give him the choice of as good a bargain in any corner of Scotland. This is a just state of the case; upon which I put the following question, Is there any equity for subjecting the vender, after restoring the price, to pay what more the land may be worth at the time of eviction? Before answering this question, let the following case be considered. Soon after the purchaser's entry to the land, a valuable lead or coal mine is accidentally discovered, for which the purchaser paid nothing, the parties having had no view to it. This mine belongs to the evictor, and to neither of the contractors. Suppose now the purchase to have been only of a few acres, the mine may intrinsically be worth a hundred times the price. Not satisfied with saying, that I see no equity for obliging the vender to pay this immense sum; I have no hesitation to affirm positively, that it would be highly unjust. This example deserves attention. Would it not require the most express terms in a clause of warrandice to oblige the vender to pay such a sum? One thing will certainly be granted me, that such a contract entered into by a facile person, or by a minor, even with consent of curators, would be voided without hesitation. There may, indeed, be good ground to demand caution from the vender to restore the price in case of eviction; considering that venders of land are seldom in opulent circumstances. More cannot justly be demanded.

The hardship is here intolerable, which no man with his eyes open will submit to. But now, supposing, for argument's sake, the purchaser's claim, however much above the price, to be well-founded; is there nothing to be said for the vender, where the

188   DEEDS AND COVENANTS.   B. I.

land happens to fall in value below the price? If
the purchaser, upon a rise of the market, be entitled
to draw from the vender more than the price, ought
not the vender to have the benefit of a falling market
to pay less than the price? I cannot invent a case
where the maxim, *Cujus commodum, ejus debet esse
incommodum,* is more directly applicable. It is evident, however, that the vender must restore the price
wholly, as the bargain was from the beginning void;
and for the same reason, the purchaser can have no
claim for more than the price.

Viewing this case with regard to expediency, it is
of importance to the public, that the commerce of
land, the most useful of all, be free, easy, and equal.
If a vender must be so deeply burdened as above,
and laid open to such consequences, no man will sell
land but in the most pinching necessity. Men at any
rate are abundantly averse to sell land, which reduces
many to low circumstances; and if this law should
obtain, there would be few sales but by public authority. Nor is this all. This law, as to meliorations, would be of no use to the purchaser, who is secured absolutely without need of oppressing the vender: he is entitled to retain possession, till the evictor
make good to him all the expence profitably laid out
upon the subject,

Hitherto of a complete progress. Very different
is the case where the progress is acknowledged to be
incomplete. If in this case the vender be unwilling
to sell under the market-price, he must submit to the
hazard of eviction, and give warrandice to make up
to the purchaser what he loses by eviction, being the
value of the subject at the time of eviction. It is a
chance bargain, importing, that if the land sink in

DEEDS AND COVENANTS.

value below the price, the purchaser is entitled to that value only; and is entitled to double or triple the price, if the land rise so high in value.

What then is the true import of a clause of absolute warrandice in a sale of land? In the sale of a moveable, there is no warrandice. The vender is held to be proprietor, of which the purchaser is satisfied without requiring warrandice. Neither is there use for warrandice against incumbrances; because a moveable passes from hand to hand, without being subjected to any incumbrance. But in a sale of land warrandice is necessary; for though there may be no doubt of the vender's right, yet it is proper that the purchaser be secured against incumbrances, to many of which, that appear not on record, land is subjected. Clauses of warrandice are different, according to the nature of the bargain. In some contracts of sale, the vender gives warrandice against his own facts and deeds only; in some, against the facts and deeds of his predecessors and authors; in some against all incumbrances whatever; and this last is termed *absolute warrandice*. But of whatever tenor the warrandice be, it will not be understood to guard against a preferable title of property, unless expressed in the clearest terms. The reason is given above, that to extend warrandice so far, where the progress is good and the price adequate, is repugnant to common law, to equity, and to expedience.

The authors of our styles have had a just conception of this matter. Every clause of warrandice I have seen engrossed in a disposition of land for a just price, and where the progress was held sufficient, is confined to incumbrances, without any mention of eviction on a preferable right of property. The style

190 DEEDS AND COVENANTS. B. I.

follows: " warranting the land from all wards, re-
" liefs, nonentries, marriages of heirs, liferent es-
" cheats, recognitions, liferent infeftments, annual-
" rents, and from all and sundry other burdens and
" incumbrances whatever, whereby the land may be
" evicted, or possession impeded, at all hands, and
" against all deadly, as law will." Nor a syllable of
eviction upon a preferable title of property; which,
as it cuts deeper than any incumbrance, would be
placed in the front were it intended. Nor let the
concluding words, *at all hands, and against all deadly*, create any doubt; it being an infallible rule in
the construction of writs, Never to extend a general
clause beyond the particulars to which it is added.
This rule holds, even where the general clause is expressed absolutely, without reference to any of the
antecedent articles in particular. In the present case,
we have scarce occasion for that rule, as the general
clause has an immediate reference to incumbrances,
and to nothing else.

It is admitted by all lawyers, that in the conveyance of claims or debts, absolute warrandice does not
secure the purchaser against eviction upon a preferable title; and I am utterly at a loss to see, that the
same precise words should have a different meaning
in a conveyance of land. Lord Stair indeed endeavours to account for this difference; but without success, as far as I can comprehend. His words are,
" Warrandice has no further effect than what the
" party warranted truly paid for the right whereby
" he was or might be distressed, though less than
" the value of the right warranted. This will not
" hold in warrandice of land; as to which land of
" equal value, or the whole worth of what is evicted,

P. I. 4.   DEEDS AND COVENANTS.   191

" as it is at the time of the eviction, is inferred; be-
" cause the buyer had the land with the hazard of
" becoming better or worse, or the rising or falling
" of rates, and, therefore, is not obliged to take the
" price he gave."* I cannot avoid observing, that
two very different subjects are jumbled together in
this passage; namely, the purchasing a competing
right in order to prevent eviction, and the effect of
warrandice where land is actually evicted. These
are different propositions depending on different principles, and entirely unconnected; yet are opposed to
each other, as if they were parts of the same proposition. Can any accuracy be expected in such a manner of handling a question? His Lordship, besides,
stops short in the middle. In the case of rising of
rates, the purchaser, says he, is not obliged to take
the price he gave. Not a word upon the case of falling of rates. His Lordship, upon maturer thinking,
would have seen, that as the subject never belonged
to the purchaser, he could have no claim for it or its
value against the vender; and he also would have
seen, that from a contract binding neither party, no
claim can arise to either party. But this is not all.
I am at a loss to conceive, that the hazard of becoming better or worse, can be of any weight in this case.
One thing I clearly conceive, that if this circumstance
have any weight, it will make absolute warrandice
to have the same effect in the conveyance of debts,
that it is said to have in the conveyance of land.
Real debts produced in a ranking, are commonly at
first of uncertain value. An adjudication is purchased for a trifle, which, by objections sustained against
competing creditors, draws at the conclusion a large

* Institut. book 2, title 3, sect. 46.

sum. There is here, perhaps, more hazard of becoming better or worse, than in the purchase of land: yet, after the purchaser of the adjudication has laid out a considerable sum in obtaining a high place in the ranking, he has, upon eviction, no claim against the vender, but for the price he paid: he must rely on the evictor for recovering the expence of process. Sensible I am, from my own experience, how difficult it is to guard against errors in the hurry of composition. Lord Stair was an able lawyer; and, not to mention the case of a mine discovered after the purchase, had he but thought on useful improvements laid out by the purchaser, he certainly would not have thought it reasonable that the vender should be liable for the value of these, considering that the evictor is bound for it. The following scene might have occurred to his Lordship. After adjusting the progress and the price, " Nothing remains," says the intended purchaser, " but that you warrant the ex-
" pence I intend to lay out upon inclosing, planting,
" and other improvements. Are you not secured by
" law?" Answers the vender: " You are entitled to
" retain possession, till you obtain full satisfaction
" from the evictor. You have thus real warrandice,
" and need not the addition of personal." " I insist
" however, for your warrandice," replies the other:
" one cannot be made too secure." After being abso-
" lutely secure," rejoins the vender, " beyond the pos-
" sibility of a disappointment, your demand for my
" warrandice has no meaning but to have it in your
" power to oppress me. A demand so irrational proves
" you either to be a fool or a knave: I reject all deal-
" ing with you." As no man of sense would advise the vender to submit to that demand, I hold it as de-

monstration, that the expence of profitable improvements cannot be understood to be comprehended in a clause of absolute warrandice. As to voluptuary expences, termed so by Roman writers, the law, it is true, gives no security in case of eviction; nor is there reason for it. A man embellishes his person, his house, his fields, in order to make a figure. In case of a voluntary sale, he reckons not upon any additional price for a fine garden, and as little in case of eviction. And were the vender to be made liable, it would oblige venders to be extremely cautious about the person they sell to; no man could sell an acre or two without the hazard of absolute ruin. Upon these acres the purchaser erects a palace, adorns his gardens with temples, triumphal arches, cascades, &c. &c. sufficient to exhaust the riches of a nabob. The poor vender all this while sits trembling at every joint for fear of eviction.

I put a case the most favourable that can be for the purchaser, to which the argument urged by Lord Stair is directly applicable. By a gradual rise of the market, without a farthing laid out on it, the land purchased thirty years ago has risen in value a third or fourth part above the price paid for it. There lies no claim against the evictor for this additional value; and it is so much lost to the purchaser if the vender be not liable. This probably is the case his Lordship had in view. If the vender, *major, sciens, et prudens*, bound himself to make up that loss, he must submit. But I state a plain question, Is there any thing in justice, or in the nature of a contract of sale, to lay this risk on the vender? In making the bargain, both parties are equally *in bona fide*, the progress is held to be good by both; and both are

194 DEEDS AND COVENANTS. B. I.

losers; not equally indeed, for the vender, who must restore the whole price, is the greatest loser. Say, what is it that entitles the purchaser to draw from the vender the present value of the land? Not the contract, for a contract that does not bind, can produce no action: not the property of the land, which did not pass to the purchaser. The only remaining foundation I can think of, is to claim that loss on the footing of damage. Neither can this hold, as there can be no claim for damage, except from express paction, or from a delict; and the case supposed admits of neither. Nor could Lord Stair have a view to either, when the opinion he gives is founded solely on the rising or falling of rates.

This interesting point of law was judicially handled in a late process, Lord Napier *contra* the Representatives of Mr. William Drummond, who sold the estate of Edinbelly to his Lordship. The progress had been held sufficient by the purchaser; and the warrandice was in the ordinary style, the same that is above mentioned. It was found, however, by decree of the Court of Session, " That the Represent-
" atives of Mr. William Drummond are liable to
" Lord Napier for the value of the estate of Edin-
" belly, evicted from him, as the same was at the
" time of eviction." * This judgment has a formidable appearance against the doctrine above inculcated. Yet as far as could be gathered from the reasoning of the judges, what moved them, was not the terms of the absolute warrandice, but the two following arguments: First, That possessors of land ought not to be discouraged from making ornamental improvements; and, next, That though many evic-

* 6th August 1776.

tions must have happened, there is not on record a single instance of a process for eviction : whence it was presumed, that the present value must have been submitted to by the vender, otherwise that it would have been demanded from him in a process. And the inference was, that it is now too late to alter a practice so long established. To the first answered, That the possessor has absolute security for profitable improvements, which, as beneficial to the public, deserve every encouragement ; but that ornamental improvements, being a species of luxury, are entitled to no favour ; and were they entitled, that the evictor only ought to be subjected, as they were occasioned by his delay or negligence.; especially as he now has the pleasure of them. . Answered to the second, The presumption lies clearly on the other side. No man who has produced a progress to the satisfaction of the purchaser, will, upon eviction, find himself bound in conscience to pay the present value of the land, including all the improvements, voluptuary as well as profitable. And as there is no instance of a decree against the vender for that value, there is the highest probability that the demand has never exceeded the price, which will always be admitted without a process. As for embellishments in particular, the taste for them is but creeping in ; and they are so rare in Scotland, as to afford no probability that they ever were claimed upon eviction.

The arguments I have endeavoured to obviate, were spoken out ; but what I conjecture chiefly influenced the judges, was the authority of Lord Stair.; which could not fail to have great weight, considering that, for a course of years, it had been inculcated into every student as a rule of law, and adopted by

196   DEEDS AND COVENANTS.   B. I.

every member of the court. Men, who, in early youth, have sucked in a maxim, whether of law or of religion, are impregnable by argument. Much superior to that of reason must the authority be, which can operate a conversion. In matters arbitrary and doubtful, I chearfully submit to the authority of eminent writers, to that especially of Lord Stair, who is our capital writer on law. But neither reason nor common sense will justify such deference, with regard to points that are resolvable into principles.

But now, waving that subject, I have another attack to make on his Lordship, and on its offspring, the late judgment of the court, which will open the eyes of our men of law, if any thing can. Though his Lordship's opinion respects voluntary sales only, yet it must equally hold in judicial sales, as the fluctuating value of land is the same, whether sold publicly or privately. Yet this opinion is not made the rule in judicial sales. The practice is, that each creditor gives warrandice against eviction to the extent of what he draws of the price; justly, because the creditors cannot retain the price, if the purchaser be deprived of the land. But warrandice is never exacted from them for the value of the land in case of eviction. This has not only been the uniform practice from the commencement of judicial sales, but is a practice authorized by an express act of sederunt,[*] declaring, " That the creditors preferred to the price, " shall, upon payment, dispone to the purchaser their " rights and diligences, with warrandice *quoad* the " sums received by them ; so that, in case of eviction " of the lands disponed, they shall be liable to refund " these sums in whole or in part effeiring to the evic-

[*] Last of March 1585.

DEEDS AND COVENANTS.

" tion. And this is declared to be the import of any
" former obligements of warrandice given by credit-
" ors in the case foresaid." Here we have constant
and uniform practice for a long course of time, authorized by the Supreme Court of the nation ; which
equals in authority an act of parliament. Now as,
with respect to the present point, no difference can be
figured between a public and a private sale, the rule
laid down for the former must equally obtain with
regard to the latter, were the case of the latter otherwise doubtful. Had the practice in public sales been
suggested to the court, or had it occurred to any of
the judges, we may rest with assurance, that a different judgment would have been given in the case of
Lord Napier.

I have insensibly been led, from the close and con-
cise manner of a didactic work, into a sort of disser-
tation. But the importance of the subject will, I hope,
plead for me.

Hitherto of errors discovered in the contract itself.
We proceed to errors arising in the performance of
a contract. Under this head comes erroneous payment, or *solutio indebiti*, as termed in the Roman law.
Of this there are two kinds ; one where payment is
erroneously made of an extinguished debt, supposed
to be subsisting ; and one where a debt really subsisting is paid by a man who mistakes himself to be
the debtor. To judge rightly of the former, the following preliminaries will pave the way. The sale of
a subject as existing, which does not exist, is void :
the vender cannot deliver a *non ens ;* and the purchaser is not bound to pay the price unless he get
what he bargained for. In like manner, where an
extinguished debt is assigned, understood to be sub-

sisting, the assignment is void ; and if the price have been paid, it must be restored on discovery of the error. This doctrine is applicable to the case in hand. As it is unjust in a creditor to take twice payment, he can have no pretext for detaining the second payment, made erroneously by the debtor. The same must follow, where the second payment has been made to the creditor's heir, who, though *in bona fide*, can have no better right than his predecessor had. The same will also follow in the case of an executorcreditor.* An assignee to a debt extinguished by payment obtains payment from the debtor's heir; both of them being ignorant of the former payment. The error is discovered *rebus integris*. The heir must have back the money he paid, being in the hands of the assignee *sine causa*; and the assignee is entitled to draw from the cedent the price he paid for a *non ens*. So far clear. But what if the error be discovered several years after, when the cedent happens to be insolvent? This intricate case is handled above, where it comes in more properly. There it is laid down, that the assignee having been deprived of his recourse against the cedent by the debtor's rashly paying the debt a second time, neglecting to look into his affairs, the loss ought to rest on him. The argument is still stronger for the assignee, where a debt is purchased on condition that the debtor's heir grant a bond of corroboration. This bond indeed, corroborating a *non ens*, cannot be effectual; but as the purchase was made on the faith of it, the loss occasioned by the cedent's bankruptcy, ought to fall on the heir, who was at least rash or incautious, not on the purchaser, who acted prudently. And when the price he paid to the cedent

* Stair, Gossford, 10th January 1673, Ramsay *contra* Robertson.

P. 1. 4.   **DEEDS AND COVENANTS.**   **199**

is made up to him by the heir, matters are restored
to their original state, as if the bargain had not been
made. There may be bargains against which there
can be no restitution; as where a bond is assigned to
a husband in name of tocher with his wife, which
happens to be corroborated by the debtor's heir before it was assigned to the husband. As the marriage was made on the faith of the bond of corroboration, the granter of the bond can have no relief,
but must pay the whole to the husband. And so
says Paulus :—" Si quis indebitam pecuniam, per er-
" rorem, jussu mulieris, sponso ejus promisisset, et
" nuptiæ secutæ fuissent, exceptione doli mali uti
" non potest. Maritus enim suum negotium gerit;
" et nihil dolo facit, nec decipiendus est: quod fit, si
" cogatur indotatam uxorem habere. Itaque adver-
" sus mulierem condictio ei competit; ut aut repetat
" ab ea quod marito dedit, aut ut liberetur, si non-
" dum solverit." *

We proceed to the case where a debt really subsisting is paid by a man who erroneously understands
himself to be the debtor. This case has divided the
Roman writers. To the person who thus pays erroneously, Pomponius gives a *condictio indebiti*.[†]
Paulus is of the same opinion.[‡] Yet this same Paulus, in another treatise, refuses action.[§] The solu-
tion of this question seems not to be difficult. Were
it the effect of the erroneous payment to extinguish
the debt, a *condictio* could not be sustained against
the creditor: a man who does no more but receive
payment of a just debt, cannot be bound to repeat.

---

* L. 9, § 1, De condict. causa data.
† L. 19, § 3, De condict. indeb.
‡ L. 65, § ult. eod.   § L. 44, eod.

DEEDS AND COVENANTS. B. I.

But the following reasons evince, that a debt is not extinguished by erroneous payment. First, There is nothing that can hinder the creditor, upon discovery of the mistake, to restore the money, and to hold by the true debtor. Second, The true debtor, notwithstanding the erroneous payment, is entitled to force a discharge from the creditor, upon offering him payment; which he could not do were the debt already extinguished. Hence it follows, that the creditor holds the putative debtor's money *sine justa causa*; and, consequently, that a *condictio indebiti* against him is well founded. But the circumstance that operates in the case first mentioned, where there exists no debt, operates equally here. Upon receiving payment *bona fide* from the putative debtor, the creditor thinks no more of a debt he considers to be extinguished; and, therefore, if the real debtor become insolvent after the payment, the inconsiderateness of the putative debtor will subject him to the loss; which may instruct him to be more circumspect, in time coming.

With respect to payment erroneously made by the debtor to one who is not the creditor, see book 2, chap. 5.

The legal consequences of the payment of a debt by a man who knows himself not to be the debtor, are handled, book 1, part 2, at the end.

SECT. VII.

*A deed or covenant being void at common Law as
ultra vires, can a court of equity afford any relief?*

A PRINCIPLE in logics, That will without power
cannot produce any effect, is applicable to matters of
law; and is thus expressed, That a deed *ultra vires*
is null and void. Common law adheres rigidly to
this principle, without distinguishing whether the
deed be wholly beyond the power of the maker, or in
part only. If it be one deed, it admits of no division at common law, but must be totally effectual, or
totally void. The distinction is reserved to a court
of equity, which gives force to every rational deed, as
far as the maker's power extends. Take the following illustrations.

If one, having power to grant a lease for ten years,
grants it for twenty, the lease is, in equity, good for
ten years.* For here there can be no doubt about
will; and justice requires, that the lease stand good
as far as will is supported by power. A tack set by
a parson, for more than three years, without consent
of the patron, is, at common law, void totally, but
in equity is sustained for the three years.† But a
college having set a perpetual lease of their teinds
for 50 merks yearly, which teinds were yearly worth
200 merks; and the lease being challenged for want
of power in the makers, who could not give such a
lease without an adequate consideration, it was found

* 1. Chancery cases, 23.

† Stair, 18th July 1669; Johaston *contra* Parishioners of Hod-
dam.

202 DEEDS AND COVENANTS. B. I.

totally null, and not sustained for any limited time or higher duty.* For a court of equity, as well as a court of common law, must act by general rules; and here there was no rule for ascertaining either the endurance of the lease, or the extent of the duty. Further, a court of equity may separate a deed into its constituent parts, and support the maker's will as far as he had power: but here the limiting the endurance, and augmenting the duty, so as to correspond to the power of the makers, would be to frame a new lease, varying in every article from the lease challenged.

By the act 80. Parl. 1579, " All deeds of great " importance must be subscribed and sealed by the " parties, if they can write; otherwise by two no- " taries, before four witnesses, present at the time, " and designed by their dwelling places; and the " deeds wanting these formalities shall make no " faith." With respect to this statute, a deed is held by the Court of Session to be of great importance, when what is claimed upon it exceeds in value £100. And upon the statute thus constructed, it has often been debated, Whether a bond for a greater sum than £100, subscribed by one notary only and four witnesses, or two notaries and three witnesses, be void; or whether it ought to be sustained to the extent of £100. A court of common law, adhering to the words of the statute, will refuse action upon it. And such was the practice originally of the Court of Session.† But a court of equity, regarding the pur-

* Stair, 13th July 1669, Old College of Aberdeen *contra* the Town.

† Hope, (Obligation), Nov. 29, 1616, Gibson *contra* Executors of Edgar; Durie, 13th Nov. 1623, Marshall *contra* Marshall.

P. 1. 4.   DEEDS AND COVENANTS.   203

pose of the legislature, which is to make additional checks against falsehood in matters of importance, will support such deeds to the extent of £100: for a deed becomes of small importance when reduced to that sum, and ought to be supported upon the ordinary checks. And, accordingly, the Court of Session, acting in later times as a court of equity, supports such bonds to the extent of £100.* But in applying the rules of equity to this case, the bond ought to be for a valuable consideration, or at least be rational: if irrational, it is not entitled to any support from equity.

Oral evidence is not sustained in Scotland to prove a verbal legacy exceeding £100, but if it be restricted to that sum, witnesses are admitted.†

When arbiters take upon them to determine articles not submitted, the award or decreet-arbitral is at common law void even as to the articles submitted. A decreet-arbitral is considered as one entire act, which must stand or fall *in totum*. Equity, prone to support things as far as rational, separates the articles submitted from those not submitted, and sustains the proceedings of the arbiters, as far as they had power. Thus, if two submit all actions subsisting at the date of the submission, and the arbitrators release all actions to the time of the award, the award shall be good for what is in the submission, and void for the residue only.‡ A decreet-arbitral being challenged, as *ultra vires compromissi* with respect to mutual general discharges, which were ordered to be granted, though some particular claims only were

* Dictionary of Decisions, (Indivisible).

† Durie, 7th July 1629, Wallace *contra* Muir; Durie, 1st Dec. 1629, executrix of Scot *contra* Raes.

‡ New Abridgment of the Law, vol. i, p. 139, 140.

DEEDS AND COVENANTS. B. I.

submitted; the decreet-arbitral was sustained as far as relative to the articles submitted, and found void as to the general discharges only.* Arbiters having decreed a sum to themselves and their clerk, for which the submission gave no authority; yet the decreet-arbitral, as far as supported by the submission, was found good even at common law, so as to have the privilege of the regulations 1695, not to be liable to any objection but falsehood, bribery, and corruption. Upon this ground, an objection of iniquity was repelled as incompetent.† Here the objection of iniquity had but an indifferent look: an objection carrying a strong appearance of justice, would probably have been better received.

Family-settlements are commonly more complex than any of the cases mentioned above, consisting of many parts interwoven so intimately, that if one be withdrawn as *ultra vires*, the rest must tumble. There is no remedy but to adjust the will to the present circumstances, in such a manner as the maker himself would have done, had he foreseen the event. Take the following examples. A man having two sons, John and James, makes a deed, settling upon them his estate, consisting of two baronies, to John one of the baronies, the other to James, John's part is evicted by one having a preferable right. The deed, as far as in favour of James, will be supported at common law, which regards the words only, without piercing deeper. But a court of equity considers, that to give to one of the brothers the whole that remains of the estate, and nothing to the other, is inconsistent with the will of the maker, who propor-

* Fountainhall, 25th Dec. 1702, Crawford *contra* Hamilton.
† March 1777, Jack *contra* Cramond.

P. I. 4. DEEDS AND COVENANTS. 205

tioned his estate between them in the same deed by a single act of will. Therefore, to support that will as far as the present circumstances can admit, the court will divide the remaining estate between the brothers, in the same proportion that the whole was divided by the maker. And this may be done boldly; as being what the granter himself would have done, had he foreseen the event. The following example is of the same kind. A man settles his estate of £1,000 yearly rent on his eldest son, burdened with £8,000 to his eight other children. A farm, making half of the estate, is evicted. The children; notwithstanding, claim their whole provision; which perhaps would be sustained at common law, as there is no condition expressed. But assuredly, the provision was not intended to be made effectual, even though there should not remain a shilling to the heir. In order to fulfil the maker's will as far as the present circumstances admit, a court of equity will restrict the provision to £4,000, which is giving to the younger children the same proportion of their father's effects that was originally intended. But let it be remarked, that the result will be different where there is a bond of provision for £8,000, and the estate settled on the heir by a different deed, or left to be taken up *ab intestato.* He will be subjected to all the debts, and to the bond of provision among the rest. Take a third example. A man having three daughters, settles his land-estate on the eldest, with competent provisions to the other two. As this settlement happened to be made on death-bed, it was reduced by the younger sisters, who by that means came to be heirs-portioners with the eldest. Can they claim their provisions over and above? Here the whole was done in the same deed, and by a single act of will. It was not the intention of the father, that the eldest should have the estate independent of her sisters provisions; and as little, that they should have their provisions independent of their eldest sister's right to the estate. A court of equity, therefore, to support the father's deed as far as possible, will reject the claim for the provisions. The younger sisters disobeying their father's will, are not permitted to take any benefit from it. Equity suffers no person to approbate and reprobate the same deed. The younger sisters, therefore, if they adhere to their reduction, must give up their provisions. The following is a similar example. John, Earl of Dundonald, by a deed of entail, settled his land-estate on his heirs-male; with the same breath, settled his moveables by a testament; and executed bonds of provision to his daughters. These several writings, done *unico contextu* in pursuance of one act of will, and making a complete settlement of his estate, real and personal, remained with him undelivered. After the Earl's death, certain lands contained in the entail being found to be still remaining *in hereditate jacente* of a remote predecessor, they were claimed by the daughters as heirs of line. It was objected, That the whole settlement was one act of will, and one deed, though in different writings; that the pursuers could not approbate and reprobate; and that, therefore, if they claimed the lands contrary to their father's will, they could take no benefit by that will. It was, accordingly, found, That the pursuers might choose either, but could not have both.*

* 20th Feb. 1729, Countess of Strathmore and Lady Catharine Cochrane contra Marquis of Clydesdale and Earl of Dundonald.

P. I. 4.   DEEDS AND COVENANTS.   227

The settlement of an estate by marriage-articles upon the heirs of the marriage, is not intended to bar the husband from a second marriage, or from making rational provisions to the issue of that marriage. A man thus bound, makes exorbitant provisions to the issue of a second marriage, such as his whole estate, or the greater part. This settlement, as a breach of engagement, is wholly void at common law; and it is a matter of delicacy for a court of equity to interpose where there is no rule for direction. It would, however, be inconsistent with common sense, that children should suffer as much by excess of affection in their father, as by his utter neglect. As it would be a reproach on law, that the children should be left without remedy, the Court of Session ventures to interpose, by sustaining the provisions to such an extent as to be consistent with the engagement the father came under in his first contract of marriage. The court, however, never interposes without necessity; and, if common law afford any means for providing the children, the matter is left to common law. The following case will illustrate this observation. Colonel Campbell, being bound by marriage-articles to provide to the issue the sum of 40,000 merks, with the conquest, did, by a death-bed-settlement, appoint his eldest son to be heir and executor; leaving it upon the Duke of Argyle and the Earl of Hay, to name rational provisions to his younger children. The referees having declined to act, the younger children insisted to have the settlement voided, as contradictory to the marriage-articles. It was urged for the heir, That the Colonel had power to divide the special sum and conquest, by giving more to one child and less to another; and

208 DEEDS AND COVENANTS. B. I.

that though the whole happens to be settled on the eldest son, by accident, not by intention, it belongs to the Court of Session to remedy the inequality, by doing what was expected from the referees, namely, to appoint rational provisions to the younger children. The court voided the settlement totally; which entitled the children, *per capita*, to an equal division of the subjects provided to them in the marriage-contract.[*]

SECT. VIII.

Where there is a failure in performance.

In order to distinguish equity from common law upon this subject, we begin with examining what power a court of common law has to compel persons to fulfil their engagements. That this court has not power to decree specific performance, is an established maxim in England, founded upon the following reason, That in every engagement there is a term for performance; before which term there can be no demand; and after the term is past, performance at the term is imprestable.[†] A court of common law, confined to the words of a writing, hath not power to substitute equivalents; and therefore all that can be done by such a court is, to award damages against the party who has failed. Even a bond of borrowed money is not an exemption; for after the term of payment, the sum is ordered to be paid by a court of

[*] 22d Dec. 1739, Campbell *contra* Campbells.
[†] See Vinnius's commentary upon § 2. De verborum obligationibus. Institutes.

common law, not as performance of the obligation, but as damage for not performance. This, it must be acknowledged, is a great defect; for the obvious intention of the parties in making a covenant, is not to have damages, but performance. The defect ought to be supplied; and it is supplied by a court of equity, upon a principle often mentioned, That where there is a right, it ought to be made effectual. By every covenant that is not conditional, there is a right acquired to each party: a term specified for performance is a mean to ascertain performance, not a condition; and when that mean fails, it is the duty of a court of equity to supply another mean, that is, to name another day.

To illustrate this doctrine, several cases shall be stated. In a minute of sale of land, a term is specified for entering the purchaser into possession, and for paying the price. The matter lies over till the term is past, without a demand on either side. At common law, the minute of sale is rendered ineffectual; because possession cannot be delivered, nor the price be paid, at a term that is now past: neither can damage be awarded for non-performance, as neither of the contractors has been *in mora*. But the remedy is easy in a court of equity; namely, to assign a new term for specific performance, which fulfils the purpose of the covenant, and makes the rights therefrom arising effectual. But the naming a new term for performance, must vary the original agreement. The price cannot bear interest from the term named in the minute, because the purchaser got not possession at that term: nor is the vender liable from that term to account for the rents, because he was not bound to yield possession till the price should be offered. These several prestations must take place from the new term named by the court of equity.

Supposing now a *mora* on one side. The purchaser, for example, demands performance at the term stipulated ; and years pass in discussing the vender's defences. These being over-ruled, the purchaser insists for specific performance. What doth equity suggest in this case ? for now, the term of performance being past, performance cannot be made in terms of the original articles. One thing is evident, that the purchaser must not suffer by the vender's failure; and, therefore, a court of equity, though it must name a new term for performance, may, at the instance of the purchaser, appoint an account to be made on the footing of the original articles. If the rent exceed the interest of the price, the balance may be justly claimed by the purchaser. But what if the interest of the price, as usual, exceed the rent ? The vender will not be entitled to the difference ; because no man is entitled to gain by his failure. In a word, the purchaser can claim damage in the former case, so far as he loses by the vender's failure, but in the latter case, he gains by the failure, and has no damage to claim. This, at first view, may seem to clash with the maxim, *Cujus commodum, ejus debet esse incommodum.* There is no clashing in reality : the vender suffers justly for his failure ; but the purchaser cannot suffer, who was always ready to perform. This gives the true sense of the maxim, That it holds only between persons who are upon an equal footing ; not between persons where the one is guilty, the other innocent. I need scarce add, that the option given to the purchaser upon the vender's *mora*, is given to the vender upon the purchaser's *mora*.

P. I. 4. DEEDS AND COVENANTS. 211

It frequently happens, that specific performance is imprestable ; as, where I sell the same horse first to John, and then to James. The performance to John becomes imprestable after the horse is delivered to James ; and, therefore, instead of specific perform-ance, a court of equity must be satisfied, like a court of common law, to decree damages to John ; accord-ing to the maxim, *Loco facti impræstabilis succedit damnum et interesse.*

This suggests an inquiry, whether, in awarding damages, there be any difference between common law and equity. An obligor, bound to perform what he undertakes, ought to make up the loss occasioned by his failure ; and such failure accordingly affords a good claim for damages at common law, as well as in equity. Thus the purchaser of an estate from an apparent heir, having, along with the disposition, re-ceived a procuratory to serve and infeft the apparent heir, employs his own doer to perform that work. By the doer's remissness, the heir-apparent dies with-out being infeft, which renders the disposition inef-fectual. The doer is bound at common law to make up the purchaser's loss, though it be *lucrum cessans* only ; and a court of equity can go no further. In cases of that nature, if skill be professed, unskilfulness will not afford a defence. " Proculus ait, si medicus " servum imperite secuerit, vel locato vel ex lege " Aquilia competere actionem.* Celsus etiam impe-" ritiam culpæ adnumerandum scripsit. Si quis vi-" tulos pascendos vel sarciendum quid poliendumve " conductix, culpum eum præstare debere ; et quod. " imperitia peccavit, culpam esse ; quippe ut artifex, " conduxit."† Upon this rule the following case was

* L. 8, § 8, Ad. legem Aquil.   † L. 9, § 5, Locati conducti.

O 2

DEEDS AND COVENANTS.

determined. An advocate being debtor to his client, wrote and delivered him a bill of exchange for the sum. Being sued for payment, he objected, That the bill was null, containing a penalty. The advocate probably was ignorant that this was a nullity; but he undertook the trust of drawing the bill, and, therefore, was bound for its sufficiency.* Where a prisoner for debt makes his escapes, it must be admitted, that the creditor is hurt in his interest; but he cannot prove any damage; for it is not certain that he would have recovered payment by detaining the debtor in prison, and it is possible he may yet recover it. But to be deprived of the security he has by his debtor's imprisonment, is undoubtedly a hurt or prejudice; and the common law gives reparation, by making the negligent jailor liable for the debt, as equity doth in similar cases. A messenger who neglects to put a caption in execution, affords another instance of the same kind. By his negligence, he is subjected to the debt, which is said to be *litem suam facere.* The undertaking an office, implies an agreement to fulfil the duty of the office: negligence, accordingly, is a breach of agreement, which subjects the officer to all consequences, whether actual damage or other prejudice. At the same time, it ought not to escape observation, that as neglect singly, without intention of mischief, is no ground for punishment, damages are the only means within the compass of law for compelling a man to be diligent in his duty. So far the remedy afforded by a court of common law is complete, without necessity of recurring to a court of equity.

Certain covenants, unknown to common law, belong to a court of equity. This was the case of a

* 26th November 1743, Garden *contra* Thomas Rigg, Advocate.

P. L. 4. DEEDS AND COVENANTS.

bill of exchange, before it was brought under common law by act of parliament; and while it continued in its original state, damages from failure of performance could not be claimed. but in a court of equity. A policy of insurance, is to this day, unknown at common law; and, consequently, every wrong relative to it must be redressed in a court of equity.

And now, as to the rules for estimating actual damage upon failure to perform a covenant. A failure of duty, whether the duty arise from a covenant, or from any other cause, is a fault only, not a crime; and, upon such failure, no consequential damage that is uncertain ought to be claimed.* There is the greatest reason for this moderation with respect to covenants, where the failure is often occasioned by a very slight fault, and sometimes by inability without any fault. This rule is adopted by writers on the Roman law:—" Cum per venditorem steterit quo
" minus rem tradat, omnis utilitas emptoris in æsti-
" mationem venit: quæ modo circa ipsam rem con-
" sistit. Neque enim, si potuit ex vino puta nego-
" tiari, et lucrum facere, id æstimandum est, non
" magis quam si triticum emerit, et ob eam rem quod
" non sit traditum, familia ejus fame laboraverit:
" nam pretium tritici, non servorum fame necatorum,
" consequitur."† " Venditori si emptor in pretio
" solvendo moram fecerit, usuras duntaxat præsta-
" bit, non omne omnino quod venditor, mora non
" facta, consequi potuit; veluti si negotiator fuit, et,
" pretio soluto, ex mercibus plus quam ex usuris
" quærere potuit."‡

* See above, p. 64.
† L. 21, § 3, Empti et venditi.
‡ L. 19, De peric. et commod. rei vend.

214   DEEDS AND COVENANTS.   B. I.

At a slight view it might be thought, that to reject uncertain damage here, is inconsistent with what is laid down above concerning a jailor or a messenger. But upon a more accurate view, it will appear, that uncertain damage is not admitted in either case. The creditor's risk upon escape of his prisoner, is certain, however uncertain the consequences may be. It is this risk only that is estimated; and it is estimated in the most accurate manner, by relieving the creditor, and laying it on the jailor or messenger. Upon the whole, with respect to estimating actual damage from breach of covenant, there appears no defect in common law more than in estimating risk, to make the interposition of equity necessary.

Hitherto of a total failure. Next where the failure is partial only. Many obligations are of such a nature as to admit no medium between complete performance and total failure. Other obligations admit a partial performance, and consequently a failure that is but partial. A bargain and sale of a horse furnishes examples of both. The vender's performance is indivisible: if he deliver not the horse, his failure is total. The obligation on the purchaser to pay the price, admits a performance by parts: if he have paid any part of the price, his performance is partial, and his failure partial.

Many obligations *ad facta præstanda* are of the last kind. A waggoner who engages to carry goods from London to Edinburgh, and yet stops short at Newcastle, has performed his bargain in part, and consequently has failed only in part. The like, where a ship freighted for a voyage, is forced, by stress of weather, to land the cargo before arriving at the destined port. In cases of that kind the ques-

P. I. 4.   DEEDS AND COVENANTS.   215

tion is, What is the legal effect of a partial failure? The answer is easy at common law, which takes the bargain strictly according to the strict meaning of the words. I am not bound to pay the price or wages till the whole goods be delivered as agreed on. But in order to answer the question in equity, a culpable failure must be distinguished from a failure occasioned by accident or misfortune: a culpable failure can expect no relief from equity; the rule being general, that equity never interposes in favour of a wrong-doer: but where the failure is occasioned by accident or misfortune, the price or wages will be due in proportion to what part of the work has been done; and the claim rests on the following maxim: *Nemo debet locupletari aliena jactura.* Thus, where a man undertakes to build me a house for a certain sum, and dies before finishing, his representatives will be entitled to a part of the sum, proportioned to the work done; for in that proportion I am *locupletior aliena jactura.* And in the case above mentioned, if the waggoner die at Newcastle, or be prevented by other accident from completing his journey, he or his executors will have a good claim *pro rata itineris.* By the same rule, the freight is due *pro rata itineris,* as was decreed Lutwidge *contra* Gray.*

A process was lately brought before the Court of Session upon the following fact. Mariners were hired at Glasgow to perform a trading voyage, first to Newfoundland, next to Lisbon, and last to the Clyde. A certain sum per month was agreed on for wages, to be paid when the voyage should be completed. The Glasgow cargo was safely landed in Newfoundland; and a cargo of fish, received there,

* See the Dictionary, title (*Periculum.*)

was delivered at Lisbon. In the homeward passage, the ship, with the Lisbon cargo, being taken by a French privateer, the mariners, when liberated from prison, claimed their wages *pro rata itineris*. This cause was compromised. It can scarce, however, admit of a doubt, but that the rule *pro rata itineris*, must hold with respect to mariners, as well as with respect to the freighter of a ship. And, accordingly, it is a common saying, that the freight is the mother of the seamen's wages; meaning, that where the former is due, the latter must also be due.

What is said above is applicable to a lease. A lease, in its very nature supposes a subject possessed by one, for the use of which he pays a yearly sum to another: the possession and rent are mutual causes of each other, and cannot subsist separately. Land set in lease happens to be swallowed up by the sea: this puts an end to the lease. Here the failure is total. A total sterility is in effect the same. Let us now suppose the sterility to be partial only. What says common law? It says, that such sterility will not entitle the lessee to any deduction of rent; that he must abandon the farm altogether, or pay the whole rent. In the following case, several rules of equity concerning sterility are opened. In January 1755, Foster and Duncan set to Adamson and Williamson a salmon-fishing in the river Tay, opposite to Errol, on the north side of a shallow, named the *Guinea-bank*, to endure for five years. The river there is broad; but the current, being narrow, passed at that time along the north side of the said bank, the rest of the river being dead water. As one cannot fish with profit but in the current, the lessees made large profits the first two years, and were not losers the third; but the fourth year the current changed, which frequently happens in that river, and instead of passing as formerly along the north side of the bank, passed along the south side, which was a part of the river let to others; by which means the fishing let to Adamson and Williamson became entirely unprofitable during the remainder of their lease. The granters of the lease having brought a process against the lessees for £36 Sterling, being the rent for the two last years, the defence was, a total sterility by the change of the current as aforesaid; and a proof being taken, the facts appeared to be what are above stated. It was pleaded for the pursuers, That whatever may be thought with respect to a total sterility during the whole years of the lease, or during the remaining years after the lease is offered to be given up, the sterility here was temporary only: for as the stream of the river Tay is extremely changeable, it might have returned to its former place in a month, or in a week; and as the lessees adhered to the lease, and did not offer to surrender the possession, they certainly were in daily expectation that the current would take its former course. A tenant cannot pick out one or other steril year to get free of that year's rent: if equity afford him any deduction, it must be upon computing the whole years of the lease; for if he be a gainer upon the whole, which is the present case, he has no claim in equity for any deduction. It was carried, however, by a plurality, to sustain the defence of sterility, and to assoilzie the defenders from the rent due for the last two years. This judgment seems no better founded in equity than at common law. And it is easy to discover what moved the plurality: In a question between a rich

218 DEEDS AND COVENANTS. B. I.

landlord and a poor tenant, the natural bias is for the latter : the subject in controversy may be a trifle to the landlord, and yet be the tenant's all. Let us put an opposite case. A widow with a numerous family of children has nothing to subsist on but her liferent of a dwelling-house, and of an extensive orchard. These she leases to a gentleman in opulent circumstances, for a rent of £15 for the house, and £25 for the orchard, He possesses for several years with profit. The orchard happens to be barren the two last years of the lease, and he claims a deduction upon that account. No one would give this cause against the poor widow. Such influence have extraneous circumstances, even where the judges are not conscious of them.

Partial failure has hitherto been considered in its consequences with respect to the person who has failed to execute a commission. I proceed to the effect of a failure with respect to those who give the commission. A submission is a proper example. It being the professed intention of a submission to put an end to all the differences that are submitted, the arbiters chosen to fulfil that intention, are bound by acceptance to perform. An award or decreet-arbitral is accordingly void at common law, if any article submitted be left undecided ; for in that case the commission is not executed. Nor will such a decreet-arbitral be sustained in a court of equity, where claims made by the one party are sustained, and the other left to a process ; which is partial and unfair. But where the claims are all on one side, and some of them only decided, equity will support the decreet-arbitral ; it being always better to have some of the claims decided than none. But in this case, the decreet-arbi-

SECT. IX.

Indirect means employed to evade performance.

AMONG persons who are swayed by interest more than by conscience, the employing indirect means to evade their engagements, is far from being rare. Such conduct, inconsistent with the candour and *bona fides* requisite in contracting and in performing contracts, is morally wrong; and a court of equity will be watchful to disappoint every attempt of that kind. Thus, if a man, subjected to a thirlage of all the oats growing on his farm that he shall have occasion to grind, sell his own product of oats, and buy meal for the use of his family, withno other view but to disappoint the thirlage; this is a wrong *contra bonam fidem contractus*, which will subject him to the multure that would have been due for grinding the oats of his own farm. The following case is an example of the same kind. A gentleman being abroad, and having no prospect of children, two of his nearest relations agreed privately, that if the estate should be disponed to either, the other was to have a certain share. The gentleman, ignorant of this agreement, settled his estate upon one of them, reserving a power to alter. The disponee sent his son privately to Denmark, where the gentleman resided: upon which the former deed was recalled, and a new one made upon the son. In a process, after the gentleman's death, for performance of the agreement, the defence was, That the agreement had not taken place, as the disposition was not in favour of the defendant, but of his son. The court judged, That the defendant had acted fraudulently in obtaining an alteration of the settlement, in order to evade performance of the agreement; and that no man can take benefit by his fraud. For which reason he was decreed to fulfil the engagement, as if the alteration had not been made.*

CHAP. V.

Powers of a Court of Equity to remedy what is imperfect in common law with respect to Statutes.

CONSIDERING the nature of a court of common law, there is no reason that it should have more power over statutes than over private deeds. With respect to both, it is confined to the words; and must not pretend to pronounce any judgment upon the spirit and meaning in opposition to the words. And yet the words of a statute correspond not always to the will of the legislature; nor are always the things enacted proper means to answer the end in view; falling sometimes short of the end, and sometimes going beyond it. Hence, to make statutes effectual, there is the same necessity for the interposition of a court of equity, that there is with respect to deeds and covenants. But, in order to form a just notion of the powers of a court of equity with respect to statutes, it is necessary, as a preliminary point, to ascertain how far they come under the powers of a court of

* Stair, 15th July 1681, Campbell *contra* Moir.

P. I. 5. STATUTES. 221

common law; and with that point I shall commence the inquiry.

Submission to government is universally acknowledged to be a duty: but the true foundation of that duty seems to lie in obscurity, though scarce any other topic has filled more volumes. Many writers derive this duty from an original compact between the sovereign and his people. Be it so. But what is it that binds future generations? for a compact binds those only who are parties to it; not to mention that governments were established long before contracts were of any considerable authority.* Others, dissatisfied with this narrow foundation, endeavour to assign one more extensive, deriving the foregoing duty from what is termed in the Roman law a *quasi-contract*. " It is a rule," they say, " in law, and in
" common sense, That a man who lays hold of a be-
" nefit, must take it with its conditions, and submit
" to its necessary consequences. Thus, one who ac-
" cepts a succession, must pay the ancestor's debts:
" he is presumed to agree to this condition, and is
" not less firmly bound than by an explicit engage-
" ment. In point of government, protection and sub-
" mission are reciprocal; and the taking protection
" from a lawful government, infers a consent to sub-
" mit to its laws." This ground of submission is not much more extensive than the former; for both proceed upon the supposition, that, without consent expressed or implied, no person owes obedience to government. At this rate, the greater part of those who live under government are left in a state of independency; for seldom is there occasion to afford such peculiar protection to private persons, as necessarily to

* See Historical law-tracts, tract 2.

222 STATUTES. B. I.

infer their consent. Consider farther, that the far greater part of those who live in society, are not capable to understand the foregoing reasoning : many of them have not even the slightest notion of what is meant by the terms *protection* and *submission*. I am inclined, therefore, to think, that this important duty has a more solid foundation ; and, comparing it with other moral duties, I find no reason to doubt, that, like them, it is rooted in human nature.* If a man be a social being, and government be essential to society, it is not conformable to the analogy of nature, that we should be left to an argument for investigating the duty we owe our rulers. If justice, veracity, gratitude, and other private duties, be supported and enforced by the moral sense, it would be strange if nature were deficient with respect to the public duty only. But nature is not deficient in any branch of the human constitution : government is no less necessary to society, than society to man; and by the very frame of our nature, we are fitted for government as well as for society. To form originally a state of society under government, there can be no means, it is true, other than compact ; but the continuance of a state, and of government over multitudes who never have occasion to promise submission, must depend on a different principle. The moral sense, which binds individuals to be just to each other, binds them equally to submit to the laws of their society ; and we have a clear conviction that this is our duty. The strength of this conviction is no where more visible than in a disciplined army. There, the duty of submission is exerted every moment at the hazard

* See Essays on the principles of morality and natural religion, part 1, ess. 2, chap. 7.

P. I. 5.   STATUTES.   **223**

of life : and, frequently, where the hazard is imminent, and death almost certain. In a word, what reason shows to be necessary in society, is, by the moral sense, made an indispensable duty. We have a sense of fitness and rectitude in submitting to the laws of our society ; and we have a sense of wrong, of guilt, and of meriting punishment, when we transgress them. *(a)*

Hence it clearly follows, that every voluntary

(*a*) In examining this matter, it would not be fair to take under consideration statutes relating to justice, because justice is binding independent of municipal law. Consider only things left indifferent by the law of nature, which are regulated by statute for the good of society ; the laws, for example, against usury, against exporting corn in time of dearth, and many that will occur upon the first reflection. Every man of virtue will find himself bound in conscience to submit to such laws. Nay, even with respect to those who by interest are moved to transgress them, I venture to affirm, that the first acts, at least, of transgression, are seldom perpetrated with a quiet mind. I will not even except what is called *smuggling ;* though private interest, authorised by example, and the trifle that is lost to the public by any single transgression, obscure commonly the consciousness of wrong ; and, perhaps, after repeated acts, which harden individuals in iniquity, make it vanish altogether. It must, however, be acknowledged, that the moral sense, uniform as to private virtue, operates with very different degrees of force with relation to municipal law. The laws of a free government, directed for the good of the society, and peculiarly tender of the liberty of the subject, have great and universal influence : they are obeyed cheerfully as a matter of strict duty. The laws of a despotic government, on the contrary, contrived chiefly to advance the power, or secure the person of a tyrant, require military force to make them effectual : for conscience scarce interposes in their behalf. And hence the great superiority of a free state, with respect to the power of the governors, as well as the happiness of the subjects, over every kingdom that in any degree is despotic or tyrannical.

,STATUTES.

transgression of what is by statute ordered to be done or prohibited, is a moral wrong, and a transgression of the law of nature. This doctrine will be found of great importance in the present enquiry.

Many differences among statutes must be kept in view in order to ascertain the powers of a court of common law concerning them. Some statutes are compulsory, others prohibitory; some respect individuals, others the public; of some the transgression occasions damage, of others not; to some a penalty is annexed, others rest upon authority.

I begin with those which rest upon authority, without annexing any penalty to the transgression. The neglect of a compulsory statute of this kind will found an action at common law to those who have interest, ordaining the defendant either to do what the statute requires, or to pay damages. If, again, the transgression of a prohibitory statute of the same kind harm any person, the duty of the court is obvious: The harm must be repaired, by voiding the act where it can be voided, such as an alienation after inhibition; and where the harm is incapable of this remedy, damages must be awarded. This is fulfilling the will of the legislature, being all that is intended by such statutes.

But from disobeying a statute, prejudice often ensues, which, not being pecuniary, cannot be repaired by awarding a sum in name of damages. Statutes relating to the public are for the most part of this nature; and many also in which individuals are immediately concerned. (a) To clear this point, we must

(a) This branch, by the general distribution, ought regularly to be handled afterward, part 2, of this first book; but by joining

P. I. 5. STATUTES. 225

distinguish as formerly between compulsory and prohibitory statutes. The transgression of a prohibitory statute is a direct contempt of legal authority, and consequently a moral wrong, which ought to be redressed; and where no sanction is added, it must necessarily be the purpose of the legislature to leave the remedy to a court of law. This is a clear inference, unless we suppose the legislature guilty of prohibiting a thing to be done, and yet leaving individuals at liberty to disobey with impunity. To make the will of the legislature effectual in this case, different means must be employed, according to the nature of the subject. If an act done *prohibente lege* can be undone, the most effectual method of redressing the wrong is to void the act. If the act cannot be undone, the only means left is punishment. And, accordingly, it is a rule in the law of England,* that an offender for contempt of the law, may be fined and imprisoned at the King's suit. *(a)*

it here to other matters with which it is intimately connected, I thought it would appear in a clearer light.

* 2. Instit, 163.

(a) If this doctrine to any one appear singular, let it be considered, that the power insisted on is only that of authorizing a proper punishment for a crime after it is committed, which is no novelty in law. Every crime committed against the law of nature, may be punished at the discretion of the judge, where the legislature has not appointed a particular punishment; and it is made evident above, that a contempt of legal authority is a crime against the law of nature. But to support this in the present case, an argument from analogy is very little necessary; for, as observed above, it is obviously derived from the will of the legislature. I shall only add, that the power of naming a punishment for a crime after it is committed, is greatly inferior to that of making a table of punishments for crimes that may be committed hereafter, which is a capital branch of the legislative authority.

P

On the other hand, the transgression of a compulsory statute ordering a thing to be done, infers, not necessarily, a contempt of legal authority. It may be an act of omission only, which is not criminal; and it will be construed to be such, unless from collateral circumstances it be made evident that there was an intention to contemn the law. Supposing, then, the transgression to be an act of omission only, and, consequently, not an object of punishment, the question is, What can be done, in order to fulfil the will of the legislature. The court has two methods: one is, to order the statute to be fulfilled; and if this order be also disobeyed, a criminal contempt must be the construction of the person's behaviour, to be followed, as in the former case, with a proper punishment. The other is, to order the thing to be done under a penalty. I give an example. The freeholders are, by statute, bound to convene at Michaelmas, in order to receive upon the roll persons qualified; but no penalty is added to compel obedience. In *odium* of a freeholder who desires to be put upon the roll, they forbear to meet. What is the remedy here, where there is no pecuniary damage? The Court of Session may appoint them to meet under a penalty. For, in general, if it be the duty of judges to order the end, they must use such means as are in their power. And if this can be done with respect to a private person, it follows, that where a thing is ordered to be done for the good of the public, it belongs to the Court of Session, upon application of the King's Advocate, to order the thing to be done under a penalty. In a process, at the instance of an heritor, entitled to a salmon-fishing in a river, against an inferior heritor, for regulating his cruive and

P. I. 5.   STATUTES.   227

cruive-dike, concluding, That he should observe the Saturday's slap; that the hecks of his cruives should be three inches wide, &c. it was decreed, That the defendant should be obliged to observe these regulations, under the penalty of £50 sterling. It was urged for the defendant, That the pursuer ought to be satisfied with damages upon contravention, because the law has imposed no penalty, and the court can impose none. Answered, That it is beyond the reach of art to ascertain damage in this case; and, therefore, that to enforce these regulations a penalty is necessary. And, if this remedy be neglected by the legislature, it must be supplied by a court of equity, upon the principle, That if there be a right, it ought to be made effectual.

What next come under consideration are statutes forbidding things to be done under a penalty; for to the omission of a thing ordered to be done, a penalty is seldom annexed. These are distinguishable into two kinds. The first regard the more noxious evils, which the legislature prohibits absolutely; leaving the courts of law to employ all the means in their power for repressing them; but adding a penalty beforehand, because that check is not in the power of courts of law. The second regard slighter evils, to repress which no other means are intended to be applied but a pecuniary penalty only. Both kinds are equally binding in conscience; for in every case it is a moral wrong to disobey the law. Disobedience, however, to a statute of the second class, is attended with no other consequence but payment of the penalty; whereas, the penalty in the first class is due, as we say, *by and attour performance*; and, for that reason, a court of law, beside inflicting the penalty,

P 2

228   STATUTES.   B. I.

is bound to use all the means in its power to make
the will of the legislature effectual, in the same manner as if there were no penalty. And even supposing that the act prohibited is capable of being voided by the sentence of a court, the penalty ought still
to be inflicted ; for, otherwise, it will lose its influence as a prohibitory means.

Prohibitory statutes are often so inaccurately expressed, as to leave it doubtful whether the penalty be
intended as one of the means for repressing the evil,
or the only means. This defect occasions in courts
of law much conjectural reasoning, and many arbitrary judgments. The capital circumstance for clear-
ing the doubt, is the nature of the evil prohibited.
With respect to every evil of a general bad tendency,
it ought to be held the will of the legislature, to give
no quarter ; and consequently, beside inflicting the
penalty, it is the duty of courts of law to use every
other mean to make this will effectual. With respect
to evils less pernicious, it ought to be held the intention of the legislature, to leave no power with judges
beyond inflicting the penalty. This doctrine will be
illustrated by the following examples. By the act
52, parl. 1587. " He who bargains for greater profit
" than 10 *per cent.* shall be punished as an usurer."
Here is a penalty without declaring such bargains
null : and yet it has ever been held the intendment of
this act to discharge usury totally ; and the penalty
is deemed as one mean only of making the prohibition effectual. There was, accordingly, never any hesitation to sustain action for voiding usurious bargains, nor even to make the lender liable for the sums
received by him above the legal interest. This then
is held to be a statute of the first class. The follow-

P. I. 5. STATUTES. 229

ing statutes belong to the second class. An exclusive privilege of printing books is given to authors and their assigns for the term of fourteen years. Any person who, within the time limited, prints or imports any such book, shall forfeit the same to the proprietor, and one penny for every sheet found in his custody; the half to the king, and the other half to whoever shall sue for the same.* With respect to the monopoly granted by this statute, it has been justly established, that a court of law is confined to the penalty, and cannot apply other means for making it effectual, not even an action of damages against an interloper.† " Members of the College of Justice are " discharged to buy any lands, teinds, &c. the pro- " perty of which is controverted into a process, under " the certification of losing their office."‡ It has been always held the sense of this statute, to be satisfied with the penalty, without giving authority to reduce or void such bargains.

But though contracts or deeds, contrary to statutory prohibitions of the kind last mentioned are not subject to reduction, it is a very different point, Whether it be the duty of courts of law to sustain action upon such a contract or deed. And yet this distinction seems to have been overlooked in the Court of Session; for it is the practice of that court, while they inflict the penalty, to support with their authority that very thing which is prohibited under a penalty. Thus, a member of the College of Justice, buying land while the property is controverted in a

---

* 8. Ann. 18.

† June 7, 1748, Booksellers of London *contra* Booksellers of Edinburgh and Glasgow.

‡ Act 216, parl. 1594.

process, is deprived of his office; and yet, with the same breath, action is given him to make the minute. of sale effectual.* This, in effect, is considering the statute, not as prohibitory of such purchases, but merely as laying a tax upon them, similar to what at present is laid upon plate, coaches, &c. I take liberty to say, that this is a gross misapprehension of the spirit and intendment of the statute. Comparing together the statutes contained in both classes, both equally are prohibited: the difference concerns only the means employed for making the prohibition effectual. To repress the less noxious evils, the statutory penalty is thought sufficient: to repress the more noxious evils, beside inflicting the statutory penalty, a court may employ every lawful mean in its power. But evidently both are intended to be repressed; and justly, because both in different degrees are hurtful to the society in general, or to part of it. This article is of no slight importance. If I have set in a just light the spirit and intendment of the foregoing statutes, it follows of consequence, that an act prohibited in a statute of the second class, ought not to be countenanced with an action, more than an act prohibited in a statute of the first class. Courts of law were instituted to enforce the will of the national legislator, as well as of the Great Legislator of the universe, and to put in execution municipal laws, as well as those of nature. What shall we say, then, of a court that supports an act prohibited by a statute, or authorises any thing contradictory to the will of the legislature? It is a transgression of

* Haddington, June 5, 1611, Cuninghame *contra* Maxwell; Durie, July 30, 1635, Richardson *contra* Sinclair; Fountainhall, December 20, 1683, Purves *contra* Keith.

P. I. 5. STATUTES. 251

the same nature, though not the same in degree, with that of sustaining action for a bribe promised to commit murder or robbery. With regard, then, to statutes of this kind, though a court is confined to the penalty, and cannot inflict any other punishment, it doth by no means follow, that action ought to be sustained for making the act prohibited effectual: on the contrary, to sustain action would be flying in the face of the legislature. The statute, for example, concerning members of the College of Justice, is satisfied with the penalty of deprivation, without declaring the bargain null; and, therefore, to sustain a reduction of the bargain, would be to punish beyond the words, and, perhaps, beyond the intention of the statute. But whether action should be sustained to make the bargain effectual, is a consideration of a very different nature: the refusing action is made necessary by the very constitution of a court of law; it being inconsistent with the design of its institution, to enforce any contract, or any deed prohibited by statute. It follows, indeed, from these premises, that it is left optional to the vender to fulfil the contract or no at his pleasure; for if a court of law cannot interpose, he is under no legal compulsion. Nor is this a novelty. In many cases beside the present, the rule is applicable, *Quod potior est conditio possidentis*, where an action will not be given to compel performance, and yet if performance be made, an action will as little be given to recal it.

Pondering this subject sedately, I can never cease wondering to find the practice I have been condemning extended to a much stronger case, where the purpose of the legislature to make an absolute prohibition is clearly expressed. The case I have in view relates to the revenue-laws, prohibiting certain goods to be imported into this island, or prohibiting them to be imported from certain places named. To import such goods, or to bargain about their importation, is clearly a contempt of legal authority; and, consequently, a moral wrong, which the smuggler's conscience ought to check him for, and which it will check him for, if he be not already a hardened sinner. And yet, by mistaking the nature of prohibitory laws, actions in the Court of Session have been sustained for making such smuggling-contracts effectual. They are not sustained at present; nor I hope will be. " Non dubium est, in legem committere eum, qui " verba legis amplexus, contra legis nititur volunta- " tem. Nec pœnas insertas legibus evitabit, qui se " contra juris sententiam sæva prærogativa verbo- " rum fraudulenter excusat. Nullum enim pactum, " nullam conventionem, nullum contractum inter eos " videri volumus subsecutum, qui contrahunt lege " contrahere prohibente. Quod ad omnes etiam le- " gum interpretationes, tam veteres quam novellas, " trahi generaliter imperamus; ut legislatori quod " fieri non vult, tantum prohibuisse sufficiat: cætera- " que, quasi expressa, ex legis liceat voluntate colli- " gere: hoc est, ut ea, quæ lege fieri prohibentur, si " fuerint facta, non solum inutilia, sed pro infectis " etiam habeantur: licet legislator fieri prohibuerit " tantum, nec specialiter dixerit *inutile esse debere* " *quod factum est.*" *

So much upon the powers of a court of common law, with respect to statutes. Upon the whole, it appears, that this court is confined to the will of the legislature, as expressed in the statutory words. It

* L. 5, C. De legibus.

P. I. 5. STATUTES. 233

has no power to rectify the words, nor to apply any means for making the purpose of the legislature effectual, other than those directed by the legislature, however defective they may be. This imperfection is remedied by a court of equity, which enjoys, and ought to enjoy, the same powers with respect to statutes that are explained above with respect to deeds and covenants. To give a just notion of these powers concerning the present subject, the following distinction will contribute. Statutes, as far as they regard matter of law, and come under the cognisance of a court of equity, may be divided into two classes. First, Those which have justice for their object, by supplying the defects, or correcting the injustice, of common law. Second, Those which have utility for their sole object. Statutes of the first class are intended for no other purpose but to enlarge the jurisdiction of courts of common law, by empowering them to distribute justice where their ordinary powers reach not : such statutes are not necessary to a court of equity, which, by its original constitution, can supply the defects, and correct the injustice of law : but they have the effect to limit the jurisdiction of a court of equity; for the remedies afforded by them must be put in execution by courts of common law, and no longer by a court of equity. All that is left to a court of equity concerning a statute of this kind, is to supply the defects, and correct the injustice of common law, as far as the statute is incomplete or imperfect; which, in effect, is supplying the defects of the statute. But it is not a new power bestowed upon a court of equity as to statutes that are imperfect : the court only goes on to exercise its wonted powers, with respect to matters of

254 STATUTES. B. I.

justice that are left with it by the statute, and not bestowed upon courts of common law. I explain myself by an example. When goods were wrongously taken away, the common law of England gave an action for restitution to none but the proprietor; and, therefore, when the goods of a monastery were pillaged during a vacancy, the succeeding abbot had no action. This defect in law, with respect to material justice, would probably have been left to the Court of Chancery, had its powers been unfolded when the statute of Marlebirge, supplying the defect, was made; * but no other remedy occurring, that statute empowers the judges of common law to sustain action. Had the statute never existed, action would undoubtedly have been sustained in the Court of Chancery: all the power that now remains with that court, is to sustain action where the statute is defective. The statute enacts, " That the successor shall " have an action against such transgressor, for re- " storing the goods of the monastery." Attending to the words singly, which a court of common law must do, the remedy is incomplete; for trees cut down and carried off are not mentioned. This defect in the statute is supplied by the Court of Chancery. And Coke observes, that a statute which gives remedy for a wrong done, shall be taken by equity. After all, it makes no material difference, whether such interposition of a court of equity be considered as supplying defects in common law, or as supplying defects in statutes. It is still enforcing justice in matters which come not under the powers of a court of common law.

Statutes that have utility for their object, are of

* 52. Henry III, cap. 29.

P. 1. 5. STATUTES. 255

two kinds. First, Those which are made for promoting the positive good and happiness of the society in general, or of some of its members in particular. Second, Those which are made to prevent mischief. Defective statutes of the latter kind may be supplied by a court of equity: because, even independent of a statute, that court hath power to make regulations for preventing mischief. But that court hath not, more than a court of common law, any power to supply defective statutes of the former kind; because it is not empowered originally to interpose in any matter that hath no other tendency but merely to promote the positive good of the society. But this is only mentioned here to give a general view of the subject: for the powers of a court of equity, as directed by utility, are the subject of the next book.

Having said so much in general, we are prepared for particulars; which may commodiously be distributed into three sections. First, Where the will of the legislature is not justly expressed in the statute. Second, Where the means enacted fall short of the end purposed by the legislature. Third, Where the means enacted reach unwarily beyond the end purposed by the legislature.

SECT. I.

Where the will of the legislature is not justly expressed in the statute.

THIS section, for the sake of perspicuity, shall be divided into three articles. First, Where the words

236 STATUTES. **B. I.**

are ambiguous. Second, Where they fall short of
will. Third, Where they go beyond will.

ART. I. *Where the words are ambiguous.*

THE following is a proper instance. By the act
250. parliament 1597, " Vassals failing to pay their
" feu-duties for the space of two years, shall forfeit
" their feu-rights, in the same manner as if a clause
" irritant were engrossed in the infeftment." The
forfeiting clause here is ambiguous : it may mean an
ipso facto forfeiture upon elapsing of the two years ;
or it may mean a forfeiture if the feu-duty be not
paid after a regular demand in a process. Every
ambiguous clause ought to be so interpreted as to support the rules of justice, because such must be constructed the intendment of the legislature : and that
by this rule the latter sense must be chosen, will appear upon the slightest reflection. The remedy here
provided against the obstinacy or negligence of an
undutiful vassal, could never be intended a trap for
the innocent, by forfeiting those who have failed in
payment through ignorance or inability. The construction chosen making the right voidable only, not
void *ipso facto,* obliges the superior to insist in a declarator of irritancy or forfeiture, in order to void the
right ; which gives the vassal an opportunity to prevent the forfeiture, by paying up all arrears. By
this method, it is true, the guilty may escape : but
this is far more eligible in common justice, than that
the innocent be punished with the guilty.

ART. II. *Where the words fall short of will.*

IN the act of Charles II, laying a tax on malt-liquors, there are no words directing the tax to be paid, but only·a penalty in case of not payment. The exchequer, which, like the session, is a court both of common law and of equity, supplies the defect; and, in order to fulfil the intendment of the statute, sustains an action for payment of the tax.

ART. III. *Where the words go beyond will.*

BY the act 5. parl. 1695, it is enacted, " That " hereafter, no man binding for and with another, " conjunctly and severally, in any bond or contract " for sums of money, shall be bound longer than " seven years after the date of the bond." It appearing to the court, from the nature of the thing, and from other clauses in the statute, that the words are too extensive, and that the privilege was intended for none but for cautioners upon whose faith money is lent, they have for that reason been always in use to restrict the words, and to deny the privilege to other cautioners.

The act 24. parl. 1695, for making effectual the debts of heirs who, after three years possession, die in apparency, is plainly contrived for debts only that are contracted for a valuable consideration. The act, however, is expressed in such extensive terms, as to comprehend debts and deeds gratuitous as well as for a valuable consideration. The court, therefore, restricting the words to the sense of the statute, never sustains action upon this statute to gratuitous creditors.

The regulations 1695, admitting no objection against a decreet-arbitral but bribery and corruption only, reach unwarily beyond the meaning of the legislature. A decreet-arbitral derives its force from the submission; and for that reason, every good objection against a submission must operate against the decreet-arbitral.

By the statute 9° *Annæ, cap.* 13. " The person " who at one time loses the sum or value of £10 " Sterling at game, and pays the same, shall be at li- " berty, within three months to sue for and recover " the money or goods so lost, with costs of suit. And " in case the loser shall not, within the time foresaid, " really and *bona fide* bring his action, it shall be law- " ful for any one to sue for the same, and triple va- " lue thereof, with costs of suit." Here there is no limitation mentioned with respect to the popular action : nor, as far as concerns England, is it necessary ; because, by the English statute, 31st Eliz. cap. 5. " No action shall be sustained upon any penal sta- " tute made or to be made, unless within one year of " the offence." A limiting clause was necessary with regard to Scotland only, to which the said statute of Elizabeth reacheth not ; and therefore, as there is no limitation expressed in the act, a court of common law in Scotland must sustain the popular action for forty years, contrary evidently to the will of the legislature, which never intended a penal statute to be prepetual in Scotland, that in England is temporary. As here, therefore, the words go beyond will, it belongs to the Court of Session to limit this statute, by denying action if not brought within one year after

P. I. 5. **STATUTES.** **239**

the offence. Hence, in the decision, January 19, 1737, Murray *contra* Cowan, where an action was sustained even after the year, for recovering money lost at play with the triple value, the Court of Session acted as a court of common law, and not as a court of equity.

The following is an instance from the Roman law with respect to the *hereditatis petitio*, of words reaching inadvertently beyond the will of the legislator. " Illud quoque quod in oratione Divi Hadriani est, " *Ut post acceptum judicium id actori præstetur, quod* " *habiturus esset, si eo tempore, quo petit, restituta* " *esset hereditas*, interdum durum est : quid enim, " si post litem contestatam mancipia, aut jumenta, " aut pecora deperierint ? Damnari debebit secundum " verba orationes : quia potuit petitior, restituta here- " ditate, distraxisse ea. Et hoc justum esse in speci- " alibus petitionibus Proculo placet : Cassius contra " sensit. In prædonis persona Proculus recte exis- " timat : in bonæ fidei possessoribus Cassius. Nec " enim debet possessor aut mortalitatem præstare, " aut, propter metum hujus periculi temere indefen- " sum jus euum relinquere." *

SECT. II.

Where the means enacted fall short of the end purposed by the legislature.

THE first instance shall be given of means that afford a complete remedy in some cases, and fall short

* L. 40. De hereditatis petitione.

240   STATUTES.   B. I.

in others *ubi par. est ratio.* In order to fulfil justice,
the will of the legislature may be made effectual by a
court of equity, whatever defect there may be in the
words. Take the following examples. In the Roman
law, Ulpian mentions the following edict. " Si quis
" id quod, jurisdictionis perpetuæ causa, in albo, vel
" in charta, vel in alia materia propositum erit, dolo
" malo corruperit; datur in eum quingentorum au-
" reorum judicium, quod populare est." Upon this
edict Ulpian gives the following opinion. " Quod
" si, dum proponitur, vel ante propositionem, quis
" corruperit; edicti quidem verba cessabunt; Pom-
" ponius autem ait sententiam edicti porrigendam
" esse ad hæc." *

" Oratio Imperatorum Antonini et Commodi, quæ
" quasdam nuptias in personam senatorum inhibuit,
" de sponsalibus nihil locuta est : recte tamen dici-
" tur, etiam sponsalia in his casibus ipso jure nul-
" lius esse momenti; ut suppleatur, quod orationi
" deest." †

" Lex Julia, quæ de dotali prædio prospexit, Ne
" id marito liceat obligare, aut alienare, plenius in-
" terpretanda est : ut etiam de sponso idem juris sit,
" quod de marito." ‡

By the statute of Glocester, " A man shall have a
" writ of waste against him who holdeth for term
" of life or of years." § This statute, which supplies a defect in the common law, is extended against
one who possesses for half a year, or a quarter. For
(says Coke) a tenant for half a year, being within the

---

* L. 7, § 2. De jurisdic.   † L. 16. De sponsalibus.

‡ L. 4. De fundo dotali.   § 6. Edward I, cap. 5.

STATUTES.

same mischief, shall be within the same remedy, though it be out of the letter of the law. *

An heir, whether apparent only, or entered *cum beneficio*, cannot act more justly with respect to his predecessor's creditors, than to bring his predecessor's estate to a judicial sale. The price goes to the creditors, which is all they are entitled to in justice; and the surplus, if any be, goes to the heir, without subjecting him to trouble or risk. The act 24, parl. 1695, was accordingly made, empowering the heir-apparent to bring to a roup or public auction his predecessor's estate, whether bankrupt or not. But as there is a solid foundation in justice for extending this privilege to the heir entered *cum beneficio*, he is understood as omitted *per incuriam*; and the Court of Session supplied the defect, by sustaining a process at the instance of the heir *cum beneficio*, for selling his predecessor's estate.†

By the common law of Scotland, a man's creditors, after his death, had no preference upon his estate; the property was transferred to his heir, and the heir's creditors came in for their share. This was gross injustice; for the ancestor's creditors, who lent their money upon the faith of the estate, ought, in all views, to have been preferred. The act 24, parl. 1661, declares, " That the creditors of the predeces-
" sor doing diligence against the apparent heir, and
" against the real estate which belonged to the de-
" funct, within the space of three years after his
" death, shall be preferred to the creditors of the ap-
" parent heir." The remedy here reaching the real

---

* 1. Instit. 54, b.

† Feb. 27, 1751, Patrick Blair.

Q

estate only, the Court of Session completed the remedy, by extending it to the personal estate, * and also to a personal bond, limited to a substitute named. † And, as being a court of equity, it was well authorised to make this extension; for to withdraw from the predecessor's creditors part of his personal estate, is no less unjust, than to withdraw from them part of his real estate.

One statute there is, or rather clause in a statute, which affords a plentiful harvest of instances. By the principles of common law, an heir is entitled to continue the possession of his ancestor; and formerly, if he could colour his possession with any sort of title, however obsolete or defective, he not only enjoyed the rents, but was enabled, by that means, to defend his possession against the creditors.‡ Among many remedies for this flagrant injustice, there is a clause in the act 62, parl. 1661, enacting, " That in " case the apparent heir of any debtor shall acquire " right to an expired apprising, the same shall be " redeemable from him, his heirs and successors, " within ten years after acquiring the same, by the " posterior apprisers, upon payment of the purchase- " money." This remedy has been extended in many particulars, in order to fulfil the end intended by the legislature. For, 1*mo*, Though the remedy is afforded to apprisers only, it is extended to personal creditors. 2*do*, It has been extended even to an heir of entail, empowering him to redeem an apprising of the entailed lands, after it was purchased by the heir of line. 3*tio*, Though no purchase is mentioned in

* Stair, Dec. 16, 1674, Kilhead *contra* Irvine.

† Forbes, Feb. 9, 1711, Graham *contra* Macqueen.

‡ See Historical law-tracts, tract 12, toward the close.

STATUTES.

this clause but what is made by the heir-apparent, the remedy, however, is extended against a presumptive heir, who cannot be heir-apparent while his ancestor is alive. *4to*, It was judged, That an apprising led both against principal and cautioner, and purchased by the heir-apparent of the principal, might be redeemed by the creditors of the cautioner. This was a stretch, but not beyond the bounds of equity : the cautioner himself, as creditor for relief, could have redeemed this apprising in terms of the statute; and it was thought, that every privilege competent to a debtor ought to be extended to his creditors, in order to make their claims effectual. *5to*, The privilege is extended to redeem an apprising during the legal, though the statute mentions only an expired apprising. And, *lastly*, Though the privilege of redemption is limited to ten years after the purchase made by the heir apparent, it was judged, that the ten years begin not to run but from the time that the purchase is known to the creditors. These decisions all of them are to be found in the Dictionary, vol. 1, p. 359.

It is chiefly to statutes of this kind that the following doctrine is applicable. " Non possunt omnes " articuli singillatim aut legibus aut senatusconsultis " comprehendi ; sed cum in aliqua causa sententia " eorum manifesta est, is, qui jurisdictioni praeest, " ad similia procedere, atque ita jus dicere debet. " Nam ut ait Pedius, quoties lege aliquid, unum vel " alterum introductum est, bona occasio est, caetera, " quae tendunt ad eandem utilitatem, vel interpreta- " tione vel certe *jurisdictione*, suppleri."*

The next branch is of means that are incomplete

* L. 12 & 13 De legibus.

in every respect, where the very thing in view of the legislature is but imperfectly remedied. Of this take the following illustrious example, which, at the same time, furnishes an opportunity to explain the nature and effect of an adjudication after its legal is expired.

An adjudication during the legal is a *pignus prætorium*: and expiry of the legal is held to transfer the property from the debtor to the creditor; precisely as in a wadset or mortgage, where the redemption is limited within a day certain. Yet the rule which, with relation to a wadset, affords an equity of redemption after the stipulated term of redemption is past,* has never been extended, directly at least, to relieve against an expired legal. This subject, therefore, is curious, and merits attention.

In a poinding of moveables, the debtor has not an equity of redemption, because the moveables are transferred to the creditor at a just value. The same being originally the case of an apprising of land, the legal reversion of seven years introduced by the act 36, parl. 1469, was, in reality, a privilege bestowed upon the debtor, without any foundation in equity; and, therefore, equity could not support an extension of the reversion one hour beyond the time granted by the statute. But the nature of an apprising was totally reversed, by an oppressive and dishonest practice of attaching land for payment of debt, without preserving any equality between the debt and the land; great portions of land being frequently carried off for payment of inconsiderable sums. An apprising, as originally constituted, was a judicial sale for a just price: but an execution, by which land at random is attached for payment of debt without any es-

* Page 62.

P. I. 5.   STATUTES.   245

timation of value, ought to have been reprobated as
flying in the face of law. By what means it happened, that creditors were indulged to act so unjustly, I cannot say; but so it is, that such apprisings
were supported even against the clearest principles
of common law. An apprising so irregular, cannot
indeed be held as a judicial sale for a just price : the
utmost indulgence that could be given it, was to hold
it to be a security for payment of debt. Accordingly, the act 6, parl. 1621, considers it in that light,
enacting, " That apprisers shall be accountable for
" their intromissions within the legal, first, in extinc-
" tion of the interest, and, thereafter, of the capital ;"
which, in effect, is declaring the property to remain
with the debtor, as no man is bound to account for
rents that are his own. And it is considered in the
same light by the act 62, parl. 1661, " ranking *pari*
" *passu* with the first effectual apprising, all other
" apprisings led within year and day of it :" creditors, real or personal, may be ranked upon a common
subject *pari passu*, or in what order the legislature
thinks proper; but such ranking evidently implies,
that the property belongs to the debtor. (*a*)

An apprising, then, or, instead of it, an adjudication, has, during the legal, sunk down to be a *pignus
prætorium*, or a judicial security for debt; and the

(*a*) Stair declares positively for this doctrine.—" An apprising
" is truly a *pignus prætorium :* the debtor is not denuded, but his
" infeftment stands. And if the apprising be satisfied within the
" legal, it is extinguished, and the debtor need not be re-invested.
" Therefore, he may receive vassals during the legal ; and if he
" die during the legal, his apparent heir, intromitting with the
" mails and duties, doth behave himself as heir." *Book 2,
til.* 10, § 1.

STATUTES. B. I.

remaining question is, Whether it be converted into a title of property upon expiry of the legal? The act 1621, above mentioned, makes apprisers accountable for their intromission within the legal; and, if they be not accountable after, ought it not to be inferred, that they must be held to be proprietors? It may, indeed, be clearly inferred from the act, that they are not accountable after the legal is expired; but it follows not, that the property must be held to be in them: I instance a proper wadsetter, who is not proprietor of the subject, and yet is not liable to account. I say further, that a court of equity, though it has no power to overturn express law, is not bound by any inference drawn from a statute, however clear, except as far as that inference is supported by the rules of justice. And, in that view, we proceed to inquire, what are the rules of justice with respect to an apprising or an adjudication after expiration of the legal.

According to the original form of an apprising, requiring a strict equality between the debt and the value of the land, it was rational and just, that the property of the land should instantly be transferred to the creditor in satisfaction of the debt; but it could no longer be rational or just to transfer the property, after it became customary to attach land at random without regarding its extent. The debtor's whole land-estate was apprised, and is now adjudged by every single creditor, however small his debt may be; and therefore, to transfer to an appriser or adjudger, the property of the land *ipso facto*, upon the debtor's failure to make payment within the legal, would be a penal irritancy of the severest kind. On the other hand, this supposed *ipso facto* transference of the pro-

P. I. 5. STATUTES. **247**

perty is penal upon the creditor, where the land adjudged by him happens to be less in value than his debt : in that case, it would be glaring injustice to force the land upon him in payment of his debt. Nay, more, it is repugnant to first principles, that a man should be compelled to take land for his debt, however valuable the land may be : it may be his choice to continue possession as creditor, after the legal as well as before; and this must be understood his choice, if he do not signify the contrary. To relieve the creditor as well as the debtor, from the foregoing hardships, equity steers a middle course. It admits not an *ipso facto* transference of the property, upon expiry of the legal; but only gives the creditor an option, either to continue in his former situation, or to take the land for his debt ; which last must be declared in a process, entituled *a declarator of expiry of the legal*. This removes all hardship : land is not imposed upon the creditor against his will : the debtor, on the other hand, has an opportunity to purge his failure, by making payment ; and if he suffer a decree to pass without offering payment, it is just that the property be transferred to the creditor in satisfaction of the debt ; for judicial proceedings ought not for ever to be kept in suspense. Thus, the law is so constructed as to make the property transferable only, and not to be transferred but by the intervention of a declarator. The declarator here, serves the same double purpose that it serves in the *lex commissoria in pignoribus :* it is a declaration of the creditor's will to accept the land for his money ; and it relieves the debtor from a penal irritancy, by admitting him to purge at any time before the declaratory decree pass.

248 STATUTES. B. I.

We proceed to examine how far the practice of the Court of Session, concerning apprisings and adjudications, is conformable to the principles above laid down. And I must prepare my reader beforehand to expect here the same wavering and fluctuation between common law and equity, that in the course of this work is discovered in many other instances. I observe, in the first place, that though the court, adhering to common law, has not hitherto sustained to the debtor an equity of redemption after expiry of the legal, yet that the same thing in effect is done indirectly, through the influence of equity. Some pretext or other of informality is always embraced to open an expired legal, in order to afford the debtor an opportunity to redeem his land by payment of the debt. And this has been carried so far, as to open the legal to the effect solely of entitling the debtor to make payment, holding the legal as expired with respect to other effects, such as that of relieving the creditor from accounting for the rents levied by him, unless during the ten years that the legal is current by statute.*

In another particular, our practice appears to deviate far from just principles. With respect to the adjudger, it is justly held, that the debt due to him cannot be extinguished without his consent; whence it necessarily follows, that, even after the legal is expired, he must have an option to adhere to his debt, or to take the land instead of it. This is established in our present practice: and what man is so blind as not to perceive what necessarily follows? An adjudger, upon whose will it depends to continue

* Forbes, Feb. 2, 1711, Guthrie *contra* Gordon.

creditor, or to take himself to the land, cannot be proprietor of that land : before the property can be transferred to him, he must interpose his will, which is done by a declarator ; and so far our practice proceeds upon just principles. But whether what is held with respect to the debtor be consistent with that practice, we next enquire. It is held, that the debtor's power of redemption is confined within the legal ; that, by expiry of the legal, he is forfeited *ipso facto* of his property ; and consequently, that he has no power to redeem, nor to purge his failure of payment. Here we find a direct inconsistency in our practice : with respect to the creditor, the property is not his, till he obtain a declarator of expiry of the legal : with respect to the debtor, the property without a declarator is lost to him *ipso facto*, by expiry of the legal. Can any man say who is proprietor in the interim ? These notions cannot be reconciled ; but the cause of them may be accounted for. In our practice, there is a strong bias to creditors in opposition to their debtors. This bias hath bestowed on an appriser the equitable privilege of an option between the debt and the land upon which he is secured : the rigor, on the other hand, with which debtors are treated, has denied them the equitable privilege of purging an irritant clause at any time before the door be shut against them by a declaratory decree.

SECT. III.

*Where the means enacted reach unwarily beyond the
end purposed by the legislature.*

BY the common law of England, ecclesiastics were
at liberty to grant leases without limitation of time.
As this liberty might be exercised greatly to the hurt
of their successors in office, the statute 13^d Eliz. cap.
10, was made, prohibiting ecclesiastics from granting
a lease for a longer time than twenty-one years, or
three lives. In the construction of this statute, it is
held, that a lease during the life of the granter is
good, were he to live a century; for not being within
the mischief, it is not within the remedy.

The act 6, parl. 1672, requires, " That all execu-
" tions of summons shall bear expressly the names
" and designations of the pursuers and defenders."
This regulation was necessary in order to connect the
execution with the summons. For as, at that period,
it was common to write an execution upon a paper
apart, bearing a reference in general to the summons,
in the following manner, " That the parties within
" expressed were lawfully cited," &c. the execution
of one summons might be applied to any other, so as
to become legal evidence of a citation that was never
given. But as there can be no opportunity for this
abuse where an execution is written upon the back of
the summons, it belongs to a court of equity, with
respect to a case where the statutory remedy is unnecessary, to relieve so far from the enacting clause;
which is done by declaring, that it is not necessary

P. i. 5.   STATUTES.   **251**

to name the pursuers and defenders where the execution is written on the back of the summons.*

By the 34th and 35th Henry VIII, cap. v, § 14, it is declared, That a will or testament made of any manors, lands, &c. by a feme covert, shall not be effectual in law. This could not be intended to render ineffectual a will made by a woman whose husband is banished for life by act of parliament. And accordingly, such will was sustained.†

The statutes introducing the positive and negative prescriptions, have for their object public utility; and the supplying defects in these statutes rests upon the same principle; a subject that belongs to the next book, which contains the proceedings of a court of equity acting upon the principle of utility. But to mitigate these statutes with respect to articles that happen to be oppressive and unjust, is a branch of the present subject; and to examples of that kind I proceed. Common law, which limits not actions within any time, affords great opportunity for unjust claims, which, however ill founded originally, are brought so late as to be secure against all detection. It is not wrong in common law to sustain an old claim, for a claim may be very old and yet very just: but to sustain claims without any limitation of time, gives great scope to fraud and forgery; and for that reason public utility required a limitation. Upon that principle the statutes 1469 and 1474 were made, denying action upon debts and other claims beyond forty years. A court of common law proceeding upon these statutes, cannot sustain action after forty

---

* Feb. 20, 1755, Sir William Dunbar *contra* John Macleod, younger of Macleod.

† 2 Vernon 104.

years, even where a claim is evidently well founded, as where it is proved to be so by referring it to the oath of the defendant. In this case, the means enacted go evidently beyond the end purposed by the legislature; which intended only to secure against suspicious and ill-founded claims, not to cut off any just debt; and in this view nothing further could be intended, than to introduce a presumption against every claim brought after forty years; reserving to the pursuer to bring positive evidence of its being a subsisting claim, and justly due. Yet the Court of Session, acting as a court of common law, did, in one instance, refuse to sustain action after the forty years, though the debt was offered to be proved by the oath of the defendant.* In another point, they act properly as a court of equity. Persons under age are relieved from the effect of these statutes, for an extreme good reason, That no presumption can lie against a creditor while under age, for delaying to bring his action.

The same construction in equity is given to the English act of limitation concerning personal actions: it is held, That a bare acknowledgment of the debt is sufficient to bar the limitation; † importing, that the legislature intended not to extinguish a just debt, but only to introduce a presumption of payment. But with this doctrine I cannot reconcile what seems to be established in the English courts of equity, " That " if a man by will or deed subject his land to the pay- " ment of his debts, debts barred by the statute of " limitations shall be paid; for they are debts in " equity, and the statute hath not extinguished the

* Fountainhall, Dec. 7, 1703, Napier *contra* Campbell.
† Abridg. of the law, vol. 3, p. 517.

P. I. 5. STATUTES. 253

"obligation, though it hath taken away the re-
"medy." * This differs widely from the equitable
construction of the statute; for if its intendment be
to presume such debts paid, they cannot, even in
equity, be considered as debts, unless the statutory
presumption be removed by contrary evidence. The
following case proceeds upon the same misapprehension of the statute:—" It hath also been ruled in
" equity, that if a man has a debt due to him by
" note, or a book-debt, and has made no demand of
" it for six years, so that he is barred by the statute
" of limitations; yet if the debtor or his executor,
" after the six years, puts out an advertisement in
" the Gazette, or any other newspaper, that all per-
" sons who have any debts owing to them may ap-
" ply to such a place, and that they shall be paid;
" this, though general, (and, therefore, might be in-
" tended of legal subsisting debts only), yet amounts
" to such an acknowledgment of that debt which was
" barred, as will revive the right, and bring it out of
" the statute again." †

To the case first mentioned of referring a debt to
the defendant's oath, a maxim in the law of England
is obviously applicable, " That a case out of the mis-
" chief, is out of the meaning of the law, though it
" be within the letter." A claim of whatever age,
referred to the defendant's oath, is plainly out of the
mischief intended to be remedied by the foregoing
statutes; and, therefore, ought not to be regulated
by the words, which in this case go beyond the end
purposed. Coke ‡ illustrates this maxim by the fol-

* Ibid. p. 518.
† Abridg. of the law, vol. 3, p. 518.
‡ 2. Instit. 106.

lowing example. The common law of England suffered goods taken by distress to be driven where the creditor pleased ; which was mischievous, because the tenant, who must give his cattle sustenance, could have no knowledge where they were. This mischief was remedied by statute 3. Edward I, cap. 16, enacting, " That goods taken by distress shall not be car- " ried out of the shire where they are taken." Yet, says our author, if the tenantcy be in one county and the manor in another, the lord may drive the distress to his manor, contrary to the words of the statute ; for the tenant, by doing of suit and service to the manor, is presumed to know what is done there.

The act 83, parl. 1579, introducing a triennial prescription of shop-accounts, &c. is directed to the judges, enacting, " That they shall not sustain action af- " ter three years," without making any distinction between natives and foreigners. Nor is there reason for making a distinction ; because every claimant, native or foreigner, must bring his action for payment in the country where the debtor resides ; and for that reason, both equally ought to guard against the prescription of that country. When such is the law of prescription in general, and of the act 1579 in particular, I cannot avoid condemning the following decision. " In a pursuit for an account of drugs, fur- " nished from time to time by a London druggist to " an Edinburgh apothecary, the court repelled the " defence of the triennial prescription, and decreed, " That the act of limitation in England, being the " *locus contractûs*, must be the rule."* There is here another error beside that above mentioned. The English statute of limitation has no authority with

* November 1731, Fulks contra Aikenhead.

P. I. 5.   STATUTES.   255

us, otherwise than as inferring a presumption of payment from the delay of bringing an action within six years; and this presumption cannot arise where the debtor is abroad, either in Scotland or beyond seas.

If the prescription of the country where the debtor dwells be the rule which every creditor, foreign or domestic, ought to have in view, it follows necessarily, that a defendant, to take advantage of that prescription, must be able to specify his residence there, during the whole course of the prescription. While the debtor resides in England, for example, or in Holland, the creditor has no reason to be upon his guard against the Scotch triennial prescription: and supposing the action to be brought the next day after the debtor settles in Scotland, it would be absurd that the creditor should be cut out by the triennial prescription. I illustrate this doctrine by a plain case. A shopkeeper in London furnishes goods to a man who has his residence there. The creditor, trusting to the English statute of limitation, reckons himself secure if he bring his action within six years; but is forced to bring his action in Scotland, to which the debtor retires after three years. It would in this case be unjust, to sustain the Scotch triennial prescription as a bar to the action; in which view, the means enacted in the statute 1579 are unwarily too extensive, forbidding action after three years, without limiting the defence to the case where the defendant has been all that time in Scotland.

Equity is also applied to mitigate the rigor of statute-law with respect to evidence. By the English statute of frauds and perjuries,* it is enacted, "That " all leases, estates, interests of freehold, or terms of

* 29. Charles II, cap. 3.

256 STATUTES. B. I.

" years, made or created by parole, and not put in
" writing, shall have the force and effect of leases or
" estates at will only." In the construction of this
statute, the following point was resolved, That if
there be a parole agreement for the purchase of land,
and that in a bill brought for a specific performance,
the substance of the agreement be set forth in the
bill, and confessed in the answer, the court will decree a specific performance; because, in this case,
there is no danger of perjury, which was the only
thing the statute intended to prevent.* Again, whatever evidence may be required by law, yet it would
be unjust to suffer any man to take advantage of the
defect of evidence, when the defect is occasioned by
his own fraud. There are, accordingly, many instances in the English law-books, where a parole
agreement, intended to be put into writing, but prevented by fraud, has been decreed in equity, notwithstanding the statute of frauds and perjuries. Thus,
upon a marriage-treaty, instructions given by the
husband to draw a settlement, are by him privately
countermanded: after which he draws in the woman,
upon the faith of the settlement, to marry him. The
parole agreement will be decreed in equity.†

Statutory irritancies in an entail are handled, book
1, part 1, chap. 4, sect. 1, art. 3.

Whether can a statutory penalty be mitigated by
a court of equity? See below, chap. 8.

* Abridg. cases in equity, ch. 4, sect. B, § 3.
† Abridg. cases in equity, ch. 4, sect. B, § 4.

CHAP. VI.

Powers of a court of equity to remedy what is imperfect in common law, with respect to matters between debtor and creditor.

With respect to this subject, we find daily instances of oppression, sometimes by the creditor, sometimes by the debtor, authorised by one or other general rule of common law, which happens to be unjust when applied to some singular case out of the reason of the rule. In such cases, it is the duty of a court of equity to interpose, and to relieve from the oppression. To trust this power with some court, is evidently a matter of necessity; for otherwise wrong would be authorised without remedy. Such oppression appears in different shapes, and in different circumstances, which I shall endeavour to arrange properly; beginning with the oppression a creditor may commit under protection of common law, and then proceeding to what may be committed by a debtor.

SECT. I.

Injustice of common law with respect to compensation.

By the common law of this land, when a debtor is sued for payment, it will afford no defence that the plaintiff owes him an equivalent sum. This sum he may demand in a separate action; but, in the meantime, if he make not payment of the sum demanded, a decree issues against him, to be followed with exe-

258 TRANSACTIONS BETWEEN B. I.

cution. Now, this is rigorous, or rather unjust. For, with respect to the plaintiff, unless he mean to oppress, he cannot wish better payment than to be discharged of the debt he owes the defendant. And, with respect to the defendant, it is gross injustice to subject him to execution for failing to pay a debt, when possibly the only means he has for payment is that very sum the plaintiff detains from him. To that act of injustice, however, the common law lends its authority, by a general rule, empowering every creditor to proceed to execution when his debtor fails to make payment. But that rule, however just in the main, was never intended to take place in the present case; and, therefore, a court of equity remedies an act of injustice occasioned by a too extensive application of the rule, beyond the reason and intention of the law. The remedy is, to order an account in place of payment, and the one debt to be hit off against the other. This is termed the *privilege of compensation*, which furnishes a good defence against payment. Compensation accordingly, was in old Rome sustained before the Prætor; and in England has long been received in courts of equity. In Scotland, indeed, it has the authority of a statute;* which it seems was thought necessary, because at that period the Court of Session was probably not understood to be a court of equity.† But perhaps there was a further view, namely, to introduce compensation as a defence into courts of common law; and with that precise view did compensation lately obtain the authority of a statute in England :‡ the defence of compensation was always admitted in the Court of Chancery; but by authority of

---

* Act 143, parl. 1592. † See the Introduction.
‡ 2. Geo. II, cap. 22, § 11.

the statute, it is now also admitted in courts of common law.

In applying, however, the foregoing statute, the powers of a court of equity are more extensive than of a court of common law. A court of common law is tied to the letter of the statute, and has no privilege to inquire into its motive. But the Court of Session, as a court of equity, may supply its defects, and correct its excesses. Yet I know not by what misapprehension the Court of Session, with regard to this statute, hath always been considered as a court of common law, and not as a court of equity; a misapprehension the less excusable, considering the subject of the statute, a matter of equity, which the court itself could have introduced had the statute never been made. I shall make this reflection plain, by entering into particulars. The statute authorises compensation to be pleaded in the original process only, by way of exception, and gives no authority to plead it, whether in the reduction or suspension of a decree. The words are, " That a liquid debt be admitted by way " of exception before decreet by all judges, but not in " a suspension nor reduction of the decreet." This limitation is proper in two views. The first is, that the omitting or forbearing to plead compensation in the original process is not a good objection against the decree. The other view is, that it would afford too great scope for litigiosity, were defendants indulged to reserve their articles of compensation as a ground for suspension or reduction. Attending to these views, a decree purely in absence ought not to bar compensation; because it is often pronounced when the party hath not an opportunity to appear. For that reason, a party who is restored to his de-

260 **TRANSACTIONS BETWEEN** **B. I.**

fences in a suspension, upon shewing that his absence was not contumacious, ought to be at liberty to plead every defence, whether in equity or at common law. And yet our judges constantly reject compensation when pleaded in a suspension of a decree in absence, though that case comes not under the reason and motive of the statute. The statute, in my apprehension, admits of still greater latitude; which is, that after a decree *in foro* is suspended for any good reason, compensation may be received in discussing the suspension; for the statute goes no farther but to prohibit a decree to be suspended merely upon compensation. Nor can it have any bad effect to admit compensation when a cause is brought under review by suspension because of error committed in the original process : on the contrary, it is beneficial to both by preventing a new law-suit.

If the decisions of the Court of Session, upon the different articles of this statute, show a slavish dependence on the common law, the decisions which regulate cases of compensation, not provided for by the statute, breathe a freer spirit, being governed by true principles of equity. The first case that presents itself, is, where one only of the two concurring debts bears interest. What shall be the effect of compensation in that case? Shall the principal and interest be brought down to the time of pleading compensation, and be set off at that period against the other debt which bears not interest? Or shall the account be instituted as at the time of the concourse, as if, from that period, interest were no longer due? Equity evidently concludes for the latter ; for it considers, that each had the use of the other's money; and that it is not just the one should have

P. I. 6.   DEBTOR AND CREDITOR.   261

a claim for interest, while the other has none : interest is a premium for the use of money, and my creditor in effect gets that premium by having from me the use of an equivalent sum. And, accordingly, it is the constant practice of the court, to stay the course of interest from the time the two debts concurred. But as it would be unjust to make a debtor pay interest for money he must retain in his hand ready to answer a demand, therefore, in such a case, compensation is excluded. Example. A tacksman lends a considerable sum to his landlord, agreeing in the bond to suspend the payment during the currency of the tack, but stipulating to himself a power to retain the interest annually out of the tack-duty. The tacksman makes punctual payment of the surplus tack-duties, as often as demanded : but, by some disorder in the landlord's affairs, a considerable arrear is allowed to remain in the hands of the tacksman. The landlord pleading to make the tack-duties in arrear operate *retrò* against the bonded debt, so as to extinguish some part of the principal annually, the *retrò* operation was not admitted : because, in terms of the contract, the tacksman was bound to keep in his hand the surplus tack-duties, ready to be paid on demand ; and, for that reason, it would be unjust to make him pay interest for this sum ; or, which comes to the same, it would be unjust to make it operate *retrò*, by applying it annually in extinction of the bonded debt bearing interest.*

In applying compensation, both claims must be pure ; for it is not equitable to delay paying a debt of which the term is past, upon pretext of a counter-claim that cannot at present be demanded, or that is

* July 21, 1756, Campbell *contra* Carruthers.

TRANSACTIONS BETWEEN B. I.

uncertain as to its extent. But what if the pursuer be bankrupt, or be *vergens ad inopiam?* The common law authorises a bankrupt to insist for payment equally with a person solvent: but it is not just to oblige me to pay what I owe to a bankrupt, and to leave me without remedy as to what he owes me. This, therefore, is a proper case for the interposition of equity. It cannot authorise compensation, in circumstances that afford not place for it; but it can prevent the mischief in the most natural manner, by obliging the bankrupt to find security to make good the counter-claim when it shall become due; and this is the constant practice of the Court of Session.

Compensation would be but an imperfect remedy against the oppression of the common law, if it could not be applied otherwise than by exception. The statute, it is true, extends the remedy no farther; but the Court of Session, upon a principle of equity, affords a remedy where the statute is silent. Supposing two mutual debts, of which the one only bears interest, the creditor in the barren debt demands his money; which the debtor pays without pleading compensation, and then demands the debt due to himself with the interest. Or let it be supposed, that payment of the barren debt is offered, which the creditor must accept, however sensible of the hardship. In these cases there is no opportunity to apply the equitable rule, That both sums should bear interest, or neither. Therefore, to give opportunity for applying that rule, a process of mutual extinction of the two debts ought to be sustained to the creditor whose sum is barren; to have effect *retrò* from the time of concourse: and this process accordingly is always sustained in the Court of Session.

P. 1. 6. DEBTOR AND CREDITOR. 263

. We next take under consideration the case of an assignee. And the first question is, Whether the process of mutual extinction now mentioned be competent against an assignee. To prevent mistakes, let it be understood, that an assignment intimated is, in our present practice, a proper *cessio in jure*, transferring the claim *funditùs* from the assignor or cedent to the assignee. This being taken for granted, it follows, that compensation cannot be pleaded against an assignee: for though one of the claims is now transferred to him, that circumstance subjects him not to the counter claim; and therefore there is no mutual concourse of debts between the parties, upon which to found a compensation.

Let us suppose, that the claim bearing interest is that which is assigned. This claim, principal and interest, must be paid to the assignee, because he is not subjected to the counter-claim. Must then the assignee's debtor, after paying the principal and interest, be satisfied to demand from the cedent the sum due to himself which bears not interest? At that rate, the creditor whose claim bears interest, will always take care, by an assignment, to prevent compensation. This hardship is a sufficient ground for the interposition of equity. If the cedent hath procured an undue advantage to himself, by making a sum bear interest in the name of an assignee, which would not bear interest in his own name, the debtor ought not to suffer; and the proper reparation is to oblige him to pay interest *ex æquitate*, though the claim at common law bears none.

But if the debt assigned be that which bears not interest, a total separation is thereby made between the two debts. And what after this can prevent the

264   TRANSACTIONS BETWEEN   B. I.

counter-claim, with its interest, from being made effectual against the cedent? No objection in equity can arise to him, seeing, with his eyes open, he deprived himself of the opportunity of compensation, the only mean he had to avoid paying interest upon the counter-claim.

In handling compensation as directed by equity, I have hitherto considered what the law ought to be, and have carefully avoided the intricacies of our practice, which in several particulars appears erroneous. To complete the subject, I must take a survey of that practice. By our old law, derived from that of the Romans, and from England, a creditor could not assign his claim; all he could do was to grant a procuratory *in rem suam;* which did not transfer the *jus crediti* to the assignee, but only intitled him *procuratoriá nomine* to demand payment. From the nature of this title, it was thought, that compensation might be pleaded against the assignee as well as against the cedent: and indeed, considering the title singly, the opinion is right; because the pleading compensation against a procurator, is in effect pleading it against the cedent or creditor himself. The opinion however is erroneous; and the error arises from overlooking the capital circumstance, which is the equitable right, that the assignee, though considered as a procurator only, hath to the claim assigned, by having paid a price for it. Equity will never subject such a procurator or assignee to the cedent's debts, whether in the way of payment or compensation. And as for the statute, it affords not any pretext for sustaining compensation against such an assignee, being made to support compensation against the rigour of common law; but to support it only as far as just. It could not, therefore, be the intention of the legislature, in defiance of justice, to make compensation effectual against an assignee who pays value. Nor must it pass unobserved, that, as our law stands at present, this iniquitous effect given to compensation is still more absurd, if possible, than it was formerly. In our later practice, an assignment has changed its nature, and is converted into a proper *cessio in jure*, divesting the cedent *funditùs*, and vesting the assignee. Whence it follows, that, after an assignment is intimated, compensation is barred from the very nature of the assignee's right, even laying aside the objection upon the head of equity. But we began with sustaining compensation against an assignee for a valuable consideration, in quality of a procurator; not adverting, that though his title did not protect him from compensation, his right as purchaser ought to have had that effect : and by the force of custom we have adhered to the same erroneous practice, though now the title of an assignee protects him from compensation, as well as the nature of his right when he pays value for it.

SECT. II.

Injustice of common law with respect to indefinite payment.

Next of oppression or wrong that may be committed by a debtor, under protection of common law.

Every man who has the administration of his own affairs, may pay his debts in what order he pleases, where his creditors interpose not by legal execution.

266 TRANSACTIONS BETWEEN B. L.

Nor will it make a difference, that several debts are due by him to the same creditor ; for the rule of law is, That if full payment be offered of any particular debt, the creditor is bound to accept, and to give a discharge.

But now, supposing a sum to be delivered by the debtor to the creditor as payment, but without apply-ing it to any one debt in particular, termed *indefinite payment*, the question is, By what rule shall the ap-plication be made when the parties afterward come to state an account ? If the debts be all of the same kind, it is of no importance to which of them the sum be applied : otherwise, if the debts be of different kinds, one, for example, bearing interest, one barren ; the rule in the Roman law is, *Quod electio est debi-toris*; a rule founded on the principles of common law. The sum delivered to the creditor is in his hand for behoof of the debtor, and, therefore, it belongs to the debtor to make the application. But though this is the rule of common law, it is not the rule of justice : if the debtor make an undue application, equity will interpose to relieve the creditor from the hardship. A debtor, it is true, delivering a sum to his creditor, may direct the application of it as he thinks proper : he may deliver it as payment of a debt bearing in-terest, when he is due to the same creditor a debt bearing none ; yet a remedy in this case is beyond the reach of equity. But where the money is alrea-dy in the hand of the creditor indefinitely, the debt-or has no longer the same arbitrary power of making the application : equity interposing, will direct the application. Thus, indefinite payment comes under the power of a court of equity.

In order to ascertain the equitable rules for applying an indefinite payment, a few preliminary consi-derations may be of use. A loan of money is a mu-tual contract equally for the benefit of the lender and borrower: the debtor has the use of the money he borrows, and for it pays to the creditor a yearly pre-mium. With respect, therefore, to a sum bearing interest, the debtor is not bound, either in strict law or in equity, to pay the capital, until the creditor make a demand. A debt not bearing interest, is in a very different condition: the debtor has the whole benefit, and the creditor is deprived of the use of his money without a valuable consideration; which binds the debtor, in good conscience, either to pay the sum, or to pay interest. Though this be a matter of duty, it cannot, however, be enforced by a court of equity in all cases; for it may be the creditor's intention to assist the debtor with the use of money without in-terest: but upon the first legal expression of the cre-ditor's will to have his money, a court of equity ought to decree interest.

Another preliminary is, that where a cautioner ac-cedes to a bond of borrowed money, the debtor is, in conscience, bound to pay the sum at the term cove-nanted, in order to relieve his cautioner, who has no benefit by the transaction. The case is different where the cautioner shews a willingness to continue his credit.

Entering now into particulars, the first case I shall mention is, where two debts are due by the same debtor to the same creditor, one of which only bears interest. An indefinite payment ought, undoubtedly, to be applied to the debt not bearing interest; be-cause this debt ought, in common justice, to be first paid, and there is nothing to oblige the debtor to pay

268 TRANSACTIONS BETWEEN B. I.

the other till it be demanded. A man of candour will make the application in this manner; and were there occasion for a presumption, it will be presumed of every debtor, that he intended such application. But the judge has no occasion for a presumption: his authority for making the application is derived from a principle of justice. The same principle directs, that where both debts bear interest, the indefinite payment ought first to be applied for extinguishing what is due of interest; and next, for extinguishing one or other capital indifferently, or for extinguishing both in proportion.*

The second case shall be of two debts bearing interest; one of which is secured by infeftment or inhibition. It is equal to the debtor which of the debts be first paid: and, therefore, the indefinite payment ought to be applied to the debt for which there is the slenderest security; because such application is for the interest of the creditor. Take another case of the same kind. A tenant in tail owes two debts to the same creditor; one of his own contracting, and one as representing the entailer. Every indefinite payment he makes ought to be ascribed to his proper debt, for payment of which there is no fund but the rents during his life. This, it is true, is against the interest of the substitutes: but their interest cannot be regarded in the application of rents which belong not to them but to the tenant in tail: and next, as they are *certantes de lucro captando*, their interest cannot weigh against that of a creditor, who is *certans de damno evitando*.

---

* The rule here laid down seems to be unknown in England. Sometimes it is found, that *electio est debitoris*, and sometimes that it is *creditoris*. *Abridg. cases in equity, cap. 22, sect. D, § 1, & 2.*

P. I. 6. DEBTOR AND CREDITOR. 269

Third case. A debtor obtains an ease, upon con-, dition of paying at a day certain, the transacted sum bearing interest: he is also bound to the same creditor in a separate debt not bearing interest. The question is, To which of these debts ought an indefinite payment to be applied? It is the interest of the debtor that it be applied to the transacted sum : it is the interest of the creditor that it be applied to the separate debt not bearing interest. The judge will not prefer the interest of either, but make the application in the most equitable manner, regarding the interest of both : he will, therefore, in the first place, consider which of the two has the greatest interest in the application ; and he will so apply the sum as to produce the greatest effect. This consideration will lead him to make the application to the transacted sum : for if the transaction be in any degree lucrative, the debtor will lose more by its becoming ineffectual, than the creditor will by wanting the interim use of the money due to him without interest. But then, the benefit ought not to lie all on one side ; and therefore equity rules, that the debtor, who gets the whole benefit of the application, ought to pay interest for the separate sum; which brings matters to a perfect equality between them. For the same reason, if the application be made to the debt not bearing interest, the transaction ought to be made effectual, notwithstanding the term appointed for paying the transacted sum be elapsed.

Fourth case. Suppose the one debt is secured by adjudication, the legal of which is near expiring, and the other is a debt not bearing interest. And, to adjust the case to the present subject, we shall also suppose, that the legal of an adjudication expires *ipso facto* without necessity of a declarator. An indefinite payment here ought to be applied for extinguishing the adjudication. And, for the reason given in the preceding case, the separate debt ought to bear interest from the time of the indefinite payment.

Fifth case. An heir of entail owes two debts to the same creditor; the one a debt contracted by the entailer not bearing interest, the other a debt bearing interest, contracted by the heir, which may found a declarator of forfeiture against him. An indefinite payment ought to be applied to the first-mentioned debt, because it bears not interest: for, with regard to the heir's hazard of forfeiture, the forfeiture, which cannot be made effectual but by a process of declarator, may be prevented by paying the debt. And the difficulty of procuring money for that purpose, is an event too distant and too uncertain to be regarded in forming a rule of equity.

Sixth case. Neither of the debts bear interest; and one of them is guarded by a penal irritancy, feu-duties, for example, due more than two years. In this case, the feu-duties ought to be extinguished by the indefinite payment; because such application relieves the debtor from a declarator of irritancy, and is indifferent to the creditor, as both debts are barren. Nor will it be regarded, that the creditor is cut out of the hope he had of acquiring the subject by the declarator of irritancy; because in equity the rule holds without exception, *Quod potior debet esse conditio ejus qui certat de damno evitando, quam ejus qui certat de lucro captando.*

Seventh case. If there be a cautioner in one of the debts, and neither debt bear interest, the indefinite payment ought undoubtedly to be applied for relieving the cautioner. Gratitude demands this from the principal debtor, for whose service solely the cautioner gave his credit. It may be more the interest of the creditor to have the application made to the other debt, which is not so well secured : but the debtor's connection with his cautioner is more intimate than with his creditor ; and equity respects the more intimate connection as the foundation of a stronger duty.

Eighth case. Of the two debts, the one is barren, the other bears interest, and is secured by a cautioner. The indefinite payment ought to be applied to the debt that bears not interest. The delaying payment of such a debt, where the creditor gets nothing for the use of his money, is a positive act of injustice. On the other hand, there is no positive damage to the cautioner, by delaying payment of the debt for which he stands engaged. There is, it is true, a risk ; but, seeing the cautioner makes no legal demand to be relieved, it may be presumed that he willingly submits to the risk.

Ninth case. One of the debts is a transacted sum that must be paid at a day certain, otherwise the transaction to be void : or it is a sum which must be paid without delay, to prevent an irritancy from taking place. The other is a bonded debt with a cautioner, bearing interest. The indefinite payment must be applied to make the transaction effectual, or to prevent the irritancy. For, as in the former case, the interest of the creditor, being the more substantial, is preferred before that of the cautioner ; so, in the present case, the interest of the debtor is for the same reason preferred before that of the cautioner.

Tenth case. An indefinite payment made after in-

272 TRANSACTIONS BETWEEN B. I.

solvency to a creditor in two debts, the one with the other without a cautioner, ought to be applied proportionally to both debts, whatever the nature or circumstances of the debts may be: for here the creditor and cautioner being equally *certantes de damno evitando*, ought to bear the loss equally. It is true, the debtor is more bound to the cautioner who lent his credit for the debtor's benefit, than to the creditor, who lent his money for his own benefit; but circumstances of this nature cannot weigh against the more substantial interest of preventing loss and damage.

SECT. III.

Injustice of common law with respect to rent levied indefinitely.

By the common law of this land, a creditor introduced into possession upon a wadset, or upon an assignment to rents, must apply the rent he levies toward payment of the debt, which is the title of his possession; because for that very purpose is the right granted. Rent levied by execution, upon an adjudication, for example, must for the same reason be applied to the debt upon which the execution proceeds. Rent thus levied, whether by consent or by execution, cannot be applied by the creditor to any other debt, however unexceptionable.

But this rule of common law may in some cases be rigorous and materially unjust; to the debtor sometimes, and sometimes to the creditor. If a creditor in possession by virtue of a mortgage or improper

P. I. 6.   DEBTOR AND CREDITOR.   273

wadset, purchase or succeed to an adjudication of the same land, it is undoubtedly the debtor's interest that the rents be applied to the adjudication, in order to prevent expiry of the legal, not to the wadset, which contains no irritancy nor forfeiture upon failure of payment. But if the creditor purchase or succeed to an infeftment of annualrent, upon which a great sum of interest happens to be due, it is beneficial to him that the rents be ascribed for extinction of that interest, rather than for extinction of the wadset-sum which bears interest. These applications cannot be made, either of them, upon the principles of common law; and yet material justice requires such application, which is fair and equitable, weighing all circumstances. No man of candour, in possession of his debtor's land by a mortgage or improper wadset, but must be ashamed to apply the rents he levies to the wadset, when he has an adjudication, the legal of which is ready to expire. And no debtor of candour but must be ashamed to extinguish a debt bearing interest rather than a debt equally unexceptionable that is barren.

Equity, therefore, steps in to correct the oppression of common law in such cases; and it is lucky that this can be done by rules, without hazard of making judges arbitrary. These rules are delineated in the section immediately foregoing; and they all resolve into a general principle, which is, "That the " judge ought to apply the rents so as to be most " equal with respect to both parties, and so as to pre- " vent rigorous and hard consequences on either " side."

But this remedy against the rigour of common law, ought not to be confined to real debts that entitle the creditor to possess. In particular cases, it may be more beneficial to the debtor or to the creditor, without hurting either, to apply the rents for payment even of a personal debt, than for payment of the debt that is the title of possession. What if the personal debt be a bulky sum, restricted to a lesser sum upon condition of payment being made at a day certain? It is the debtor's interest, that the rents be applied to this debt in the first place; as, on the other hand, it is the creditor's interest that they be applied to a personal debt which is barren. A court of equity, disregarding the rigid principles of common law, and considering matters in the view of material justice, reasons after the following manner. A personal creditor has not access to the rents of his debtor's land till he lead an adjudication. But if the creditor be already in possession, an adjudication is unnecessary: such a title, it is true, is requisite to complete the forms of the common law; but equity dispenses with these forms, when they serve no end but to load the parties with expence. And thus where the question is with the debtor only, equity relieves the creditor in possession from the ceremony of leading an adjudication upon his separate debt: and no person can hesitate about the equity of a rule, that is no less beneficial to the debtor, by relieving him from the expence of legal execution, than to the creditor, by relieving him from trouble and advance of money. Thus an executor in possession, is, by equity, relieved from the useless ceremony of taking a decree against himself, for payment of debt due to him by the deceased; and for that reason, an executor may pay himself at short-hand. In the same manner, a wadsetter in possession of his debtor's land, has no

P. I. 6. DEBTOR AND CREDITOR. 275

occasion to attach the rents by legal execution for payment of any separate debt due to him by the proprietor : his possession, by construction of equity, is held a good title ; and by that construction, the rents are held to be levied indefinitely ; which makes way for the question, To which of the debts they ought to be imputed ? The same question may occur where possession is attained by legal execution, without consent of the debtor. A creditor, for example, who enters into possession by virtue of an adjudication, acquires or succeeds to personal debts due by the same debtor : these, in every question with the debtor himself, are justly held to be titles of possession, to give occasion for the question, To what particular debt the rent should be imputed ?

Having said so much in general, the interposition of equity to regulate the various cases that belong to the present subject, cannot be attended with any degree of intricacy. The road is in a good measure paved in the preceding section ; for the rules there laid down with regard to debts of all different kinds, may, with very little variation, be readily accommodated to the subject we are now handling. For the sake, however, of illustrating a subject that is almost totally overlooked by our authors, I shall mention a few rules in general, the application of which to particular cases, will be extremely easy. Let me only premise what is hinted above, that the creditor in possession can state no debts for exhausting the rents, but such as are unexceptionably due by the proprietor : for it would be against equity, as well as against common law, that any man should be protected in the possession of another's property, during the very time the question is depending, whether he

276 TRANSACTIONS BETWEEN B. I.

be or be not a creditor. Let such debts then be the only subject of our speculation. And the first rule of equity is, That the imputation be so made, as to prevent, on both hands, irritancies and forfeitures. A second rule is, That, *in pari casu*, personal debts ought to be paid before those which are secured by infeftment. And, thirdly, with respect to both kinds, That sums not bearing interest be extinguished before sums bearing interest.

It is laid down above, that where the legal of an adjudication is in hazard of expiring, equity demands that the rents be wholly ascribed to the adjudication. But it may happen, in some instances, to be more equitable, that the creditor be privileged to apply the rents to the bygone interest due upon his separate debts; and this privilege will be indulged him, provided he renounce the benefit of an expired legal.

The foregoing rules take place between creditor and debtor. A fourth rule takes place among creditors. The creditor who attains possession by virtue of a preference decreed to him in a competition with co-creditors, cannot apply the rents to any debt but what is preferable, before those debts which, by the other creditors, were produced in the process of competition: for, after using his preferable right to exclude others, it would be unjust to apply the rents to any debt that is not effectual against the creditors who are excluded. This would be taking an undue preference upon debts that have no title to a preference.

Hitherto I have had nothing in view but the possession of a single fund, and the rules for applying the rent of that fund, where the possessor hath claims of different kinds. But, with very little variation,

P. I. 6.   DEBTOR AND CREDITOR.   277

the foregoing rules.may be applied to the more involved case of different funds. A creditor, for example, upon an entailed estate, has two debts in his person; one contracted by the entailer, upon which an adjudication is led against the entailed estate; another contracted by the tenant in tail, which can only affect the rents during his life. It is the interest of the substitutes, that the rents be imputed toward extinction of the entailer's debt, because they are not liable for the other. The interest of the creditor in possession upon his adjudication is directly opposite: it is his interest that the personal debt be first paid, for which he has no security but the rents during his debtor's life. Here equity is clearly on the side of the creditor: he is *certans de damno evitando*, and the substitutes *de lucro captando*. And this coincides with the second case stated in the foregoing section of indefinite payment.

CHAP. VII.

Powers of a court of equity to remedy what is imperfect in common law, with respect to a process.

UNDER the shelter of common law, many act imprudently, many indecently, and not a few act against conscience and moral honesty. The two first are repressed by censure, public and private: the last, a more serious matter, is repressed by a court of equity; which will not sustain either a claim or a defence against conscience, however well founded it may be at common law. The party will be repelled *personali objectione* from insisting on his claim or defence. This personal objection is, with respect to the pursuer, the same with what is termed *exceptio doli* in the Roman law. I proceed to examples; and, first, of the personal objection against a claimant. An informal relaxation of a debtor denounced rebel on a horning, is no relaxation; and, therefore, will not prevent single escheat. But the creditor on whose horning the escheat had fallen, craving preference on the escheated goods; it was objected, That he had consented to the relaxation, which removed the informality as to him; and that equity will not suffer him to act against his own deed. The court accordingly excluded him *personali objectione* from quarrelling the relaxation.* In a competition between two annualrenters, the first of whom was bound to the other as cautioner: it was objected to the first claiming preference, That it was against conscience for him to use his preferable infeftment against a creditor whose debt he was bound to pay. The Court refused to sustain this personal objection; leaving the second annualrenter to insist personally against the first as cautioner.† This was acting as a court of common law, not as a court of equity. The preferable annualrenter ought to have been barred *personali objectione* from obstructing execution for payment of a debt, which he himself was bound to pay as cautioner. In the Roman law, he would have been barred by the *exceptio doli.*

Next as to personal objections of this kind against defendants. A cautioner for a curator being sued for a sum levied by the curator, the cautioner objected, That the person for whom he stands bound as cau-

* Forbes, Feb. 10, 1710, Wallace *contra* Creditors of Spot.
† Forbes, June 28, 1711, Baird *contra* Mortimer.

tioner could not be curator, as there is a prior act of curatory standing unreduced. An endeavour to break loose from a fair engagement being against conscience, the cautioner was repelled *personali objectione* from insisting in his objection.* A verbal promise to dispone lands is not made effectual in equity; because a court of equity has no power to overturn common law, which indulges repentance till writ be interposed. But a disponee to land insisting upon performance, the disponer objected a nullity in the disposition. He was barred *personali objectione* from pleading the objection, because he had verbally agreed to ratify the disposition.†

There is one case in which the personal objection cannot be listened to, and that is, where an objection is made to the pursuer's title. The reason is, that it is *pars judicis* to advert to the pursuer's title, and never to sustain process upon an insufficient title, whether objected to or not. Thus, against a poinding of the ground, which requires an infeftment, it being objected, That the pursuer was not infeft, it was answered, That the defendant, who is superior, has been charged by the pursuer to infeft him; and that the defendant ought to be barred *personali objectione* from pleading an objection arising from his own fault. The Court judged, That it is their duty to refuse action, unless upon a good title; and that no personal objection against a defendant can supply the want of a title.‡

* Durie, Dec. 5, 1627, Rollok *contra* Crosbie.

† Feb. 22, 1745, Christies *contra* Christie.

‡ Durie, June 20, 1627, Laird Touch *contra* Laird Hardiesmill; Stair, Gosford, June 25, 1668, Heriot *contra* Town of Edinburgh.

CHAP. VIII.

Powers of a court of equity to remedy what is imperfect in common law with respect to legal execution.

THIS chapter splits naturally into two sections. First, Where the common law is defective. Second, Where it is oppressive or unjust.

SECT. I.

Where the common law is defective.

IT is natural to believe, and it holds in fact, that the different executions for payment of debt founded on common law, relate to those cases only which most frequently occur in practice. Upon a debtor's failing to make payment, his land is attached by an apprising, his moveables by poinding, and the debts due him by arrestment and forthcoming. But experience discovered many profitable subjects that cannot be brought under any of the foregoing executions. And even with respect to common subjects, several peculiar circumstances were discovered, to which the executions mentioned are not applicable. A court of common law, which cannot in any article exceed the bounds of common law, has not power to supply any of these defects. This power is reserved to a court of equity, acting upon a principle of justice often above mentioned, namely, That wherever there is a right it ought to be made effectual.

This section comprehends many articles. 1st, Sub-

jects that cannot be attached by the executions of
common law. 2d, Circumstances where even common subjects are withdrawn from these executions.
3d, These executions are in some cases imperfect.
4th, They serve only to make debts effectual, and
give no aid to other claims.

ART. I. *Subjects that cannot be attached by the executions of common law.*

THE common law is defective with respect to a
variety of subjects that cannot be attached by any of
its executions; a reversion, for example, a bond secluding executors, a sum of money with which a disposition of land is burdened, &c. These are all carried by an adjudication invented by the sovereign
court. They could not be carried by an apprising
in the form of common law: nor can they be carried
by an adjudication put in place of an apprising by
the act 1672, which, by the act itself, is confined to
land, and to what rights are properly accessory to
land, real servitudes, for example, and such like.
But this is not all. There are many other rights and
privileges, to attach which no execution is provided.
A debtor has, for example, a well-founded claim for
voiding a deed granted by him in his minority,
greatly to his hurt and lesion; but he is bankrupt,
and perversely declines a process, because the benefit
must accrue to his creditors; he will neither convey
his privilege to them, nor insist on it himself. A
reduction on the head of deathbed is an example of
the same kind. There are many others. If a man
fail to purge an irritancy, the common law admits
not his creditors to purge in his name; and they can-

not in their own, unless the privilege be conveyed to them. A court of equity supplies these defects of common law; and, without necessity either of a voluntary or judicial conveyance, entitles creditors at short-hand to avail themselves of such privileges. They are empowered to prosecute the same for their own advantage; in the same manner as if the debtor had done them justice, by making a conveyance in their favour.

Art. II. *Circumstances where even common subjects are withdrawn from these executions.*

I give the following instances. First, The apprisings of common law reach no land but where the debtor is infeft. The apprising a minute of sale of land, and a disposition without infeftment, was introduced by the sovereign court.

Second, John is creditor to James, and James to William. To convey the last-mentioned debt to John, common law requires an arrestment and process of forthcoming. But what if, before John proceed to execution, William die, and no person is found to represent him? In this case there is no place for an arrestment; and yet John ought not to be disappointed of his payment. The Court of Session must supply the defect, by adjudging to John the debt due by William to James.

Third, Execution for payment of debt supposes a *mora* on the debtor's part; and a judge cannot warrantably authorise such execution where there is no *mora*. This holds even in a process for payment. Nor is there any foundation in equity, more than at

P. 1. 8. LEGAL EXECUTION. 283

common law, for a process before the term of payment. Where the debtor is ready to fulfil his engagement at the term covenanted, and is guilty of no failure, justice will not suffer him to be vexed with a process. But with respect to an annuity, or any sum payable at different terms, if the debtor be once *in mora* to make a process necessary for payment of a part actually due, a decree may not only be pronounced for payment of that part, but also for what will afterward become due, superseding execution till the debtor be *in mora*. Equity supports this extension of the common law, which is beneficial to the creditor by easing him of trouble, and no less to the debtor, by preventing the costs that he would otherwise be subjected to in case of future *mora*.

From these principles it appears, that a process for poinding the ground before the term of payment, ought not to be sustained, more than a process against the debtor personally for payment. I observe, indeed, that a process of maills and duties has been sustained after the legal term of Martinmas, though Candlemas be the customary term of payment.* But the reason of this singularity is, that originally Martinmas was the conventional term of corn-rent, and for that reason was established to be the legal term. It crept in by practice to delay payment till Candlemas, in order to give the tenant time to thrash out his corns. And for some centuries, this delay was esteemed an indulgence only, not a matter of right. But, now that long custom has become law, and that a tenant is understood not to be bound to pay his corn-rent before Candlemas, a court, whether of com-

* Durie, Feb. 5, 1624, Wood *contra* Waddel.

284 LEGAL EXECUTION. B. I.

mon law or of equity, will not readily sustain the process before Candlemas.

A process of forthcoming is in a different condition; for being held necessary to complete the right of the arrester, it may in that view proceed before the term of payment of the debt arrested.* The same holds in a process for poinding the ground, if it be necessary to complete a base infeftment by making it public.†

There is one general exception to the foregoing rule, That if a debtor be *vergens ad inopiam*, execution may in equity proceed against him for security. Thus, arrestment in security was sustained, where the debtor was in declining circumstances.‡ The defendant's testator gave the plaintiff £1,000, to be paid at the age of twenty-one years. The bill suggested, that the defendant wasted the estate; and prayed he might give security to pay this legacy when due; which was decreed accordingly.§

Fourth, In the common law of England, there is one defect that gives access to the most glaring injustice. When a man dies, his real estate is withdrawn from his personal creditors, and his personal estate from his real creditors. The common law affords not to a personal creditor execution against the land of his deceased debtor, nor to a real creditor execution against the moveables; and by this means a man may die in opulent circumstances, and yet

* Durie, Feb. 21, 1624, Brown *contra* Johnston. Durie, July 3, 1628, Scot *contra* Laird of Drumlanrig.

† Gilmour, Feb. 1662, Douglas *contra* Tenants of Kinglassie.

‡ Stair, July 17, 1678, Laird Pitmedden *contra* Patersons. Home, Feb. 27, 1758, Meres *contra* York-buildings Co.

§ 1. Chancery Cases, 121.

LEGAL EXECUTION.

P. I. 8.

many of his creditors be forfeited. Whether the Court of Chancery interposes in this case, I am uncertain. In the following case it cannot, I am certain, fail to interpose; and that is, where a debtor, having a near prospect of death, bestows all his money on land, in order to disappoint his personal creditors. The common law affords not a remedy, because the purchasing land is a lawful act; and the common law looks not beyond the act itself. But the Court of Chancery is not so circumscribed. If the guilt appear from circumstances, the court will relieve against the wrong, by decreeing satisfaction to the personal creditors out of the real estate.

Fifth, A process at common law reacheth no man but within the jurisdiction. If a debtor, therefore, be in foreign parts, a judgment cannot pass against him, because he cannot be cited to appear in court; and execution cannot be issued against his effects without a judgment. This defect, which interrupts the course of justice, is in Scotland remedied by a citation at the market-cross of Edinburgh, pier and shore of Leith, introduced by the sovereign court, acting upon the foregoing principle, That where there is a right, it ought to be made effectual. In England, a person abroad cannot be cited to appear even in the Court of Chancery. This Court, however, affords a remedy. It will not warrant a citation against any person who is not within the jurisdiction of the court, but it will appoint notice to be given to the debtor; and if he appear not in his own defence, the court will out of his effects decree satisfaction to the creditor. Thus, upon an affidavit that the defendant was gone into Holland to avoid the plaintiff's demand against him, and he having been arrested on an attachment, and a

286 LEGAL EXECUTION. B. 1.

cepi corpus returned by the sheriff, the Court of Chancery granted a sequestration of the real and personal estate.* By virtue of the same power supplying the defects of common law, the Court of Session gives authority to attach moveables in this country belonging to a foreigner, in order to convert them into money for payment to the creditor who applies for the attachment. And as the foreigner cannot be cited to appear in the Court of Session, notice will be appointed to be given him, that he may appear if he think proper. Where a debtor, lurking somewhere in Scotland, cannot be discovered, the Court of Session makes no difficulty to order him to be cited at that head borough with which he appears to have the greatest connection.

ART. III. *These executions are in some cases imperfect.*

THE executions of common law, even where there is sufficiency of effects, fall sometimes short of the end proposed by them, that of operating payment. I give for example the English writ *Elegit*, that which corresponds the nearest to our adjudication. The chief difference is, that an *Elegit* is a legal security only, and transfers not the property to the creditor. Hence it follows, that though the interest of the debt exceed the rent of the land, the creditor must be satisfied with the possession ; and hath no means at common law to obtain payment of his capital, or in place of it to obtain the property of the land. But as in this case, the execution is obviously imperfect, hurting the

* 1. Vernon 344.

creditor without benefiting the debtor, the Court of Chancery will supply the defect, by ordering the land to be sold for payment of the debt.

ART. IV. *They serve only to make debts effectual, and give no aid to other claims.*

BESIDE for payment of debt, execution sometimes is necessary for making other claims effectual; and here also the common law is imperfect. To remedy this imperfection, adjudications in implement, declaratory adjudications, &c. were in Scotland invented by the sovereign court. The following case shews the necessity of a declaratory adjudication.

Sir Robert Munro, debtor to Andrew Drummond, banker, assigned to John Gordon, " in trust, and for " the use of the said Andrew Drummond," certain subjects, and, in particular, an adjudication led by him against Mackenzie of Redcastle's estate. After Gordon's death, Andrew Drummond, upon this adjudication, as his title, brought a process of mails and duties against the tenants of Redcastle. The objection was, That the pursuer, having no conveyance from Gordon, has no title to carry on this process. The judges agreed upon the following propositions: 1st, That the trust being given to John Gordon only, and not to his heirs, was at an end by his death; for there cannot be a trust without a trustee. 2d, That Sir Robert Munro being divested by the trust-deed, the adjudication returns not to him by the death of the trustee. 3d, That though the person for whom the trust is created may, in his own name, insist in every personal action flowing from the trust, yet none

288   LEGAL EXECUTION.   B. I.

but the trustee can insist in any real action founded on the adjudication; because the trustee only is vested in it. These points being settled, the difficulty was, to find out a legal method for establishing the adjudication in the person of Andrew Drummond; and the judges came all into the following opinion, That Andrew Drummond's only method was, to raise a declaratory adjudication, calling all parties that may appear to have interest, namely, the representatives of John Gordon, and of Sir Robert, and concluding, that the adjudication thus left *in medio* should be adjudged to him, in order to make effectual the purposes of the trust. This can be done by the Court of Session supplying defects in common law. An action was competent to Andrew Drummond against John Gordon himself, to denude of the adjudication; and the declaratory adjudication comes in place of that action.*

The common law is defective with respect to those who are *in meditatione fugæ*, in order to avoid payment of their debts; but a court of equity lends a helping hand, by granting warrant for seizing the debtor, and incarcerating him, unless he find bail for his appearance. But this is not done rashly, upon the naked complaint of the creditor. He is bound first to give evidence of his debt: he is bound next to explain the reasons of his suspicion; and if these be found groundless, or no sufficient cause of suspicion, the warrant will be refused: he is bound to give his oath of credulity, that he verily believes his debtor to be *in meditatione fugæ*. And, in the last place, he is bound to give security for damages, in

---

* Andrew Drummond *contra* Mackenzie of Redcastle, June 30, 1758.

P. I. 8.   LEGAL EXECUTION.   289

case of wrongous detention.* Damages will be awarded accordingly, if upon trial it be found, either that his claim of debt was groundless, or that he fail to prove the facts alleged by him to justify his suspicion of a *meditatio fugæ*.

SECT. II.

Where the common law with respect to execution is oppressive or unjust.

EXECUION for payment of debt is the operation of the judge or magistrate, interposing in behalf of a creditor to whom the debtor refuses or neglects to do justice. It is the duty of a debtor to convert his effects into money in order to pay his debts; and if he prove refractory or be negligent, it is the duty of the judge to interpose, and, in his stead, to do what he himself ought to have done.† Hence it appears, that the judge ought not to authorise execution against any subject which the debtor himself is not bound to surrender to his creditors. But a court of common law, confined by general rules, regards no circumstance but one singly, Whether the subject belong to the debtor: if it be his property, execution issues; and it is not considered whether it would be just in the debtor to apply this subject for payment of his debts. A man who, by fraud or other illegal means, has acquired the property of a subject, is not bound to convey that subject to his creditors: on the contrary, he is in conscience bound to restore it to the

* See act of sederunt, Dec. 16, 1613.
† Historical law-tracts, tract 12, at the beginning.

T

LEGAL EXECUTION.

person injured, in order to repair the wrong he has done. And in such a case, a court of law ought not to interpose in behalf of the creditors, but in behalf of the person injured. A court of equity, accordingly, correcting the injustice of common law, will refuse its aid to the creditors, who ought not to demand from their debtor what in conscience he ought to restore to another; and will give its aid to that other for recovering a subject of which he was unjustly deprived.

Having thus given a general view of the subject, I proceed to particulars; and shall first state a case, where a merchant, in immediate prospect of bankruptcy, purchases goods and takes delivery without any view of paying the price. This is a gross cheat in the merchant, which binds him in common justice to restore the goods. A court of common law, however, regardless of that circumstance, will authorise the bankrupt's creditors to attach these goods for their payment, as being his property. This act of injustice ought to be redressed by a court of equity: if the goods be claimed by the vender, the court of equity, barring execution by the creditors, will decree the goods to be restored to him. Thus, a reduction upon the head of the cheat mentioned, was sustained against the bankrupt's creditors, arresting the subject purchased in the hands of the person to whom it was delivered for behoof of the purchaser.* Mrs. Rolland obtained a *cessio bonorum*, anno 1748, and began again to trade as formerly. In the year 1749, she purchased a cargo of wine from Main and Company

---

* Stair, Fountainhall, December 22, 1680, Prince *contra* Pallat; Dalrymple, Bruce, January 18, 1715, Main *contra* Maxwell; December 8, 1736, Sir John Inglis *contra* Royal Bank.

P. I. 8.   LEGAL EXECUTION.   291

in Lisbon. She commissioned another cargo from them, May 1750, which was arrested at Leith by one of her creditors, against whom she had obtained the *cessio bonorum.* The venders appeared in the forthcoming, and were preferred to the cargo for payment of the price, upon the following medium, That it was fraudulent in Mrs. Rolland to commission goods from her foreign correspondents, when she must have been conscious that they would not have trusted her had they been informed of the *cessio.**

The same must hold with respect to land, when purchased fraudulently: when the purchaser's creditor commences his adjudication, the vender will be admitted for his interest, and the following objection will be sustained in equity, " That the land ought " not to be adjudged to the creditor, but restored to " him, the vender, to repair the wrong done him." I put another case. In a process of adjudication, a man who had purchased the land by a minute of sale before the adjudication was commenced, appears for his interest: ought he not to be preferred? His objection against the adjudger appears good in two respects: it would, in the first place, be unjust in the proprietor to grant to his creditor a security upon that subject; and it is, therefore, unjust in the creditor to demand the security by legal execution: in the next place, it would be unjust in the court to authorise execution against a subject which the debtor is not bound to surrender to his creditors; but, on the contrary, is strictly bound to convey it in terms of the minute of sale.

I illustrate this doctrine by applying it to a subject of some importance that has been frequently canvas-

* Andrew Forbes *contra* Main and Company, Feb. 25, 1752.

LEGAL EXECUTION. B. I.

sed in the Court of Session. A factor having sold
his constituent's goods, took the obligation for the
price in his own name, without mentioning his constituent. The factor having died bankrupt, the
question arose, Whether the sum in this obligation was to be deemed part of his moveable
estate affectable by his creditors; or whether he
was to be deemed a nominal creditor only, and a
trustee for his constituent. The common law, regarding the words only, considers the obligation as
belonging to the deceased factor: but equity takes
under consideration the circumstances of the case,
which prove that the obligation was intended to be
taken *factorio nomine*, or ought to have been so intended; and that the factor's creditors are in equity
barred from attaching a subject which he was bound
to convey to his constituent. The constituent was
accordingly preferred.* A employs B as his factor
to sell cloth. B sells on credit, and, before the money
is paid, dies bankrupt. This money shall be paid to
A, and not to the administrator of B: for a factor is
in effect a trustee only for his principal.† Hugh
Murray, named executor in Sir James Rochead's testament, appointed a factor to act for him. At clear-
ing accounts there was a balance of £268 sterling in
the hands of the factor, for which he granted bill to
Murray, his constituent, and of the same date obtained from him a discharge of the factory. Murray,
the executor, having died insolvent, the said bill, as
belonging to him, was confirmed by his creditors.
Sir James's next of kin claimed the sum in the bill

* Stair, June 9, 1669, Street *contra* Home. The like, Forbes,
March 15, 1707, Hay *contra* Hay.
† 2. Vernon, 638.

P. I. 8.   LEGAL EXECUTION.   293

as part of his executry, or as the produce of it. They urged, That though the bill was taken payable to Murray singly, yet the circumstances of the case evince, that it was taken payable to him in quality of executor, and that he was bound to account for it to Sir James's next of kin. They accordingly were preferred.* For the same reason, if an executor, instead of receiving payment, take a new bond from a debtor of the deceased with a cautioner, and discharge the original bond, this new bond, being a *surrogatum* in place of the former, will be considered in equity as part of the effects of the deceased : and will not be affectable by the creditors of the executor.† And if the debt be lost by the bankruptcy of the debtor and his cautioner, equity will not charge the executor with it, but will only decree him to assign the security.‡ Boylstoun having given money to one Makelwood to buy a parcel of linen-cloth for him, she bought the goods, but without mentioning her employer. Her creditors having arrested these goods, Boylstoun appeared for his interest. The vender deposed, that he understood Makelwood to be the purchaser for her own behoof. She deposed upon the commission from Boylstoun, and that with this money she bought the cloth for his behoof. The court, in respect that the goods being sold to Makelwood for her own behoof, became her property, therefore preferred her creditors the arresters.§ This was acting as a court of common law. The property no doubt vested in Makelwood, because the goods were sold and delivered to her for her own behoof : but

---

* January 4, 1744, Sir John Baird *contra* Creditors of Murray.
† Stair, book 3, tit. 8, § 71.   ‡ 1. Chancery cases, 74.
§ Stair, January 24, 1672, Boylstoun *contra* Robertson.

that circumstance is far from being decisive in point of equity. It ought to have been considered, that though the transference of property be ruled by the will of the vender, yet that it depends on the will of the purchaser whether to accept delivery for his own behoof or for behoof of another. Here it clearly appeared, that Makelwood bought the goods for behoof of Boylstoun ; and that, in effect, she was trustee only in the subject : the legal right was indeed in her, but the equitable right clearly in Boylstoun. It ought to have been considered further, that Makelwood having laid out Boylstoun's money in purchasing the cloth, was bound in justice to deliver the cloth to Boylstoun ; and therefore, that he in equity ought to have been preferred to her creditors, even though she had been guilty of making the purchase for her own behoof.

Such is the relief that, by a court of equity, is afforded to the person who has the equitable claim, while matters are entire, and the subject *in medio*. But now, supposing the execution to be completed, and the property to be transferred to the creditor ignorant of any claim against his debtor, as, for example, by a poinding or by an adjudication with a decree declaring the legal to be expired ; what shall be the operation of equity in that case ? In answer to this question, it holds in general without a single exception, That a *bona fide* purchaser lies not open to a challenge in equity more than at common law ; because no man can be deprived of his property except by his consent or his crime.

I proceed to another branch of the subject. Execution, both personal and real, for payment of debt, is afforded by the law of all countries : but execution in-

P. I. 8.   LEGAL EXECUTION.   295

tended against the refractory only, is sometimes extended beyond the bounds of humanity ; and equity is interposed against rigorous creditors, where it can be done by some rule that is applicable to all cases of the kind.   Two rules have been discovered, which judges may safely apply without hazard of becoming arbitrary.   The first governs those cases where there is such a peculiar connection between the debtor and creditor, as to make kindness or benevolence their reciprocal duty.   In such cases, if the creditor carry his execution to extremity, and deprive the debtor of bread, he acts in contradiction to his positive duty, and a court of equity will interpose to prevent the wrong.   The rule is, That a competency must be left to the debtor to preserve him from indigence.   Thus, in the Roman law, parents have *beneficium competentiæ* against their children, and a patron against his client ;* a man against his wife ;† and the same obtains in an *actio pro socio.*‡   The rule was applied by the Court of Session to protect a father against his children, February 21, 1745, Bontein of Mildovan, where two former decisions on the other side were overruled.   The common law, in affording execution against a debtor, intends not to indulge the rigour of creditors, acting in direct contradiction to their duty. But as, in making laws, it is impracticable to foresee every limitation, the rule must be made general, leaving to a court of equity to make exceptions in singular cases.

The other rule is more general, and still more safe in the application.   Personal execution was contrived to force the debtor, by the terror and hardship

* L. 17, De re judicata.   † § 37, Instit. de actionibus.
‡ L. 16, De re judicata.

296　　LEGAL EXECUTION.　　**B. I.**

of personal restraint, to discover his effects, and to do justice to his creditors. But if the *squalor carceris*, a species of torture, cannot draw a confession of concealed effects, the unhappy prisoner must be held innocent; and upon that supposition, personal restraint is no less inconsistent with justice than with humanity. Hence the foundation of the *cessio bonorum*, by which the debtor, after his innocence is proved by the torture of personal restraint, recovers his liberty, upon conveying to his creditors all his effects. And in Scotland this action was known as far back as we have any written law.

APPENDIX to Chap. VIII.

WHEN a creditor leads an adjudication for a greater sum than is due, it is held, that, at common law, the adjudication is totally void. The reason given is, That an adjudication, being an indivisible right, cannot subsist in part, and fall in part. At the same time it is admitted, that where the *pluris petitio* is occasioned by an innocent error, without any *mala fides* in the creditor, the adjudication ought to be supported as a security for what is justly due, not only in accounting with the debtor, but even in a competition with co-creditors; and that, in fact, it receives this support from the Court of Session, acting as a court of equity. If this be the true foundation of the practice, it belongs to the present chapter; being an example of equity correcting the rigour of common law with respect to execution.

But that this practice cannot be founded on equity, appears to me clear from the following considera-

P. I. 8.   LEGAL EXECUTION.   297

tions. In the first place, it is made evident above, than one *certans de damno evitando* may take advantage of an error committed by another; and that equity prohibits not such advantage to be taken, except where positive gain is made by it.* This rule is applicable to the present case. A creditor demanding his payment in a competition, is *certans de damno evitando*: and that, in order to obtain preference, he may lawfully avail himself of an error committed by a co-creditor; and, consequently, that to support a void adjudication against him, is not agreeable to any rule of equity. In the next place, an adjudication *ex facie* null, as proceeding without citing the debtor, is not supported to any effect whatever, either against a competing creditor, or even against the debtor himself. Nor is there any support given to an adjudication against an apparent heir, when it proceeds without a special charge, or where the lands are not specified in the special charge. This leads me to reflect upon the difference between intrinsic objections, which render the adjudication void and null, and intrinsic objections, which only tend to restrict it. If the *pluris petitio* be an objection of the former sort, the adjudication, being void totally at common law, cannot be supported in equity, more than an adjudication that proceeds without calling the debtor: if it be an objection of the latter sort, there may possibly be a foundation at common law for supporting the adjudication in part, even against a competing creditor, though there be no foundation in equity. The question then is, To which class this objection belongs?

Intrinsic objections, generally speaking, resolve

* See *suprá*, p. 141.

298   LEGAL EXECUTION.   B. I.

into an objection of want of power. A judge, unless the debtor be called into court, cannot adjudge his land to his creditor; and if he proceed without that solemnity, he acts *ultra vires*, and the adjudication is void. The case is the same, where an adjudication is led against an apparent heir, without charging him to enter to the estate of his ancestor. To determine what must be the effect of a *pluris petitio*, an adjudication shall be considered in two lights; first, as a judicial sale, and next as a *pignus prætorium*. If a man voluntarily give off land to his creditor for satisfaction of £1,000, understood at the time to be due, though the debt be really but £900, the sale is not void; nor is it even voidable. The property is fairly transferred to the creditor, of which he cannot be forfeited when he is guilty of no fault; and all that remains is, that the *quondam* creditor, now proprietor, be bound to make good the difference. A judicial sale of land for payment of debt, stands precisely on the same footing: it cannot be voided upon account of a *pluris petitio* more than a voluntary sale. I illustrate this doctrine, by comparing an adjudication considered as a judicial sale, with a poinding, which is really a judicial sale. A man poinds his debtor's moveables for payment of £100, and the poinding is completed by a transference of these moveables to the creditor, for satisfaction of the debt. It is afterward discovered, that £90 only was due. Will this void the execution, and restore the goods to the debtor? No person ever dreamed that an innocent *pluris petitio* can have such effect with respect to a poinding. By the original form of this execution, the debtor's goods were exposed to public auction, and the price was delivered to the creditor

LEGAL EXECUTION.

in payment *pro tanto* : the purchaser surely could not be affected by any dispute about the extent of the debt; and the result must be the same where the goods are adjudged to the creditor for want of another purchaser. With regard to all legal effects, he is held the purchaser, and is in reality so ; and if it shall be found that the execution has proceeded for a greater sum than was really due, this circumstance will found a personal action to the *quondam* debtor, but by no means a *rei vindicatio*.

But too much is said upon an adjudication considered as a judicial sale ; for during the legal at least, it is not a judicial sale, but a *pignus prætorium* only ; and this I have had occasion to demonstrate above.* If a man shall grant to his creditor real security for £1,000 when in reality £900 is only due, will this *pluris petitio* void the infeftment? There is not the least pretext for such a consequence : the sum secured will indeed be restricted, but the security stands firm and unshaken. It will be evident at first glance, that the same must be the case of an adjudication led innocently for a greater sum than is due : a *pignus prætorium* must, with respect to the present point, be precisely of the same nature with a voluntary pledge.

Hence it clearly appears, that the sustaining an adjudication for what is truly due, notwithstanding a *pluris petitio*, is not an operation of equity, to have place regularly in the present treatise ; but truly an operation of common law, which sustains not a *pluris petitio* to any other effect than to restrict the sum secured to what is truly due, without impinging upon the security. And this was the opinion of the court, given in the case of the creditors of Easterfearn, 6th

* See *suprà*, p. 274.

300 LEGAL EXECUTION. B. I.

November 1747, engrossed in Lord Kilkerran's collection. An adjudication was objected to upon a most dishonest *pluris petitio*. The adjudication, however, was sustained as a security for the sum truly due. Equity could afford no aid to such an adjudication. What the court went upon was, That at common law a *pluris petitio* is not sufficient to annul a right in security, but only to restrict it. This is not a vain dispute; for, beside resting the point upon its true foundation, which always tends to instruction, it will be found to have considerable influence in practice. At present, an adjudication, where there is a *pluris petitio*, is never supported against competing creditors further than to be a security for the sums due in equity, striking off all penalties: and this practice is right, supposing such adjudication to be null at common law, and to be supported by equity only. But, if a *pluris petitio* have not the effect at common law to void the adjudication, but only to restrict the sum secured, there is no place for striking off the penalties, more than where there is no *pluris petitio*. Equity, indeed, interposes to restrict penalties to the damage that the creditor can justly claim by delay of payment; but this holds in all adjudications equally, not excepting those that are free of all objections.

That it is lawful for one *certans de damno evitando* to take advantage of another's error, is an universal law of nature; that it has place in covenants, is shown in a former chapter; and that it should have place among creditors, is evidently agreeable to justice, which dictates, that if there must be a loss, it ought to rest upon the creditor who hath been guilty of some error, rather than upon the creditor

P. I. 8.   LEGAL EXECUTION.   301

who hath avoided all error. When matters of law are taken in a train, and every case is reduced to some principle, judges seldom err. What occasions so many erroneous judgments, is the being swayed by particular circumstances in every new case, without thinking of recurring to principles or general rules. By this means we are extremely apt to go astray, carrying equity sometimes too far, and sometimes not far enough. Take the following remarkable instance.—Among the creditors of the York-Buildings Company, a number of annuitants for life, infeft for their security, occupied the first place; and next in order came the Duke of Norfolk, infeft for a very large sum. These annuities were frequently bought and sold; and the purchasers, in some instances, instead of demanding a conveyance of the original bonds secured by infeftment, returned these to the company, and took new personal bonds in their stead, not imagining, that by this method the real security was unhinged. These new bonds being objected to by the Duke of Norfolk, as merely personal, and incapable to compete with his infeftment, the court pronounced the following interlocutor:—" In " respect that the English purchasers, ignorant of " the laws of Scotland, had no intention to pass from " their real security ; and that the Duke of Norfolk, " who had suffered no prejudice by the error, ought " not to take advantage of it ; therefore, find the " said annuitants preferable, as if they had taken as-" signments to the original bonds, instead of deliver-" ing them up to the company." This was stretching equity beyond all bounds ; and, in effect, judging that a creditor is barred by equity from taking advantage of any error committed by a co-creditor.

302　　　LEGAL EXECUTION.　　　B. I.

Upon a reclaiming petition, the interlocutor was altered, and the Duke of Norfolk preferred.* And this judgment was affirmed in the House of Lords.

CHAP. IX.

Power of a court of equity to inflict punishment, and to mitigate it.

IT is an inviolable rule of justice, as well as of expediency, That no man be allowed to reap the fruits of his fraud, nor to take benefit by any wrong he has done. If, by the tortious act, another be hurt in his rights or privileges, there is ground for reparation at common law; which subject is handled in the beginning of this work. But wrong may be done without impinging upon any right or privilege of another; and such wrongs can only be redressed in a court of equity, by inflicting punishment in proportion to the offence. In slight offences, it is satisfied with forfeiting the wrong-doer of his gain: in grosser offences, it not only forfeits the gain, but sometimes inflicts a penalty over and above. I begin with cases of the first kind.

A man having two estates, settles them upon John and James, his two sons. John discovering, accidentally, a defect in his father's titles, to the estate settled on James, acquires a preferable title, and claims that estate from his brother. This palpable transgression, not only of gratitude, but of filial affection, was never committed by any person with a

* Feb. 14, 1752, Duke of Norfolk *contra* Annuitants of the York-Buildings Company.

quiet mind; and yet, upon the principles of common law, this odious man must prevail. But a court of equity will interpose, and bar him from taking any benefit from this immoral act, by limiting his claim to the sum laid out upon the purchase.

If a gratuitous disposition be granted with a proviso that the disponee shall perform a certain fact, his acceptance of the disposition subjects him at common law to performance. But let us suppose, that a man makes a settlement of his estate, burdening his heir with a legacy to a certain person named; and that afterward, in a separate deed, he appoints that person to be tutor to his children. Here the legacy being given without any condition, is due at common law, whether the legatee undertake the tutory or not. But every one must be sensible, that it is an act of ingratitude in the legatee to decline the trust reposed in him, and that he is in conscience bound either to undertake the tutory or to surrender the legacy. If, therefore, he be so unjust as to claim the legacy without undertaking the trust, a court of equity will punish him with the loss of his legacy.* Many examples of the same kind are found in the Roman law. A *libertus* claiming a legacy left him by his patron, will be removed *personali objectione*, or *exceptione doli* in the language of the Roman law, if he have been guilty of ingratitude to his patron; even where the act of ingratitude is otherwise laudable, as where, after the death of the patron, the *libertus* informed against him as a smuggler.† But the connection between a master and his manumitted slave was so intimate, as to make a step of this kind

---

* See Dirleton, 16th June 1675, Thomson *contra* Ogilvie.

† L. 1. De his quæ ut indign.

304 PUNISHMENT. B. I.

to be reckoned highly ungrateful. Again, a legatee who conceals a testament in order to disappoint it, is, for his ingratitude to the testator, removed *personali objectione* from claiming his legacy.* I shall add but one other example : " Meminisse autem oporte-
" bit, eum, qui testamentum inofficiosum improbè
" dixit, et non obtinuit, id quod in testamento acci-
" pit perdere, et id fisco vindicari quasi indigno ob-
" latum. Sed ei demum aufertur quod testamento
" datum est, qui usque ad sententiam, lite improba,
" perseveraverit : cæterum, si ante sententiam desti-
" tit vel decessit, non ei aufertur quod datum est."†

When a man is thus forfeited of a good claim, the question is, What becomes of the subject claimed ; whether doth it accrue to the fisk as *bona vacantia*, or is it left with the person against whom the claim is laid ? Ulpian, in the text last cited, gives his opinion for the fisk ; thinking probably that the legacy becomes a subject without a proprietor ; and that if no person can claim, it must go to the fisk. Paulus takes the other side : " Amittere id quod testa-
" mento meruit, et eum, placuit, qui tutor datus ex-
" cusavit se a tutela. Sed hoc legatum, quod tutori
" denegatur, non ad fiscum transfertur, sed filio relin-
" quitur cujus utilitates desertæ sunt."‡ And this seems to be the more solid opinion. The legatee is not guilty of any wrong with respect to the crown, but only with respect to the testator and his heir. Nor can the legacy be ranked *inter bona vacantia* ; for the legatee continues proprietor, and is only barred from the use of his property by an exception competent to the heir, not against the legatee's right,

* L. 25. C. De legatis.   † L. 8. § 14. De inoff. test.
‡ L. 5. § 2. De his quæ ut indign.

P. I. 9. PUNISHMENT. 305

but only to defend himself against payment. There is an additional reason for this defence against payment, which is, that the heir should have some compensation as a *solatium* for that distress of mind he must feel, when treated ill by those who owed gratitude to his father or ancestor. In our law, accordingly, the heir is relieved from the legacy.

But supposing both parties equally criminal, Ulpian's opinion upon that supposition seems to be well founded. I give for an example an obligation granted *ob turpem causam*, paid and discharged. Here both parties are equally guilty ; and hence the maxim in the Roman law, *Quod in turpi causa potior est conditio possidentis ;* meaning that the obligee is barred *personali objectione* from demanding payment ; and that if payment be made, the *quondam* obligor is equally barred from claiming restitution. This maxim may hold between the parties ; but not against the fisk.

Stellionate, which consists in' aliening to different persons the same subject, is a crime punishable by statute.* I sell my land to John by a minute of sale. I sell it a second time to James, who is first infeft. If James was ignorant of my bargain with John, his purchase will stand good in equity as well as at common law ; because he made a lawful purchase, and had no intention to hurt John. But what shall be the consequence, supposing James, when he made his purchase, to have been in the knowledge of my bargain with John ? It will make no difference at common law, which only considers that James is preferable by his first infeftment, and that John is not more

* Act 105, parl. 1540.

U

306 PUNISHMENT. B. I.

hurt than if his bargain had been unknown to James. But it was a tortious act in James to receive from me what I could not lawfully give ; and he is punished for the tortious act by voiding his purchase. Thus, if A, having notice that lands were contracted to be sold to B, purchase these lands, such purchase will be voided in equity.* Again, in a case of two purchasers of the same land in Yorkshire, where the second purchaser, having notice of the first purchase, and that it was not registered, went on and purchased, and got his purchase registered, it was decreed, that the first purchaser was preferable. † A, who purchased land, though he knew that the vender was but tenant for life, and that the property was in his son, sold the land afterward to B, who had no notice of the settlement. Upon a bill brought by the son after the death of his father against A and B, it was decreed, That as to B, who was purchaser without notice, the bill should be dismissed ; but that A should account for the purchase-money he received, with interest from the death of the tenant for ‡ life. (a)

* Abridg. cases in equity, chap. 42, sect. A, § 1.

† Ibid. chap. 47, sect. B, § 12.

‡ Abridg. cases in equity, chap. 42, sect. A, § 5.

(a) From this and other similar cases, contained in the Chancery Reports, one would imagine it to be a rule established in England, that a *bona fide* purchaser, even from a person who has no right, is secure in equity. But if such purchaser be secure, it cannot be upon any principle in equity ; for equity forfeits no man of his property, unless he be guilty of some wrong; and though a *bona fide* purchase be an equitable title, the title of the true proprietor claiming his subject is no less so. If a *bona fide* purchaser, from a person who has no right, be preferred before the former proprietor, this preference can have no foundation but the common law. That such was once the common law, is certain, *Historical law-tracts, tract* 3 : and, from the decrees above

PUNISHMENT.

Next, of conveying a subject attached by inchoated execution. The conveying a subject, thus legally attached, is not stellionate, because it comes not under the. definition of granting double rights. But the disponer is guilty of a moral wrong, in attempting to disappoint his creditor, by withdrawing the subject from his execution, to which wrong the purchaser is accessory, if he had notice of the execution ; and, for that reason, though the purchaser's title be first completed, he will be postponed to the creditor in a court of equity, as a punishment. Thus, the porteur of a bill of exchange, having indorsed the same for ready money, after it was attached by an arrestment, laid in the hands of the acceptor, the arrestor was preferred before the indorsee, for the reason above mentioned, that the latter, when he took the indorsation, was in the knowledge of the arrestment.* This lays open the foundation of a proposition established in practice, That inchoated execution renders the subject litigious. After an adjudication, for example, is commenced, it is wrong in the debtor to sell the land ; and it is wrong for any one to purchase.

We proceed to the case of a creditor, who, for his security, takes a conveyance to a subject, which he knows was formerly disponed to another for a valuable consideration. What pleads for this creditor's preference, is the necessity of providing for his security, when he cannot otherwise obtain payment. But the debtor is undoubtedly criminal in granting the security : he is guilty of stellionate, and the cre-

mentioned, it would appear, that the law of England continues the same to this day.

* June 1728, Competition between Logan and M'Caul.

ditor is accessory to the crime. This circumstance ought to bar him in equity from taking the benefit of his real security against the first disponee; for I hold it to be clear in principles, that the motive of preventing loss, is in no case a sufficient excuse for doing an unjust act, or for being accessory to it.

Such is the relief that is afforded to the equitable claim against a purchase made *malâ fide*. Let us now suppose, that a purchase is fairly made without notice, and that the property is transferred to the purchaser. I put a strong case, that a man is guilty of stellionate, by selling his land a second time, and that the second purchaser, ignorant of the other, obtains the first infeftment. To make the question of importance, let it also be supposed, that the price is paid by the first purchaser, and that the common author is now bankrupt. Some circumstances at first view, seem to weigh against the second purchaser: The common author is guilty of stellionate; and though the second purchaser is not accessory to the crime, he takes, however, the benefit of an iniquitous deed; which may be reckoned not altogether fair. But upon mature reflection, it will be found, that justice militates not against him. By obtaining the first infeftment, he becomes proprietor: and it only remains to be considered, whether there be any ground in equity or justice to forfeit him of his property. Such forfeiture cannot otherwise be just than as a punishment for a crime, and, therefore, it cannot be applied against the innocent. Hence, an inviolable rule of justice, That the innocent cannot be deprived of their property, unless by their own consent. By this rule, the second purchaser first infeft, is secure: he is secure by the common law, because he has the

PUNISHMENT.

first infeftment; and he is secure by equity, because, having purchased *bonâ fide*, he is innocent.

A is tenant in tail, remainder to his brother B in tail. A, not knowing of the entail, makes a settlement on his wife for life as a jointure, without levying a fine, or suffering a recovery. B, who knew of the entail, engrosses this settlement, but does not mention any thing of the entail; because, as he confessed in his answer, if he had spoken of it, his brother, by a recovery, might have cut off the remainder, and barred him. B, after the brother's death, recovered an ejectment against the widow by force of the entail. She was relieved in chancery; and a perpetual injunction granted for this wrong done by B in concealing the entail; for if the entail had been disclosed, the settlement would have been made good by a recovery.* The connection which B had with the parties, partly by blood, and partly by being employed to engross the settlement, made it his duty to inform them of the entail. And his wilful transgression of this duty was a moral wrong, which justly deprived him of the benefit he projected to himself by concealing the entail.

In a case that has some analogy to the foregoing, the Court of Session, as a court of equity, stretched their powers a great way further, further, I am persuaded, than can be justified. An heiress's infeftment upon a service to her predecessor, being, after her death, challenged in a reduction as null and void, with the view to disappoint her husband of his courtesy; the court decreed, That the heiress's infeftment not having been challenged till after her death, it was sufficient to support the courtesy, upon the following

* Proced. chan. 35. Raw *contra* Potts.

PUNISHMENT. B. I.

ground of equity, That had it been challenged during her life, the nullity might and would have been supplied.* One is prone to approve this judgment; and yet there appear unsurmountable difficulties. For, 1st, it is not said that the pursuer of the reduction was in the knowledge of these nullities during the life of his predecessor, the heiress. 2dly, What if they had been known to him? Can silence alone be considered as criminal, where there is no other connection but that of predecessor and successor?

In the foregoing instances, the ill-doer is deprived of the gain he made: in what follow, a punishment is inflicted upon him. A defendant, sued for his rent, deposed that he had no lease: being afterward sued to remove, he produced a current lease. He was barred *personali objectione* from founding any defence upon it.† Which in effect was forfeiting him of his lease as a punishment for his perjury. A man by adding a seal to a note, which is sufficient without a seal, was punished with the loss of his security.‡ And, accordingly, it is a rule, " That a wrongful ". manner of executing a thing shall void a matter " that might have been executed lawfully."§ A bond being vitiated in the sum by superinduction of pounds for merks, was not sustained for the original sum, but was found null *in totum.*‖ It is not clear what was the *ratio decidendi*; whether a penalty was intended for falsifying the bond, or whether the court

* June 1716, Hamilton *contra* Boswell.

† Maitland, 7th December 1563, Laird Innerquharitie *contra* Ogilvies.

‡ 2. Vern. 162.

§ New abridg. of the law, vol. 2, p. 594.

‖ November 26, 1723, Macdowal of Garthland *contra* Kennedy of Glenour.

P. I. 9. **PUNISHMENT.** **311**

meant only to refuse action upon a bond that was vi-tiated; which they might well do, because the word *pounds* was an evident vitiation, by being superinduced over another word that could not be known to be *merks* but by conjecture. The trying case would have been a reference to the defender's oath, that he really borrowed the sum originally contained in the bond. Would the Court of Session have refused to sustain this claim, yea or no? They could not have refused upon any footing but *per modum pœnæ*. The Court of Session denied action upon a bond that was purposely antedated in order to save it from an * inhibition.(a)

What is the legal effect of bribery in the election of a member to serve in parliament, or of magistrates to serve in boroughs? Common law, with respect to electors, considers only whether the man was entitled to vote, disregarding the motive that induced him to prefer one candidate before another; and, therefore,

* Durie, February 10, 1636, Edmonston *contra* Syme.

(a) This judgment has not a foot to stand upon but that of punishment; and yet the *ratio decidendi* was very different, if we can trust the compiler, namely, " Quia quod non est verum de " data quam præ se fert, præsumitur non esse omninò verum, nec " ullo tempore fuisse gestum." It is amusing to observe how well an argument passes in Latin, that would make but a shabby figure in English. But to judge well, and to give a solid reason for one's judgment, are very different talents. There is in the mind of man a disposition to let nothing pass without a reason; but that disposition is easily gratified, for, with the plurality, any thing in the form of a reason is sufficient. Mascardus, *de probationibus*, lays down the following rule :—" That a thousand witnesses, without " being put upon oath, afford not evidence in a court of justice." What is the reason given? It is, that numbers do not supply the want of an oath; which is no more but the same assertion in different words.

312   PUNISHMENT.   B. I.

this matter comes under a court of equity. And as
good government requires a freedom and independency in voting, a court of equity will set aside every
vote obtained by bribery; for the candidate who is
guilty of bribery, will not be permitted to benefit
himself by his crime: and even the candidate's own
vote is set aside, though not obtained by bribery, as
a punishment justly inflicted upon him for corrupt-
ing others.

By the common law of England, the wife's adultery did not deprive her of her dower, even though a
divorce had followed.* Upon this account the act
13° Edward I, cap. 34, was made, enacting, " That
" if a wife willingly leave her husband, and continue
" with her adulterer, she shall be barred for ever of
" her dower, unless her husband willingly, and with-
" out coercion of the church, be reconciled to her."
Elisabeth Clement, after living with her husband for
three months, deserted him, and lived in open adultery with another man, by whom she had a child.
Being cited before the kirk-session of Crieff, she confessed her guilt, and suffered public penance in presence of the congregation. After her husband's decease, she claimed from his representatives the third
part of his moveables, and the terce of his land. Her
claim was sustained, notwithstanding her adultery,
which was not denied. What moved the plurality
of the judges was, that since there was no divorce,
the pursuer's adultery did not deprive her of her
quality of relict, nor, consequently, of her legal provisions. This may be right at common law; but it
ought to have been considered, that a woman who
hath behaved so undutifully as a wife, is justly de-

* Coke, 2. Instit. p. 435.

P. I. 9.   PUNISHMENT.   313

prived of the privileges of a wife; and that she ought not to have the aid of a court of equity to make these privileges effectual. The English statute rests obviously upon this equitable foundation; and now that the principles of equity are ripened, the same ought to obtain with us without a statute.*

. A statutory penalty cannot be extended beyond the words; but it may be limited within the words, upon circumstances that infer innocence. Captain Forbes, who had no land in the shire of Cromarty, was, however, by act of parliament, appointed commissioner of supply for that shire, under the name and designation of " Captain John Forbes of New, factor " upon the annexed estate of Cromarty." A complaint being exhibited against him for acting as commissioner of supply, without having the qualification of £100 valued rent, the court judged, That he had no title to act. But in respect he had acted many years without challenge, *qua* factor, upon the said estate, as former factors had done, and in respect the objection against him was not clear, and, in a similar case, had been found by the court to be no objection, his *bona fides* was sustained to free him from the penalty. And yet, upon a reclaiming petition, this interlocutor was altered, and he was found liable for the penalty. The judges continued in their former opinion, that he acted *bonâ fide*; but the plurality thought that they had no power to mitigate the statutory penalty; which was in effect maintaining a very absurd proposition, That a punishment may be inflicted on an innocent person for an error in judgment. merely. The doctrine of *bona fides* will only hold in statutory penalties; for in a crime against the law of nature,

. * Elisabeth Clement *contra* Sinclair, 4th March 1762.

bona fides will never be supposed. And with respect to statutory penalties, many of them are enacted in terms so ambiguous, as to make it extremely doubtful in what cases the penalty is incurred. A man happens to mistake the statute : or rather, happens to judge differently from what is afterward found to be its meaning in a court of law : is it consistent with the rules of morality, or of common justice, to subject this innocent person to the penalty ?

Upon the same ground, a conventional penalty is equally subject to mitigation. But in that case, it is sometimes difficult to say, what is to be held a penalty, what not. Take the following instance. A proprietor lets a farm, two-thirds to be in grass ; but with liberty to the tenant to add to the corn part upon paying five shillings for each acre taken from grass. This paction has nothing penal in it. But what if, instead of five shillings, £50 be stipulated ? This cannot be called properly an oppressive bargain, because the tenant may keep free of it. Nor can it be oppressive in the landlord to afford his tenant an option, however unequal. But now suppose an express prohibition against adding to the corn part, and stipulating a penalty of £50 each acre in case of contravention. This penalty would undoubtedly be mitigated by the Court of Session ; and yet the two cases mentioned are fundamentally the same, differing in the form of words only.

PART II.

Powers of a court of equity to remedy the imperfections of common law with respect to matters of justice that are not pecuniary.

THE goods of fortune, such as admit an estimation in money, are the great source of controversy and debate among private persons. And, for that reason, when civil courts were instituted, it was not thought necessary to extend their jurisdiction beyond pecuniary matters : the improvement was indeed so great as to be held complete. But time unfolded many interesting articles that are not pecuniary. Some of them, making a figure, are distributed among different courts : a claim of peerage, for example, is determined in the House of Lords ; of bearing arms, in the Lyon Court ; and of being put upon the roll of freeholders in the court of Barons. Even after this distribution, there remain many rights established by law, and wrongs committed against law, that are not pecuniary ; which being left unappropriated, must be determined in a court of equity : for the great principles so often above mentioned, That where there is a right it ought to be made effectual, and where there is a wrong it ought to be repressed, are equally applicable, whether the interest be pecuniary or not pecuniary.

To collect all the rights established and wrongs committed that are not pecuniary, would be an endless labour : it would be useless as well as endless ; for the remedy is not at all intricate. The only question of difficulty is, In what courts such matters are to be tried ? and to this question no general answer

316 JUSTICE IN MATTERS B. I.

can be given, other than that the Chancery in England and Session in Scotland, are the proper courts, where there is no peculiar court established for determining the point in controversy. Take the following example. The qualifications of a man claiming to be a freeholder, must be judged by the freeholders of the county, convened at their Michaelmas head-court : but the law has provided no remedy for a wrong that may be committed by the freeholders, namely, their forbearing to meet at the Michaelmas head-court in order to prevent a man from applying to be put upon the roll ; and, therefore, it is incumbent upon the Court of Session to redress this wrong, by ordering the freeholders to meet under a penalty.

Two branches of law come under this part of the work, so extensive as to require different chapters. In the first is treated, how far a covenant or promise in favour of an absent person, is effectual. In the other, immoral acts that are not pecuniary.

CHAP. I.

How far a covenant or promise in favour of an absent person, is effectual.

I AM aware that the interest which arises to the absent from a promise or covenant, being commonly pecuniary, ought in strict form to have been handled above. But the interest of the person who obtains the obligation for behoof of the absent, is not pecuniary; and the connection of these different interests, arising from the same promise or covenant, makes it necessary that they should be handled together.

NOT PECUNIARY. 317

Promises and covenants are provided by nature for obliging us to be useful to others, beyond the bounds of natural duty. They are perfected by an act of the will, expressed externally by words or by signs. And they are binding by the very constitution of our nature, the moral sense dictating that every rational promise ought to be performed.

No circumstance shows more conspicuously our destination for society than the obligation we are laid under by our very nature to perform our promises and covenants. And to make our engagements the more extensively useful in the social state, we find ourselves bound in conscience, not only to those with whom we contract, but also to those for whose benefit the contract is made, however ignorant of the favour intended them. If John exact from me a promise to pay £100 to James, I stand bound in conscience to perform my promise. It is true, that the promise being made to John, it is in his power to discharge the same; and therefore, if he be silent, without requiring me to perform, my obligation is in the mean time suspended, waiting the result of his will. But as John's death puts an end to his power of relieving me from my obligation, the suspension is thereby removed, and from that moment it becomes my indispensable duty to pay the £100 to James.

The binding quality of a promise goes still farther. If I promise John to educate his children after his death, or to build a monument for him, conscience binds me also in this case: which is wisely ordered by the Author of our nature; for a man would leave this world discontented, if he could not rely upon the promises made to him of fulfilling his will after his death. And though my friend dies without an

318 JUSTICE IN MATTERS. B. I.

heir to represent him, I find myself, however, bound in conscience to execute his will. Here, then, comes out a singular case, an obligor without an obligee. And if it be demanded what compulsion I am under to perform, when a court of law cannot interpose unless there be an obligee to bring an action? the answer is, that I stand bound in conscience, as men were by a covenant before courts of law were instituted. Nor is this case altogether neglected by law. It is extremely probable, that a court of equity would compel me to execute the will of my deceased friend, upon a complaint brought by any of his relations, though they could not state themselves as obligees.

Such are the binding qualities of a promise, and of a covenant, by the law of our nature. We proceed to shew how far these qualities are supported by municipal law.

For a long period after courts of law were instituted, covenants and promises were left upon conscience, and were not enforced by any action. This in particular was the case among our Saxon ancestors: they did not give an action even upon buying and selling, though the most necessary of all covenants. The Romans were more liberal; and yet they confined their actions to a few covenants that are necessary in commerce. At the same time, the action given to enforce these covenants was confined within the narrowest bounds. In the first place, as only pecuniary interest was regarded, no action was given upon a covenant, unless the plaintiff could shew that it tended to his pecuniary interest.* And, accordingly, an action was denied upon a contract to pay a sum of money to a third person. In the next

* L. 38. § 17. De verborum oblig.

P. II. 1.   NOT PECUNIARY.   319

place, though that person had a pecuniary interest to have the contract performed, yet action was not given him : because, in the Roman law, no action was given upon a contract but to those who were parties to it.* And hence the noted Roman law maxim, *Quod alii per alium non acquiritur obligatio.*

But by confining the actions upon a covenant within so narrow bounds, many moral rights and obligations are left unsupported by law. The Roman law, in particular, is signally defective in denying support to any right but what terminates upon pecuniary interest. If I exact a promise in favour of a stranger, action for performance is denied me, it being held, that I am not interested to have it performed. Is the case the same where the promise is in favour of a friend, or of a distant relation? Perhaps it may. Let us then suppose the promise to be made in favour of my benefactor, or of my child, perhaps my heir. Have not I, to whom the promise was made, an interest to exact performance? No person of feeling can answer with confidence in the negative. Intricate questions of this kind lead to a general doctrine founded on human nature, That the accomplishment of every honest purpose is a man's interest. And, accordingly, in the affairs of this world, it is far from being uncommon to prefer the interest of ambition, of glory, of learning, of friendship, to that of money. This doctrine, by refinement of manners, prevails now universally. In the case stated, that I have an equitable interest to exact the promise in favour of my friend, is acknowledged ; and a court of equity will accordingly afford

---

* L. 11. De obligationibus et actionibus.

320 JUSTICE IN MATTERS B. I.

me an action to compel performance. But has my friend an action if I forbear to interpose? He has no action at common law, because the promise was not made to him. And as little has he an action in equity during my life; for the following reason, that it depends on me, to whom the promise was made, whether it shall be performed or not. It is in my power to pass from or discharge the promise made to me; and as this power continues for life, the obligor cannot be bound to pay to my friend, while it remains uncertain whether it may not be my will to discharge the obligation.*

I illustrate this doctrine by the following examples. I give to my servant money to be delivered to my friend as a gift, or to my creditor as payment. The money continues mine till delivery; and I have it in my choice to take it back, or to compel delivery. The friend or creditor has no action. He has not a real action, because the property of the money is not transferred to him: he has not a personal action, while it continues in my power to recal the money. If delivery be delayed, he will not naturally think of any remedy other than of making his complaint to me. Yet the Court of Session taught a very different doctrine in the following case. In a minute of sale of land, the purchaser was taken bound to pay the price to a creditor of the vender's: action was sustained to this creditor for payment to him of the price: though it was pleaded for the vender, That the pursuer not being a party to the minute of sale, no right could arise to him from it, and that the vender's mandate or order might be recalled by him at

* L. 3. De servis exportandis. L. 1. C. Si mancipium ita fuerit alienat.

P. II. 1. NOT PECUNIARY. 321

his pleasure.* But the court afterward determined more justly in the following cases, founded on the same principle. A proprietor having resigned his estate in favour of his second son and his heirs-male, with power to his eldest son and the heirs-male of his body to redeem; did afterward limit the power of redemption, that it should not be exercised unless with the consent of certain persons named; and empowering those persons to discharge the reversion altogether if they thought proper, which, accordingly, they did after the father's death. In a declarator at the instance of the second son to ascertain his right to the estate, it was objected by the eldest, That, by the settlement, he had a *jus quæsitum*, which could not be taken from him. The discharge was sustained. † Sir Donald Baine of Tulloch disponed his estate to his eldest son, John; and took from him bonds of provision in name of his younger children. It was found, that as these bonds were never delivered, it was in Sir Donald's power to discharge or cancel them at pleasure. ‡ The like was found 2d July 1755, Hill *contra* Hill.

To return to the case figured of a promise exacted by me in favour of an absent person. My death makes a total change, by giving him an action which he had not during my life; for if the obligor, who formerly was bound at my instance, remain still bound in conscience, as is made evident above, it follows, that the person in whose favour the promise was made, must be entitled to demand performance.

* Stair, July 7, 1664, Ogilvie *contra* Ker; Durie, January 9, 1627, Supplicants *contra* Nimmo.

† Fountainhall, Jan. 2, 1706, Dundas *contra* Dundas.

‡ July 6, 1717, Rose *contra* Baine of Tulloch.

X

322 JUSTICE IN MATTERS **B. I.**

This will readily be yielded where the paction is for a valuable consideration: if John give a sum to James, for which James promises to John, that he will build a house to William, James cannot both retain the money and refuse performance. The same must follow though the paction be gratuitous; for James is in conscience bound to perform his promise; and William, of course, must be entitled to demand performance.

From these premises it follows, that the man who thus makes a contract for the benefit of an absent person, may renounce his power of discharging the contract; which renunciation delivered, will instantly entitle that person to demand performance. Such renunciation may also be inferred *rebus et factis*. As for example, where a man dispones his estate to his eldest son, and takes from him a bond of provision to his younger children by name: while the bond is in the father's custody, it continues under his power; but if he deliver the bond to his children, he is understood to renounce his power, which will entitle them to demand payment.*

In the Roman law, a stipulation in favour of the heir was early made effectual, by sustaining an action to the heir.† By that law, a son might stipulate in favour of his father, and a slave in favour of his master. In the progress of equity, this privilege was further extended. Where a man stipulated in favour of his daughter, an *utilis actio* was given to the daughter, which is an action in equity.‡ Yet a daughter's paction in favour of her mother, did not avail the

---

* Dirleton, Nov. 20, 1667, Trotters *contra* Lundy.

† L. 38, § 12 & 14, De verborum oblig.

‡ L. 45, § 2, De verborum oblig.

mother.* A man's stipulation in favour of his grand-children profited them.† Where there was a *rei interventus*, an *utilis actio* was given to the absent person, whoever he was.‡ But among the Romans, a gratuitous stipulation in favour of a stranger never produced an action to the stranger.‖

The foregoing doctrine unfolds the nature of *fideicommissary* settlements among the Romans. Of these settlements, Justinian § gives the following history, That they were a contrivance to elude a regulation that rendered certain persons incapable of taking benefit by a testament; that it being in vain to settle upon such a person an estate by testament, another person was named heir, to whom it was recommended to settle the estate as intended; and that Augustus Cæsar gave here a civil action to make the settlement effectual. But did Augustus make effectual a settlement executed in defraud of the law? I can hardly be of that opinion. If the law was inexpedient, why not openly rescind it? Augustus was too wise a prince to set thus a public example of eluding law. Justinian, I suspect, did not understand the nature of these settlements. It was a maxim in the Roman law, derived from the nature of property, That a man cannot name an heir to succeed to his heir.¶ Because this could not be done directly, it was attempted indirectly by a *fideicommissary* settlement: I name my heir regularly in my testament, and I or-

---

* L. 26, § 4, De pactis dotal.
† L. 7, C. De pactis conven.
‡ L. 3, C. De donat. quæ sub modo.
‖ § 4, Instit. de inutil. stipul.
§ § 1, Inst. de fideicommiss. hæred.
¶ See Historical law-tracts, tract 3.

JUSTICE IN MATTERS

der him to make a testament in favour of the person I incline should succeed him. Such settlements did at first depend entirely on the faith of the heir in possession, who, upon that account, was termed *Hæres fiduciarius*: the person appointed to succeed him, termed *Hæres fideicommissarius*, had not an action at common law to compel performance; for the fiduciary heir was not bound to him, but to the testator solely. But here was a *rei interventus*, a subject in the hands of the fiduciary heir, which, by accepting the testament, he bound himself to settle upon the *fideicommissary* heir; and he is, therefore, bound in conscience to settle it accordingly. The *fideicommissary* heir has, beside, an equitable claim to the subject, founded on the will of the testator. These things considered, it appears to me plain, that Augustus Cæsar, with respect to such settlements, did no more but supply a defect in common law, by appointing an action to be sustained to the *fideicommissary* heir.

What is just now said, serves to explain the nature of trusts, where a subject is vested in a trustee for behoof of a third party; the children *nascituri* of a marriage, for example. A trust of this nature, analogous to a *fideicommissary* settlement among the Romans, comes not under the cognizance of a court of common law; because the person in whose favour the trust is established, not being a party to the agreement, has not at common law an action to oblige the trustee to fulfil his engagement: but he hath an action in equity as above mentioned. And hence it is, that in England such trusts must be made effectual in the Court of Chancery.

Reviewing what is said above, I am in some pain about an objection that will readily occur against it.

P. II. 1.　　NOT PECUNIARY.　　325

A legatee, by the common law of the Romans, had an action against the heir for performance; and yet a legatee is not made a party in the testament; nor is the heir, by accepting the testament, bound to him, but to the testator solely. To remove this objection, it will be necessary to give an account of the different kinds of legacies well known in the Roman law; and upon setting this subject in its true light, the objection will vanish. In the first place, where a legacy is left of a *corpus*, the property is transferred to the legatee *ipso facto* upon the testator's death, conformable to a general rule in law, That subjects are transferred from the dead to the living without necessity of delivery: for after the proprietor's death, there is no person who can make delivery; and if will alone, in this case, have not the effect to transfer property, it never can be transferred from the dead to the living. Upon that account, a legatee of a *corpus* has no occasion to sue the heir for delivery: he hath a *rei vindicatio* at common law. The next kind of legacy I shall mention, is where a bond for a sum of money is bequeathed directly to Titius. The subject here, as in the former case, vests in the legatee *ipso facto* upon the testator's death. The legatee has no occasion for an action against the heir; for in quality of creditor he has at common law an action against the debtor for payment. A third sort of legacy is, where the testator burdens his heir to pay a certain sum to Titius. This is the only sort, resembling a *fideicommissary* settlement, to which the maxim can be applied *Quod alii per alium non acquiritur obligatio*. But as an action at common law for making other legacies effectual was familiar, the influence of connection, without making nice distinctions, produced an action at common law for this sort also. Therefore, all that can be made of this instance, is to prove, what will appear in many instances, that common law and equity are not separated by any accurate boundary.

Our entails upon the common law are, in several respects, similar to the Roman *fideicommissary* settlements ; and so far are governed by the principles above established. I give the following instances. A man makes an entail in favour of his son or other relation, disponing the estate to. him, substituting a certain series of heirs, and reserving his own liferent. The institute, though fettered with irritant and resolutive clauses, is however, vested in the full property of the estate ;* and the substitutes, for the reason above given, have not an action at common law, to oblige the institute to make the entail effectual in their favour. But the institute resembles precisely. a Roman *hæres fiduciarius*, and is bound in equity to fulfil the will of the entailer, by permitting the substitutes to succeed in their order.

I give a second instance, in order to clear up a celebrated question often debated in the Court of Session, namely, Whether an entail, such as that above mentioned, after being completed with infeftment, can be altered or discharged even by the joint deed of the entailer and institute. Our lawyers have generally leaned to the negative. The institute, they urge, fettered by the entail, has not power to alter or discharge ; and the will of the entailer, who is not now proprietor, cannot avail. This reasoning is a mere sophism. The full property is vested in every tenant in tail, no less than in him who inherits a fee-simple.

* See Historical law-tracts, tract 5, toward the close.

P. II. 1.   NOT PECUNIARY.   327

A tenant in tail is indeed limited as to the exercise
of his powers of property : he must not alien, and
he must not alter the order of succession.   But
these, and such like limitations, proceed not from defect of power *qua proprietor*, but from being bound
personally, by acceptance of the entail, not to exercise these powers.* This distinction, with respect
to the present question, is of moment. A man cannot exercise any power beyond the nature of his
right : such an act is void, and every person is entitled to object to it. But no person, other than
the obligee, is entitled to object to the transgression
of a covenant or personal obligation. The entailer,
in the case stated, is the obligee : it is he who took
the institute bound to limit as above the exercise of
his property ; and he, therefore, has it in his choice
to keep the heir bound, or to release him from his
obligation. To be in a condition to grant such release, it is necessary indeed that he be obligee, but it
is not necessary that he be proprietor.

Hence it appears, that the substitutes have no title,
while the entailer is alive, to restrain the institute
from the free use of his property. They have no claim
personally against the institute ; who stands bound
to the entailer, not to them : nor have they any other
ground for an action, seeing the full property of the
estate is vested in the institute, and no part in them.
In a word, it depends entirely upon the entailer, during his life, whether the entail shall be effectual or no ;
and while that continues to be his privilege, the substitutes evidently can have no claim. Nay more, I
affirm, that the entailer cannot deprive himself of this

---

* This doctrine is more fully explained in tract 3, above cited.

privilege, even though he should expressly renounce it in the deed of entail. The substitutes are not made parties to the entail, and the renunciation, though in their favour, is not made to them. The renunciation is at best but a gratuitous promise, which none are entitled to lay hold of but that very person to whom it is made.

A great change indeed is produced by the entailer's death. There now exists no longer a person who can loose the fetters of the entail. The institute must for ever be bound by his own deed, restraining him from the free exercise of his property; and as the substitutes, by the entailer's will, have in their order an equitable claim to the estate, a court of equity will make this claim effectual.

But here a question naturally arises, Why ought not the entailer's privilege to discharge the fetters of the entail, descend to his heirs. The solid and satisfactory answer is what follows. No right or privilege descends to an heir, but what is pecuniary, and tends to make him *locupletior* : but the privilege of discharging the fetters of an entail makes not the heir *locupletior*, and, therefore, descends not to him.

Similar to the rule above explained, *Alii per alium non acquiritur obligatio*, is the following rule, *Alii per alium non acquiritur exceptio*. These rules, governed by the same principle, throw light upon each other, and ought, therefore, to be handled together. I obtain from a man a promise to discharge his debtor ; the question is, What shall be the effect of that promise ? The Roman lawyers answer, that I cannot have an action to compel performance, because I have no interest that performance should be made ; and that the debtor cannot have an action to compel

P. II. 1. NOT PECUNIARY. 329

performance, because he was not a party to the agreement.*

But the Roman writers were certainly guilty of an oversight in not distinguishing here a *pactum liberatorium* from a *pactum obligatorium*. Admitting the latter to be limited as above by the common law of the Romans; it can be made evident from the principles of that very law, that the former cannot be so limited, but must be effectual to him for whose behoof it is made, whether the person who obtained it be connected with him or no. The difference indeed with respect to the present point between these pactions, arises not from any difference in their nature, but from the nature of a court of law. Courts of law, as above mentioned, were originally circumscribed within narrow bounds; and with respect to the Roman courts in particular, many *pacta obligatoria* were left upon conscience unsupported by these courts. Such a constitution indeed confines courts within too narrow limits with respect to their power of doing good; but then it does not lead them to do any wrong. The case is very different with respect to *pacta liberatoria* : it is unjust in the creditor to demand payment, after he has promised, even gratuitously, to discharge the debt; and a court of law would be accessory to that act of injustice, if it sustained action after such a promise. The court, therefore, must refuse to sustain action; or rather must sustain the *pactum liberatorium* as a good exception to the action.† And it makes no difference, whether the person who obtained the promise be dead or alive. For while the promise subsists, it must bar the creditor from claiming pay-

---

* L. 17, § 4, De pactis.

† See Historical law-tracts, tract 2.

ment; and must bar every court from supporting such a claim. It is true, indeed, that while the person who obtained the promise is alive, it is in his power to discharge the promise; and, consequently, to entitle the creditor to an action: but, till that discharge be obtained, it would be unjust in any court to sustain action.

Some of the Roman writers, sensible that an action for payment ought not to be sustained to a creditor who has passed from his debt, endeavour to make this opinion consistent with the rule *Alii per alium non acquiritur exceptio*, by a subtilty that goes out of sight. They insist, that the debtor cannot found a defence upon a paction to which he was not a party: but they yield, that the paction, though not effectual to the debtor, is effectual against the creditor; and they make it effectual against him, by sustaining to the debtor an *exceptio doli*.[*]

Upon the same principle, if a third person pay a debt knowingly, and take a discharge in name of the debtor, the debtor, though the discharge be not delivered to him, can defend himself by an *exceptio doli* against the creditor demanding payment from him: for the creditor who has received payment from the third person, cannot, in conscience, demand a second payment from the debtor. But though he be barred from demanding a second payment, it does not follow, that the debt is extinguished. That it remains a subsisting debt will appear from considering, 1mo, That the transaction between the creditor and the third person may be dissolved as it was established, namely, by mutual consent, and by cancelling the discharge.—2do, The debtor, notwithstanding the er-

[*] L. 25, § 2, l. 26, De pactis; l. 26, § 4, De pactis dotalibus.

roneous payment, has it in his power to force a discharge from the creditor, upon offering him payment: neither of which could happen, were the debt extinguished. It only remains to be observed, that, when a debt is thus paid by a third person, it is in the debtor's choice to refund the money to the third person, or to pay it to the creditor. But if he defend himself against the creditor by an *exceptio doli*, which imports his ratification of the payment, the sustaining this exception hath two effects: 1st, It operates to him a legal extinction of the debt; and, next, It entitles the third person to demand the sum from him.

CHAPTER II.

Powers of a court of equity, to repress immoral acts that are not pecuniary.

I HAVE had occasion to mention above, that an attempt to correct all the wrongs that are not pecuniary, would be endless; and in a measure useless, as the method of repressing them all is the same, which is to declare them void. One species of immoral acts deserves peculiar notice, not only as a transgression of duty, but as tending to corrupt our morals.

Individuals in society, are linked together by various relations, that require a suitable conduct. The relations, in particular, that imply subordination, make the corner-stone of government, and ripen men gradually for behaving in it with propriety. The reciprocal duties that arise from the relation of parent and child, of preceptor and scholar, of master and seryant, of the high and low, of the rich and poor, and such like, accustom men both to rule and to be ruled. It is, for that reason, extremely material, that the duties arising from subordination be preserved from encroaching on each other: to reverse them, would reverse the order of nature, and tend to unhinge government. To suffer, for example, a young man to assume rule over his father, is to countenance an immoral act and breach of duty; having, at the same time, a tendency to destroy subordination.

A young man, in his contract of marriage, consented to be put under interdiction to his father and father-in-law; and in case of their failure, to the eldest son of the marriage. They having failed, the court refused to sustain an interdiction where the father is interdicted, and the son interdictor.* A bond was granted by a man to his wife, bearing, " That " by his facility, he might be misled to dispose of a " liferent he had by her, and, therefore, binding him- " self not to dispone without her consent." Upon this bond followed an inhibition; which was, in effect, putting the husband under interdiction to his wife. The court refused to sustain this act; because a married woman, being *sub potestate viri,* cannot be a curator to any person; and to make her a curator to her husband, would be to overturn the order of nature.†

Other acts, tending to, or arising from depravation of manners, are also rejected by a court of equity. Thus, a man who had fallen out with his mother, settled his mansion-house on his brother; and took from him a bond in his sister's name, that he

* Durie, 18th January 1622, Silvertonhill *contra* his Father.
† Stair, 27th February 1663, Lady Milton *contra* Milton.

P. II. 2. NOT PECUNIARY. 333

should not permit his mother to set foot in the house. The bond was set aside.*

BOOK II.

Powers of a Court of Equity, founded on the Principle of Utility.

JUSTICE is applied to two particulars, equally capital; one to make right effectual, and one to repress wrong. With respect to the former, utility coincides with justice: with respect to the latter, utility goes farther than justice. Wrong must be done, before justice can interpose; but utility lays down measures to prevent wrong. With respect to measures for the positive good of society, and for making men still more happy in a social state, these are reserved to the legislature. (*a*) It is not necessary that such extensive powers be trusted with courts of law : the power

---

* 1. Vernon, 413.

(*a*) And to interpose for advancing the positive good of but one or a few individuals, is still farther beyond the powers of a court of equity; though the Court of Chancery has sometimes ventured to exert itself for this narrow purpose, actuated by a laudable zeal to do good, carried, indeed, beyond proper bounds. I give the following instance.—Eighteen tenants of a manor have right to a common, and fifteen of them agree to inclose. The inclosing will be decreed, though opposed by three; for it shall not be in the power of a few wilful persons to oppose a public good. *Abrid. cases in equity, cap.* 4, *sect.* D, § 2.

334 OF ACTS THAT TEND TO THE **B. II.**

of making right effectual, of redressing wrong, and of preventing mischief, are sufficient.

As the matters contained in this book come within a narrow compass, I shall not have occasion for the multiplied subdivisions necessary in the former. A few chapters will exhaust the whole; beginning with those mischiefs or evils that are the most destructive, and descending gradually to those of less consequence. I reserve the last place for the power of a court of equity, to supply defects in statutes preventive of harm, whether that harm be of more or less importance: it is proper that matters, so much connected, should be handled together.

CHAP. I.

Acts in themselves lawful, reprobated in equity, as having a tendency to corrupt morals.

SOCIETY cannot flourish by pecuniary commerce merely: without benevolence, the social state would neither be commodious nor agreeable. Many connections there are altogether disinterested; witness the connection between a guardian and his infant, and, in general, between a trustee and the person for whose behoof the trust is gratuitously undertaken. In such a case, to take a premium for executing any article of the trust, being a breach of duty, will be discountenanced even at common law. Thus, a bond for 500 merks, granted to an interdictor by one who purchased land from the person interdicted, was voided.* If the sale was a rational measure, it was the

* Haddington, penult. July 1662, Carnousie *contra* Achmachie.

CH. I.   CORRUPTION OF MORALS.   335

interdictor's duty to consent to it without a bribe: if a wrong measure, the interdictor's taking a sum for his consent, was taking a bribe to betray his trust.

Equity goes farther: it prohibits a trustee from making any profit by his management, directly or indirectly. An act of this nature may, in itself, be innocent; but is poisonous with respect to consequences; for if a trustee be permitted, even in the most plausible circumstances, to make profit, he will soon lose sight of his duty, and direct his management chiefly for making profit to himself. It is solely on this foundation that a tutor is barred from purchasing a debt due by his pupil, or a right affecting his estate. The same temptation to fraudulent practice, concludes also against a trustee who has a salary, or is paid for his labour. A *pactum de quota litis* between an advocate and his client, which tends to corrupt the morals of the former, and to make him swerve from his duty, is discountenanced by all civilized nations. A bargain betwixt such persons may be fair, and may even be advantageous to the client: but utility requires that it be prohibited; for if indulged in any circumstances, it must be indulged without reserve. It is for the same reason, that a member of the College of Justice is prohibited by statute * from purchasing land that is the subject of a law-suit; and that a factor on a bankrupt estate is prohibited by an act of sederunt † from purchasing the bankrupt's debts. The same rule is extended against private factors and agents, without an act of sederunt. Debts due by a constituent, purchased by his factor or agent, will be held as purchased for be-

* Act 216, parl. 1594; the same, 13. Edward I, cap. 49.
† 25th December 1708.

336 OF ACTS THAT TEND : **B. II.**

hoof of the constituent : and no claim be sustained but for the transacted sum. It was decreed in chancery, That a bond for £500, for procuring a marriage between two persons equal in rank and fortune, is good. But on an appeal to the House of Lords, the decree was reversed. * Such a bond to a matchmaker, tending to ruin persons of fortune and quality, ought not to be sustained ; and the countenancing such bonds would be of evil example to guardians, trustees, servants, who have the care of persons under age.

CHAP. II.

Acts and covenants in themselves innocent, prohibited in equity, because of their tendency to disturb society, and to distress its members.

THE spirit of mutiny shewed itself some time ago among the workmen in the city of London, and rose to such a height as to require the interposition of the legislature. The same spirit broke out afterward among the journeymen-tailors of Edinburgh, who erected themselves into a club or society, keeping, in particular, a list of the journeymen out of service, under pretext of accommodating the masters more easily with workmen, but, in reality, to enable themselves to get new masters, if they differed with those they served. Any of them that deserted their service, entered their names in that list, and were immediately again employed by other masters who wanted hands. The master-tailors suffered many

* Abridg. cases in equity, chap. 13, sect. F, § 3.

inconveniences from this combination, which, among other hardships, produced increase of wages from time to time. The journeymen, for saving time, had always breakfasted in the houses of their masters; but, upon a concert among them, they all of them deserted their work about nine in the morning, declaring their resolution to have the hour between nine and ten to themselves, in all time coming : a desertion that was the more distressing, as it was made when the preparing clothing for the army required the utmost dispatch. This occasioned a complaint to the bailies of Edinburgh ; who found, " That the defenders, and other journeymen tailors " of Edinburgh, are not entitled to an hour of recess " for breakfast; that the wages of a journeyman " tailor in the said city ought not to exceed one shil- " ling per day ; and that if any journeyman tailor, " not retained or employed, shall refuse to work, " when required by a master, on the foresaid terms, " unless for some sufficient cause to be allowed by " the magistrates, the offender shall, upon convic- " tion, be punished in terms of law." This cause being brought to the Court of Session by advocation, it was thought of sufficient importance for a hearing in presence ; and the result was, to approve of the regulations of the magistrates.

The only difficulty was, whether the foresaid regulations did not encroach upon the liberty of the subject. It was admitted, that they did in some measure ; but the court was satisfied of their necessity, from the following considerations. Arts and manufactures are of two kinds. Those for luxury and for amusement are subjected to no rules, because

358 OF ACTS THAT TEND **B. II.**

a society may subsist comfortably without them.
But those which are necessary to the well-being of
society must be subjected to rules; otherwise it may
be in the power of a few individuals to do much mischief. If the bakers should refuse to make bread, or
the brewers to make ale, or the colliers to dig coal,
without being subjected to any control, they would
be masters of the lives of the inhabitants. To remedy such an evil, which is of the first magnitude,
there must be a power placed somewhere; and this
power has been long exercised by magistrates of boroughs and justices of peace, under review of the sovereign court. The tailors, by forbearing to work,
cannot do mischief so suddenly: but people must be
clad; and if there be no remedy against the obstinacy of tailors, they may compel people to submit to
the most exorbitant terms.

Another point debated was the propriety of the
foregoing regulations. Upon which it was observed,
that the regulation of the wages is even admitted by
the defenders themselves to be proper, because they
have acquiesced in it without complaint. And yet if
this article be admitted, the other regulations follow
of necessary consequence; for it is to no purpose to
fix wages, without also fixing the number of working
hours; and it is to no purpose to fix either, if the
defenders have the privilege to work or not at their
pleasure. Their demand of a recess between nine
and ten, which they chiefly insist for, is extremely
inconvenient, because of the time it consumes, especially in a wet day, when they must shift and dry
themselves to avoid sullying the new work they have
on hand. And as for health, they will never be de-

CH. II. TO DISTURB SOCIETY. 339

nied, either by their masters or by the judge, a whole day at times for exercise.[*]

When the malt-tax was ordered to be levied in Scotland, the Edinburgh brewers, dissatisfied with the same, entered into a combination to forbear brewing. The Court of Session, upon the principle above mentioned, ordered them to continue their brewing as formerly under a severe penalty.

The journeymen woolcombers in Aberdeen did, in the year 1775, form themselves into a society, exacting entry-money, inflicting penalties, &c. to be under the management of stewards, chosen every month: and though their seeming pretext was to provide for their poor, yet, under that pretext, several regulations were made, cramping trade, and tending to make them independent of their employers. A complaint against the society, by the procurator-fiscal of the bailie-court of Aberdeen, being removed to the Court of Session by advocation, the following interlocutor was pronounced:—" The Lords, having considered " the plan upon which the society of woolcombers is " erected, the regulations at first enacted, though af- " terward abrogated, and the rules still subsisting, " find, That such combinations of artificers, where- " by they collect money for a common box, inflict " penalties, impose oaths, and make other by-laws, " are of dangerous tendency, subversive of peace and " order, and against law: therefore, they prohibit and " discharge the defenders, the woolcombers, to conti- " nue to act under such combination or society for the " future, or to enter into any suchlike new society " or combination, as they shall be answerable: but

[*] Tailors of Edinburgh *contra* their Journeymen, December 10, 1762.

340 OF ACTS THAT TEND B. II.

" allow them, at the sight of the magistrates of
" Aberdeen, to apply the money already collected,
" for discharging the debts of the society: the re-
" mainder to be distributed among the contributors,
" in proportion to their respective contributions."

Upon a reclaiming petition, answers, replies, and
duplies, the court adhered to the foregoing interlocutor, as far as it finds the society complained of to be
of dangerous tendency, and consequently *contra bonos mores;* but they remitted to the Ordinary to hear
the parties, Whether the woolcombers may not be
permitted, under proper regulations, to contribute
sums for maintaining their poor.[*]

The journeymen weavers in the town of Paisley,
emboldened by numbers, began with mobs and riot-
ous proceedings, in order to obtain higher wages.
But these overt acts having been suppressed by authority of the Court of Session, they went more cun-
ningly to work, by contriving a kind of society termed the *defence-box;* and a written contract was subscribed by more than six hundred of them, containing many innocent and plausible articles, in order to
cover their views, but chiefly contrived to bind them
not to work under a certain rate, and to support out
of their periodical contributions those who, by insisting on high wages, might not find employment.
Seven of the subscribers being charged upon the contract, for payment of their stipulated contributions,
brought a suspension, in which it was decreed, That
this society was an unlawful combination, under the

[*] Procurator-fiscal *contra* Woolcombers in Aberdeen, December 15, 1762.

CH. II. TO DISTURB SOCIETY. 341

false colour of carrying on trade; and that the contract was void, as *contra utilitatem publicam.*[*]

CHAP. III.

Regulations of commerce, and of other public concerns, rectified where wrong.

It belongs to a court of police to regulate commerce and other public matters. The Court of Session is not a court of police; but it is a court of review, to take under consideration the proceedings of courts of police and to rectify such as are against the public interest. This jurisdiction is inherent in the Court of Session as the supreme court in civil matters, founded on the great principle, That every wrong must have a remedy.

In the year 1703, the magistrates and town-council of Stirling, made an act confirming a former act of council, in favour of the town weavers, and prohibiting all country weavers from buying woollen or linen yarn brought to the town for sale, except in public market, after eleven forenoon, under the pain of confiscation. This act of council was not a little partial: the weavers in the neighbourhood were confined to the market, while the town weavers were left at liberty to make their purchases at large. The former brought a process before the Court of Session, insisting to have the market at an earlier hour, in order that they might not be prevented by the latter from purchasing; and also, that the prohibition of purchasing yarn privately should be made general, to

[*] January 21, 1766, Barr *contra* Curr, &c.

342 OF REGULATIONS B. II.

comprehend the town weavers, as well as those of the country. The court not only appointed an earlier hour for the market; but put both parties upon an equal footing, by prohibiting yarn to be purchased before the opening of the market.*

Regulations that encroach on freedom of commerce, by favouring some to the prejudice of others, is what renders a monopoly odious in the sight of law. However beneficial a monopoly may be to the privileged, it is a wrong done to the rest of the people, by prohibiting them arbitrarily from the exercise of a lawful employment. Monopolies, therefore, ought to be discountenanced by courts of justice, not excepting those granted by the crown. And I am persuaded, that the monopolies granted by the crown last century, which were not few in number, would have been rejected by our judges, had their salaries been for life, as they now happily are. I venture a bolder step, which is to maintain, that even the Parliament itself cannot legally make such a partial distinction among the subjects. My reason is, that admitting the House of Commons to have the powers of a Roman dictator *ne quid respublica detrimenti capiat*, it follows not that such a trust will include a power to do injustice, or to oppress the many for the benefit of a few. How crude must have been our notions of government in the last century, when monopolies granted by the king's sole authority, were generally thought effectual to bind the whole nation! I am acquainted with no monopolies that may be lawfully granted but what are for the public good, such as, to the authors of new books and new machines, li-

* 14th November 1777, Paterson and others *contra* Rattray and others.

CH. III. OF COMMERCE. 343

mited to a time certain. The profit made in that period is a spur to invention: people are not hurt by such a monopoly, being deprived of no privilege enjoyed by them before the monopoly took place; and after expiry of the time limited, all are benefited without distinction.

In the year 1722, certain regulations were made in the bailie-court of Leith, concerning the forms of procedure in the administration of justice, and the qualification of practitioners before that court; among other articles, providing, " That when the procura- " tors are not under three in number, none shall be " allowed to enter, except such as have served the " clerk or a procurator for the space of three years " as an apprentice, and one year at least after; be- " side undergoing a trial by the procurators of court, " named by the magistrates for that effect." John Young, craving to be entered procurator, as having served an apprenticeship to an agent of character before the Court of Session, this regulation of the bailie-court of Leith was objected. The bailies having found the petitioner not qualified, in terms of the regulations, the cause was advocated; and the court found the said article void, as *contra utilitatem publicam*, by establishing a monopoly.*

* 21st December 1765, John Young *contra* Procurators of the bailie-court of Leith.

CHAP. IV.

Forms of the common law dispensed with, in order to abridge law-suits.

RETENTION, which is an equitable exception resembling compensation, was introduced by the Court of Session, without authority of a statute. The statute 1592, authorising compensation, speaks not of an obligation *ad factum præstandum*, nor of any obligation but for payment of money; and yet it would be hard, that a man should have the authority of a court to make his claim effectual against me, while he refuses or delays to satisfy the claim I have against him. So stands, however, the common law, which is corrected by a court of equity for the public good. Supposing parties once in court upon any controversy, the adjusting, without a new process, all matters between them that can at present be adjusted, is undoubtedly beneficial, because it tends to abridge law-suits. This good end is attained, by bestowing on the defendant a privilege to withhold performance from the pursuer, till the pursuer, *simul et semel*, perform to him. This privilege is exercised by pleading it as an exception to the pursuer's demand; and the exception, from its nature, is termed *Retention*.

Compensation, as we have seen, is founded on the principle of equity. And it is also supported by that of utility; because the finishing two counter-claims in the same process tends to lessen the number of law-suits. Retention is founded solely on utility,

CH. IV. FORMS DISPENSED WITH, &c. 345

being calculated for no other end but to prevent the multiplication of law-suits. The utility of retention has gained it admittance in all civilized nations. In the English Court of Chancery particularly, it is a well-known exception, of which I give the following instance. " If the plaintiff mortgage his estate to " the defendant, and afterward borrow money from " the defendant upon bond, the redemption ought " not to take place, unless the bonded debt be paid " as well as the mortgage-money." *

From what is said, every sort of obligation affords, as it would appear, a ground for retention, provided the term of performance be come, and no just cause for withholding performance. It shall only be added, that for the reasons given with respect to compensation,† retention cannot be pleaded against an assignee for a valuable consideration.

A directed B to pay C what sums C should want. C accordingly received two sums (among others) from B, for which he gave receipts, as by the order of A. A and C came to account, which, being stated, they gave mutual releases. But the two sums not being entered in the books of A, were not accounted for by C. B not having received any allowance from A for the two sums, prefers his bill against C to have the money returned to him. C confessed the receipts, but insisted, that the money was delivered to him by the order of A, and that B, being a hand only, had no claim. But the court decreed, That the plaintiff had a fair claim against the defendant to avoid circuity of suits : for otherwise it would turn the plaintiff on A, and A again on the defendant in equity to set aside the release, and to have an

---

* 1. Vernon, 244. † See *supra*, p. 257.

346   FORMS DISPENSED WITH,   B. II.

allowance of these sums. And the decree was affirmed in the House of Lords. *

By the common law of this land, a creditor introduced into possession upon a wadset, upon an assignment to rents, or upon an adjudication, is bound to surrender the possession as soon as the debt is paid by the rents levied. He obtained possession, in order to levy the rents for his payment; and when payment is obtained, he is no longer entitled to possess. He perhaps is creditor in other debts that may entitle him to apprehend possession *de novo :* but these will not, at common law, empower him to detain possession one moment after the debt that was the title of his possession is paid. He must first surrender possession; and he may afterward apply for legal authority to be repossessed for payment of these separate debts. A court of equity views matters in a different light. The debtor's claim to have his land restored to him is certainly not founded on utility, when such claim can serve no other end but to multiply expence, by forcing the creditor to take out execution upon the separate debt, in order to be repossessed. A maxim in the Roman law concludes in this case with force, *Frustrà petis quod mox es restituturus ;* and this maxim accordingly furnisheth to the creditor in possession a defence that is a species of retention. There is, indeed, the same reason for sustaining the exception of retention in this case, that there is in personal debts, namely, utility, which is interposed to prevent the multiplying of law-suits, prejudicial to one of the parties at least, and beneficial to neither.

But this relief against the strictness of common law, ought not to be confined to real debts which en-

* Shower's cases in Parliament, 17.

Ch. v.   REGULATED BY UTILITY.   347

title the creditor to possess. It may sometimes happen, as demonstrated above,* to be more beneficial to the debtor or to the creditor, without hurting either, that the rents be applied for payment even of a personal debt, than for payment of the debt which is the title of possession. And wherever the rents may be applied for payment of a personal debt, the creditor must be privileged to hold possession till that debt be paid.

CHAP. V.

Bona fides, *as far as regulated by utility*.

My first head shall be *bona fide* payment. It may happen by mistake that payment is made, not to the person who is really the creditor, but to one understood to be the creditor. However invincible the error may be, payment made to any but to the creditor avails not at common law ; because none but the creditor can discharge the debt. What remedy can be afforded by a court of equity where a debt is *bona fide* paid to another than the true creditor, I proceed to explain.

It is an observation verified by long experience, That no circumstance tends more to the advancement of commerce, than a free circulation of the goods of fortune from hand to hand. In this island, commercial law is so much improved, as that land, moveables, debts, have all of them a free and expedite currency. A bond for borrowed money, in particular, descends to heirs, and is readily transferable to assignees vo-

* See *suprà*, p. 275.

348 . BONA FIDES AS B. II.

luntary or judicial. But that circumstance, beneficial
to commerce, proves, in many instances, hurtful to
debtors. Payment made to any but the creditor, frees
not the debtor at common law : and yet circumstances may be often such, as to make it impracticable for
the debtor to discover that the person who produceth
a title, fair in appearance, is not the creditor. Here
is a case extremely nice in point of equity. On the
one hand, if *bona fide* payment be not sustained, the
hardship will be great upon the debtor, who must
pay a second time to the true creditor. On the other
hand, if the exception of *bona fide* payment be sustained to protect the debtor from a second payment,
the creditor will be often forfeited of his debt without his fault. Here the scales hang even, and equity
preponderates not on either side. But the principle
of utility affords relief to the debtor, and exerts all
its weight in his scale : for, if a debtor were not secure by voluntary payment, no man would venture
to pay a shilling by any authority less than that of
the sovereign court : and how ruinous to credit this
would prove, must be obvious without taking a moment for reflection.

To bring this matter nearer the eye, we shall first
suppose, that the putative creditor proceeds to legal
execution, and in that manner recovers payment.
Payment thus made by authority of law, must undoubtedly protect the debtor from a second payment.
And this leads to another case, That the debtor, to
prevent legal execution, which threatens him, makes
payment voluntarily. The payment here is made
indeed without compulsion, because there is no actual
execution : but then it is not made without authority ; for, by the supposition, execution is awarded, and

nothing prevents it but payment. The third case is of a clear bond, upon which execution must be obtained as soon as demanded; and the debtor pays, knowing of no defence. Why ought not he also to be secure in this case? That he be secure, is beneficial to creditors as well as to debtors, because otherwise there can be no free commerce of debts. This exception, then, of *bona fide* payment, is supported by the principle of utility in two different respects: it is beneficial to creditors, by encouraging debtors to make prompt payment; and by removing from them the pretext of insisting upon anxious and scrupulous defences, which, under the colour of paying securely, would often be laid hold of to delay payment: it is beneficial to debtors, who can pay with safety without being obliged to suffer execution.

But here the true creditor is not left without a remedy. The sum received by the putative creditor is in his hand *sine justa causa*, and he is answerable for it to the true creditor. In this view, the operation of *bona fide* payment is only to substitute one debtor for another, which may as often be beneficial to the true creditor, as detrimental.

An executor under a revoked will, being ignorant of the revocation, pays legacies; and the revocation is afterward proved: he shall be allowed these legacies.[*]

If, in making payment to the putative creditor, the debtor obtain an ease, the exception of *bona fide* payment will be sustained for that sum only which was really paid.[†] This rule is founded on equity; for

---

[*] 1. Chancery cases, 126.

[†] Stair, July 19, 1665, Johnston *contra* Macgregor.

352 BONA FIDES AS, &c. B. II.

that it was *in rem versum* of the infant heir. The favourableness of this case had, I conjecture, no slight influence in procuring the judgment. It lies open to objections that seem not easily solved. First, What room was there for *bona fides* while it remained uncertain whether the widow might not be pregnant? and surely the debts could not be so pressing as not to bear the delay of a few months. Next, Had the interest of the debts exceeded the rents of the estate, to make it necessary to dispose of the whole, a sale upon that supposition might be held to be *in rem versum* of the infant heir: but it does not appear so clearly, that the sale of a part could be *in rem versum*; because, by exact and frugal management during the minority of the heir, the debts might have been so much reduced as to make it proper to preserve the estate entire.

I close this chapter with the acts and deeds of a putative judge; of which the case of Barbarius Philippus is an illustrious instance.[*] Having been elected a Roman Prætor, he determined many causes, and transacted every sort of business that belonged to the office. He was discovered to be a slave, which rendered all his acts and deeds void at common law; because none but a freeman was capable to be a Roman Prætor. With respect to third parties, however, their *bona fides* supported all his acts and deeds as if he really had been a Prætor.

[*] L. 3, De officio Præt.

CHAP. VI.

Interposition of a court of equity in favour even of a single person to prevent mischief.

THIS subject is so fully explained in the introduction, as to require very little addition. It exhibits a court of equity in a new light, shewing that this court, acting upon the principle of utility, is not confined to what is properly termed *jurisdiction*; but, in order to prevent mischief even to a single person, may assume magisterial powers. It is by such power that the Court of Session names factors to manage the estates of those who are in foreign parts, and of infants who are destitute of tutors. The authority interposed for selling the land-estate of a person under age, is properly of the same nature; for the inquiry made about the debts, and about the rationality of a sale, though in the form of a process, is an expiscation merely.

By the Roman law, a sale made by a tutor, of his pupil's land-estate, without authority of a judge, was void *ipso jure*, as *ultra vires*. This seems not to have been followed in Scotland. Maitland reports a case,[*] where it is decreed, that such a sale *sine decreto* is not void, but that it is good if profitable to the infant. And I must approve this decision as agreeable to principles and to the nature of the thing. The interposition of a court beforehand, is not to bestow new powers upon a tutor, but to certify the necessity of a sale, in order to encourage purchasers, by rendering them secure. But if, without anthority of a court,

[*] Dec. 1, 1565, Douglas *contra* Foreman.

354 STATUTES PREVENTIVE B. II.

a purchaser be found who pays a full price, and if the sale be necessary, where can the objection lie? So far, indeed, a court may justly go, as to presume lesion from a sale *sine decreto*, until the tutor justify the sale as rational, and profitable to the infant.

CHAP. VII.

Statutes preventive of wrong or mischief, extended by a court of equity.

STATUTES, as hinted above,[*] that have utility for their object, are of two kinds: First, Statutes directed for promoting the positive good of the whole society, or of some part: Second, Statutes directed to prevent mischief only. Defective statutes of the latter kind may be supplied by a court of equity; because, independent of a statute, it is empowered to prevent mischief. But that court has not, more than a court of common law, any power to supply defective statutes of the former kind; because it belongs to the legislature only to make laws or regulations for promoting good positively.

Usury is in itself innocent, but to prevent oppression, it is prohibited by statute. Gaming is prohibited by statute; as also the purchasing lawsuits by members of the College of Justice. These in themselves are not unjust; but they tend to corrupt the morals, and prove often ruinous to individuals. Such statutes, preventive of wrong and mischief, may be extended by a court of equity, in order to complete the remedy intended by the legislature. It is chiefly

[*] See *supra*, p. 220, 221.

CH. VII.   OF WRONG, EXTENDED.   355

with relation to statutes of this kind, that Bacon delivers an opinion with great elegance : " Bonum pub-
" licum insigne rapit ad se casus omissos.   Quamo-
" brem, quando lex aliqua reipublicæ commoda not-
" abiliter et majorem in modum intuetur et procurat,
" interpretatio ejus extensiva esto et amplians."*

In this class, as appears to me, our statute 1617, instituting the positive prescriptive, ought to be placed.   For it has not, like the Roman *usucapio*, the penal effect of forfeiting a proprietor for his negligence, and of transferring his property to another : it is contrived, on the contrary, to secure every man in his land-property, by denying action upon old obsolete claims, which, by common law, are perpetual. A claim may be very old, and yet very just ; and it is not, therefore, wrong in the common law to sustain such a claim.   But the consequences ought to be considered : if a claim be sustained beyond forty or fifty years, because it may be just, every claim must be sustained, however old ; and experience discovered, that this opens a wide door to falsehood.   To prevent wrong and mischief, it was necessary that land-property should, by lapse of time, be secured against all claims ; and as, with respect to antiquated claims, there is no infallible criterion to distinguish good from bad, it was necessary to bar them altogether by the lump.   The passage quoted from Bacon is applicable in the strictest manner to this statute, considered in the light now mentioned ; and it hath, accordingly, been extended, in order to complete the remedy afforded by the legislature.   To secure land-property against obsolete claims, it must be qualified, that the proprietor has possessed peaceably forty

* De augmentis scientiarium, l. 8, cap. 3, aphor. 12.

356 STATUTES PREVENTIVE B. II.

years, by virtue of a charter and seisin. So says the statute; and if the statute be taken strictly, no property is protected from obsolete claims, but where infeftment is the title of possession. But the Court of Session, preferring the end to the means, and consulting its own powers as a court of equity, to prevent mischief, secures by prescription every subject possessed upon a good title, a right to tithes for example, a long lease of land, or of tithes, which are titles that admit not infeftment.

As the foregoing statute was made to secure land from obsolete and unjust claims, the statute 1469, introducing the negative prescription of obligations, was made to secure individuals personally from claims of the same kind. As this statute is preventive of mischief, it may be extended by a court of equity, to complete the remedy. It has, accordingly, been extended to mutual contracts, to decrees *in foro contradictorio*, and to reductions of deeds granted on deathbed.(a)

Considering the instances above mentioned, it must, I imagine, occasion some surprise, to find a proposition cherished by our lawyers, That correctory statutes, as they are termed, ought never to be extended. We have already seen this proposition contra-

(a) I am aware, that the statutes, introducing the negative prescription, have, by the Court of Session, been considered in a different light. They have been held as a forfeiture even of a just debt: for it was once judged, that after the forty years, the defendant was not bound to give his oath upon the verity of the debt: and that, though he should acknowledge the debt to be just, yet he was not liable *in foro humano*, however he might be liable *in foro poli et conscientiæ*; Fountainhall, December 7, 1703, Napier contra Campbell. That this is a wrong construction of these statutes, I have endeavoured to show above, p. 252, 253.

CH. VII. OF WRONG, EXTENDED. 357

dicted, not only by solid principles, but even by the Court of Session in many instances. With relation to statutes, in particular, correctory of injustice or of wrong, no man can seriously doubt, that a court of equity is empowered to extend such statutes, in order to complete the remedy prescribed by the legislature: and the same is equally clear with relation to statutes supplying defects in common law. As to the statutes under consideration, intended to prevent mischief, it might, I own, have once been more doubtful, whether these could be extended; for, of all the powers assumed by a court of equity, it is probable, that the power of preventing mischief was the latest. But in England, this power has been long established in the Court of Chancery; and experience has proved it to be a salutary power. Why, then, should we stop short in the middle of our progress? No other excuse can be given for such hesitation, but that our law, considered as a regular system, is of a much later date than that of England.

The foregoing are instances, where the Court of Session, without hesitation, have supplied defects in statutes, made to prevent mischief. But to show how desultory and fluctuating the practice of the court is in that particular, I shall confine myself to a single case on the other side, which makes a figure in our law. In the transmission of land-property, by succession, as well as by sale, we require infeftment. An heir, however, without completing his right by infeftment, is entitled to continue the possession of his ancestor.* In this situation, behaving as proprietor, he contracts debts; and, unless he be reduced to the necessity of borrowing large sums, those

* See Historical Law-tracts, tract 5.

358 STATUTES PREVENTIVE **B. II.**

he deals with are seldom so scrupulous, as to inquire
into his title. By the common law, however, the
debtor's death, before infeftment, is, as to the real
estate, a forfeiture of all his personal creditors. This
is a mischief, which well deserved the interposition
of the legislature; and a remedy was provided by
act 24. parl. 1695, enacting, " That if an apparent
" heir have been in possession for three years, the
" next heir, who, by service or adjudication, connects
" with the predecessor last infeft, shall be liable to
" the apparent heir's debts *in valorem* of the herit-
" age." There can be no doubt, that this statute
was intended to procure payment to those who deal
bonâ fide with an heir-apparent. And yet, if we regard the words only, the remedy is imperfect; for
what if the next heir-apparent, purposely to evade
the statute, shall content himself with the possession
and enjoyment of the heritage, without making up
titles by service or adjudication? Taking the statute
strictly according to the words, the creditors will reap
little benefit: if the debts be considerable, no heir will
subject himself by completing his titles, when he has
full enjoyment of the rents, without that solemnity.
Formerly, the heir-apparent in possession had no interest to forbear the completing his titles: his forbearing must have proceeded from indolence or inat-
tention. But if the remedy, intended by the statute,
reach not an heir-apparent, though in possession, a
strong motive of interest will make him forbear to
complete his titles. In this view, the statute, if confined to the words, is perfectly absurd; for what can
be more absurd, than to leave it in the power of the
heir-apparent to disappoint the creditors of the remedy intended them? It is always in his power, by

satisfying himself with a possessory title, to disappoint them: and, as by a possessory title, he has the full enjoyment of the estate, he will always disappoint them, if he regard his own interest. The legislature, in this case, undoubtedly intended a complete remedy; and the consideration now mentioned, peculiar to this case, is a strong additional motive for the interposition of a court of equity, to fulfil the intendment of the legislature. And yet, misled by the notion, that correctory laws ought not to be extended, the Court of Session hath constantly denied action to the creditors of an heir who dies in apparency, against the next heir in possession, unless he has completed his title to the estate by service or adjudication.

There is another palpable defect in this statute, which ought also to be supplied. A predecessor may have a good title to his estate, without being infeft; and yet, regarding the words only, the heir-apparent is not liable upon this statute, unless where he connects with a predecessor infeft. I put the following case.—John purchases an estate, takes a disposition with procuratory and precept, but dies without being seised. James, his heir-apparent, enters into possession, without making up titles, and contracts debt, after being in possession three years. After his death, William, the next heir-apparent, makes up his titles by a general service. This case comes not under the words of the statute; but as it undoubtedly comes under the mischief which the legislature intended to remedy, it is the duty of a court of equity to complete the remedy.

In one case, the court, from a due sense of their equitable powers, ventured upon a remedy where this statute was defective. Some acres and houses having been disponed for a valuable consideration by an heir-apparent, three years in possession, the next heir-apparent, foreseeing that he would be barred, by the act 1695, from objecting to this alienation, if he should enter heir, bethought himself of a different method. He sold the subject for twenty guineas, and granted bond to the purchaser, who led an adjudication against the estate, and upon that title brought a reduction of the disposition in his own name. But the court decreed, that this case fell under the meaning of the statute, though not under the words; and, therefore, that the pursuer was barred from challenging the disposition.*

What if the heir forbearing to enter, in order to evade the act 1695, shall contract debt to the value of the subject, upon which adjudications are led *contra hæreditatem jacentem?* Here the estate is applied for payment of the heir's debts, and consequently converted to his use as much as if he were entered. Would the Court of Session give no relief in this case to the creditors of the interjected heir-apparent? Would they suffer the purpose of the statute to be so grossly eluded?

A word or two upon statutes contrived to advance the positive good of the society in general, or of individuals in particular, making them *locupletiores*, as termed in the Roman law. To supply defects in such a statute, is beyond the power even of a court of equity. The statute 1661, act 41, obliging me to concur with my neighbour in erecting a march-dike, is of that nature. There is no provision in the act for upholding the march-dike after it is made; and

* Burns of Dorator *contra* Pickens, July 11, 1758.

CH. VII.   OF WRONG, EXTENDED.   361

the defect cannot be supplied by any court. Upon
my neighbour's requisition, I must join with him to
build a march-dike; but I am bound no further; and
therefore, the burden of upholding must rest upon
himself. Monopolies or personal privileges, cannot
be extended by a court of equity;* because that court
may prevent mischief, but has no power to advance
the positive good of any person. As to penal statutes, it is clear, in the first place, that to augment a
penalty beyond that directed by a statute, is acting
in contradiction to the statute, which enacts that precise penalty, and not a greater. In the next place, to
extend the penalty in a statute to a case not mentioned, is a power not trusted with any court, because
the trust is not necessary. A penalty is commonly
added to a statutory prohibition, for preventing
wrong or mischief. A court of equity may extend
the prohibition to similar cases, and even punish the
transgression of their own prohibition.† But with
respect to a prohibition that regards utility only, not
justice, it is a prerogative peculiar to the legislature,
to annex beforehand a penal sanction.

CONCLUSION OF BOOK II.

Justice and Utility compared.

THE principle of justice, though more extensive in
its influence than that of utility, is in its nature more
simple: it never looks beyond the litigants. The
principle of utility, on the contrary, not only regards

* L. 1, § 2, De constitut. princ.
† Book 1, part 1, cap. 5.

362   JUSTICE AND   B. II.

these, but also the society in general; and comprehends many circumstances concerning both. Being
thus in its nature and application more intricate than
justice, I thought it not amiss to close this book with
a few thoughts upon it. In the introduction there
was occasion to hint, that utility co-operates sometimes with justice, and sometimes is in opposition to
it. There are several instances of both in the first
book, which I propose to bring under one view, in
order to give a distinct notion of the co-operation and
opposition of these principles.

It is scarce necessary to be premised, that in op-
posing private utility to justice, the latter ought always to prevail. A man is not bound to prosecute
what is beneficial to him: he is not even bound to
demand reparation for wrong done him. But he
is strictly bound to do his duty; and for that reason
he himself must be conscious, that in opposition to
duty, interest ought to have no weight. It is beside
of great importance to society, that justice have a
free course; and accordingly, public utility unites
with justice to enforce right against interest. Private interest, therefore, or private utility, may, in the
present speculation, be laid entirely aside; and it is
barely mentioned to prevent mistakes.

Another limitation is necessary. It is not every
sort of public utility that can outweigh justice: it is
that sort only which is preventive of mischief, affecting the whole or bulk of the society : public utility,
as far as it concerns positive additional good to the
society, is a subject that comes not within the sphere
of a court of equity.

Confining our view then to public utility, that
which is preventive of mischief to the whole, or great

part of the society, I venture to lay down the following proposition, That wherever it is at variance with justice, a court of equity ought not to enforce the latter, nor suffer it to be enforced by a court of common law. In order to evince this proposition, which I shall endeavour to do by induction, the proper method will be, to give a table of cases, beginning with those where the two principles are in strict union, and proceeding orderly to those where they are in declared opposition.

These principles for the most part are good friends. The great end of establishing a court of equity is, to have justice accurately distributed, even in the most delicate circumstances; than which nothing contributes more to peace and union in society. As this branch, therefore, of utility is inseparable from justice, it will not be necessary hereafter to make any express mention of it. It must be always understood when we talk of justice.

We proceed to other branches of utility, which are not so strictly attached to justice, but sometimes coincide with it, and sometimes rise in opposition. One of these is the benefit accruing to the society by abridging law-suits. In the case of compensation, utility unites with justice to make compensation a strong plea in every court of equity. Retention depends entirely upon the utility of abridging law-suits. But if it have no support from justice, it meets, on the other hand, with no opposition from it.

In the case of *bona fide* payment, the utility is different. It is the benefit that arises from a free course to money-transactions, which would be obstructed, if debtors, by running any risk in making payment, were encouraged to state anxious or frivolous defences. The exception of *bona fide* payment is sustained upon no ground but that of preventing the mischief here described. Justice weighs equally on both sides; for if the exception be not sustained, the honest debtor bears the hazard of losing his money; if it be sustained, the hazard is transferred upon the creditor.

But there are cases where justice and utility take opposite sides: which, in particular, is the case where a transaction, extremely unequal, is occasioned by error. Here the justice of affording relief is obvious: but then a transaction, by putting an end to strife, is a favourite of law; and it is against the interest of the public to weigh a transaction in the nice balance of grains and scruples. A man, by care and attention in making a transaction, may avoid error; but the bad consequences of opening transactions upon every ground of equity cannot be avoided. Justice, therefore, must in this case yield to utility; and a transaction will be supported against errors sufficient to overturn other agreements. I give another example. In the Roman law, *læsio ultra duplum* was sustained to avoid a bargain: but, in Britain, we refuse to listen to equity in this case; for if complaints of inequality were indulged, lawsuits would be multiplied, to the great detriment of commerce.

If the discouraging law-suits be sufficient to withhold relief in equity, the hazard of making judges arbitrary is a much stronger motive for withholding that relief. However clear a just claim or defence may be, a court of equity ought not to interpose, unless the case can be brought under a general rule. No sort of oppression is more intolerable than what is done under the colour of law; and, for that reason, judges ought to be confined to general rules, the only method invented to prevent legal oppression. Here the refusing to do justice to a single person makes no figure, when set in opposition to an important interest that concerns deeply the whole society. And it seems to follow, from the very nature of a court of equity, that it ought to adhere to general rules, even at the expence of forbearing to do justice. It is, indeed, the declared purpose of a court of equity, to promote the good of society by an accurate distribution of justice: but the means ought to be subordinate to the end; and, therefore, if, in any case, justice cannot be done but by using means that tend to the hurt of society, a court of equity ought not to interpose. To be active in such a case, involves the absurdity of preferring the means to the end.

Thus we may gather by induction, that in every case where it is the interest of the public to withhold justice from an individual, it becomes the duty of a court of equity in that circumstance, not only to abstain from enforcing the just claim or defence, but also to prevent its being enforced at common law. But the influence of public utility stops here, and never authorises a court of equity to enforce any positive act of injustice.* For, first, I cannot discover that it ever can be the interest of the public to require the doing an unjust action. And, next, if even self-preservation will not justify any wrong done by a private person, † much less will public utility justify any wrong done or enforced by a court of equity.

* See this doctrine illustrated, Historical Law-tracts, tract 2.
† Sketches of the History of Man, vol. 4, p. 31.

366   JUSTICE AND UTILITY, &c.   B. II.

It is inconsistent with the very constitution of this court, to do injustice, or to enforce it. (a)

(a) The following case is an illustrious instance of this doctrine. A ship-cargo of negroes, young and old, being imported into Jamaica for sale, Mr. Wedderburn purchased a boy not above twelve years of age, educated him for a house-servant, and employed him as his slave while he continued in Jamaica. The negro being now fully grown, was brought to Scotland by his master, where he got a wife, and had children. Never having received any wages, he became uneasy for want of means to maintain his family. He absented, and endeavoured to procure money by a lawful employment. Mr. Wedderburn applied to the sheriff of Perth to oblige his slave to return to him. The sheriff found, " That slavery is not recognised by the law of this king-" dom, and is inconsistent with the principles thereof; that the " regulations in Jamaica, concerning slaves, extend not to this " kingdom; and, therefore, repelled Mr. Wedderburn's claim to " perpetual service from the negro." The cause being advocated to the Court of Session, was held to be of such importance as to demand a hearing in presence. The sum of the argument for the negro was what follows. It was premised, that not one of the causes assigned by writers for justifying slavery is applicable to the negro in question. It is not alleged that he was taken captive in war; and he was too young for committing any crime that deserved so severe a punishment. As to consent, it is not said that he ever consented or shewed any willingness to be a slave. He could expect no redress in Jamaica; but when he came to a land of liberty, where he could hope for protection, he left his master, and asserted his claim to be free. Now, as all men are born free, and in a state of independence, except upon their parents, and as the negro in question has done no act to deprive him of that valuable right, he is protected by the law of nature, and by every principle of justice, from being made a slave. Slavery, it is true, is supported by the practice of Jamaica. But even supposing it to be authorised by the municipal law of that country, yet the judges in Scotland do not give blind obedience to any foreign law. If a foreign decree or a foreign statute be brought here for execution, our judges listen cordially to any objection in equity that may

BOOK III.

HITHERTO our plan has been, to set forth the different powers of a court of equity; and to illustrate these powers by apt examples selected from various subjects where they could be best found. Our plan in the present book is, to shew the application of these powers to various subjects, handled each as an entire whole; and the subjects chosen are such as cannot easily be split into parts to be distributed under the different heads formerly explained. Beside, as the various powers of a court of equity have been sufficiently illustrated, as well as the principles on which they are founded, I thought it would be pleasant as well as instructive to vary the method, by shewing the operation of these powers upon particular subjects. The first and second books may be considered as theoretical, explaining the powers of a court of equity: the present book is practical, shewing the application of these powers, to several important subjects.

lie against it; and never interpose their authority for execution, unless where it is founded on material justice. Mr. Wedderburn can have no pretext other than the law of Jamaica for claiming this man as a slave. And as this claim is repugnant to the law of nature and to every just principle, the Court of Session would be accessory to a gross wrong if they should enforce that claim. Courts were instituted to make justice effectual, and never to transgress it.—The court accordingly remitted the cause to the sheriff; which, in effect, was refusing to interpose their authority in behalf of Mr. Wedderburn's claim. But they avoided the giving any opinion with respect to the law or practice of Jamaica, how far effectual by long custom for the sake of commerce. (15th January 1778, John Wedderburn *contra* Joseph Knight, a negro.)

CHAP. I.

What equity rules with respect to rents levied upon an erroneous title of property.

WITH respect to land possessed upon an erroneous title of property, it is a rule established in the Romon law, and among modern nations, That the true proprietor asserting his right to the land, has not a claim for the rents levied by the *bona fide* possessor, and consumed. But though this subject is handled at large both by the Roman lawyers and by their commentators, we are left in the dark as to the reason of the rule, and of the principle upon which it is founded. Perhaps it was thought, that the proprietor has not an action at common law for the value of the product consumed by the *bona fide* possessor : or perhaps, that the action, as rigorous, is rendered ineffectual by equity. So far, indeed, it is evident, that as no title of property can absolutely be relied on, sad would be the condition of land-holders, were they liable forty years back, for rents which they had reason to believe their own, and which, without scruple, they bestowed on procuring the necessaries and conveniences of life.

Though, in all views, the *bona fide* possessor is secure against restitution, it is, however, of importance to ascertain the precise principle that affords him security ; for, upon that preliminary point, several questions depend. We shall, therefore, without further preface, enter into the enquiry.

The possessor, as observed, must be protected either by common law or by equity. If common law afford to the proprietor a claim for the value of his

CH. I.   AN ERRONEOUS TITLE.   369

rents consumed, it must be equity correcting the rigour of common law that protects the possessor from this claim: but if the proprietor have not a claim at common law, the possessor has no occasion for equity. The matter, then, is resolvable into the following question, Whether there be or be not a claim at common law? And to this question, which is subtile, we must lend attention.

Searching for materials to reason upon, what first occurs is the difference between natural and industrial fruits. The former, owing their existence not to man but to the land, will readily be thought an accessary that must follow the land. The latter will be viewed in a different light; for industrial fruits owe their existence to labour and industry, more than to land. Upon this very circumstance does Justinian found the right of the *bona fide* possessor: " Si quis a non domino quem dominum esse credi- " derit, bona fide fundum emerit, vel ex donatione, " aliave qualibet justa causa æquè bona fide accepe- " rit; naturali rationi placuit, fructus, quos perce- " pit, ejus esse pro cultura et cura. Et ideo, si " postea dominus supervenerit, et fundum vindicet, " de fructibus ab eo consumptis agere non potest." * And upon this foundation Pomponius pronounces, that the *bona fide* possessor acquires right to the industrial fruits only: " Fructus percipiendo, uxor " vel vir, ex re donata, suos facit: illos tamen quos " suis operis adquisierit, veluti serendo. Nam si po- " mum decerpserit, vel ex sylva cedit, non fit ejus : " sicuti nec cujuslibet bonæ fidei possessoris; quia " non ex facto ejus is fructus nascitur." † Paulus goes further. He admits not any distinction between.

§ 35. I nstit. De rer. divisione.   † L. 45. De usuris.

2 A

370 OF RENTS LEVIED UPON B. III.

natural and industrial fruits; but is positive, that both kinds equally, as soon as separated from the ground, belong to the *bona fide* possessor: Bonae fi. " dei empter non dubie percipiendo fructus, etiam " ex aliena re, suos interim facit, non tantum eos " qui diligentia et opera ejus pervenerunt, sed om. " nes; quia quod ad fructus attinet, loco domini pe. " ne est. Denique etiam, priusquam percipiat, sta. " tim ubi a solo separati sunt, bonae fidei emptoris " fiunt." *

But now, after drawing so nigh in appearance to a conclusion, we stumble upon an unexpected obstruction. Is the foregoing doctrine consistent with the principle, *Quod satum solo cedit solo?* If corns, while growing, make part of the land, and, consequently, belong to the proprietor of the land, the act of separation cannot have the effect to transfer the property from him to another. And if this hold as to fruits that are industrial, the argument concludes with greater force if possible, as to natural fruits. What, then, shall be thought of the opinions delivered above by the Roman writers? Their authority is great I confess, and yet no authority will justify us in deviating from clear principles. The fruits, both industrial and natural, after separation as well as before, belong to the proprietor of the land. He has undoubtedly an action at common law to vindicate the fruits while extant: and, if so, has he not also a claim for the value after consumption?

However prone to answer the foregoing question in the affirmative, let us however suspend our judgment till the question be fairly canvassed. It is indeed clear, that the fruits, while extant, the *percepti*

* L. 48. pr. De acquir. rer. dom.

CH. I.   AN ERRONEOUS TITLE.   371

as well as *pendentes*, belong to the proprietor of the land, and can be claimed by a *rei vindicatio*. (*a*) But is it equally clear, that the *bona fide* possessor who consumes the fruits is liable for their value? Upon what medium is this claim founded? The fruits are indeed consumed by the possessor, and the proprietor is thereby deprived of his property : but it cannot be subsumed, that he is deprived of it by the fault of the possessor ; for, by the supposition, the possessor was *in bona fide* to consume, and was not guilty of the slightest fault. Let us endeavour to gather light from a similar case. A man buys a horse *bona fide* from one who is not proprietor : upon urgent business he makes a very severe journey ; and the horse, unable to support the fatigue, dies. Is the purchaser answerable for the value of the horse? There is no principle upon which that claim can be founded. In general, a proprietor deprived of his goods by the fact of another, cannot claim the value upon any principle but that of reparation : but it is a rule established both in the law of nature and in municipal law, That a man free from fault or blame, is not liable to repair any hurt done by him : one in all respects innocent, is not subjected to reparation more than to punishment.* And thus it comes out clear, that there is no action at common law against the *bona fide* possessor for the value of the fruits he consumes : such an action must resolve into a claim of damages, to which the innocent cannot be subjected,

And if *bona fides* protect the possessor when he

(*a*) Whether he may not in equity be liable for some recompence to the person by whose labour the industrial fruits were raised, is a different question.

* See Sketches of the History of Man, vol. iv, p. 71.

2 A 2

372　　OF RENTS LEVIED UPON　　B. III.

himself consumes the fruits, it will equally protect his tenants. A man who takes a lease from one who is held to be proprietor of the land, is *in bona fide* as well as his landlord. The fruits, therefore, that the tenant consumes or disposes of, will not subject him to a claim of damages ; and if the proprietor have no claim for their value, he can as little claim the rent paid for them.

As common law affords not an action in this case, equity is still more averse. The proprietor no doubt is a loser ; and, which is a more material circumstance, what he loses is converted to the use of the *bona fide* possessor. But then, though the proprietor be a loser, the *bona fide* possessor is not a gainer : the fruits or rents are consumed upon living, and not a vestige of them remains. (a) Thus, equity rules even where the claim is brought recently. But where it is brought at a distance of time, for the rents of many years, against a possessor who regularly consumed his annual income, and had no reason to dread or suspect a claim, the hardship is so great, that were it founded in common law, the *bona fide* possessor would undoubtedly be relieved by equity.

What is now said suggests another case. Suppose the *bona fide* possessor to be *locupletior* by the rents he has levied. It is in most circumstances difficult to ascertain this point : but circumstances may be supposed that make it clear. The rents for example, are assigned by the *bona fide* possessor for payment of his debts : the creditors continue in possession till their claims are extinguished ; and then the true pro-

(a) The *bona fide* possessor cannot be reached by an *actio in rem versum* ; for this action takes place only where the goods applied to my use are known by me to belong to another.

CH. I.   AN ERRONEOUS TITLE.   373

prietor discovering his right, enters upon the stage.
Here it can be qualified, that the *bona fide* possessor
is *locupletior*, and that he has gained precisely the a-
mount of the debts now satisfied and paid. Admitting then, the fact, that the *bona fide* possessor is en-
riched by his possession, the question is, Whether
this circumstance will support any action against
him? None at common law, for the reason above
given, that there is nothing to found an action of reparation or damages in this case, more than where
the rents are consumed upon living. But that equity affords an action is clear; for the maxim, *Nemo
debet locupletari aliená jacturá* is applicable to this
case in the strictest sense : the effects of the proprietor are converted to the use of the *bona fide* possess-
or : what is lost by the one, is gained by the other ;
and, therefore, equity lays hold of that gain to make
up the loss. This point is so evidently founded on
equity, that even after repeated instances of wandering from justice in other points, I cannot help testi-
fying some surprise, that the learned Vinnius, not to
mention Voet and other commentators, should reject
the proprietors claim in this case, And I am the
more surprised, that, in this opinion, they make a step
no less bold than uncommon, which is, to desert their
guides who pass for being infallible, I mean the Roman lawyers, who justly maintain, that the *bona fide*
possessor is liable *quatenus locupletior.*—" Consuluit
" senatus bonæ fidei possessoribus, ne in totum dam-
" no adficiantur, sed in id duntaxat teneantur in quo
" locupletiores facti sunt. Quemcunque igitur sump-
" tum fecerint ex hæreditate, si quid dilapidaverunt,
" perdiderunt, dum re sua se abuti putant, non præs-
" tabunt : nec si donaverint, locupletiores facti vide-

374   OF RENTS LEVIED UPON   B. III.

" buntur, quamvis ad remunerandum sibi aliquem
" naturaliter obligaverunt." *

Where the *bona fide* possessor becomes *locupletior*
by extreme frugality and parsimony, it may be more
doubtful whether a claim can lie against him. It must
appear hard, that his starving himself and his family,
or his extraordinary anxiety to lay up a stock for his
children, should subject him to a claim, which his
prodigality would free him from ; and yet I. cannot
see that this consideration will prevent the operation
of the maxim, *Nemo debet locupletari alienâ jacturâ.*

The foregoing disquisition is not only curious but
useful. Among other things, it serves to determine
an important question, Whether *bona fides*, which relieves the possessor from accounting for the rents,
will, at the same time, prevent the imputation of these
rents towards extinction of a real debt he has upon
the land. A man, for example, who has claims upon
an estate by infeftments of annualrent, adjudications,
or such like, enters into possession upon a title of
property, which he believes unexceptionable. When
the lameness of his title is discovered, his *bona fides*
will secure him from paying the rents to the true
proprietor : but will it also preserve his debts alive,
and save them from being extinguished by his possession of the rents ? The answer to this question depends upon the point discussed above. If the proprietor have, at common law, though not in equity, a
claim for the value of the rents consumed by the *bona
fide* possessor, this value, as appears to me, must go in
extinction of the debts affecting the subject. For where
the proprietor, instead of demanding the money to be
paid to himself, insists only, that it shall be applied

* L. 25, § 11, De hæred. pet.

to extinguish the real incumbrances; equity inter-poseth not against this demand, which is neither rigor-ous nor unjust! and if equity interpose not, the ex-tinction must take place. If, on the other hand, there be no claim at common law for the value of the rents consumed, I cannot perceive any foundation for ex-tinguishing the real debts belonging to the possessor; unless the following proposition can be maintained, That the very act of levying the rents extinguishes *ipso facto* these debts, without necessity of applying to a judge for his interposition. This proposition holds true, where a real debt is the title for levying the rents; as, for example, where they are levied up-on a poinding of the ground, or upon an adjudication completed by a decree of mails and duties. But it cannot hold in the case under consideration; because, by the very supposition, the rents are levied upon a title of property, and not by virtue of the real debts.

I illustrate this point, by stating the following case. An adjudger, infeft, enters into possession of the land adjudged, after the legal is expired, considering his adjudication to be a right of property. After many years' possession, the person against whom the ad-judication was led, or his heir, claims the property; urging a defect in the adjudication, which prevented expiration of the legal. It is decreed, accordingly, that the adjudication never became a right of property, but that the legal is still current. Here it comes out in fact, that the land has all along been possessed upon the title of a real debt, extinguishable by levy-ing the rents, though, by the possessor, understood to be a title of property. Even in this case, the le-vying the rents will not extinguish the debt. I give my reason. To extinguish a debt by voluntary payment, two acts must concur; first, delivery by the debtor, in order to extinguish the debt; and, next, acceptance by the creditor as payment. In legal payment by execution, there must also be two acts; first, the rent levied by the creditor, in order to be applied for payment of the debt; and, next, his holding the same as payment: neither of which acts are found in the case under consideration. The rent is levied, not by virtue of execution, in order to extinguish a debt, but upon a title of property: neither is the rent received by a creditor, as payment, but by a man who conceives himself to be proprietor.

The foregoing reasoning, which, because of its intricacy, is drawn out to a considerable length, may be brought within a narrow compass. A *bona fide* possessor, who levies and consumes the rents, is not liable to account to the proprietor, whose rents they were; nor is subjected to any action, whether in law or in equity; and for that reason, his possession of the rents will not extinguish any debt in his person affecting the subject. But if it can be specified, that he is *locupletior* by his possession, that circumstance affords to the proprietor a claim against him in equity; of which the proprietor may either demand payment, or insist that the sum be applied for extinguishing the debts upon the subject.

In these conclusions, I have been forced to differ from the established practice of the Court of Session, which indeed protects the *bona fide* possessor from payment; but always holds the possession as sufficient to extinguish the real debts belonging to the possessor. But I have had the less reluctance in differing from the established practice, being sensible that this matter has not been examined with all the

CH. I. AN ERRONEOUS TITLE. 377

accuracy of which it is susceptible. In particular, we are not told upon what ground the practice is founded: and if it be founded on the supposition, that the proprietor has a legal claim for his rents levied by the *bona fide* possessor, I have clearly proved this a supposition to have no foundation.

Another important question has a near analogy to that now discussed. If the *bona fide* possessor have made considerable improvements upon the subject, by which its value is increased, will his claim be sustained as far as the proprietor is benefited by these improvements, or will it be compensated by the rents he has levied? Keeping in view what is said upon the foregoing question, one will readily answer, that the proprietor, having no claim for the rents levied and consumed by the *bona fide* possessor, has no ground upon which to plead compensation: But upon a more narrow inspection, we perceive, that this question depends upon a different principle. It is a maxim, suggested by nature, That reparations and meliorations bestowed upon a house, or upon land, ought to be defrayed out of the rents. Governed by this maxim, we sustain no claim against the proprietor for meliorations, if the expence exceed not the rents levied by the *bona fide* possessor. It is not properly compensation; for the proprietor has no claim to found a compensation upon. The claim is rejected upon a different medium: the rents, while extant, belong to the proprietor of the land: these rents are not consumed, but are bestowed upon meliorations; and the *bona fide* possessor, who thus employs the proprietor's money, and not a farthing of his own, has no claim either in law or in equity. Such, accordingly, is the determination of Papinian, the most

378 EQUITY WITH RESPECT TO B. III.

solid of all the Roman writers :—" Sumptus in præ-
" dium, quod alienum esse apparuit, a bona fide pos-
" sessore facti, neque ab eo qui prædium donavit,
" neque a domino peti possunt: verum exceptione
" doli posita, per officium judicis æquitatis ratione
" servantur: scilicet si fructuum ante litem contes-
" tatam perceptorum summam excedant. Etenim,
" admissâ compensatione, superfluum sumptum. me-
" liore prædio facto, dominus restituere cogitur."*

CHAP. II.

Powers of a court of equity with respect to a conven-
tional penalty.

A PENAL sum is inserted in a bond or obligation
as a spur on the debtor to perform. With respect to
an obligation *ad factum præstandum*, no law can compel the obligor to perform, otherwise than indirectly
by stipulating a penal sum in case of failure. This
is explained by Justinian in the following words.
" Non solum res in stipulatum deduci possunt, sed
" etiam facta; ut si stipulemur aliquid fieri vel non
" fieri. Et in hujusmodi stipulationibus optimum
" erit pœnam subjicere, ne quantitas stipulationis in
" incerto sit, ac necesse sit actori probare quod ejus
" intersit. Itaque si quis, ut fiat aliquid, stipule-
" tur; ita adjici pœna debet, *si ita factum non erit,*
" *tunc pœnæ nomine decem aureos dare spondes.*"†
This sum comes in place of the fact promised to be
done; and when paid, relieves from performing the
fact. The only thing that a court of equity has to

---

* L. 48. De rei vindicatione.　　† § 7. Inst. De verb. oblig.

CH. II. A CONVENTIONAL PENALTY. 379

mind with respect to a stipulation of this kind, is, that advantage be not taken of the obligant to engage him for a much greater sum than the damage, on failure of performance, can amount to. If exorbitant, it is so far penal, and will be mitigated by the court. But unless the excess be considerable, the court will not readily interpose. Thus, a farm being let to a tenant, under the condition, that if he entered not, he should pay a year's rent; the whole was decreed against him on his failure : for the landlord's damage might have amounted to a year's rent.*

As payment of a bond for money can be compelled by legal execution, the penal clause in such a bond differs from the former. In our bonds for borrowed money, the debtor is taken bound to pay the principal and interest, and " to pay over and above a fifth " part more of liquidate expences, in case of failzie." This lump sum is a modification or liquidation of the damage the creditor may happen to suffer by delay of payment, advantageous to both parties, by saving the trouble and expence of proving the quantum of the damages. Here, as in the former case, if the penal sum correspond in any moderate degree to the damage that may ensue from the delay, equity will not interpose. But as money-lenders in Scotland were, not long ago, in condition to give law to the borrowers, their practice was to stipulate exorbitant sums as liquidate expences, which, as rigorous and oppressive, are always mitigated in equity. " The " Court of Session (says Lord Stair) modifies ex- " orbitant penalties in bonds and contracts, even " though they bear the name of liquidate expences, " with consent of the parties, which necessitous debt-

† Durie, 15th July 1637, Skene.

380 EQUITY WITH RESPECT TO B. III.

" ors yield to. These the Lords retrench to the
" real expence and damage of the parties."* This
penal sum is now constantly made the fifth part
of the principal sum ; from which our scribes
never swerve, though nothing can be more absurd.
It is commonly no less expensive to recover £5 than
to recover £5,000 ; yet, in the former, the penalty is
no more but twenty shillings, in the latter no less
than £1,000. How disproportioned are these sums
to their destined purpose ? and yet, for preventing
such inequality, the Court of Session has not hitherto ventured to interpose. Why not an act of sederunt, confining the penalty in a bond to £100, or
some such moderate sum, however great the principal may be?

An English double bond has the effect of a conventional penalty. It was originally intended to evade
the common law, which prohibits the taking interest
for money. That prohibition is no longer in force :
the double bond, however, is continued, as it supplies
the want of a conventional penalty. The penal sum is,
upon failure, due at common law ; but in equity it is
restricted to damages. " After the day of payment,
" the double sum becomes the legal debt ; and there
" is no remedy against such penalty, but by appli-
" cation to a court of equity, which relieves on pay-
" ment of principal, interest, and costs."†

A debtor who, by failure of payment, draws a process upon him, and has no defence that he can urge
bona fide, must submit to the penalty restricted to
the pursuer's expense. No other excuse will avail
him. Failure is often occasioned by want of money :

* Book 4, tit. 3.
† New abridgment of the law, vol. 3, p. 691.

CH. II.   A CONVENTIONAL PENALTY.   381

but were such an excuse admitted, it would never be wanting; and the conventional penalty would lose its effects. Imprisonment on suspicion of treason would not be sustained as an excuse, were the debtor even refused the use of pen, ink, and paper, to request aid from his friends. The creditor goes on with all the artillery of the law; and must have his expenses out of the penalty, because the misfortune of his debtor cannot affect him.

The only doubt is, where the debtor or his heir, trusting to a defence in appearance good, ventures to stand a process, and at last is overruled; whether the creditor be entitled to the modified penalty. This question merits a deliberate discussion; in order to which, it will be necessary to examine what ground there is for costs of suit, abstracting from a conventional penalty. Any voluntary wrong is a foundation for damages, even at common law; but a man free from fault or blame, is not liable for damages, or liable to repair any hurt he may have occasioned:* whence it follows, that there is no foundation, even at common law, for subjecting to costs of suit a defendant who is *in bona fide*. Equity is still more averse from subjecting an innocent person to damages; and, considering the fallibility of man, his case would be deplorable, were he bound to repair all the hurt he may occasion by an error or mistake. What then shall be said of the act 144. parl. 1592, appointing, " That damage, interest, and expences of plea, be " admitted by all judges, and liquidated in the de- " cree, whether condemnator or absolvitor?" If this regulation could ever be just, it must have been among a plain people, governed by a few simple

* See the chapter immediately foregoing.

EQUITY WITH RESPECT TO B. III.

rules of law, supposed to be universally known. Law, in its present state, is too intricate for presuming that every person who errs is *in mala fide*; and yet, unless *mala fides* be presumed in every case, the regulation cannot be justified.

These things being premised, we proceed to examine, whether a defender who is *in bona fide* can be subjected to costs by virtue of a conventional penalty. Suppose a defence urged against payment, so doubtful in law as to divide the judges, who at last gave it against the defendant by the narrowest plurality : Or suppose the cause to depend on an obscure fact requiring a laborious investigation ; as where I owe £1,000 by bond to my brother, who dies without children, so far as known to his relations. A woman appears with an infant, alleging a private marriage. I stand a process : the proof, drawn out to a great length, appears still dark and doubtful : judgment is at last pronounced against me by a plurality. Will justice permit me to be loaded with an immense sum of costs for not submitting to the claim without trial ? To extend a conventional penalty to such cases, would be in effect to punish men, for adhering, after the best advice, to what appears their rights and privileges : the grievance would be intolerable. Many a man, through the dread of costs, would be deterred from insisting on a just defence, and tamely submit to be wronged.

It appears, therefore, clear, that to extend against a *bona fide* defendant the penal clause in a bond, would be rigorous and unjust. And to make it still more clear, I put the following question. Let us suppose, that in a bond of borrowed money the debtor is taken expressly bound to pay the costs of suit, however

Ch. II. A CONVENTIONAL PENALTY. 383

plausible his defence may be, however strong his *bona fides*: would not such a clause be rejected by the Court of Session, as exacted from a necessitous debtor by a rigorous and oppressive creditor? If the question be answered in the affirmative, which cannot be doubted, the necessary consequence is, that the penal clause, in its ordinary style, cannot be understood to have that meaning.

But at that rate, it will be urged, a conventional penalty is of no use to the creditor where it is most needed, namely, in a process for recovering payment; that if the debtor be *in bona fide*, the penalty will not reach him; and if he be litigious, that there is no use for the penalty, as he is subjected to costs at common law. I answer, That the penal clause is of use even in a process. Litigiosity must be evident, to infer costs at common law; but the slightest fault, or even doubt, on the defendant's part, though far from amounting to litigiosity, will subject him to the modified penalty. And Lord Stair, accordingly, in the passage partly quoted above, says, " That in liquid-
" ating the pursuer's expence, the Lords take slen-
" der probation of the true expence, and do not con-
" sider whether it be necessary or not, provided it
" exceed not the sum agreed on; whereas, in other
" cases, they allow no expence but what is necessary
" or profitable."

384 WHAT OBLIGATIONS, &c. B. III.

CHAP. III.

What obligations and legacies transmit to heirs.

IF the obligee's heirs be named in the obligation, they will succeed whether he die before or after the term of payment, because such is the will of parties. The present question relates to obligations where the obligee's heirs are not named. Such obligations by the common law transmit not to heirs; because the common law regards what is said to be the only proof of will: but equity is not so peremptory nor superficial. It considers, that in human affairs errors and omissions are frequent, and that words are not always to be absolutely relied on: it holds, indeed, words to be the best evidence of will, but not to be the only evidence. If, therefore, any suspicion lie, that the will is not precisely what is expressed, every rational circumstance is laid hold of to ascertain, with all the accuracy possible, what really was the will of the granter, or of the contractors.*

With respect to this point, the motive that produced the obligation is one capital circumstance. Where there is no motive but good-will merely, the words are strictly adhered to; as there is nothing to infer that more was intended than is expressed. Therefore my gratuitous promise of a sum to John, is void at common law, if he die without receiving payment; for as heirs are not named, they have no claim. Nor in equity have they any claim, if the obligee die before the term of payment. But where the obligee survives the term, without receiving payment, his

* See *suprà*, p. 146, 147.

CH. III. TRANSMIT TO HEIRS. 385

heirs have a good claim upon the following rule in equity, That what ought to have been done is held as done. * If payment had been made, as ought to have been done, at the term specified in the deed, the sum would have been an addition to the stock of the obligee, which would have accrued to his representatives; and it would be a reproach to justice, were they left to suffer by the obstinacy or neglect of the obligor. It would be a reproach still greater, that the obligor's fault, in postponing payment, should liberate him from his obligation. The sum is, In a deed flowing from a motive of pure benevolence, the granter's will must govern, which is understood to be in favour of the grantee only, if heirs be not mentioned. In commercial obligations, on the contrary, where there is *quid pro quo*, the obligee's will governs; and he is understood to purchase for his heirs as well as for himself, if the contrary be not expressed. The not mentioning heirs is an omission, which will be supplied by a court of equity; as justice will not permit the obligor to enjoy the valuable consideration, without performing the equivalent pactioned. Thus, a bond for borrowed money, though the creditor only be mentioned, and not heirs, descends to his heirs, where he dies before the term of payment, as well as after.

Men are bound to educate their children till they be able to provide for themselves; and any further provision is understood to be gratuitous. Hence, a bond of provision to children is deemed a gratuitous deed; and, for that reason, if the children die before the term of payment, equity gives no aid to their heirs. If heirs be named in the bond, they have

* See Elucidations of Common and Statute law, p. 62.

2 B

WHAT OBLIGATIONS, &c. B. III.

right at common law : if not named, neither equity nor common law gives them right. Thus, in a contract of marriage, certain provisions being allotted to the children, the portions of the males payable at their age of twenty-one years, and of the females at eighteen, without mentioning heirs or assignees ; the assignees and creditors of some of the children who died before the term of payment, were judged to have no right.* I cannot so readily acquiesce in the following decision, where a bond of provision payable to a daughter at her age of fourteen, and to her heirs, executors, and assignees, was voided by her death before the term of payment. † The addition of *heirs, executors, and assignees,* was thought to regard the child's death after the term of payment ; and not to be an indication of the granter's will that the bond should be effectual though the child died before the term of payment. The clause, I admit, is capable of that restricted meaning : but I can find no reason for this restriction ; and, in all cases, it is safest to give words their natural import, unless it be made clear, that the granter's meaning was different. And, accordingly, Chalmers having settled his estate upon his nephew, with the burden of a sum certain to Isabel Inglis, wife of David Millar, and to her heirs, executors, or assignees, payable year and day after his death, with interest after the term of payment ; and Isabel having died before Chalmers, leaving a son who survived him ; the sum was decreed to that son as a conditional institute.‡

Even a bond of provision, or any gratuitous deed,

---

* Stair, January 17, 1665, Edgar *contra* Edgar.

† Stair, February 22, 1677, Belsches *contra* Belsches.

‡ Millar *contra* Inglis, July 16, 1760.

CH. III.   TRANSMIT TO HEIRS.   387

will descend to heirs, as above said, if such was the
granter's intention.   Nor is it necessary in equity
that such intention be expressed in words : it is sufficient that it be made evident from circumstances.

What is said above seems a more clear and satisfactory reason for excluding heirs where the creditor
in a bond of provision dies before the term of payment,
than what is commonly assigned, that the sum in the
bond, being destined as a stock for the child, ceases
to be due, since it cannot answer the purpose for
which it was intended.   Were this reason good, it
would hold equally whether the child die before or
after the term of payment ; and, therefore, in proving
too much it proves nothing.

In what cases a legacy descends to heirs, is a question that takes in a great variety of matter.   To have
a distinct notion of this question, legacies must be
divided into their different kinds.   I begin with the
legacy of a *corpus*.   The property here is transferred
to the legatee *ipso facto* upon the testator's death.
The reason is, that will solely must in this case have
the effect to transfer property, otherwise it could never
be transferred from the dead to the living : a proprietor after his death cannot make delivery ; and no
other person but the proprietor can make a legal delivery.   Now if the legatee be vested in the property of the subject legated, it must, upon his death, descend to his heirs even by common law.

But what if the legatee die before the testator ?
In this case the legacy is void.   The testator remains
proprietor till his death, and the subject legated cannot by his death be transferred to a person who is no
longer in existence.   Nor can it be transferred to that

2 B 2

person's heirs, because the testator did not exert any act of will in their favour.

The next case I put is of a sum of money legated to Titius. A legacy of this sort, giving the legatee an interest in the testator's personal estate, and entitling him to a proportion, vests in the legatee *ipso facto* upon the testator's death. And, for the same reason that is given above, the legacy, even at common law, will transmit to heirs, if the legatee survive the testator; if not, it will be void. But what if the legacy be ordered to be paid at a certain term? It is to be considered, whether the term be added for the benefit of the testator's heir, in order to give him time for preparing the money; or whether it be added to limit the legacy. A term for payment given to the testator's heir, will not alter the nature of the legacy, nor prevent its vesting in the legatee upon the testator's death; and, consequently, such a legacy will transmit to heirs, even where the legatee dies before the term of payment, provided he survive the testator. *Dies cedit etsi non venerit.* But where the purpose of naming a term for payment is to limit the legacy, the legatee's death before that term will bar his heirs, because he himself had never any right. Here *dies nec cedit nec venit.* In order to determine what was the intention of the testator in naming a day for payment, the rule laid down by Papinian is judicious: *Dies incertus conditionem in testamento facit.** A day certain for performance is commonly added in favour of the testator's heir, in order to give him time for providing the money. An uncertain day respects commonly the condition of the legatee; as where a legacy is in favour of a boy to be claimed

* L. 75, De condition. et demon.

CH. III. TRANSMIT TO HEIRS. 389

when he arrives at eighteen years of age, or of a girl to be claimed at her marriage. In such instances, it appears to be the will of the testator, that the legacy shall not vest before the term of payment. The *dies incertus* is said to make the legacy conditional; not properly, for the naming a day of payment, certain or uncertain, is not a condition. But as the uncertain term for payment has the effect to limit the legacy in the same manner as if it were conditional; for that reason, the uncertain term is said to imply a condition, or to make the legacy conditional.

A third sort of legacy is where the testator burdens his heir to pay a certain sum to Titius singly, without the addition of heirs. The heirs at common law have no right even where Titius survives the testator, because there is not here, as in the former cases, any subject vested in Titius to descend to his heirs; nor can heirs, at common law, claim upon an obligation which is not in their favour. But equity sustains an action to them: for no day being named, the death of the testator is the term of payment; and equity will not suffer the testator's heir to profit by delaying payment. Where a term of payment is added by the testator, the case becomes the same with that of a gratuitous obligation *inter vivos.*

CHAPTER IV.

Arrestment and process of forthcoming.

CURRENT coin is the only legal subject for payment of debt, which, accordingly, the creditor is bound to accept of. Sometimes, however, for want of current

ARRESTMENT AND' B. III.

coin, the creditor submits to take satisfaction in goods; and sometimes he is put off with a security, an assignment to rents, for example, or to debts, which empowers him to operate his payment out of these subjects. Legal execution, copying voluntary acts between debtor and creditor, is of three kinds. The first, compelling payment of the debt, resembles voluntary payment. This was the case of poinding in its original form;* and it is the case of a decree for making *corpora* forthcoming, as will be seen afterwards. The second, resembles voluntary acceptance of goods for satisfying the debt; which is the case of poinding according to our present practice. The goods are not sold as originally; but after being valued, are delivered *ipsa corpora* to the creditor. The third, resembles a voluntary security: it gives the creditor a security upon his debtor's funds, and enables him to operate his payment accordingly. This is the case of an adjudication during the legal; which empowers the creditor to draw payment out of the debtor's rents by a decree of mails and duties against the tenants. A decree for making forthcoming sums of money due to the debtor, is of the same nature: it is a security only, not payment; and, consequently, if my debtor, against whom the decree of forthcoming is obtained, prove insolvent, the sum is lost to me, not to my creditor who obtained the decree: his security indeed is gone; but the debt which was secured remains entire.

So much for preliminaries. And as to the subject of the present chapter, I begin with the several kinds of arrestment. The first I shall mention is, that which proceeds on a judicial order to secure the per-

* Historical Law-tracts, tract 10.

CH. IV. PROCESS OF FORTHCOMING. 391

son of one accused of a crime. The next is for securing moveable effects in the hands of the possessor, till the property be determined. This arrestment, termed *rei servandæ causa*, is a species of sequestration: it is a sequestration in the hands of the possessor. The goods are thus secured till the property be determined; and the person declared proprietor, takes possession *viâ facti*. A third arrestment is, that which is preparatory to a process of forthcoming raised by a creditor for recovering payment out of his debtor's moveables, whether *corpora* or *debita*.

A debtor's corporeal moveables in his own possession, are attached by poinding, corresponding to the *Levari facias* in England. But where such moveables are in the possession of any other, and the particulars unknown, there can be no place for poinding. The creditor obtains a warrant or order from a proper court to arrest them in the hands of the possessor, to hinder him from delivering them up to the proprietor. The service of this order is termed an *arrestment*; and the person upon whom it is served, is termed the *arrestee*. The first step of the process of forthcoming, consequent upon the arrestment, is an order to sell the goods secured by the arrestment. The price is delivered to the creditor for his payment; and the debt is thereby extinguished in whole or in part, which completes the process. A process of forthcoming upon sums arrested, is in the same form; with this only difference, that instead of selling *corpora*, a decree of forthcoming goes out against the arrestee, and payment is recovered from him accordingly.

An arrestment of this kind is not to be considered as necessary to found a process of forthcoming. This process is founded on common law; and may proceed without an arrestment; which will appear from the following consideration. If I have not money to pay my debt, I ought to convey to my creditor what other things I am master of, that he may convert them into money for his payment. If I refuse to do him that act of justice, a court of law will interpose, and do what I ought to have done. The court will adjudge my land to belong to him; or they will ordain my effects to be made forthcoming to him. An arrestment, indeed, commonly precedes; but its only purpose is, to secure the subject in the hands of the arrestee, till a process of forthcoming be raised. In that respect, an arrestment resembles an inhibition, which is not a step of execution, but only an injunction to the debtor, prohibiting him to alien his land, or to contract debt, in order to preserve the fund entire for the creditor's adjudication. A forthcoming is of the same nature with an adjudication: an heritable subject is attached by the latter; a moveable by the former. A process of adjudication is carried on every day without a preparatory inhibition; and a process of forthcoming may be carried on equally without a preparatory arrestment.

Though what is above laid down belongs to common law, it is, however, proper here, as an introduction to the matters of equity that follow. The subject to be handled, is the operations of common law and of equity, with respect to a competition between an arrestment and other rights, voluntary or legal. With respect to the arrestment of a *corpus*, all are agreed, that it is a sequestration merely in the hands of the possessor, and transfers no right to the creditor. The goods secured by the arrestment, are in

CH. IV.   PROCESS OF FORTHCOMING.   393

the process of forthcoming sold as the property of the debtor; and the price is applied for payment of the debt due by him to the arrester.' For that reason, an arrestment cannot bar a poinding carried on by another creditor. If the subject belong to the debtor; poinding goes on of course by the authority of common law.

It is natural to assimilate the arrestment of a debt to that of a moveable, in being prohibitory only, and in transferring no right to the creditor. Yet many hold, that the former has a stronger effect than the latter, by transferring to the creditor some sort of right, signified by the term *nexus realis*. To ascertain the nature and effect of such an arrestment, the best way is to give an accurate analysis of it. The letter or warrant for arrestment, to which the arrestment itself is entirely conformable, is' in the following words :—" To fence and arrest all and sundry the " said A. B. his readiest goods, gear, debts, &c. in " whosoever hands the same can be apprehended, to " remain under sure fence and arrestment, at the in- " stance of the said complainer, ay and while pay- " ment be made to him." Upon this warrant and arrestment following upon it, it will be observed, first, That no person is named but the arrester and his debtor. It is not a limited warrant to arrest in the hands of any particular person; but an authority to arrest in the hands of any person that the creditor suspects may owe money to his debtor. Secondly, The arrestee is not ordered or authorised to make payment to the arrester: the order he receives, is to keep the money in his hand till the arrester be satisfied. These particulars make it plain, that an arrestment, like an inhibition, is merely prohibitory;

and that it transfers not any right to the arrester. And this point is put out of doubt by the summons of forthcoming, concluding, " That the defender " should be decerned and ordained to make forth- " coming to the complainer the sum of " resting and owing by him to A. B. (the com- " plainer's debtor against whom the execution passes,) " and arrested in the defender's hands at the complain- " er's instance." It is the decree of forthcoming, therefore, that entitles the creditor to demand the sum arrested, to be applied for payment of the debt upon which the arrestment and forthcoming proceed- ed; and the preparatory arrestment has no other ef- fect, but to prevent alienation before the process of forthcoming is raised.

If it hold true, that arrestment is prohibitory only, and that my creditor arresting in the hands of my debtor, hath no right to the sum arrested till he ob- tain a decree of forthcoming, it follows, upon the principles of common law, that this sum, belonging to me after arrestment, as well as before, lies open to be attached by my other creditors; and that, in a competition among these creditors, all of them ar- resters, the first decree of forthcoming must give pre- ference. For the first order served upon my debtor binds him to the creditor who obtained the order; after which he cannot legally pay to any other. Thus stands the common law, which is followed out in a course of decisions, mostly of an old date, giving pre- ference, not to the first arrestment, but to the first decree of forthcoming.

Whether equity make any variation, shall be our next inquiry. It is the privilege of a debtor, with respect to his own funds, to apply which of them he

CH. IV.   PROCESS OF FORTHCOMING.   395

pleases for payment of his debts. Upon the debtor's failure, this choice is transferred to the creditor, who may attach any particular subject for his payment. In that case, the debtor is bound to convey to his creditor the subject attached, for his security: it is undoubtedly the duty of the debtor to relieve his creditor from the trouble and expence of execution; and, consequently, to relieve him from execution against any particular subject, by surrendering it voluntarily, unless he find other means of making payment. The creditor's privilege to attach any particular subject for his payment, and the debtor's relative obligation to save execution by surrendering that subject to his creditor, are, indeed, the foundation of all execution. A judge authorising execution, supplies only the place of the debtor; and, consequently, cannot authorise execution against any particular subject, unless the debtor be antecedently bound to surrender the same to his creditor.* This branch of the debtor's duty explains a rule in law, " That the inchoated " execution makes the subject litigious, and ties up " the debtor's hands from aliening." If it be his duty to prevent execution by surrendering this subject to his creditor, it is inconsistent with his duty to dispose of it to any other person.

In applying the rules of equity to an arrestment, the duty now unfolded is of importance. If the debtor ought to convey to his creditor the subject arrested, no other creditor who knows the debtor to be so bound, can justly attach that subject by legal execution: for it is unjust to demand from a debtor a subject he is bound to convey to another.† And if a creditor shall act thus unjustly, by arresting a subject

* See *suprà*, p. 289.   † See *suprà*, p. 290.

which he knows to be already arrested by another creditor, a court of equity will disappoint the effect of the second arrestment, by giving preference to the first.

Our writers, though they have not clearly unfolded the debtor's obligation to the first arrester, have, however, been sensible of it; for it is obviously with reference to this obligation, that an arrestment is said to make a *nexus realis* upon the subject. I know but of two ways by which a man can be connected with a debt: one is, where he has the *jus exigendi*, and one, where the creditor is bound to make it over to him. It will be admitted, that an arrestment has not the effect of transferring to the arrester the debt arrested: the arrester has not even the *jus exigendi* till he obtain a decree of forthcoming. And if so, a *nexus realis* applied to the present subject, cannot import other than the obligation which the creditor is under to make over the debt to the arrester. Thus, by the principles of equity, the first arrestment is preferable, while the subject is *in medio*; but if a posterior arrester, without notice of a former, obtain payment upon a decree of forthcoming, he is secure in equity, as well as at common law; and his discovery afterward of a prior arrestment will not oblige him to repay the money.* This equitable rule of preferring the first arrestment, while the subject is *in medio*, is accordingly established at present, and all the late decisions of the Court of Session proceed upon it.

An arrestment, as observed above, hath not the effect at common law to bar poinding; but, in equity, for the reason now given, an arrestment made known to the poinder, ought to bar him from proceeding in

* See *suprà*, p. 293.

CH. IV.   PROCESS OF FORTHCOMING.   397

his execution, as well as it bars a posterior arrestment. A creditor ought not, by any sort of execution, to force from his debtor what the debtor cannot honestly convey to him. And yet, though in ranking arrestments, the Court of Session follows the rules of equity, it acts as a court of common law in permitting a subject to be poinded after it is arrested by another creditor. I shall close this branch of my subject with a general observation, That the equitable rules established above, hold only where the debtor is solvent: it will be seen afterward, that, in the case of bankruptcy, all personal creditors ought to draw equally.

So much about arresters competing for the same debt. Next about an arrester competing with an assignee. Touching this competition, one preliminary point must be adjusted, namely, How far an arrestment makes the subject arrested litigious; or, in other words, How far it bars voluntary deeds. It is obvious, in the first place, that an arrestment makes the subject litigious with respect to the arrestee, because it is served upon him: the very purpose of the arrestment is, to prohibit him from paying the debt arrested, or from giving up the goods. In the next place, as a creditor may proceed to arrestment without intimating his purpose to his debtor, an arrestment cannot bar the debtor's voluntary deeds, till it be notified to him: the arrestment deprives him not of his *jus crediti*, nor of his property; and while he continues ignorant of the arrestment, nothing bars him, either in law or in equity, from conveying his right to a third party. Upon that account, intimation to him is an established practice in the country from whence we borrowed an arrestment: " Quamvis

"debitor debitoris mei a me arrestari nequeat, cum
"mihi nulla ex causa obligatus sit, tamen, quod
"Titius debitori meo debet, per judicem inhibere
"possum, ne debitori meo solvatur, sine mea vel ju-
"dicis voluntate. De quo arresto debitorem meum
"certiorem facere debeo eique diem dicere; quo si
"compareat, nec justam causam alleget ob quam ar-
"restum relaxari debeat, vel si non compareat, judex
"ex pecunia arrestata mihi solvendum decernet."*
The same doctrine is laid down by Balfour,† "That
"an arrestment of corns, goods, or gear, ought to be
"intimated to the owner thereof; and that, if no in-
"timation be made, it is lawful for the owner to dis-
"pose of the same at his pleasure." Thirdly, With
respect to others, an arrestment, though notified to
the arrester's debtor, makes not the subject litigious;
for any person ignorant of the arrestment, is at liberty to take from the arrester's debtor a conveyance to
the subject arrested. The cedent aliens, indeed, *malâ
fide*, after the arrestment is notified to him; but the
purchaser is secure if he be *in bona fide:* the property is legally transferred to him; and there is nothing
in law nor in equity to deprive a man of a subject
honestly acquired. That an arrestment makes not
the subject litigious with regard to third parties, will
be clear from considering, that an effect so strong is
never given to any act, unless there be a public notification: a process in the Court of Session is supposed to be known to all; and as it is a rule, *Quod nihil
innovandum pendente lite,* any person who transacts
either with the plaintiff or defendant, so as to hurt
the other, does knowingly an unlawful act, which for

* Sande Decis. Fris. l. 1, tit. 17, def. 1.
† Title Arrestment, cap. 3.

CH. IV.   PROCESS OF FORTHCOMING.   309

that reason will be voided : an inhibition and interdiction are published to all the lieges, who are thereby put *in mala fide* to purchase from the person inhibited or interdicted : an apprising renders the subject litigious as to all, because the letters are publicly proclaimed or denounced, not only upon the land, but also at the market-cross of the head-borough of the jurisdiction where the land lies ;* and an adjudication has the same effect, because it is a process in the Court of Session. A charge of horning bars not the debtor from aliening, till he be publicly proclaimed or denounced rebel ; and it must be evident, that an arrestment served upon my debtor, cannot hurt third parties dealing with me, more than a horning against myself. In a word, litigiosity, so as to affect third parties, never takes place without public notification.

Were we to draw an argument from an inhibition, it might be inferred, that even the actual knowledge of an arrestment should not bar one from purchasing the subject arrested. But the argument from an inhibition concludes not with respect to an arrestment ; and in order to shew the difference, it will be necessary to state the nature of an inhibition in a historical view.

This writ prohibits the alienation of moveable subjects as well as of immoveable ; and to secure against alienation, the writ is published to the lieges, to put every man upon his guard against dealing with the person inhibited. This writ must have been the invention of a frugal age, before the commerce of money was far extended. While inhibitions were rare, their publication could be kept in remembrance ; a debtor inhibited would be a remarkable person, to make every one avoid dealing with him. But when

* Stair, lib. 3, tit. 2, § 14.

400   ARRESTMENT AND   **B. III.**

the commerce of money was further extended, and debts were multiplied, an inhibition was no longer a mark of distinction. And as inhibitions could no longer be kept in memory, they became a load upon the commerce of moveables past enduring; for no man was in safety to purchase from his neighbour a horse, or a bushel of corn, till first the records of inhibitions were consulted. A Lycurgus intending to bar commerce, in order to preserve his nation in poverty, could not have invented a more effectual scheme. This execution, inconsistent with commerce, as far as it affects moveables, is also inconsistent in itself, tending directly to disappoint its own end. The purpose of an inhibition is to force payment; and the effect of it is to prevent payment, by locking up the debtor's moveables, which commonly are the only ready fund for procuring money.

These reasons have prevailed upon the Court of Session to refuse any effect to an inhibition as far as it regards moveables. An inhibition indeed, with respect to its form and tenor, continues the same as originally; and, accordingly, every debtor inhibited is to this hour discharged to alien his moveables, no less peremptorily than to alien his land. This inconsistence cannot be remedied but by the legislature; for the Court of Session cannot alter a writ of the common law, more than it can alter any other branch of the common law. But the Court of Session, as a court of equity, can redress the rigour, injustice, or oppression of the common law: and though it hath no power to alter the style of an inhibition, it acts justly in refusing to give force to it as far as it affects moveables; because so far it is an oppressive and inconsistent execution. This argument, as above hinted,

CH. IV.   PROCESS OF FORTHCOMING.   401

may seem to apply to an arrestment, that even the knowledge of this execution ought not to bar any person from purchasing the subject arrested, whether it be a debt, or a *corpus.* But this holds not in practice : and there is good reason for distinguishing, in this particular, an arrestment from an inhibition : the latter prohibits, in general, the debtor to alien any of his moveables, and for that reason, is rigorous and oppressive : the former is of particular subjects only ; nor doth it affect any moveables in the debtor's own possession, for which reason, the execution so limited, is neither rigorous nor oppressive. An arrestment, therefore, as to the subjects affected by it, is allowed in practice to have the full effect that is given it at common law. But with respect to a third party, it has a more ample effect in equity than at common law : for though a man who *bona fide* purchases a subject arrested, is secure in equity as well as at common law ; yet a *mala fide* purchase, though effectual at common law, will undoubtedly be voided in a court of equity.

Having discussed preliminary points, we proceed to the subject proposed, competition between an arrester and an assignee. I begin with arrestment of a moveable bond, assigned before the arrestment, but intimated after. The intimation by our law, makes a complete conveyance of the bond into the person of the assignee; after which, the sum cannot be made forthcoming to the arrester for his payment: the very foundation of his claim is gone ; for neither law nor equity will permit any subject to be taken in execution that belongs not to the debtor. Many decisions, it is true, prefer the arrester ; upon what medium, I cannot comprehend. Our decisions, how-

2 c

402 ARRESTMENT AND B. III.

ever, are far from being uniform upon this point. I give the following example. John assigns the rent of his land for security and payment of a debt due by him. He hath another creditor, who afterward raises a process of adjudication affecting the same land. The assignee intimating his right after the citation, but before the decree of adjudication, is preferred before the adjudger.* An arrestment surely makes not a stronger *nexus* upon the subject than is made by a citation upon a summons of adjudication; and if an assignment be preferred before the latter, it ought also to be preferred before the former. But I say more. Let it be supposed, that after the citation upon the summons of adjudication, but before intimation of the assignment, the rent is arrested by a third creditor. The decree of adjudication is preferred before the arrestment.† If so, here is a circle absolutely inextricable, an adjudication preferred before an arrestment, the arrestment before an assignment, and the assignment before the adjudication. This proves demonstrably, that the assignee ought to be preferred before the arrester, as well as before the adjudger. The court went still further, in preferring an assignee before an arrester. An English assignment, to this day, is a procuratory *in rem suam* only, carrying the equitable right indeed, but not the legal right. And yet, with respect to a bond due to Wilson residing in England, by the Earl of Rothes in Scotland, an English assignment by Wilson of the said bond was of itself, without intimation, preferred before an arrestment served afterward upon the Earl. The preference thus given was clearly founded on

---

* Durie, March 2, 1637, Smith *contra* Hepburn.

† Dalrymple, June 26, 1705, Stewart *contra* Stewart.

CH. IV.   PROCESS OF FORTHCOMING.   403

equity; because, the Court of Session, as a court of equity, could not justly make forthcoming to a creditor of Wilson for his payment, a subject that Wilson had aliened for a valuable consideration, and to which the purchaser had the equitable, though not the legal right. But if this be a just decision, which it undoubtedly is, nothing can be more unjust, than to prefer an arrestment before a Scotch assignment of a prior date, even after it is completed by intimation; for here the assignee has both the equitable and legal right.

The next case I put, is where, in a process of forthcoming upon an arrestment, an assignee appears with an assignment prior to the arrestment, but not intimated. I have already given my reason for preferring the assignee, as the court did with respect to an English assignment: and yet, the ordinary practice is to prefer the arrestment; which one will have no hesitation to believe, when an arrestment is preferred even where the assignment is intimated.

The preference due to the assignee is, in this case, so clear, that I am encouraged to carry the doctrine further, by preferring an assignee even before a poinder; provided the assignee appear for his interest before the poinding be completed. The poinder, no doubt, is preferable at common law, because, till an assignment be completed by intimation, the debtor continues proprietor. The assignee, however, has the equitable right; and justice will not permit goods that the debtor has aliened for a valuable consideration to be attached by any of his creditors. The result will be different, where the poinding is completed, and the property of the goods is transferred to the creditor, before the assignee appears. In this

2 c 2

404 ARRESTMENT AND B. III.

case, the poinder is secure; because no man can be forfeited of his property who has committed no fault.

I proceed to an assignment, dated after arrestment, but intimated before competition. Supposing the assignee to be *in bona fide*, he is clearly preferable; for the intimation vests in him the legal as well as equitable right; which bars absolutely the cedent and his creditors: and this reason is good at common law to prefer the assignee, even supposing he had notice of the arrestment before he took the assignment. But in equity, the arrester is preferable where the assignee is *in mala fide*, for the following reason. The debtor, after his subject is affected by an arrestment, is bound in duty to make over the subject to his creditor the arrester: if he transgress by conveying the subject to one who knows of the arrestment, both are guilty of a moral wrong, which equity will redress by preferring the arrester.

Let us drop now the intimation, by putting the case, that in a process of forthcoming upon an arrestment, an assignee appears for his interest, craving preference upon an assignment bearing date after the arrestment, but before the citation in the process of forthcoming. Supposing the assignee *in mala fide*, he will, in equity, be postponed to the arrester for the reason immediately above given. But what shall be the rule of preference, where the assignee purchases *bona fide?* The arrester and he have each of them an equitable right to the subject; neither of them has the legal right. This case resembles that of stellionate, where a proprietor of land sells to two different purchasers ignorant of each other: neither of whom has the legal right, because there is no infeftment; but each of them has an equitable right.

CH. IV.   PROCESS OF FORTHCOMING.

In these cases, I cannot discover a rule for preference; nor can I extricate the matter otherwise than by dividing the subject between the competitors. And, after all, whether this may not be cutting the Gordian knot instead of untying it, I pretend not to be certain.

Upon the whole, an arrestment appears a very precarious security till a process of forthcoming be commenced. This process indeed is a notification to the debtor not to alien in prejudice of the arrestor, and at the same time a public notification to the lieges not to purchase the subject arrested. And by this process the subject is rendered litigious ; though the same privilege is not indulged to an inhibition as far as moveables are concerned.

CHAPTER V.

Powers of a court of equity with relation to Bankrupts.

In the two foregoing books are contained many instances of equity remedying imperfections in common law as to payment of debt. But that subject is not exhausted: on the contrary, it enlarges upon us, when we take under consideration the law concerning bankruptcy. And this branch was purposely reserved, to be presented to the reader in one view ; for the parts are too intimately connected to bear a separation without suffering by it.

This branch of law is of great importance in every commercial country ; and in order to set it in a clear light, I cannot think of a better arrangement than

406 OF BANKRUPTS. B. III.

what follows. First, To state the rules of common law. Second, To examine what equity dictates. Third, To state the regulations of different countries. And to conclude with the proceedings of the Court of Session.

The rules of common law are very short, but very imperfect. Any deed done by a bankrupt is effectual at common law, no less than if he were solvent; nor is legal execution obstructed by bankruptcy; a creditor, after his debtor's bankruptcy, having the same remedy for recovering payment, that he had before. The common law considers only whether the subject conveyed by the bankrupt, or attached by his creditors, was his property: if it was, a court of common law supports both. Let him alien his moveables, or his land, intentionally, to defraud his creditors, common law, however regardless of intention, considers such acts as legal exertions of property, and consequently effectual.

In order to determine what justice dictates in this case, it becomes necessary, in the first place, to ascertain what circumstances make bankruptcy in the common sense of mankind. A man, while he carries on trade, or hath any business that affords him a prospect of gain, is not bankrupt though his effects may not be sufficient to pay his debts; for he has it in view to pay all; but if his business fail him, and leave him no prospect of paying his debts, he is, in the common sense of mankind, insolvent or bankrupt; his creditors must lose by him.

This situation, though not uncommon, is yet singular in the eye of justice. *Property* and *interest*, for the most part strictly united, are here disjoined: the bankrupt continues proprietor of his estate, but

CH. V.   OF BANKRUPTS.   **407**

his creditors are the only persons interested in it: they have the equitable right, and nothing remains with him but the legal right. In this view, a bankrupt may not improperly be held as a trustee, bound to manage his effects for behoof of his creditors: the duty of a bankrupt is in effect the same with that of a trustee, as both of them ought to make a faithful account of the subjects under their management. While a debtor continues solvent, he may pay his creditors in what order he pleases; because no creditor suffers by the preference given to another. But upon his bankruptcy or insolvency, that privilege vanishes: he is bound to all his creditors equally; and justice dictates, that he ought to distribute his effects among them equally. A creditor demanding payment from his debtors, or from their cautioners, bound conjunctly and severally, ought to behave with impartiality:* much more is this incumbent upon a bankrupt in making payment to his creditors. No distinction ought to be made but between real and personal creditors: a real security fairly obtained from a debtor in good circumstances, is not prejudicial to the other creditors; and if unexceptionable originally, it cannot be voided by what may afterward happen to the debtor. There is no injustice, therefore, in the preference given to real creditors before personal.†

To confirm this doctrine, I appeal to the general sense of the nation, vouched by act 5. parl. 1696,

* *Vid. supra*, p. 112, et seq.

† The following rule is contained in a code of Hindostan laws. " When several men are creditors to the same debtor, they shall " make a sort of common stock of their debts, and receive their " respective shares of each payment. If any creditor refuse to " accede to this agreement, he shall lose his share."

408 OF BANKRUPTS. B. III.

which, taking for granted that a bankrupt ought to behave with impartiality to his creditors, prohibits him to prefer any of his creditors before the rest, and annuls every one of his deeds giving such undue preference. And I appeal also to the English bankrupt-statutes, which evidently rest upon the same foundation.

Thus stands the duty of a bankrupt with respect to his creditors, founded on the rules of justice. The duty of the creditors with respect to each other may seem not so evident. It is the privilege of a creditor who obtains not satisfaction, to draw his payment out of the debtor's effects: and it will not readily occur, that the debtor's insolvency, the very circumstance which enhances the value of the privilege, should be a bar to it. This way of thinking is natural; and hence the following maxims that have obtained an universal currency: *Prior tempore potio jure: Vigilantibus non dormientibus jura subveniunt.* In rude times, before the connections of society have taken deep root, selfish principles prevail over those that are social. Thus in the present case, a creditor, partial to his own interest, is apt to confine his thoughts to the power he hath over his debtor; overlooking, or seeing but obscurely, that where the debtor is bankrupt, his creditors, connected now with each other by a common fund, ought to divide that fund equally among them. But by refinement of manners, man becomes more a social than a selfish being; and, by the improvement of his faculties, he discovers the lawful authority of social duties, as what he is bound to fulfil even in opposition to his own interest. By such refinement it is at last perceived, that by the debtor's

CH. V. OF BANKRUPTS. 409

insolvency, his personal creditors have all of them an equal claim upon his effects ; that a creditor, taking measures to operate his payment, ought to consider the connection he has with his fellow creditors, engaged equally with him upon the same fund ; and, therefore, that justice requires an equal distribution. In every view we take of the subject, we become more and more satisfied that this rule is agreeable to justice. To make the distribution of the common fund depend on priority of execution, exhibits the appearance of a race, where the swiftest obtains the prize : a race is a more manly competition, because there is merit in swiftness ; none in priority of execution, which depends upon accident more frequently than upon expedition. It is natural for savage animals to fall out about their prey, and to rob each other ; but social beings ought to be governed by the principle of benevolence : creditors in particular, connected by a common fund, and equally interested, should not, like enemies, strive to prevent each other ; but, like near relations, should join in common measures for the common benefit.

This proposition is put past doubt by the following argument. A debtor, after his insolvency, is bound to distribute his effects equally among his creditors ; and it would be an act of injustice in him to prefer any of them before the rest. It necessarily follows, that a creditor cannot be innocent, who, knowing the bankruptcy, takes more than his proportion of the effects : if he take more by voluntary payment, he is accessory to an unjust act done by the bankrupt ; and it will not be thought that he can justly take more by execution than by voluntary pay-

410 OF BANKRUPTS. B. III.

ment. If he should attempt such wrong, it is the duty of the judge to refuse execution.*

That creditors having notice of their debtor's bankruptcy are barred from taking advantage of each other, shall now be taken for granted. It is not so obvious what effect bankruptcy ought to have against creditors who are ignorant of it. I begin with payment made by a bankrupt in money or effects, which transfers the property to his creditor. It is demonstrated above,† that even in the case of stellionate, the second purchaser, supposing him *in bona fide*, and not partaker of his author's fraud, is secure by getting the first infeftment; and that his purchase cannot be cut down in equity more than at common law. The reasoning there concludes with equal if not superior force in the case of bankruptcy: it is unjust in a bankrupt to prefer one creditor before another; but if he offer payment, the creditor who accepts, supposing him ignorant of the bankruptcy, is innocent, and therefore secure: the property of the money or effects being transferred to him in lieu of his debt, there is no rule in equity more than at common law to forfeit him of his property. The same reasoning concludes in favour of a creditor, who, ignorant of the bankruptcy, recovers payment by a poinding, or by a forthcoming upon an arrestment.

Next comes the case of a real security, which transfers not the property of the subject. It is observed above, that a real security, obtained before bankruptcy, is in all events a preferable debt. But what if it be obtained after bankruptcy? The creditor, who,

* See book 1, p. 1, chap. 8, sect. 2.
† P. 308, 309.

CH. V.   OF BANKRUPTS.   **411**

ignorant of his debtor's bankruptcy, obtains from him such security, whether by legal execution, or by voluntary deed, is, indeed, not culpable in any degree. But before this security existed, each of the creditors had an equitable right to a proportion of the bankrupt's effects; which right cannot be hurt by legal diligence, and still less by a partial deed of the bankrupt, who acts against conscience in preferring one of his creditors before the rest. Where payment is actually made, a court of equity can give no relief, for two reasons: first, the innocent creditor, to whom the money was paid, cannot be deprived of his property; and next, a debt extinguished by payment, cannot be reared up in order to compel the *quondam* creditor to enter the lists again with the remaining creditors. But where the creditor is still *in petitorio*, demanding preference by virtue of his real security, the court cannot listen to his claim; because to prefer him, would be to forfeit the other creditors of what they are justly entitled to.

If, in a bankrupt, it be unjust to divide his effects unequally among his creditors, it is still more unjust to hurt his whole creditors by gratuitous alienations or gratuitous bonds. A gratuitous alienation, transferring the property, cannot, it is true, be voided, if the donee be not in the knowledge of the bankruptcy: but he is liable for the value to the bankrupt's creditors, upon the rule of equity, *Nemo debet locupletari alienâ jacturâ;* which is not applicable to an alienation before bankruptcy, because, by such an alienation, the creditors are not hurt. But against a gratuitous bond claimed after bankruptcy, though executed and delivered while the granter was solvent, the rule *Nemo debet locupletari alienâ jacturâ* is applicable;

412 OF BANKRUPTS. B. III.

because the taking payment is a direct prejudice to the creditors, by lessening their fund ; and for that reason, a court of equity will not interpose to make such a bond effectual. It deserves attention, that this principle operates in favour of a creditor who lent his money even after the date of the gratuitous bond. *

The equitable right to the debtor's effects, which, upon his insolvency, accrues to his creditors, makes it a wrong in him to sell any of his effects privately without their consent. The sale indeed is effectual at common law ; but the purchaser, supposing his knowledge of the bankruptcy, is accessory to the wrong, and the sale is voidable upon that ground. The principle of utility also declares against a sale of that nature : for to permit a bankrupt to alien his effects privately, even for a just price, is throwing a temptation in his way to defraud his creditors, by the opportunity it affords him to walk off with the money.

Thus we see, that in applying the rules of equity to the case of bankruptcy, two preliminary facts are of importance ; first, the commencement of the bankruptcy ; and next, what knowledge creditors or others have of it : the former is necessary to be ascertained in every case ; the latter frequently. The necessity of such proof tends to darken and perplex law-suits concerning bankruptcy. To ascertain the commencement of bankruptcy, must always be difficult, considering that it depends on an internal act of the debtor's mind, deeming his affairs irretrievable : and the difficulty is greatly increased, when the knowledge of the bankruptcy comes also to be a point at issue ; for such knowledge must be gathered commonly from a variety of circumstances that are scarce

* Dirleton, January 21, 1677, Ardblair contra Wilson.

CH. V. OF BANKRUPTS. 413

ever the same in any two cases. To avoid such in-tricate expiscation, which tends to make law-suits endless, and judges arbitrary, it has been a great aim of the legislature, in every commercial country, to specify some overt act, that shall be held not only the commencement of bankruptcy, but also a public no-. tification of it.

But if the specifying a legal mark of bankruptcy be of great importance, the choice of a proper mark is no less nice than important. Whether, in any country, a choice, altogether unexceptionable, has been made, seems doubtful. It ought, in the first place, to be some act that cannot readily happen except in bankruptcy : for to fix a mark of bankruptcy on one who is not a bankrupt, would be a great punishment without a fault. Secondly, It must be an act that will readily happen in bankruptcy, and which a bankrupt cannot prevent : for if it be in his power to suppress it altogether, or for any time, he may, in the interim, do much wrong, that will not admit a remedy.

Having thus gone through the rules of common law, and the rules of equity concerning bankruptcy, we are, I presume, sufficiently prepared for the third article proposed, namely, to state the regulations of different countries upon that subject. And to bring the present article within reasonable compass, I shall confine myself to the Roman law, the English law, and to that of Scotland, which may be thought sufficient for a specimen. I begin with the Roman law. A debtor's absconding, entitled his creditors to apply to the court for a *curator bonis* ; and after the creditors were put in possession by their *curator*, no creditor could take

414 OF BANKRUPTS. **B. III.**

payment from the bankrupt.* This *missio in possessionem*, however, seems not to have been deemed a public notification of bankruptcy; for even after that period, a purchaser from the bankrupt was secure, if it could not be proved that he was *particeps fraudis*.† But every gratuitous deed was rescinded, whether the acquirer was accessory to the wrong or no ;‡ and in particular, a gratuitous discharge of a debt.§

Before the *missio in possessionem*, the debtor continued to have the management as while he was solvent ; and particularly, was entitled to pay his creditors, in what order he thought proper. It is accordingly laid down, That a creditor, who, before the *missio in possesionem* receives payment, is secure, though he be in the knowledge of his debtor's insolvency. *Sibi enim vigilavit*, says the author : ‖ a doctrine very just with respect to a court of common law, but very averse to Prætorian law, or that of equity.

The defects of the foregoing system are many ; but so obvious, as to make a list unnecessary. I shall mention two particulars only, being of great importance. The first is, that the necessity of establishing a public mark of bankruptcy, which every one is presumed to know, seems to have been altogether overlooked by the Romans. Even the *missio in possessionem*, as mentioned above, was not held such a mark. It is true, that after such possession, no creditor could take payment from the bankrupt. But

---

* L. 6, § 7, Quæ in fraud. cred. L. 10, § 16, eod.
† L. 9, eod. ‡ L. 6, § 11, eod.
§ L. 1, § 2, eod. ‖ L. 6, § 7, Quæ in Fraud. cred.

CH. V. OF BANKRUPTS. 415

why? Not because of the creditor's *mala fides*, but because of the creditors, in general, being put in possession of the bankrupt's funds, acquired thereby a *jus pignoris*; and in the division of the price, were accordingly entitled each to a rateable proportion. I observe next, that it is a great oversight in the Roman law, to neglect that remarkable period, which runs between the first act of bankruptcy and the *missio in possessionem*. In that period, generally, all contrivances are set on foot to cover the effects of the bankrupt, or to prefer favourite creditors.

In England, the regulations concerning bankrupts are extended further than in the Roman law, and are brought much nearer the rules of equity above laid down. The nomination of commissioners by the chancellor, upon application of the creditors, is, in effect, the same with the nomination of a *curator bonis* in the Roman law. But the foregoing defects of the Roman law are supplied, by declaring a debtor's absconding or keeping out of the way, termed *the first act of bankruptcy*, to be a public mark or notification of bankruptcy, of which no person is suffered to plead ignorance. From that moment, the hands, both of the bankrupt and of his creditors, are fettered : he can do no deed that is prejudicial to his creditors in general, or to any one in particular : they, on the other hand, are not permitted to receive a voluntary payment, nor to operate their payment by legal execution.

It is perhaps not easy to invent a regulation better calculated for fulfilling the rules of equity, than that now mentioned. It may be thought indeed, that the absconding, or keeping out of the way, supposing it momentary only, is a circumstance too slight and

416 OF BANKRUPTS. B. III.

too private to be imposed upon all the world as notorious. But the English bankrupt statutes are confined to mercantile people, who live by buying and selling : and with respect to a merchant, his absconding or keeping out of the way is a mark of bankruptcy, neither slight nor obscure. Merchants converse regularly in the exchange ; a retailer ought to be found in his shop or warehouse ; and their absconding or absence, without a just cause, is conspicuous. A creditor may happen, for some time, to be ignorant of the first act of bankruptcy ; but a singular case must not be made an exception : justice must be distributed by general rules, though at the expence of a few individuals ; in order to prevent judges from becoming arbitrary, and law-suits endless. There is, indeed, a hardship in this regulation, with respect to commerce, which is softened by a late statute,* enacting, That money received from a bankrupt in the course of trade and dealing before the commission of bankruptcy sued forth, whether in payment of goods sold to the bankrupt, or of a bill of exchange accepted by him, shall not be claimed by the assignees to the bankruptcy, unless it be made appear, that the person so receiving payment, was in the knowledge of the debtor's bankruptcy. This is in effect declaring with respect to payment received in the course of trade, that the issuing the commission of bankruptcy is to be deemed the first public mark or notification of bankruptcy, and not what is called the first act of bankruptcy.

The first bankrupt-act we have in Scotland, is an act of sederunt, ratified by statute 1621, cap. 18, intituled, " A ratification of the act of the Lords of

* 19. Geo. II, cap. 32.

CH. V. OF BANKRUPTS. 417

" Council and Session, against unlawful dispositions
" and alienations, made by dyvours and bankrupts."
In this act of sederunt, two articles only are brought
under consideration. First, Fraudulent contrivances, to withdraw a bankrupt's effects from his creditors, by making simulate and feigned conveyances.
Second, The partiality of bankrupts, by making payment to favourite creditors, neglecting others. With
respect to the first, it is set forth in the preamble,
" That the fraud, malice, and falsehood of dyvours
" and bankrupts was become so frequent, as to be in
" hazard of dissolving all trust and commerce among
" the subjects of this kingdom ; that many, by their
" apparent wealth in land and goods, and by their
" shew of conscience and honesty, having obtained
" credit, intend not to pay their debts, but either live
" riotously, or withdraw themselves or their goods
" forth of this realm, to elude all execution of justice:
" and to that effect, and in manifest defraud of their
" creditors, make simulate and fraudful aliena-
" tions, dispositions, and other securities of their
" lands, reversions, teinds, goods, actions, debts, and
" other subjects belonging to them, to their wives,
" children, kinsmen, allies, and other confident and
" interposed persons, without any true, lawful, or
" necessary cause, and without any just or true price ;
" whereby the creditors and cautioners are falsely
" and godlessly defrauded of their just debts, and
" many honest families are ruined." For remedying
this evil, it is ordained and declared, " First, That
" all alienations, dispositions, assignations, made by
" the debtor, of any of his lands, teinds, reversions,
" actions, debts, or goods, to any conjunct or confi-
" dent person, without true, just, and necessary

2 D

418 OF BANKRUPTS. B. III.

" causes, and without a just price really paid,
" shall be of no force or effect against prior credit-
" ors. Second, Whoever purchases from the said
" interposed persons, any of the bankrupt's lands or
" goods, at a just price, or in satisfaction of debt,
" *bond fide*, without being partaker of the fraud, shall
" be secure. Third, The receiver of the price shall
" make the same forthcoming to the bankrupt's cre-
" ditors. Fourth, It shall be sufficient evidence of
" the fraud intended against the creditors, if they
" verify by writ, or by oath of the party-receiver,
" of any right from the dyvour or bankrupt, that
" the same was made without any true, just, and ne-
" cessary cause, or without any true price ; or that
" the lands or goods of the bankrupt, being sold by
" the interposed person, the price is to be converted
" to the bankrupt's profit and use. Fifth, All such
" bankrupts, and interposed persons, for covering or
" executing their frauds, and all others who shall
" give counsel and assistance to the said bankrupts,
" in devising and practising their frauds and godless
" deceits, to the prejudice of their true creditors,
" shall be reputed and holden dishonest, false, and
" infamous persons, incapable of all honours, digni-
" ties, benefices, and offices, or to pass upon an in-
" quest or assize, or to bear witness in judgment or
" outwith, in any time coming."

The clause, restraining a bankrupt's partiality, in
making payment to favourite creditors, and neglecting others, is expressed in the following terms :—" If
" any bankrupt or interposed person, partaker of his
" fraud, shall make any voluntary payment or right
" to any person, in defraud of the more timely dili-
" gence of another creditor, having served inhibi-

CH. V.　　OF BANKRUPTS.　　419

"tion, or used horning, arrestment, comprising, or
"other lawful mean, to affect the bankrupt's lands,
"goods, or price thereof: in that case, the bank-
"rupt, or interposed person, shall be bound to make
"the same forthcoming to the creditor, having used
"the more timely diligence. And this creditor shall
"likewise have good action to recover from the co-
"creditor posterior in diligence what was voluntari-
"ly paid to him in defraud of the pursuer."

With respect to the article concerning fraud, this
act is an additional instance of what I have had more
than one opportunity to observe, that the Court of
Session, for many years after its institution, acted as
a court of common law only. No wrong calls louder
for a remedy than frauds committed by bankrupts,
in withdrawing their effects from their creditors;
and yet, from the preamble of the act, it appears,
that the Court of Session had not, before that period,
assumed the power to redress any of these frauds.
Nor is it clear, that the power was assumed by the
Session as a court of equity: it is more presumable,
that the court considered itself as a court of common
law, acting by legislative authority; first, by authority of its own act, and afterward, by authority of
the act of parliament :—I say by authority of its own
act; for the Court of Session being empowered by
parliament to make regulations for the better administration of justice, an act of sederunt originally
was held equivalent to an act of parliament.(a)

(a) Acts, by a bankrupt defrauding his creditors, as mentioned
at the beginning of this chapter, are left without remedy by common law. As bankruptcy does not divest a man of his property,
he is understood, at common law, to have the same power over

2 D 2

420 OF BANKRUPTS. B. III.

This act, framed, as we ought to suppose, by the wisest heads of the nation, is, however, not only shamefully imperfect, but in several particulars grossly unjust. No general regulations are established concerning the conduct of the bankrupt, of his creditors, or of the judges: no overt act is fixed as a public notification of bankruptcy: nor is there any regulation barring the creditors from taking advantage of each other by precipitancy of execution. Such blindness is the less excusable in judges, to whom the Roman law was no stranger; and who, in an English bankrupt-statute, passed a few years before, had a good model to copy after, and to improve. But this act, which has occasioned many irregular and even unjust decisions, must be examined more particularly.

In the first place, There cannot be a more pregnant instance of unskilfulness in making laws, than the clause confining the evidence of fraud to the writ or oath of the person who benefits by it. A very little insight into human nature would have taught our judges, that it is in vain to think of detecting fraud by such evidence. Covered crimes must be detected by circumstances, or not at all; and such matters, being beyond the reach of a general rule, ought to be left with judges, without any rule other than to determine every case according to its peculiar circumstances. We shall, accordingly, have occasion to see, that the Court of Session were forced to abandon the evidence established by themselves; and, in every instance, to indulge such proof as the nature

his estate that he had before, however prejudicial to his creditors his acts and deeds may be, and however ill intended.

of the case will admit. In the second place, With respect to deeds done against creditors, it must appear strange, that the act of sederunt should be confined to actual fraud; a crime that merits punishment, and to which, accordingly, a punishment is annexed in the act itself. It bars not a gratuitous deed in favour of children or others, however prejudicial to creditors; provided it be not granted purposely to hurt them, but to benefit the donees. This palpable defect in the act will be accounted for by an observation one has occasion to make daily, that in reforming abuses, there is commonly a degree of diffidence, which prevents the innovation from being carried its due length. The repressing actual fraud was a great improvement, which filled the mind, and scarce left room for a thought of further improvement. And, in all probability, it appeared a bolder step to supply the defect of common law by voiding frauds committed by bankrupts, than to supply the defect of the statute by voiding also gratuitous deeds.

So much upon the first article. With respect to the second, contrived to restrain the bankrupt from acting partially among his creditors, it is not in my power to give it any colour, either of justice or expediency. I have been much disposed to think, that an inchoated act of execution was intended by the legislature to be the public notification of bankruptcy, so often mentioned. But I am obliged to relinquish that thought, when I consider, that our statute 1621 is not confined to merchants, but comprehends the whole body of the people; and that an inchoated act of horning or arrestment is scarce a mark of bankruptcy at present, far less when the act was made, with respect especially to landed men. And that, in fact, it was not intended a mark or notification of bankruptcy, is clear from the following considerations, that creditors are not barred by it from forcing payment by legal execution; nor even the bankrupt from acting partially among his creditors, except with regard to those only who have commenced execution : all the other creditors are left at his mercy as much as before the act was made. This, however, is an omission only ; and I could wish, for the honour of my country, that nothing but an omission could be objected to this clause : but it is fruitless to disguise that it is grossly unjust. There ought, no doubt, to be a remedy against the creditor who obtains payment by the bankrupt's partiality : but to make him surrender the whole to the creditor who has got the start in execution, is an unjust remedy ; for justice only requires that he should surrender a part, that both may be upon a level. To make him surrender the whole, is indeed an effectual cure to the bankrupt's partiality, but a cure that is worse than the disease ; worse, I say, because the partiality of an individual is a spectacle much less disgusting than is the partiality of law. This regulation is unjust, even supposing the bankruptcy to be known to the creditor who receives payment. But how much more glaring the injustice, where he happens to be ignorant of that fact : the money he receives becomes undoubtedly his property ; and justice forfeits no man of his property without a fault. Nor is this all. The regulation, in itself unjust, is no less so with respect to consequences. Voluntary payment effectually binds up the creditor from legal execution : in the meantime, the funds of the bankrupt are swept away by other creditors : and the creditor is forfeited for

CH. V.   OF BANKRUPTS.   442

condescending to take payment, being left without a
remedy. Viewing now this regulation with respect
to utility, it appears no less inexpedient than unjust ;
to excite creditors to take the start in execution, it
holds out a premium, to which they are not entitled
by the rules of justice ; a premium that tends to a
very unhappy consequence, namely, to overwhelm
with precipitant execution honest dealers, who, treated with humanity, might have emerged out of their
difficulties, and have become bold and prosperous
traders.

The next bankrupt statute, in order of time, is the
act 62, parl. 1661, ranking, *pari passu* with the first
effectual apprising, all apprisings of a prior date, and
all led within year and day of it ; for I shall have
occasion to shew afterward, that this statute ought
to be classed with those concerning bankruptcy,
though not commonly considered in that light. But
the connection of matter, more intimate than that of
time, leads me first to the act 5, parl. 1696, intended
evidently to supply the defects of the act 1621. Experience discovered in the act 1621 one defect mentioned above, that no overt act is ascertained to be
held the first act of bankruptcy, as well as a public
notification of it. This defect is supplied by the act
1696, in the following manner. An insolvent debt-
or, under execution by horning and caption, is declared a notour bankrupt, provided he be imprisoned, or retire to a sanctuary, or fly, or abscond, or defend his person by force. This is one term, and
counting sixty days back, another term is fixed ; after which all partial deeds by a bankrupt among his
creditors are prohibited. The words are, " All dis-
" positions, assignations, or other deeds, granted by

OF BANKRUPTS. B. III.

" the bankrupt at any time within sixty days before
" his notour bankruptcy, in favour of a creditor, di-
" rectly or indirectly, for his satisfaction or further
" security, preferring him to other creditors, shall
" be null and void."

It will be observed, that this statute, with respect to the legal commencement of bankruptcy, differs widely from those made in England. And, indeed, to have copied these statutes, by making absconding, or keeping out of the way, the first act of bankruptcy would, in this country, have been improper. In England, arrestment of the debtor's person till he find bail, being commonly the first act of execution, a debtor, to avoid imprisonment, must abscond or keep out of the way, the moment his credit is suspected ; and, therefore, in England, absconding or keeping out of the way is a mark of bankruptcy not at all ambiguous. But in Scotland, this mark of bankruptcy would always be too late; for with us there must be several steps of execution before a bankrupt be forced to abscond, letters of horning, a charge, a denunciation, a caption. In this country, therefore, it was necessary to specify some mark of bankruptcy antecedent to absconding. The mark that would correspond the nearest to absconding in England, is denunciation upon a horning ; for, after receiving a charge, the debtor, if he have any credit, will be upon his guard against denunciation, supposing it to be established as a public notification of bankruptcy. But our legislature perhaps showed greater penetration, in commencing bankruptcy from a term of which even the bankrupt must be ignorant. Sudden bankruptcy is so rare, as scarce to deserve the attention of the legislature. A man commonly becomes

CH. V.   OF BANKRUPTS.   425

bankrupt long before he is publicly known to be so by ultimate execution; and considering that the suspicious period, during which a debtor is tempted to act fraudulently, commences the moment he foresees the ruin of his credit, which is generally more than two months before his notour bankruptcy, it appears the safest course to tie up a bankrupt's hands during that period. Such retrospect from notour bankruptcy cannot be productive of any wrong, if it have no other effect but to void securities, which creditors obtain by force of execution, or by the voluntary deed of their debtor. And, therefore, the statute 1696, as far as concerns the commencement of bankruptcy, seems wise and political; and perhaps the best that is to be found in any country.

The statute adheres strictly to the principles of equity above laid down, as far as it voids every security granted to one creditor in prejudice of the rest, within sixty days before notour bankruptcy. But I must add, with regret, that it goes unwarily too far when it voids also, without distinction, conveyances made in satisfaction or payment of debt. To deprive a man of a subject, the property of which he has obtained *bonà fide* in lieu of a debt, is, as observed above, inconsistent with an inviolable rule of justice, That an innocent man ought never to be forfeited of his property: and, therefore, a conveyance of this nature ought not to be voided, unless the creditor receiving satisfaction be in the knowledge of his debtor's bankruptcy.

But this is an error of small importance compared with what follows. After the commencement of bankruptcy, ascertained as above, a bankrupt is prohibited to act partially among his creditors; and yet

426 OF BANKRUPTS. B. III.

creditors are permitted, as in the act 1621, to act partially among themselves, and to prevent each other by legal execution. To permit a creditor to take by legal execution what he is prohibited to receive voluntarily, is a glaring absurdity. Payment or satisfaction obtained *bond fide*, whether from the bankrupt himself, or by force of execution, ought to be sustained : but after the commencement of bankruptcy, there is the same justice for voiding a security obtained by execution, that there is for voiding a security obtained voluntarily from the bankrupt. And yet our legislature has deviated so widely from justice, as to give full scope to execution even after notour bankruptcy. Nothing can be conceived more gross. It had been a wise regulation, that, upon notour bankruptcy a factor should be appointed, to convert the bankrupt's effects into money, and to distribute the same among the creditors at the sight of the Court of Session. This regulation, established in Rome and in England, ought not to have been overlooked. But if it was not palatable, our legislature ought at least to have prohibited more to be taken by any execution, than a rateable proportion ; for after notour bankruptcy no creditor can be *in bona fide* to take payment of his whole debt.

The injustice and absurdity of permitting a creditor to take by execution what he is discharged to receive from his debtor voluntarily, though left without remedy by our two capital bankrupt-statutes, have not however been altogether overlooked. And I now proceed to the regulations made to correct that evil, which, for the sake of connection, I have reserved to the last place, though one of these regulations comes in point of time before the act 1696. The

CH. V. OF BANKRUPTS. 427

great load of debt contracted during our civil wars in the reign of Charles I, and the decay of credit occasioned thereby, produced the act 62. parl. 1661, laying down regulations suited to the times, for easing debtors and restoring credit. Among other articles, " All apprisings deduced since the 1st of Ja-" nuary 1652, before the first effectual apprising, or " after, but within year and day of the same, are ap-" pointed to come in *pari passu*, as if one apprising " had been deduced for the whole." This regulation is general without respect to bankruptcy. But whatever stretches may be necessary for a particular exigency, it is evident, that the regulation cannot be justified as a perpetual law, except upon supposition that all the apprisings are deduced after the debtor is insolvent. A debtor, while he is in good circumstances, may pay his debts or grant real securities in what order he pleases. By using this privilege, he harms none of his creditors : they have no ground for challenging such a deed at the time when it is granted ; and his supervening bankruptcy cannot afford them a ground of challenge which they had not at first. A security obtained by an apprising or adjudication is precisely similar. If the debtor be solvent when an adjudication is obtained by a creditor, the other creditors suffer not by it ; and the adjudger who has thus fairly obtained a security, must be entitled to make the best of his right, whether the debtor afterward become insolvent or no. I have reason, therefore, to place the foregoing statute, considered as perpetual, among those which have been enacted in the case of bankruptcy: and in order to fulfil the rules of justice, the Court of Session, as a court of equity, will consider it in that light. The

428 OF BANKRUPTS. B. III.

involved circumstances of debtors and creditors at the time of the statute, made it a salutary regulation to bring in apprisers *pari passu*, even where the debtor was solvent, though evidently a stretch against justice : but to adhere strictly to the regulation at present, when there is not the same necessity, is to adhere rigidly to the words, against the mind and intendment of the legislature ; for surely it could not be intended, that a creditor should for ever be deprived of the preference he obtains by being the first adjudger, even where the other creditors are not hurt by that preference. That after the debtor's bankruptcy a creditor should not have more than his proportion of the common fund, is extremely just ; and so far the statute ought to be held perpetual. What further is enacted to answer a particular purpose, ought to be considered as temporary ; because the legislature could not mean it to be perpetual.

If then the foregoing statute be held to be perpetual, it must be confined to the case of bankruptcy ; and in that view it deserves to be immortal. The first adjudication may be justly held a public mark or notification of the debtor's bankruptcy, warning the other creditors to bestir themselves : and a year commonly is sufficient for them to lead adjudications, which, by authority of the statute, will entitle each creditor to a proportion of the debtor's real estate. This was a happy commencement of a much-wanted reformation. The Court of Session, taking example, ventured to declare by an act of sederunt,* That the priority of a creditor's confirmation shall afford no preference in competition with other creditors confirming within six months of the death of their debt-

* Feb. 28, 1662.

CH. V. OF BANKRUPTS. 429

or. By another act of sederunt,* All arrestments within sixty days preceding the notour bankruptcy, or within four months thereafter, are ranked *pari passu;* and every creditor who poinds within sixty days preceding the notour bankruptcy, or within four months thereafter, is obliged to communicate a proportion to the other creditors suing him within a limited time.† In the heat of reformation, the last-mentioned regulation is carried too far. Poinding operates at once a transference of the property and a discharge of the debt; and supposing a poinder to be ignorant of his debtor's insolvency, which is frequently the case, where the execution precedes the notour bankruptcy, there is no rule in equity more than at common law to oblige the poinder to communicate any proportion to the other creditors. Nay it is possible that a debtor may be solvent within sixty days of his notour bankruptcy : a poinding against him in that case, which wounds not the other creditors, ought not to afford them the shadow of a claim.(a)

The principles of equity ripening gradually, our zeal for the act 1661 has increased; and there is a visible tendency in our judges to make the remedy still more complete. In order to that end, the Court

---

* August 9, 1754. † Act of sederunt, August 9, 1754.

(a) Experience soon suggested, that the two last-mentioned acts of sederunt required several emendations; for which reason, being temporary only, they were allowed to run out. And thus again we were laid open to the rapacity of creditors endeavouring to prevent one another by legal execution; till a remedy was provided by a British statute, that shall be mentioned at the end of this chapter *cum elogio,* being the most perfect bankrupt-statute that ever was contrived by the wit of man, as far as moveables are concerned.

OF BANKRUPTS.

of Session, as a court of equity, might have enlarged the time given by the statute for leading adjudications. The principles of justice authorise a still bolder step, which is, to put upon an equal footing all adjudications led upon debts existing before the first adjudication. But the Court of Session, wavering always as to their equitable powers, have not hitherto ventured so far. Not adverting to an obvious doctrine, That, in order to fulfil justice, it is lawful to improve means laid down in a statute, the Court of Session hath not attempted directly to enlarge the time for bringing in adjudgers *pari passu:* but they do the same thing every day indirectly; for, upon the application of any creditor, setting forth, " That if " the common *induciæ* required in the processes of " constitution and adjudication be not abridged in " his favour, he cannot hope to complete his adjudi- " cation within year and day of the adjudication first " effectual," the court, without requiring any cause to be assigned for the delay, give authority for adjudging summarily; which, in effect, is declaring, that all adjudgers shall have the benefit of the statute, provided the summons of adjudication be within year and day of the first effectual adjudication. It may be questioned, whether this be not too indulgent: the extraordinary privilege of shortening the forms, ought not to be permitted, unless the creditor can assign some good cause for his delay; because law ought not to be stretched in favour of those who suffer by their own fault or neglect. It is curious at the same time to observe, that a court, like an individual, afraid of a bold step, will, to shun it, venture upon one no less bold in reality, though perhaps less so in appearance: for, to abridge or dispense with forms, salu-

CH. V. OF BANKRUPTS. 431

tary in themselves, and sanctified by inveterate practice, is an act of authority no less extraordinary, than to enlarge the time afforded in a statute for ranking adjudgers *pari passu.*

But after all, the foregoing regulations for putting creditors upon a level in the case of bankruptcy, are mere palliatives : they soften the disease, but strike not at the root. The Court of Session tried once a bolder and more effectual remedy, borrowed from the law of Rome and of England, that of naming a factor for managing and disposing of the bankrupt's moveable funds, in order that the price may be equally distributed among the creditors. It was made for a trial, and, in that view, was made temporary. Why it was not renewed and made perpetual, I cannot guess, if it was not that the court, doubting of its powers, thought a statute necessary. One thing is certain, that the late bankrupt-statute, mentioned below was framed by the judges of that court, and procured upon their application.

According to the method proposed in the beginning, nothing now remains but the operations of the Court of Session, to which I proceed, beginning with decisions relative to the statutes, and concluding with decisions founded on equity, independent of the statutes. And first, the statute 1621 has been extended to a lease of land set to a trustee at an undervalue, in order that the bankrupt himself might enjoy the profits. A lease of this nature, though not comprehended under the words of the act, comes plainly under its spirit and intention ; and, therefore, it was the duty of the court to extend the act to that case. A fraudulent bond granted by a bankrupt, in order to withdraw from the true creditors a part of the fund for

432 · OF BANKRUPTS. B. III.

the bankrupt's own behoof, is another example of the same kind. For, as Sir George Mackenzie observes in his explication of this act, " Though neither tacks " nor bonds be comprehended under the letter of the " law, yet the reason of the law extends to them; and " in laws founded on the principles of reason, exten- " sions from the same principles are natural. And " in laws introduced for obviating of cheats, exten- " sions are most necessary, because the same subtle " and fraudulent inclination that tempted the debtor " to cheat his creditors, will tempt him likewise to " cheat the law, if the wisdom and prudence of the " judge do not interpose." A discharge granted by the bankrupt, in order to cover a debt from his cre-ditors for his own behoof, will also come under the act by an equitable interpretation.

With respect to the evidence required in the first article of the statute 1621, for detecting fraudulent deeds, the Court of Session hath assumed a power proper and peculiar to a court of equity. It has been forced to abandon the oath or writ of the partaker of the fraud, being a means altogether insufficient to answer the purpose of the statute, and, in place of it, to lay hold of such evidence as can be had. It is, accordingly, the practice of the court, after weighing circumstances, to presume sometimes in favour of the deed till fraud be proved, and sometimes against the deed till a proof be brought of its being fair and honest. Thus, a bond bearing borrowed money, granted by a bankrupt to a conjunct and confident person, was presumed to be fairly granted for the cause expressed; and the burden of proving it to have been granted without any just cause, was, in terms of the act, laid upon the pursuer of the reduc-

CH. V. OF BANKRUPTS. 433

tion.* A disposition by a bankrupt of his whole heritage to his son-in-law, upon the narrative of a price paid, was found probative, unless redargued by the disponee's oath.† A disposition by a bankrupt to his brother, bearing to be for security of a sum instantly borrowed, was sustained; but admitting the cause expressed to be redargued by the disponee's oath. And the judges distinguished this case from that of a disposition bearing a valuable consideration in general, which must be otherwise verified than by the disposition.‡

On the other hand, in a reduction upon the act 1621, of a bond bearing borrowed money granted by a bankrupt to his brother, the judges thought, that though bonds *inter conjunctos* may prove where commercial dealings appear; yet as no such dealings were alleged, and as the creditor's circumstances made the advancement of so large a sum improbable, the bond was not sustained as probative of its cause.§ A disposition of land by a bankrupt to his brother, bearing a valuable consideration in general, was not sustained as probative of its narrative in prejudice of prior creditors; and it was laid on the disponee to astruct the same.‖ And he having specified, that it was for a sum of money advanced in specie to his brother, which he offered to depone upon, the court found this not relevant.¶ In a similar case, the disponee having produced two bonds due to him by the

* Durie, Jan. 22, 1630, Hope-Pringle *contra* Carre.
† Durie, Jan. 17, 1632, Skene *contra* Beatson.
‡ Gosford, Nov. 28, 1673, Campbell *contra* Campbell.
§ Fountainhall, Forbes, Dec. 5, 1707, Maclearie *contra* Glen.
‖ Stair, Nov. 29, 1671, Whitehead *contra* Lidderdale.
¶ Stair, Dec. 14, 1671, inter eosdem.

2 E

disponer, and offering to give his oath, that these were the cause of the disposition, the court thought this sufficient.*

A disposition by a bankrupt to a conjunct or confident person, referring to a prior engagement as its cause, is not sustained, unless the prior engagement be instructed. Thus, an assignment made by a bankrupt to a conjunct and confident person, bearing to be a security for sums due to the assignee, was presumed to be *in fraudem creditorum*, unless the assignee would bring evidence of the debts referred to in the deed.† And the assignee specifying, that he took the assignment for behoof of a third party, one of the bankrupt's creditors, the assignment was sustained.‡ An assignment by a bankrupt to his brother, bearing to be a security for debts owing to him, was presumed gratuitous, unless the assignee would instruct otherwise than by his own oath, that he was creditor.§ To support the narrative of a disposition by a bankrupt to his son, bearing for its cause certain debts undertaken by the son, it was judged sufficient, that the son offered to prove by the creditors mentioned in the disposition, that he had made payment to them in terms of the disposition.‖ A disposition by a bankrupt to his brother, bearing to be a security for certain sums due by bond, was thought sufficiently supported by production of the bonds, unless the pursuer would offer to prove, that the bonds were granted

---

* Stair, Dec. 15, 1671, Duff *contra* Forbes of Culloden.

† Durie, Haddington, Feb. 12, 1622, Dennison *contra* Young.

‡ Hope, (De creditoribus), Feb. 27, 1622, inter eosdem.

§ Durie, Jan. 29, 1629, Auld *contra* Smith; Stair, July 15, 1670, Hamilton *contra* Boyd.

‖ Stair, Jan. 9, 1672, Robertson *contra* Robertson.

CH. V.   OF BANKRUPTS.   435

after insolvency. Here no suspicious circumstances occurred, other than the conjunction itself; and, if such a proof of a valuable consideration be not held sufficient, all commerce among relations will be at an end. It might, upon the same footing, be doubted, whether even a proof by witnesses of the actual delivery of the money would be sufficient, which might be done simulately, in order to support a bond, as well as a bond be granted simulately in order to support a disposition.* It will be observed, that some of the foregoing cases are of bonds granted after bankruptcy, as for borrowed money, which ought not to be sustained in equity. But the Court of Session, as will be seen afterward, is in the practice of sustaining such bonds, for no better reason than that they are not prohibited by the bankrupt-statutes.

With respect to the second article of the act 1621, prohibiting payment to be made in prejudice of a creditor who is *in cursu diligentiæ*, the Court of Session ventured to correct the injustice of this article, by refusing to oblige a creditor who had obtained payment, to deliver the money to the creditor first in execution; unless it could be verified, that at the time of the payment, the debtor was commonly reputed a bankrupt.† A debtor commonly reputed a bankrupt, will always be held such by his creditors; and a creditor knowing of his debtor's bankruptcy, cannot justly take more than his proportion. Where payment is made before inchoated execution, and yet within threescore days of notour bankruptcy, the Court of Session hath no occasion to extend its equitable powers to support such payment, which stands

* Fountainhall, Feb. 22, 1711, Rule *contra* Purdie.
† Dalrymple, Bruce, June 7, 1715, Tweedie *contra* Din.

2 E 2

free of both statutes; for the statute 1621 challenges no payments but what are made after inchoated execution, and payments are not at all mentioned in the statute 1696. Payments after notour bankruptcy are in a different case: they are barred in equity, though not by this statute.

The second branch of the act 1621, securing a creditor who has commenced execution against the partiality of his debtor, is so strictly interpreted by the Court of Session, that where a security is voided by a creditor prior in execution, the whole benefit is given to him. And the act 1696 is so strictly interpreted, that moveables being delivered to a creditor in satisfaction of his debt, the transaction was voided because delivery was made within sixty days before notour bankruptcy;[*] though, abstracting from the injustice of depriving an innocent man of his property, the court, in interpreting a rigorous statute, ought to have limited the words within their narrowest meaning, by finding, that moveables, the commerce of which ought to be free, are not comprehended in the statute.

By the act 1696, as above observed, " All dispo-
" sitions, &c. granted by a debtor within sixty days
" before his notour bankruptcy, in favour of a cre-
" ditor, for his satisfaction or security, preferring
" him before other creditors, are declared null and
" void." This clause admits a double meaning: it may import a total nullity, or it may import a nullity as far only as that creditor is preferred before others. The former meaning would be·rational, supposing the creditors to be barred from execution, as the bankrupt is from alienation: but,

[*] Dalrymple, Jan. 27, 1715, Forbes of Ballogie; July 19, 1728, Smith contra Taylor.

CH. V.   OF BANKRUPTS.   **437**

as they are left free, the latter meaning ought to be adopted, as what answers the purpose of the legislature, and fulfils the rules of justice. And yet, I know not by what misapprehension, the former is adopted by the Court of Session. A disposition accordingly of this kind was voided totally, without even giving the disponee the benefit of a *pari passu* preference with the other creditors, who had attached the subject by legal execution.* This is laying hold of the words of a statute, without regarding its spirit and intendment. It is worse: it is giving a wrong sense to an ambiguous clause, in opposition to the spirit and intendment. The obvious purpose of the act 1696, is not to deprive a bankrupt altogether of the management of his affairs, for in that case a *curator bonis* must have been appointed; but only to bar him from acting partially. It clearly follows, that a court of equity, supporting the spirit of the law, ought not to have carried the reduction further than to redress the inequality intended by the disposition. Yet the Court of Session, in this case, was no less partial to the pursuers of the reduction, than the disposition was to the defendant; and their decree exceeded the bounds of justice on the one side, as much as the bankrupt's disposition did on the other. The solidity of this reasoning will be clearly apprehended, in applying it to a security granted by a debtor in good credit, but who, within sixty days after, becomes a notour bankrupt. The creditor, being *in optima fide* to take a security in these circumstances, merits no punishment. Another creditor, however, anxious about his debt, attaches the

* Fountainhall, Dalrymple, Dec. 4, 1704, Man *contra* Reid; July 19, 1738, Smith *contra* Taylor,

438　　　OF BANKRUPTS.　　　B. III.

subject by legal execution ; and thus gets the start of the disponee, whose hands, by the disposition, are tied up from execution. Could one listen with patience to a decision that voided the disposition altogether, and preferred the other creditor ?

With respect to particulars that come not under either of the bankrupt statutes, but are left to be regulated by equity, it is distressing to observe the never-ceasing fluctuation of the Court of Session between common law and equity. In many instances, the court hath given way to the injustice of common law, without affording a remedy; for a very odd reason indeed, That no remedy is provided by statute. In other instances, the court, exerting its equitable powers, has boldly applied the remedy. I proceed to examples of both.

A sale by a notour bankrupt, after the act 1696, was supported for the following reason, That it is not prohibited by the act.* Very true. But, as above demonstrated, it is prohibited by justice and by utility; and, upon these *media*, it ought to have been voided. And a bond for money was sustained, though lent to a known bankrupt. † In those days, it seems to have been assumed as a maxim, That every exercise of property, even by a notour bankrupt, however destructive to his creditors, is lawful, except what are prohibited in express terms by the bankrupt statutes. Upon the statutes 1696, it has been disputed, whether an act be challengeable where no subject is aliened, and yet a partial preference is given. The case was as follows. An heir-apparent having given infeftments of annualrent, did thereaf-

---

* Bruce, January 1, 1717, Burgh *contra* Gray.

† Stair, June 28, 1665, Monteith *contra* Anderson.

CH. V. OF BANKRUPTS. 459

ter grant a procuratory to serve himself heir, that his infeftment might accresce to the annualrent-rights. In a competition between these annualrent-ers and posterior adjudgers, it was objected against the procuratory, That it was granted by a notour bankrupt, and, therefore, null by the statute 1696; the purpose of which is to annul every partial pre-ference by a bankrupt, *direct or indirect*. It was an-swered, That the statute mentions only alienations made by the bankrupt, and reaches not every act that may be attended with a consequential damage or benefit to some of the creditors. The court pre-ferred the annualrenters. * Had the service been before the bankruptcy, there could be no reason in equity against it : but a man who, conscious of his own bankruptcy, performs any act in order to prefer one creditor before another, is unjust ; and the cre-ditor who takes advantage of that act, knowing his debtor to be bankrupt, is partaker of the wrong. The court, therefore, denying a remedy in this case, acted as a court of common law, overlooking its equit-able powers.

Opposite to the foregoing instances, I shall men-tion, first, a donation, the motive of which is love and favour to the donee, without any formed intention to wrong the creditors, though in effect they are wronged by it. That this case is not provided for in the statute 1621, is evident from every clause in it. Fraud only is repressed : not fraud in a lax sense, signifying every moral wrong by which a cre-ditor is disappointed of his payment ; but fraud in its proper sense, signifying a deliberate purpose to cheat creditors ; that sort of fraud which is criminal

* February 1728, Creditors of Graitney competing.

and merits punishment : which is put beyond doubt by the final clause, inflicting a punishment fully adequate to fraud in its proper sense. But a gratuitous bond or alienation, of which the intention is precisely what is spoken out, without any purpose to cover the effects from the creditors, is not a fraud in any proper sense, at least not in a sense to merit punishment. This, then, is left upon equity : and the Court of Session, directed by the great principle of equity, *Nemo debet locupletari alienâ jacturâ*, makes no difficulty to cut down a gratuitous bond or alienation granted by a bankrupt. With respect to a gratuitous bond, the court, I believe, has gone further : it has preferred the creditors upon an eventual bankruptcy, even where the granter was solvent when he made the donation. And, indeed, the court cannot do otherwise, without deviating from the principle now mentioned.

Next comes a security given by a bankrupt in such circumstances as not to be challengeable upon either of the statutes ; being given, for example, before execution is commenced against the bankrupt, and more than sixty days before his bankruptcy becomes notorious. It is made out above, that a court of equity ought to void such a security, even though the creditor, ignorant of his debtor's bankruptcy, obtained the same *bonâ fide*. The Court of Session, it is true, hath not hitherto ventured to adopt this equitable regulation in its full extent ; but it hath made vigorous approaches to it, by voiding such security wherever any collateral circumstance could be found that appeared to weigh in any degree against the creditor. Thus, a security given by a bankrupt to one of his creditors, who was his near relation,

CH. V.   OF BANKRUPTS.   441

was voided, though the disposition came not under either of the bankrupt-statutes.* In the same manner, a disposition *omnium bonorum*, as a security to a single creditor, is always voided. And here it merits observation, that the Court of Session, acting upon principles of equity, is more correct in its decrees, than where it acts by authority of the statutes; witness the following case. "A debtor, against whom "no execution was commenced, having granted a "disposition *omnium bonorum* as a security to one "of his creditors, another creditor arrested in the "disponee's hands, and in the forthcoming insisted, "that the disposition was null, and that the subject "ought to be made forthcoming to him upon his arrestment. The court reduced, to the effect of bringing in the arrester *pari passu.*"† The following case, though varying in circumstances, is built upon the same foundation. Robert Grant, conscious of his insolvency, and resolving to prefer his favourite creditors, executed privately in their favour a security upon his land estate, which, in the same private manner, he completed by infeftment. This security being kept latent, even from those for whom it was intended, gave no alarm, and Robert Grant did not become a notour bankrupt for many months after. But the peculiar circumstances of this case, a real security bestowed on creditors who were not making any demand, seisin given clandestinely, &c. were clear evidence of the granter's consciousness of his bankruptcy, as well as of his intention to act partially and unjustly among his creditors; and the court accordingly voided the security as far as it gave preference

* Fount. January 28, 1696, Scrymzeour *contra* Lyon.
† February 25, 1737, Cramond *contra* Bruce.

442 OF BANKRUPTS. B. III.

to the creditors therein named ; *November* 10, 1748, *Sir Archibald Grant contra Grant of Lurg.*

The principle upon which this decision is founded, was admitted in the following case ;* though the judgment was laid on a specialty. Fenwick Stow, merchant in Berwick, having been employed by the Thistle Bank of Glasgow as an agent for circulating their notes, was indebted to them, February 1768, the sum of £2,000. Finding himself insolvent, without hope of retrieving his circumstances, he set on foot a most unjust plan, that of securing his favourite creditors, at the expence of the rest. In that view, he executed privately three heritable bonds on his land-estate in Scotland, two to his near relations, and the third to the Thistle Bank, for the said £2,000. These bonds were kept latent, even from the persons concerned, till late in June 1768; at which time, be-in *in actu proximo* of absconding, the bond to the Thistle Bank was sent to them by post 29th of that month. Upon the 3d July 1768, he left Berwick abruptly, and fled to London; and infeftment was taken upon the bond to the Thistle Bank 13th July. By the debtor's sudden elopement, his other Scotch creditors were deprived of an opportunity to render him notour bankrupt: but upon notice of his absconding, border-warrants were taken out for apprehending his person; and sundry inhibitions were raised and executed 12th and 13th July. In a competition among the bankrupt's creditors, the case between the Thistle Bank and the adjudging creditors was debated in presence ; and the following argument was urged for the latter.

* 4th August 1774, Creditors of Fenwick Stow *contra* Thistle Bank of Glasgow.

CH. V.   OF BANKRUPTS.   443.

A merchant in the course of business purchases goods, draws bills, grants securities. He may even pay one creditor before another, as long as he has a prospect to pay all. But where he is so far dipt as to despair of retrieving his circumstances, and yet delays to declare himself insolvent till he has distributed his effects among his favourite creditors; such management is grossly unjust: it is a fraud which no court of equity will countenance; and it is the very fraud which is the inductive cause of the bankrupt-act 1696. For what other reason are partial preferences cut down by that act, but because they are unjust or fraudulent? And what is remarkable in that act, even the *bona fides* of a creditor who obtains a preference, does not secure him, if the preference be granted by the debtor within threescore days of his notour bankruptcy. Nor ought *bona fides* to be regarded in this case: it is fraudulent to prefer a favourite creditor: the *bona fides* of that creditor vanisheth when he is made acquainted with the condition of his debtor; and he is *particeps fraudis* if he pretend to hold the security.

It is a gross mistake, that the act 1696 is the only law we have for repressing the partial deeds of a bankrupt. It required indeed a statute to make bankruptcy operate *retrò ;* and it required a statute to cut down a partial preference *funditùs,* so as not even to rank it *pari passu* with other debts. Such effects are far above the power of any court. But though the characteristics of notour bankruptcy are necessary, each of them, to produce these extraordinary effects, yet the act says not, nor insinuates, that any bankrupt who falls not precisely under the description of the statute; may, without control, commit the grossest injustice by preferring one creditor before another. It would be strange indeed, to annul *in totum* all partial deeds by one who is a bankrupt in terms of the act 1696, if granted within sixty days antecedent to the notour bankruptcy; and yet to leave a bankrupt at freedom to distribute his effects as he pleases, if but a single circumstance be wanting of those specified in the statute. Our law is not so imperfect. For every wrong there ought to be a remedy; and the Court of Session, directed by the great principle of justice, will correct every wrong a bankrupt can do to his creditors. So far as the bankrupt statutes extend, they act as a court of common law: beyond these bounds, they act as a court of equity. Take the following instances of the latter. A debtor advertises his insolvency in the newspapers, and appoints a day for the meeting of his creditors; who meet and name trustees. The bankrupt surely will not after this be suffered to give a real security to one of his creditors in prejudice of the rest; and yet all these steps may have been taken without a single execution against him. A person insolvent having been charged with horning, retires to the sanctuary, or steps over the border. Though this case falls not under the act 1696, yet no one can doubt but that every partial preference granted by him will be cut down by the Court of Session. A peer cannot be brought under the description of the statute, nor a member of the House of Commons during the sitting of parliament. Are such persons under no control with respect to their creditors? Our law would be miserably defective if they were not. Nor is it a novelty for the Court of Session to undertake the redressing of such wrongs. To cut down

CH. V. OF BANKRUPTS. 445

funditùs a security granted by a bankrupt any of the sixty days that precede his bankruptcy, requires that he be a bankrupt in terms of the statute; but as it is repugnant to common justice, that a person insolvent should take upon him to parcel out his effects among his creditors unequally, the Court of Session will rectify this act of injustice by bringing them all in *pari passu*. Thus, a disposition *omnium bonorum* to one creditor has always been cut down as being a partial preference by a debtor who virtually acknowledges himself to be insolvent. A disposition to a near relation suffers the same fate, where the disponer appears to be insolvent. Now, of all the cases that have happened, there is not one that bears more evident marks of partiality and injustice in preferring some creditors to the ruin of others. The fact here is the same that occurred in the case, Sir Archibald Grant *contra* Grant of Lurg, namely, a person insolvent granting of his own motive a security for a large sum to creditors who were not pressing him for payment; with the addition, in the present case, of being granted the moment before absconding. There cannot be a more bare-faced act of injustice, and none that requires more to be redressed by the court: the remedy is easy, which is to rank all the creditors *pari passu*.

It was the opinion of the court, that an insolvent person cannot prefer one creditor before another; and that every such partial preference ought to be cut down. But the plurality of the judges voted for supporting the infeftment of the Thistle Bank, on the following ground, " That the Thistle Bank trusted " their notes with Fenwick Stow to be put into cur- " rency for their behoof, and not with an inten-

446 OF BANKRUPTS. B. III.

" tion to lend him money; and that Fenwick
" Stow became their debtor by a breach of trust,
" in using these notes as his own, which bound
" him for reparation." This argument occurred in
the course of reasoning, and made a sudden impression, which I am convinced would have been
found insufficient had the cause been brought under
review. For, at that rate, if a man should burn
my house, spuilzie my goods, run away with my
money, or commit any other delict entitling me to
reparation, I ought to be preferred before all his
other creditors. He is, indeed, bound in conscience
to repair the hurt he has done me; but is he not
equally bound in conscience to pay the sums he has
borrowed? Let it be supposed, that Fenwick Stow,
instead of taking upon him arbitrarily to prefer one
creditor before another, had made a fair surrender of
his effects, would the Thistle Bank, in a competition,
have been preferred *primo loco?* This would be a
new ground of preference, hitherto unknown. If so,
it is a clear consequence, that the bankrupt, by his
voluntary deed, could not give a preference to the
Thistle Bank, which they would not have been entitled to in a competition before the Court of Session.

After finishing the instances promised, another
point demands our attention. With respect to an
alienation bearing to be granted for love and favour,
or made to a near relation bearing a valuable consideration; a doctrine established in the Court of Session by a train of decisions, appears singular. It is
held, that the purchaser from such disponee, though
he pay a full price, is in no better condition than his
author; and that a reduction at the instance of the

bankrupt's creditors will reach both equally. This doctrine ought not to pass current without examination; for its consequences are terrible. At that rate, every subject acquired upon a lucrative title is withdrawn from commerce for the space at least of forty years. What shall become of those who purchase from heirs, if this doctrine hold? And if a purchaser from an heir of provision, for example, be secure, why not a purchaser from a gratuitous disponee? The only reason urged in support of this doctrine is, That a purchaser cannot pretend to be *in bona fide* when his author's right bears to be gratuitous, or is presumed to be so. I do not feel the weight of this reason. The act 1621 gives no foundation for such reduction: for if, even in the case of a fraudulent conveyance to an interposed person, a purchaser *bona fide* from that person be secure, what doubt can there be that a purchaser from a gratuitous disponee is also secure, especially where the gratuitous disponee is innocent of any fraud? And considering this matter with relation to equity, a gratuitous deed is not subject to reduction, unless granted by a bankrupt; and to put a man who purchases from a gratuitous disponee *in mala fide*, the bankruptcy ought also to be known to him. And yet I find not that the purchaser's knowledge of the bankruptcy has ever been held a necessary circumstance; one case excepted, reported by Fountainhall:* " It is " not sufficient to reduce the purchaser's right that " he knew his author's relation to the bankrupt, un- " less he was also in the knowledge of the bankrupt- " cy; because there is no law to bar a man in good " circumstances from making a donation to a near

* Nov. 28, 1693, Spence *contra* Creditors of Dick.

OF BANKRUPTS. B. III.

" relation. And knowledge, an internal act, must
" be gathered from circumstances, the most pregnant
" of which is, that the granter of the gratuitous deed
" was at the time held and reputed a bankrupt."
But now, supposing the bankruptcy known to the
purchaser, I deny that this circumstance can support
the reduction either at common law or in equity: it
is made evident above, that a gratuitous disponee,
ignorant of his author's bankruptcy, is not bound to
yield the subject to the bankrupt's creditors, but only
to account to them for the value; and when he disposes of the subject for a full price, this sale, far from
disappointing the obligation he is under to the bankrupt's creditors, enables him to perform it. In one
case only will the purchaser's right be voided in
equity; and that is, where the gratuitous disponee
and the purchaser from him, are both of them *in mala
fide:* a man who takes a gratuitous disposition knowing his author to be bankrupt, is guilty of a wrong,
which binds him in conscience to restore the subject
itself to the bankrupt's creditors; and the person who
purchases from him knowing that he is so bound, being also guilty, is for that reason bound equally to
restore.

The statute 1696, voiding all dispositions, assignments, or other deeds, granted by a bankrupt to a
favourite creditor, appears to have no subjects in
view but what are locally in Scotland, within the
jurisdiction of the Court of Session. And, indeed,
it would be fruitless to void a disposition of foreign
effects granted by a Scotch bankrupt; because such
effects will be regulated by the law of the place, and
not by a decree pronounced in Scotland. Supposing,
then, such a disposition to be granted, is there no

CH. V.   OF BANKRUPTS.   ·   **449**

remedy? It is certainly a moral wrong for a bankrupt to convey to one of his creditors what ought to be distributed among all ; and the creditor, who accepts such security, knowing his debtor's insolvency, is accessory to the wrong. Upon that ground, the Court of Session, though they cannot void the security, may ordain the favourite creditor to repair the loss that the other creditors have sustained by it, which will oblige the favourite creditor either to surrender the effects, or to be accountable for the value. And this was decreed in the Court of Session, July 18, 1758, Robert Syme, clerk to the signet, *contra* George Thomson, tenant in Dalhousie.

Of late it has been much controverted, whether a disposition *omnium bonorum* by a notour bankrupt, to trustees for behoof of his whole creditors, be voidable upon the bankrupt-statutes. Formerly such dispositions were sustained, as not being prohibited by any clause in either of the statutes. But the Court at last settled in the following opinion, " That no dis-" position by a bankrupt can disable his creditors " from doing diligence."* This opinion, founded on justice and expediency, though not upon the bankrupt-statutes, ought to govern the Court of Session as a court of equity. It belongs not to the bankrupt, though proprietor, to direct the management of his funds ; but to his creditors, who are more interested in that management than he is. It belongs, therefore, to the creditors to direct the method by which the funds shall be converted into money for their payment; and if they choose to have the effects managed by trustees, it is their privilege, not the bank-

* July 12, 1734, Snee *contra* Trustees of Anderson. February 3, 1736, Earl of Aberdeen *contra* Trustees of Blair.

2 F

450 OF BANKRUPTS. B. III.

rupt's, to name the trustees. It follows, however, from this consideration, that those trust-rights only which are imposed by bankrupts upon their creditors, ought to be voided. There lies evidently no objection, either at common law or in equity, against a disposition *omnium bonorum*, solicited by the creditors, and granted by the bankrupt to trustees of their naming. On the contrary, a trust-right of that nature, which saves the nomination of a *curator bonis*, as in Rome, or of commissioners, as in England, merits the greatest favour, being an expeditious and frugal method of managing the bankrupt's funds, for behoof of his creditors. And supposing such a measure to be concerted among the bulk of the creditors, a court of equity ought not to regard a few dissenting creditors, who incline to follow separate measures. The trust-right is good at common law, being an alienation by a proprietor; and it is good in equity, as being a just act. It must accordingly afford a preference to the creditors who lay hold of it. A dissenting creditor may, if he please, proceed to execution against his debtor, and he may attach the imaginary reversion implied in the trust-disposition : but such peevish measures cannot hurt the other creditors, who are secured by the trust-right; for if that right be not voidable, it must be preferred before an adjudication, or any other execution by a dissenting creditor.

I close this chapter, with observing, that since the former edition of this work, all the defects above mentioned of our bankrupt-statutes, are remedied by a British statute, 12th Geo. III, cap. 72; of which the summary follows. Upon application of any of the bankrupt's creditors, or upon his own application,

CH. V. OF BANKRUPTS. 451

his moveable estate is sequestrated, and provision made for a fair and equal distribution of the same among the creditors. In the next place, to bar the preference, that a creditor formerly had access to obtain against others by legal execution, the act has a retrospect of thirty days; within which time an arrestment or poinding gives no preference. And now it may with confidence be pronounced, that no other country can vie with Scotland in the perfection of its bankrupt-laws.

CHAP. VI.

Powers and Faculties.

EVERY right, real or personal, is a legal power. In that extensive sense, there are numberless powers. Every individual hath power over his own property, and over his own person; some over another's property or person. To trace all these powers, would be the same with writing an institute of law. The powers under consideration are of a singular kind. They are not rights, properly speaking, but they are means by which rights can be created, a power, for example, to make a man debtor for a sum, a power to charge his land with debt, a power to redeem land from the purchaser.

These powers are of two kinds; powers founded on consent, and powers founded on property. A disposition by a proprietor of land to his heir, containing a clause, empowering a third person to charge the heir or the land with a sum, is an example of the first kind : a power, thus created, is founded on the

2 F 2

452 POWERS AND FACULTIES. B. III.

consent of the heir, signified by his acceptance of the disposition. A power reserved in a settlement of a land estate, to alter the settlement, or to burden the land with debt, is an example of the other kind : by such settlement, the property is so far understood to be reserved to the maker, as to empower him to alter or to burden. These powers may be termed *personal* and *real*.

To explain a power of the first kind, which is commonly termed *a faculty*, in contradistinction to a power founded on property, it must be considered, 1st, That with regard to pecuniary interest, a man may subject himself to the power of another : he may gratuitously bind himself to pay a sum of money ; or he may empower any person to burden him with a sum. 2d, He may also subject his property to the power of another : a proprietor can empower any person to charge his land with an infeftment of annual-rent ; and a real right, thus established, is good even at common law. Thus, it is laid down by our writers, that the proprietor's consent will validate a resignation made by one who hath no right,* and will validate also an annualrent-right, granted by one who is not proprietor.† 3d, Though an annualrent-right thus granted by a person having a faculty to burden the land, is a real right, no less complete than if granted by the proprietor ; yet the faculty itself is not a real right. It may indeed be exerted, while the granter continues proprietor ; his consent makes it effectual : but his consent cannot operate, after he is divested of his property, more than if he never had been proprietor : it is a consent by one to burden the

* Stair, tit. Extinction of Infeftments, § 7.
† Durie, Dec. 15, 1630, Stirling *contra* Tenants.

CH. VI.   POWERS AND FACULTIES.   453

property of another; an act that can have no effect
in law. Thus, a power granted by a proprietor, to
charge his land with a certain sum, ceases by his selling the land, before the faculty is exerted. Nor,
in strict law, can such faculty be exerted after the
granter's death. Whether equity may not interpose,
is more doubtful. Let us suppose that a man makes
a deed, empowering certain persons to name provisions to his younger children after his death, and to
burden his heir and land-estate with the payment;
leaving at the same time his estate to descend to his
heir-at-law by succession. This deed cannot be effectual at common law; because it is inconsistent
with the nature of property, that a burden can be
imposed upon the estate of any man, without his consent. It seems, however, just, that a court of equity
should interpose, to make so rational a faculty effectual against the heir, though not to charge the estate.
The faculty, it is true, cannot be considered as a debt
due by the ancestor to subject the heir by representation: but it is the will of the ancestor to burden the
heir with provisions to his younger children; and in
equity the will of the ancestor ought to be a law to
the heir who succeeds by that very will, implied,
though not expressed. In the law of England, accordingly, where lands are devised to be sold for
younger childrens' portions, and the executor dies
without selling, the heir is compelled to sell. And
where lands were ordered to be sold, for payment of
debts, without empowering any person to sell, it was
decreed that the heir should sell.* But a settlement
of an estate made by the proprietor upon any of his
blood-relations, that his wife should think proper to

* 1, Chancery Cases, 176.

454 POWERS AND FACULTIES. B. III.

nominate after his death, is effectual at common law: for there is nothing in reason or in law to bar a proprietor from making a settlement upon any person he has a mind, whether named by himself, or by another having his authority. The settlement excludes the heir-at-law, and the person named has a good title by his deed.*

That sort of power, which is a branch of property, is in a very different condition. It is in its nature effectual against all singular successors, even *bona fide* purchasers; for a disponee, to whom the property is conveyed to a limited effect only, cannot bestow upon another a more extensive right than he himself has.

It may be laid down as a general rule, That powers reserved in a disposition of land, the most limited, as well as the most extensive, are all of them branches of the property. To justify this rule, it must be premised, that all the powers a man hath over his own subject are included in his right of property; and that the meaning of a reservation is not to create a new right, but only to limit the right that is conveyed. The reservation, accordingly, of any power over the land, implies, so far, a reservation of the property; and this must hold, however limited the reserved power be, or however extensive, unless it be expressed in clear terms, that a faculty only is intended. A separate argument concurs for this rule. Human nature, which, in matters of interest, makes a man commonly prefer himself before others, founds a natural, and, therefore, a legal presumption, that when a disponer reserves to himself any power over the subject disponed, his intention is to reserve it in

* Nov. 28, 1729, Murray *contra* Fleming.

CH. VI.   POWERS AND FACULTIES.   455

the amplest and most effectual manner.   And hence, *in dubio*, a power properly so called, will be presumed, in opposition to a faculty.   Thus, a reserved power to charge the estate disponed with a sum, though the most limited power that can be reserved, is held to be a reservation of the property, so as to make the reserved power good, even against a purchaser from the disponee.   A man disponed his estate to his eldest son, reserving a power " to affect or " burden the same with a sum named for provisions " to his children."   The son's creditors apprised the estate and were infeft.   Thereafter, the disponer exerted his reserved power, by granting to his children heritable bonds, upon which they also were infeft; and, in a competition, they were preferred : * the reserved power was justly deemed a branch of property, which made every deed done in pursuance of it a preferable right upon the land.   James Henderson, in his eldest son's contract of marriage, disponed to him the lands of Grange, " reserving to himself " power and faculty, even *in articulo mortis*, to bur- " den the land with 8,000 merks to any person he " should think fit."   In his testament he legated the said 8,000 merks to his three younger sons ; who, in a ranking of the eldest son's creditors, were preferred before all of them. †

But though a faculty regularly exerted, while the granter continues proprietor, will lay a burden on the land, effectual against purchasers, and though a power will have the same effect at whatever time ex-

* Stair, Dirleton, Jan. 6, 1677, Creditors of Mouswell *contra* Children.   Stair, Dec. 16, 1679, inter eosdem.

† Hendersons *contra* Creditors of Francis Henderson, July 8, 1760.

456 POWERS AND FACULTIES. B. III.

erted, it follows not that every exertion of a power
or faculty will be so effectual : which leads us to examine in what manner they must be exerted, in order to be effectual against purchasers. That land
may be charged with debt without infeftment, or
without giving a title in the feudal form, is evident
from a rent-charge, and from a clause in a conveyance of land, burdening the land with a certain sum.*
That, without infeftment, such a burden may be laid
on land by means of a power or faculty to burden,
seems equally consistent : and were there a record
of bonds granted in pursuance of such powers, there
would be nothing repugnant to utility more than to
law, in sustaining them as real rights. But as no
record is appointed for bonds of this kind, it is a
wise and salutary regulation to sustain none of them
as real rights, unless where created in the feudal form
to produce infeftment ; which brings them under the
statute 1617, requiring all seisins to be recorded.
Where land stands charged with a sum by virtue
of a clause contained in the disposition, no inconvenience arises from supporting this right, according to its nature, against all singular successors ; for
a purchaser from the disponee is put upon his guard
by the disposition containing the burden, which disposition makes part of his title-deeds. But a power
or faculty, could it be exerted without infeftment,
might occasion great embarrassment : the power or
faculty, it is true, appears on the face of the disposition, which is a title-deed that must be delivered to
a purchaser ; but then a purchaser has no means to
discover whether the power or faculty be exerted, or
to what extent. Nay, further, if a bond be held an

* See Historical Law-tracts, tract 4, p. 244.

CH. VI.   POWERS AND FACULTIES.   457

exertion, there can be no limitation: for bonds referring to the faculty may be granted for £10,000, though the faculty be limited to the tenth part of that sum. Such uncertainty would put the land *extra commercium* during the space of the long prescription, commencing at the death of the disponer who reserved to himself the power of burdening the land. The foregoing regulation is accordingly in strict observance. By the decision mentioned above, Creditors of Mouswell *contra* Children, it appears, that when a reserved power to burden land is regularly exerted, by granting an infeftment of annualrent, such annualrent-right is preferred even before a prior infeftment derived from the disponee: but a bond simply is never so preferred. Thus, a man who disponed his estate to his eldest son, reserving to himself a power to burden the same with 5,000 merks, granted thereafter bonds for that sum to his wife and children, proceeding upon the narrative of the reserved power. After the date of these bonds, the disponee contracted debts, which were established upon the estate by infeftments. A competition arising between these two sets of creditors after the disponer's decease, the disponee's creditors were preferred upon their infeftments.* In a disposition to the eldest son, the father having reserved power to charge the estate with wadsets or infeftments of annualrent to the extent of a sum specified, a bond referring to the faculty was not deemed a real burden; and for that reason it was not held to be effectual against the donator of the son's forfeiture.† But where the disponer reserves a power to burden the

* June 26, 1735, Ogilvies *contra* Turnbull.
† Stair, July 12, 1671, Lermont *contra* Earl of Lauderdale.

458   POWERS AND FACULTIES.   **B. III.**

land with a sum to a person named, the heir-male of
a second marriage, for example; and thereafter grants
a bond to that person referring to the reserved power;
it seems not unreasonable that this bond should be
deemed a real burden effectual against purchasers.
For here there is no uncertainty to put the land *extra commercium:* the burden can never exceed the
sum specified in the disposition; and after the disponer's death, a purchaser, by inquiring at the person named, has access to know whether and to what
extent the power has been exerted.

If the foregoing regulation hold in reserved powers,
there can be no doubt of it with respect to the faculties properly so called. The following decisions I
think belong to this class. A purchaser of land took
the disposition to himself in liferent, and to his son
nominatim in fee, with power to himself to dispone,
wadset, &c. He afterward granted a bond, upon
which the creditor adjudged the estate after the son
was divested, and a purchaser infeft. The adjudication was evidently void, and the bond was decreed
not to be a proper exertion of the faculty to be effectual against singular successors.* This is properly an instance of a faculty, because the power which
the father provided to himself, could not be a branch
of the property which was never in him. Again, a
purchaser of land having taken the disposition to
himself in liferent, and to his son *nominatim* in fee,
with a faculty " to burden, contract debt, and to sell,
" or otherwise dispose at his pleasure," did first grant
a bond, declaring it a burden on the land, and after-

* Home, February 1719, Rome *contra* Creditors of Graham.
November 1725, Sinclair *contra* Sinclair of Barrack.

CH. VI.   POWERS AND FACULTIES.   459

ward sold the land. The purchaser was preferred, the bond not being a real burden on the land.*

The cases above mentioned are governed by the rules of common law. Let us next see what equity dictates. Where a man in a gratuitous disposition of a land-estate reserves a power to burden the subject with certain sums, every question relative to such reservation must be governed by his will; for an obvious reason, that the deed and every clause in it were created by him. Common law, indeed, adhering to the precise words, will not entitle the granter to burden the disponee personally. But it will be considered, that in burdening the land for his own behoof, he could have no intention to exempt the disponee; and, therefore, that this was a pure omission, which ought to be supplied by a court of equity, in order to fulfil the will of the granter. In the decisions, accordingly, Rome *contra* Creditors of Graham, Sinclair *contra* Sinclair of Barrack, and Ogilvies *contra* Turnbull, now mentioned, though a bond granted in pursuance of a power to burden the land was held not to be a real right, it was held, however, to be a burden upon the disponee personally. And in like manner, a bond granted in pursuance of a reserved power to burden the land disponed, was found effectual against the disponee personally, so as to support an adjudication of the land against the disponee after the disponer's death.† In the cases mentioned, nothing is considered in equity but the will of the granter. But where a price is paid, the will of the purchaser ought to have equal

---

* Forbes, December 16, 1708, Davidson *contra* Town of Aberdeen.

· † January 17, 1723, Creditors of Rusco *contra* Blair of Senwick.

460 POWERS AND FACULTIES. **B. III.**

weight; and if he have not agreed to be bound personally, equity will not bind him more than common law.

With respect to faculties, there is not the same latitude of interpretation. A faculty granted to a third person gratuitously, cannot be extended against the granter beyond the precise words. And it will be the same though the faculty has been granted for a valuable consideration.

A disponer, who had reserved a power to burden the disponee with a sum, grants a bond for that sum, without referring to the reserved faculty. Will this bond be in equity deemed an exertion of the faculty, yea or not? If the granter have no other fund of payment, it will be presumed in equity that he intended an exertion of the faculty: if he have a separate fund, the presumption ceases, and that fund only is attachable for payment. But what if the separate fund be not altogether sufficient? A court of equity may interpose to make what is deficient effectual by means of the reserved faculty, in order to fulfil the will of the person who granted the bond. Thus, a man, upon the narrative of love and favour, having disponed his estate to his eldest son, reserving a power to burden the estate to the extent of a sum named, granted afterward a personal bond of provision to his children, without any relation to the reserved power. In a suit for payment against the disponee's representatives, it was objected, That the disponer at the date of the bond had an opulent fund of moveables; and that there is no presumption he intended to charge with this debt either his son or the estate disponed. The disponer's will was presumed to be, that the bond should burden his execu-

CH. VI.   POWERS AND FACULTIES.   561

tors in the first place, and the disponee in the second place.* By marriage-articles, the estate was provided to heirs-male, with power to burden it with a sum named for the heirs of a second marriage. The proprietor made a provision for the children of a second marriage, burdening his heir with the same, but not charging his estate in terms of the reserved power. At common law, the estate was not subjected, because the provision was not made a burden upon it; nor was the heir subjected, because the reserved power entitled the granter to burden the estate only. The court steered a middle course in equity: the heir was made liable *ultimo loco*, after his father's other estate should be discussed.†

It has been questioned, whether a reserved power to charge with a sum the land disponed, can benefit a creditor whose debt was contracted before the reserved power was created. The court thought it reasonable that this power should be subjected to the disponer's debts, whether prior or posterior.‡ A power to charge an estate with debt, being strictly personal, is incommunicable to a creditor, or to any other, even during the life of the person privileged; not to talk of his or her death. Equity, however, rules, that a power or faculty should be available to creditors, prior as well as posterior: for it is the duty of a debtor to use all lawful means for paying his debts, whether by selling his goods or exerting his faculties;

---

* Stair, Dirleton, June 21, 1677, Hope-Pringle *contra* Hope-Pringle.

† Fountainhall, Dalrymple, June 23, 1698, Carnegie *contra* Laird Kinfauns.

‡ Fountainhall, Dalrymple, Dec. 16, 1698, Eliot of Swinside *contra* Eliot of Meikleden.

462 POWERS AND FACULTIES. B. III.

and if he unjustly refuse, equity will hold the faculty as exerted for the benefit of the creditors. In the present case, the creditors will have access to the land for their payment, as if the debtor had exercised his faculty, and burdened the land with the sum mentioned, payable to them. But if the creditors lie dormant during their debtor's life, and make no step to avail themselves of his reserved faculty, the faculty dies with him, and they can take nothing by it. A man disponed to his sons of the second marriage several parcels of land, " Reserving to himself full " power and faculty to alter and innovate, and to " contract debt, as fully and freely as if the entire " fee were in him." The question occurred, Whether these disponees were liable to their father's personal debts contracted before the existence of the said power; and the affirmative was decreed.* But in cases of this nature, the disponee, even where he is heir-apparent, is liable *in valorem* only :† for the disponee is. not liable at common law; and equity subjects no man further than *in valorem* of the subject he receives.

Whether and in what cases a reserved power or faculty can effectually be exercised on deathbed, has frequently been agitated in the Court of Session. One point appears clear, that a reserved power to alter or burden on deathbed, contained in a disposition to a stranger, may be exercised on deathbed; supposing always the granter to be *sanæ mentis*. And the reason is, that the stranger, laying hold of the disposition, must submit to its qualities, and cannot object to the conditions upon which it is granted.

* July 21, 1724, Creditors of Rusco, *contra* Blair of Senwick.
† Dalrymple, January 18, 1717, Abercromby *contra* Graham.

CH. VI.   POWERS AND FACULTIES.   463

The matter is far from being clear, where the settlement is upon the heir, who is *alioqui successurus*; as to which our decisions seem not to be uniform ; nor is any good rule laid down by our writers. If the heir have not, by acceptance of the disposition, consented to the burdening clause, his privilege of challenging a burden laid upon him on deathbed, remains entire. But if he have taken infeftment upon the disposition, and be in possession, which implies his consent to every clause in the deed, will not this consent bar him from objecting to the faculty, though exerted on deathbed ? This requires deliberation. What distinguishes an heir from a stranger, is his dependence upon the predecessor for the estate, leaving him no freedom of choice : he must submit to the will of his predecessor under the peril of exheredation. But does this dependence presume co-action in every transaction between a man and his heir ? This can hardly be maintained ; for what if the reserved faculty be to burden the estate with a moderate provision to younger children, or to do any other pious or rational act ? In such a case, no good man will withhold his consent ; and, therefore, in such a case, there is no ground for presuming the heir's consent to have been extorted from him. This hint leads us to a distinction in answering the foregoing question. If the heir's consent be voluntary, such as he would have given in a state of independence, it must be effectual both in law and equity to support the death-bed-deed. If it be extorted by fear of exheredation, it may be good at common law, but it will be voided by a court of equity.

But this distinction, however clear in theory, seems to be not a little dark in practice ; for what criterion

464   POWERS AND FACULTIES.   B. III.

have we for judging in what cases this consent is voluntary, in what cases extorted? The explication may be intricate, but it is necessary. Where a man settles his estate upon his eldest son, with a reserved power to alter even on deathbed, no rational man will willingly submit to be in so precarious a state; and, therefore, the heir's consent will be presumed the effect of extortion. On the other hand, where a man, settling his estate upon his eldest son, reserves only power to burden it with a moderate sum to his younger children; this is a fair settlement, by which the heir gets more than he gives; and therefore his consent may safely be presumed voluntary. Hence in general, the heir's consent to a reserved power that bears hard upon him, will always be presumed to have been extorted: his consent, on the contrary, to a reserved power that is proper and rational, will always be presumed voluntary.

This distinction gives me the greater satisfaction, when I find that it has had an influence upon the decisions of the Court of Session. A reserved power to alter upon deathbed a disposition granted to an eldest son, has in no instance been supported against the heir's reduction, even where he accepted the disposition. But the exercise upon deathbed of a reserved power that is proper and rational has generally been supported. Take the following examples.—The exercise of a reserved faculty to burden with a moderate sum an estate disponed to an heir, was sustained, though the faculty was exerted upon deathbed.* A man having disponed his estate to his eldest son, with the burden of all provisions to his

---

* Stair, June 28, 1662, Hay *contra* Seton; Stair, June 22, 1670, Douglas *contra* Douglas.

CH. VI.   POWERS AND FACULTIES.   465

younger children granted or to be granted, a bond
granted to one of his daughters *in lecto*, was sustained against the heir who had accepted the disposition.*

I shall close this chapter with a separate point,
concerning powers given to a plurality, whether in
exercising such powers the whole must concur, or
what number less than the whole may be sufficient.
If the persons be named jointly, the will of the granter is clear, that the whole must concur, because such
is the import of the word *jointly*. To say that any
number less than the whole may be sufficient, is, in
other words, to say, that a nomination to act jointly
is the same with a nomination to act separately.

But though all must concur, it follows not that
they must all agree. If they be all present, the will
of the maker naming them jointly is fulfilled ; and
what remains, is, that the opinion of the majority
must govern the whole body. Celsus, lib. 2, Diges-
torum, writes,—" Si in tres fuerit compromissum,
" sufficere duorum consensum, si præsens fuerit et
" tertius : alioquin, absente eo, licèt duo consentiant,
" arbitrium non valere ; quia in plures fuit compro-
" missum, et potuit præsentia ejus trahere eos in
" ejus sententiam.   Sicuti tribus judicibus datis,
" quod duo ex consensu, absente tertio, judicaverunt,
" nihil valet : quia id demum, quod major pars om-
" nium judicavit, ratum est, cum et omnes judicâsse
" palàm est." †

The next question is, When a plurality are named,
without adding the term *jointly*, what is the legal import of such nomination ? Whether is it understood

* Fountainhall, Forbes, Feb. 8, 1706, Bertram *contra* Weir.
† L. 17, § 7, l. 18.   De receptis qui arbitr.

2 G

POWERS AND FACULTIES. B. III.

by the will of the maker, that they must act jointly, or that they may act separately? Stair* resolves this question by an argument no less plain than persuasive:—" A mandate (says he) given to ten cannot be " understood as given to a lesser number. To give " a mandate to Titius, Seins, and Mævius, cannot be " the same with giving it to any two of them." Hence it may be assumed, as a rule at common law, That a number of persons named in one deed to act in the same affair, are understood to be named jointly, where the contrary is not expressed.

How far in this matter common law is subjected to the correction of equity, we next proceed to inquire. When a number of persons are named *jointly* to perform any work, the whole must concur in equity, as well as at common law. For here the will is clearly expressed, and a court of equity hath no power to vary from will. Thus, two tutors being named *jointly* by a man to his heir, it was decreed, That the office was vacated by the death of one of them.†

A plurality named for carrying on any particular affair, without the addition of *jointly*, affords a large field for equitable considerations. We have seen that at common law the term *jointly* is always implied or presumed. But in particular cases there are many circumstances, which a court of equity will lay hold of to overbalance this presumption; to reduce which, under any general rule, is scarce practicable: circumstances are seldom precisely the same in any two cases, and for that reason each case must be ruled by

---

* Book i, tit. 12, 13.

† Stair, January 17, 1671, Drummond *contra* Feuars of Bothkennar.

Ch. VI. POWERS AND FACULTIES. 487

its own circumstances. All that can be said in general, is, that the common law ought to take place, unless it can be clearly shown, that the maker did not intend to confine his nominees to act jointly.

Since general rules cannot be expected, what remains, is to state cases the most opposed to each other, and which, therefore, admit of different considerations. And, first, If I name a plurality to perform any act that is to bind or affect me, equity, as well as common law, requires that the nominees act jointly. In cases of that nature, there cannot readily occur any circumstance to infer it to be my will, that they may act separately: for if any one of the nominees refuse to accept, or die after acceptance, it is my privilege to make a second nomination, or to forbear altogether; and it is not presumable, that any man will give away his privilege, unless it be so declared. Thus, an award pronounced by two arbiters and an oversman named by them, was declared void; because it proceeded upon a submission to four arbiters, who were empowered to name an oversman.[*] And when a plurality are constituted sheriffs in that part by the Court of Session, no sentence can be pronounced by any of them without the rest; because (as the author expresses it) he being but one colleague joined to others, hath no power to pronounce sentence, without their consent.[†] This holds in curators, because they are elected by the minor himself: if any of them refuse to accept, or die after acceptance, it is no hardship that the nomination should be void, because it is in the minor's power to renew the commission. But where the curators named are many in number,

[*] Fountainhall, Nov. 18, 1696, Watson contra Myln.
[†] Balfour, (Of Judges), cap. 26.

468 POWERS AND FACULTIES. **B. III.**

it will scarce be held the minor's intention to adhere to the common law, by confining them to act jointly. It appears a more natural presumption, that the purpose of naming so great a number, was to provide against death or non-acceptance. And accordingly an act of curatory was sustained, though seven only accepted of the eight that were named.* Where in an act of curatory, a *quorum* is named, there can be no doubt that the act is void, if a sufficient number do not accept to make the *quorum*.† For here the will of the minor is expressed in clear terms.

There is much greater latitude for interpretation of will with respect to powers intended to be exercised after the granter's death. Stair explains this matter extremely well in the following words : " A " mandate *inter vivos*, giving power, is strictly to be " interpreted, because the nominees failing, the power " returns to the mandant. But power given by a " man, in contemplation of death, cannot return, and, " therefore, he is presumed to prefer all the persons " nominated to any other that may fall by course of " law."‡ This doctrine is finely illustrated in a nomination of tutors. Where a number of tutors are named simply, without confining them to act jointly, the preference given to them, exclusive of the tutor-in-law, manifests the will of the deceased, that the management should be carried on by any one of the nominees, rather than by the tutor-in-law. " For " were it otherwise, the more guardians are appoint-" ed for the security of the infant, the less secure he " would be, because, upon the death of any one of

* Hope, (Minor), March 11, 1612, Airth.
† Stair, Jan. 25, 1672, Ramsay *contra* Maxwell.
‡ Book 1, tit. 12, § 13.

CH. VI.   POWERS AND FACULTIES.   469

" them, the guardianship would be at an end."* Thus, three tutors being named, without specifying, *conjunctly* or *severally*, and one only having accepted, it was decreed, That the whole office was devolved on him:† And five tutors being named as above, without specifying *conjunctly* or *severally*, the nomination was sustained, though two only accepted.‡

Where a number of tutors are named *jointly*, it is more doubtful what is intended by such a nomination. It may have been the intention of the deceased, that no act of administration should be valid, unless every person named by him did concur; and, consequently, that the death or non-acceptance of any one nominee should void the nomination, leaving place to the tutor-in-law. Or it may have been his intention, that all the nominees accepting and alive must concur in every act. The argument above mentioned, urged by Lord Stair, concludes strongly for the latter interpretation ; unless the former be so clearly expressed, as to avoid all ambiguity. *In dubio*, it will always be presumed, that the deceased would put greater trust in his own nominees than in any person not chosen by himself.

With respect to a *quorum*, will the nomination fall altogether, where, by death or *non-acceptance*, there are not left a number of tutors sufficient to make a *quorum ?* In this case, as in the former, the will of the deceased may be interpreted differently. It may have been his will to void the nomination, if there remain not a number of tutors to make a *quorum*. Or it may have been his will only, that supposing a

---

* New Abridg. of the law, vol. 2, p. 677.

† Haddington, Dec. 12, 1609, Fawside *contra* Adamson.

‡ Stair, Feb. 14, 1672, Elies *contra* Scot.

470   POWERS AND FACULTIES.   B. III.

sufficient number of acting tutors to make a *quorum*, a *quorum* should be necessary to every act. The latter interpretation, for the reason above given, ought to be adopted, unless the former be clearly expressed. But now, admitting this interpretation, the falling of the number below a *quorum*, is a *casus incogitatus*, about which the deceased has interposed no act of will. To supply that defect, the court will do what they conjecture the deceased would have done, had the event occurred to him. About this there can be no hesitation ; as it is always to be presumed, that a man will have more confidence in a trustee named by himself, than in one that is not of his nomination. Suppose, for example, ten tutors are named, the tutor-in-law one of them, five to be a *quorum*. By death or non-acceptance, the number is reduced to four, of which number the tutor-in-law is one. Can so whimsical a thing have been intended, as to trust the tutor-in-law by himself, instead of confining him to act with the other three. And the argument concludes *a fortiori*, where the tutor-in-law is left out of the nomination. The same reasoning is applicable, where a *sine quo non* is named. This doctrine is finely illustrated in the following case. A gentleman having named his spouse, his brother, and several others, to be tutors and curators to his only child, " appointed, that
" of those who should accept and survive, the major
" part should be a *quorum* ; that his spouse should
" be *sine qua non* ; and in case of her death or inca-
" pacity, his brother ; but that by the death or inca-
" pacity of either, the tutory and curatory should
" not be dissolved, but be continued with the other
" persons named, as long as any one of them remain-
" ed alive." The only event omitted to be provided

CH. VI.   POWERS AND FACULTIES.   471

for was that which happened, namely, the widow's refusal to undertake the office; which brought on the question, Whether the nomination did notwithstanding, subsist; or, Whether it was void, to make way for the tutor-in-law? The court was of opinion, That it appeared the intention of the father to continue his nomination as long as any of the persons named should exist; which is expressed in clear terms with respect to the death or incapacity of the *sine quibus non*; and which must hold equally in the case of their non-acceptance, as no distinction can be made. The nomination accordingly was decreed to subsist. * In several other instances, neither the failure of a *quorum*, nor of a *sine quo non* was deemed sufficient to void the nomination. The court conjectured it to be the will of the deceased, to trust any of the persons named, rather than the tutor-in-law. † But the court adopted the opposite opinion in the following instances, A man, in a nomination of tutors to his children, declared his wife to be *sine qua non*. She, by a second marriage, having rendered herself incapable of the office, the court declared the nomination void. ‡

I proceed to examples of a different kind. A man having left 2,500 merks to his children, empowered four friends named to divide the same among the children. After the death of one of the four, a division made by the three survivors was not sustained,

* June 16, 1742, Dalrymple of Drummore *contra* Mrs. Isabel Somervell.

† Fountainhall, 22d Dec. 1692, Watt *contra* Scrymgeour; Fountainhall, 22d Feb. 1693, Countess of Callender *contra* Earl of Linlithgow.

‡ Fountainhall, 24th June 1708, Aikenhead *contra* Durham; 14th Feb. 1735, Blair *contra* Ramsay.

472 POWERS AND FACULTIES. B. III.

and the children accordingly were decreed to have each of them an equal share. * Here the four being named in the same deed, and to concur in the same act, were understood to be named jointly ; and as there was no circumstance to infer that the granter intended to empower any number less than the whole to make the division, there could be no reason for varying from the rule of common law.

Helen Cunningham left 4,000 merks to her grandchildren, to be employed for their behoof, at the sight of five persons named, of which number their father and mother were two. This sum was lent out, with the approbation of all, including the father and mother, one of the nominees excepted, who was abroad at the time. The ultimate purpose of this settlement was evidently to secure the grandchildren in the sum settled upon them ; and if this was done, by lending the money to a person of unexceptionable credit at the time, the granter's will and purpose was fulfilled. By naming so many persons, he made it easy for the executor to get the approbation of a sufficient number ; and it could not be his intention to require rigidly the concurrence of every person named. And yet the court, adhering to the words as a court of common law, found that the money was not employed as it ought to have been, and therefore decreed the executor to be liable.†

A reference being made by a man and his son to three friends, empowering them to name a sum to the father, when he should be in want, which the son should be obliged to pay ; and two having concurred,

* Fountainhall, Feb. 10, 1693, Moir *contra* Grier.
† Spottiswoode, (Legacy,) Feb. 13, 1624, Hunters *contra* Executors of Mamichael.

CH. VI.   POWERS AND FACULTIES.   473

in absence of the third, to name the sum, it was objected by the son, That the clause, importing a joint nomination, required the concurrence of the whole. The objection was overruled, and the determination of the two referees sustained.* The reference to the three friends was the means chosen for ascertaining the father's claim, but it was certainly not intended to make that claim depend on their life or acceptance. The father had a just claim, whenever he came to be in want; and supposing none of the referees had interposed, it was the duty of the Court of Session to make the claim effectual.

CHAP. VII.

Of the power which officers of the law have to act extra territorium.

A COURT of equity not only varies from common law, in order to fulfil the great principles of justice and utility, but countenances such variations in the conduct of individuals. The present chapter is intended as an illustration of this observation; for several examples shall be given, of supporting positive infringements of common law, done even by its own officers.

The legal authority of magistrates and officers of the law being territorial, is confined within precise limits. In strict reasoning, nothing can be pronounced with greater certainty, than that an officer of the law acting beyond the bounds of his commission, acts illegally: and yet in practice we admit several exceptions from this rule. If goods once ap-

* Fountainhall, July 27, 1694, Riddle *contra* Riddle.

474   OFFICERS OF THE LAW.   B. III.

pretended in order to be poinded, be driven out of
the sheriffdom purposely to disappoint the poinding,
it is lawful for the officer to follow and complete his
poinding, in the same manner as if the goods had not
been driven away.* By the statute 52, Henry III,
cap. 15, "No man, for any manner of cause, can take
" a distress out of his fee, or in the king's highway."
But if the lord coming to distrain, have the view of
the beasts within his fee, and before distraining the
tenant chases them into the highway, it hath been
found, that the lord, notwithstanding the statute, may
distrain them there.† With regard to the power of
apprehending delinquents, one instruction is, That if
a delinquent fly without the bounds of a constable's
charge, the constable, being in hot pursuit, may follow and apprehend him.‡ And, by the same rule, a
stranger committing a riot within a barony, may, by
the officers of the barony, be pursued and apprehended out of the barony.§

Sir Matthew Hale, in his history of the pleas of
the crown,‖ handles this matter with care, and
traces it through various cases. " If a warrant or
" precept to arrest a felon come to an officer or
" other, if the felon be arrested, and after arrest
" escape into another county, yet he may be pur-
" sued and taken upon fresh pursuit, and brought
" before the justice of the county where the war-
" rant issued ; for the law adjudged him always

* Balfour, (Poinding,) March 22, 1560, Home contra Sheill.
† Abridg. of the Law, vol. ii, p. 111.
‡ Act 8, parl. 1617. Act 38, parl. 1661.
§ Nicolson, (Forum competens,) Jan 8, 1661, Baillie contra
Lord Torphichen.
‖ Vol. ii, p. 115.

CH. VII: ACTING *extra Territorium.* 475

" in the officer's custody by virtue of the first arrest.
" But if he escape before arrest into another county,
" if it be a warrant barely for a misdemeanour, it
" seems the officer cannot pursue him into another
" county; because out of the jurisdiction of the
" justice who granted the warrant. But in case of
" felony, affray, or dangerous wounding, the officer
" may pursue him, and use hue and cry upon him
" into any county. But if he take him in a foreign
" county, he is to bring him to the jail or justice of
" that county where he is taken. For he doth not
" take him purely by the warrant of the justice, but
" by the authority that the law gives him; and the
" justice's warrant is a sufficient cause of suspicion
" and pursuit." Here several cases are distinguished, and different degrees of power indulged to the officer, all of them flatly contradictory to the strict
rules of common law : and yet we cheerfully acquiesce
in the doctrine, having an impression that it is just
and salutary.

Let us try what will the most readily occur, in reflecting on this subject. If a felon be once arrested
and in the hands of the officer, a notion of property
arises, and suggests a right similar to that of the first
occupant of land. Though the felon escape, the officer, in fresh pursuit, is understood to retain a sort of
possession *animo*, entitling him to pursue the felon
till he compass his aim, to wit, a second arrest. We
naturally conclude, that the felon, being in some sense
the property of the officer, may be seized wherever
he can be found; and, by virtue of that *quasi* property, may be carried before the judge who granted
the warrant. This reasoning will appear still more
satisfactory when it is applied to the case cited above.

476 . .OFFICERS OF THE LAW B. III.

from Balfour, where a poinding is inchoated by apprehension of the goods ; a circumstance which undoubtedly produces some faint notion of right to the goods, entitling the poinder to seize them wherever found.

Again, " where a felon escapes without being arrested, if the warrant be barely for a misdemeanour, it seems the officer cannot pursue him into another county. But in case of felony, affray, or dangerous wounding, the officer may pursue him into another county." Here is a distinction made which appears to have a foundation in human nature. As this distinction cannot arise from the nature of the warrant, which is no more extensive in the one case than in the other, it must arise from the nature of the delinquence. Felony, or any capital crime, inflames the mind, and creates a strong desire of punishment : the heated imagination is hurried along, and cannot be restrained by the slight fetters of strict form. And, accordingly, in weighing an abstract principle against the impulse of an honest passion, the mind, giving way to the latter, embraces the following sentiment, That the officer ought not to be confined within the limits of his commission. In the case of a slight misdemeanour, the result is different. Strict principles have a stronger effect upon the mind than any impulse that can arise from a venial transgression ; and, therefore, in judging of this case, the mind naturally rests on the limitation of the warrant.

And what is further mentioned in the foregoing quotation, will support these reflections. " A delinquent once arrested, may, upon a second arrest, be brought from another county to the judge who gave the warrant. But if arrested for the first time

CH. VII. ACTING *extra Territorium.* 477

" in a foreign county, the criminal must be carried
". before the judge of the county where he is taken."
The distinction here made, arises from the principles
above explained. It has already been observed, that
the notion of a *quasi* property supplies the want of a
second warrant. But an arrest for the first time in
a foreign county must be governed by a different
rule : the mind figuring a hot pursuit of the criminal, easily surmounts any obstruction that may arise
from mere form ; but when the end is gained by
having the felon in safe custody, the impulse of passion being over, the mind subsides ; and in this condition, perceiving the defect of power, it takes the
first opportunity of supplying the defect, by an application to the judge of the place. (*a*)

With respect to the two cases now mentioned, a
remarkable difference is observable in the operations
of the mind. However strong the impulse of a passion may be when it agitates the mind, yet as soon
as it subsides by gratification, the mind is left free
to the government of reason. Thus, where a felon
who was never arrested, is pursued into a foreign
county, the defect of power is scarce perceived during the heat of pursuit : but immediately upon the
arrest, the defect of power makes an impression ; and
reason demands that the defect be forthwith supplied.
The mind is differently influenced in the case of an

(*a*) This form is now rendered unnecessary by act 24° Geo. II,
cap. 55. " If a person, upon a warrant indorsed, be apprehend-
" ed in another county for an offence not bailable, or if he shall
" not find bail, he shall be carried back into the first county, and
" be committed by the justices in that county, or be bailed there,
" if the crime be bailable."

478   OFFICERS OF THE LAW   B. III.

escape after arrest. If once a resemblance be discovered between two objects, there is a natural propensity to make the resemblance as complete as possible, which in reasoning produces an error extremely common, that of drawing the same inferences as if the resemblance were altogether complete. Thus, by getting possession of the body of a felon, a faint notion of property being suggested, the mind proceeds to form all its conclusions, as if the felon were truly the property of the officer.

It is extremely curious to observe, how men sometimes are influenced by principle and emotions that they themselves at the time scarce attend to; which is remarkable in writers upon law, who, little apt to regard the silent operations of the mind, are not satisfied but with reasonings drawn from principles of law. This proceeds from studying law too much as an abstract science, without considering, that all its regulations ought to be founded upon human nature, and be adapted to the various operations of the mind. If one of the greatest lawyers in modern times furnish this censure, few can hope to escape. And that the censure is just, will appear from considering the reasoning of our author, which is by no means satisfactory. With regard to the felon who has been once arrested, he assigns the following reason for the regulation, " That the law adjudgeth him always in " the officer's custody by virtue of the first arrest." But why does the law give this judgment, when it is contrary to the fact? This question ought to have been prevented in accurate reasoning: instead of which, we are left in the dark, precisely where light is the most wanted. The true answer to this ques-

CH. VII.   ACTING *extra Territorium*.   479

tion is given above, that the right of possession once fairly acquired, cannot be lost by stealth or force, and therefore is retained *animo*.

Upon the other branch, the reasoning appears still more lame. The case is of a felon apprehended for the first time out of the jurisdiction; upon which, our author's reasoning is, " That the officer doth not " act purely by the warrant of the justice, but by the " authority which the law gives him; and that the " justice's warrant is a sufficient cause of suspicion " and pursuit." This is extremely obscure and unsatisfactory, as far as intelligible. In the first place, it is obvious, that the reasoning, if just, is equally applicable whatever be the nature of the crime: the justice's warrant is not a sufficient cause of suspicion and pursuit where the crime is atrocious, more than where it is of the slightest kind. In the next place, supposing the justice's warrant to be a sufficient cause of suspicion, and consequently of pursuit, the person upon whose information the warrant was issued, has a better cause of suspicion, and yet the law empowers not that person to apprehend or to pursue. Neither doth a sufficient cause of suspicion give authority to an officer of the law out of the jurisdiction, more than to a private person. But let a man, having authority to apprehend, be figured in hot pursuit of a noted criminal, the mind hurries him on till he reach his quarry wherever found: no such impression is made by the slighter transgressions. And this difference of feeling is the foundation of our author's doctrine; a difference, that, undoubtedly, made an impression on him, though overlooked in his reasoning.

Thus, we have endeavoured to trace out the foundation of several nice conclusions in law, that depend

480   OFFICERS OF THE LAW   B. III.

not on abstract reasoning, but on sentiment. In one of the cases, an imagined right over the person of a felon arrested, suggested by a slight resemblance it hath to property, is in reality the only foundation of our conclusion. In the other, what in reality deter-mines us, is the anxiety we have to prevent the felon's escape. And whoever examines laws and decisions with due attention, will find many of them founded on impressions or emotions still more slight than those above mentioned.

To complete the subject, nothing further seems necessary but to observe, that the foregoing principles and operations of the mind, are countenanced by courts of justice, so as even to dispense with the clearest rules of law. These principles and operations merit regard as virtuous and laudable ; but their merit chiefly depends on their utility. By overcom-ing that scrupulous nicety of law, which often is an impediment to the administration of justice, they tend in an eminent degree to the good of society.

CHAP. VIII.

Jurisdiction of the Court of Session with respect to foreign matters.

The subjects hitherto treated, falling within the bounds of common law, come of course under the equitable jurisdiction of the Court of Session, sup-plying defects or correcting injustice in common law. Foreign matters, as will by and by be explained, fall not within the bounds of common law ; and for that reason come not under the jurisdiction of the ses-

CH. VIII. - FOREIGN MATTERS. 481

sion, either as a court of common law, or as a court of equity. Why then should the present subject be brought into a treatise of equity? Not necessarily, I acknowledge. It is, however, so intimately connected with matters of equity, that the Session, acting, whether as a court for foreign affairs, or as a court of equity, is governed by the same principles, namely, those above laid down. Of these, accordingly, we shall see many beautiful illustrations in handling the present subject; which, in that view, will make a proper appendix to a treatise on equity, if not a necessary part.

Such tribes as relinquished the wandering state for a settled habitation, came under new rules of law. The laws of a tribe or clan governed originally each individual belonging to it, without relation to place.* But after nations became stationary, place became the capital circumstance. Laws were made to regulate all matters at home, that is, within the territory of the state; and legislators extended not their view to what was done or suffered in a foreign country, whether by their own people or by others. Thus, laws, originally *personal*, became strictly *territorial*; and hence the established maxim, That law hath no authority *extra territorium*. This confined notion of jurisdiction corresponded to the manners of early times: mutual fear and diffidence in days of barbarity, prevented all intercourse among nations; and individuals seldom ventured beyond their own territory. But regular government introduced more social manners: the appetite for riches unfolded itself; and individuals were put in motion to seek gain where the prospect was the fairest. In most coun-

* See Historical Law-tracts, tract 6.

2 H

482 FOREIGN MATTERS. B. III.

tries, accordingly, there are found many foreigners, who have an occasional residence there for the sake of commerce. This change of manners discovered the imperfection of territorial jurisdiction: a man, by retiring abroad, is secure against a prosecution, civil or criminal, for what he has done at home; and by returning home, he is secure against a prosecution for what he has done abroad: common law reacheth no person but who is actually within the territory of the state; and reacheth no cause of action but what happens within the same territory.*

The common law of England is strictly territorial in the sense above described:† nor have we reason to believe that the common law of Scotland was more extensive. When, therefore, the foregoing defect was discovered, it became necessary to provide a remedy: and the remedy was, to bring foreign matters under jurisdiction of the king and council; to which, originally, as a paramount court, all extraordinary matters were appropriated. In Scotland, particularly, the act 105, parl. 1487, declares the king and council to be the only court for *the actions of strangers of other realms.*

With respect to foreign matters, the jurisdiction of the king and council in both kingdoms, was distinguished from that of the ordinary courts of law in two particulars.—First, The jurisdiction of the latter was territorial with respect to causes, as well as with respect to persons: the jurisdiction of the former was, indeed, territorial, with respect to persons, no person in foreign parts being subjected to the jurisdiction; but with respect to causes, it was the opposite

* Historical Law-tracts, tract 7.
† See Statute-law of Scotland abridged, note 7.

CH. VIII.   FOREIGN MATTERS.   483

to territorial, no cause but what happened in foreign parts being competent. Next, The ordinary courts are confined to common law; but with respect to foreign matters this law can be no rule, for the reason above given, that it regulates nothing *extra territorium*. The king and council accordingly, judging of foreign matters, could not be governed by the common law of any country: the common law of *Britain* regulates not foreign matters; and the law of a foreign country hath no authority here. Whence it follows, that foreign matters must be governed by the rules of common justice, to which all men are subjected, or *jure gentium*, as commonly expressed.

This extraordinary jurisdiction, confined originally in both kingdoms to the same court, is now exercised very differently in the two kingdoms. In Scotland, it was derived by intermediate steps from the King and council to the Court of Session: and accordingly, by the regulations laid down soon after the institution of that court, a jurisdiction is bestowed upon it as to foreign matters; and the actions of foreigners are privileged.* In England, this extraordinary jurisdiction made a different progress. The extensive territories in France possessed by the English Kings, and the great resort of Englishmen there, occasioned numberless lawsuits before the King and council. To relieve that court from an oppressive load of business, the constable and marshal court was instituted; and to this new court were appropriated foreign matters, to be tried *jure gentium*.† After the

* Act 45, parl. 1587.

† See Duck De Authoritate juris Civilis, lib. 2, cap. 8, part 3, § 15, &c.

2 H 2

484 FOREIGN MATTERS. B. III.

English conquests in France were wrested from them, this court had very little business. We find scattered instances of its acting as a criminal court, down to the reign of Charles II.; but none for centuries before of its acting as a civil court. The Court of Chancery, with respect to its power of supplying the defects and mitigating the rigour of common law, had succeeded to the King and council: and it would have been a natural measure to transfer to the same court the extraordinary jurisdiction under consideration, the rule of judging being the same in both. But the Court of Chancery being at that time in its infancy, and its privileges as to extraordinary matters not clearly unfolded, the courts of common law, by an artifice or fiction, assumed foreign matters to themselves. The cause of action is feigned to have existed in England,* and the defendant is not suffered to traverse that allegation. This may be justly considered as an usurpation of the courts of common law upon the Court of Chancery; which, like most usurpations, has occasioned very irregular consequences. I shall not insist upon the strange irregularity of assuming a jurisdiction upon no better foundation than an absolute falsehood. It is more material to observe, that foreign matters ought to be tried *jure gentium*, and yet that the judges who usurp this juridiction have no power to try any cause otherwise than by the common law of England. What can be expected from such inconsistency, but injustice in every instance? Lucky it is for Scotland, that chance, perhaps more than good policy, hath appropriated foreign matters to the Court of

* See Duck De authoritate juris Civilis, lib. 2, cap. 8, part 3, § 18.

CH. VIII.   FOREIGN MATTERS.   485

Session, where they can be decided on rational principles, without, being absurdly fettered, as in England, by common law.

To form a distinct notion of the jurisdiction of the Court of Session with respect to foreign matters, it may be proper to state succinctly its different jurisdictions, and to ascertain the limits of each. Considered as a court of common law, those actions only belong to it where the cause of action did arise in Scotland. With regard to persons, this court was originally limited like the courts of common law in England: it had no authority over any man but during the time he was locally in Scotland. But in this respect the court hath in latter times acquired, by prescription, an enlargement of jurisdiction : every Scotchman, at home or abroad, is subjected to the jurisdiction of the court ; and, when abroad, may, by a citation at the market-cross of Edinburgh, pier and shore of Leith, be called to defend in any action before the court.* In the next place, considering this court as a court of equity, empowered to supply the defects and mitigate the rigour of common law, its jurisdiction is and must be the same with what it enjoys as a court of common law. To give it a more extensive jurisdiction would be useless ; and to confine it within narrower bounds would not fully answer the end of its institution, which is to redress common law when justice demands redress. In the last place, this court, with relation to foreign matters, has the same jurisdiction over persons that it has as a court of common law or of equity. And, accordingly, the court had no difficulty to sustain a process for payment of an account contracted at

* See Statute-law of Scotland abridged, note 7.

Campvere in Zealand, though the defendant, a Scotch merchant residing there, was not in this country any time during the suit.*

The rules that govern the Session as a court for foreign matters, are the same that govern it as a court of equity; for these rules are derived from the principles of justice. But it must not be held that these rules are applied precisely in the same manner: as a court of equity, the Session will not venture to interpose against common law, unless authorised by some general rule of equity that is applicable to all cases of the kind; but as to foreign matters, which belong not to common law, every case must be judged upon its own merits. And, therefore, the court here is less under restraint, than in supplying the defects of common law, or in correcting its rigour.

Though with respect to foreign matters, there is, strictly speaking, but one rule for judging, namely, natural justice; yet this rule, in its application to different matters, brings out very different conclusions. And should one undertake to unfold all the various cases to which the rule may be applied, the work would be endless. Avoiding, therefore, this endless task, I confine my speculations to some few leading cases that have been debated in the Court of Session; and these, for the sake of perspicuity, shall be divided into different sections.

* June 27, 1760, Hog *contra* Tennent.

SECT. I.

Personal actions founded on foreign covenants, deeds, or facts.

ACCORDING to the principles above laid down, a foreigner's covenant will produce an action against him here, provided he be found in Scotland. It would be a great defect in law, were there no redress against a foreigner who retires with his effects to this country, in order to screen himself from debts contracted at home. But a momentary residence here will not presume against him : he cannot be called into court till a domicil be fixed upon him by a residence of forty days. The Court of Session, accordingly, refused to sustain an action brought by one foreigner against another for payment of debt contracted abroad ; for the parties were here occasionally only, and the debtor had no domicil in Scotland.* A foreigner is subjected to our courts for a crime committed here, or a contract made here ; but to subject him instantly to answer for a debt contracted abroad, would put it in the power of malice to confine a man at home. Our law, for the facility of travelling, requires a residence of forty days to subject a foreigner to our courts.

When a foreign bond, stipulating the interest of the country where granted, is made the foundation of a process here, it has been doubted, whether that interest, or the legal interest of this country, ought to be decreed. This doubt is easily solved. An agreement to pay the interest of the country where the

* Haddington, Nov. 23, 1610, Vernor *contra* Elvies.

488 FOREIGN MATTERS. B. III.

money is borrowed, is undoubtedly binding in conscience, and, therefore, ought to be made effectual in every country. Nor do we meet with any obstruction in the Scotch statutes regulating the interest of money, which are not intended to reach foreign interest. And this accordingly is the rule in the law of England.* Hence it appears, that the Court of Session erred in refusing the interest of 10 *per cent.* upon a double bond executed in Ireland, and in restricting the penal part of the bond to 6 *per cent.* the legal interest here.† This error will be no less evident from another consideration. The penalty of a double bond put in suit here, ought to be sustained to the extent of damage and costs of suit: but the damage is plainly the interest of the country where the money is lent; because, had payment been duly made, the money again lent out would have produced that interest. For the same reason, supposing the rate of interest to be lower in England than here, our judges, in relieving from the penalty of a double bond, will make the English interest the rule; for the lender could not have a view to greater interest than that of his own country.

The case is different where interest is stipulated greater than is permitted in the *locus contractûs.* Such stipulation is usury in that country, and a moral wrong every where: I say a moral wrong, because, as every man is bound to give obedience to the laws of his own country, it is a moral wrong to transgress these laws.‡ When action, therefore, is brought in a foreign country for payment of the stipulated in-

* Abridg. cases in equity, ch. 36, sect. E, § 1.
† Fountainhall, Jan. 27, 1710, Savage *costra* Craig.
‡ See *Suprâ*, p. 224.

CH. VIII.   FOREIGN MATTERS.   489

terest, it would be unjust to make a claim founded
on an immoral paction; and the judge who should
sustain the claim, would be accessary to the wrong.
But now, admitting that the interest stipulated ought
not to be sustained, it comes next to be considered,
whether the interest of the *locus contractús* should be
the rule, or that of the country where the action is
brought, or, lastly, whether interest should be rejected altogether. This is a puzzling question. One,
at first view, will naturally reject interest altogether,
as a just punishment for the wrong done. But it is
not clear, that a judge can punish for a wrong committed in a foreign country. One thing indeed is
clear, that action cannot be sustained upon the immoral stipulation; and, therefore, if there be any
claim for interest, it must be upon the maxim, *Nemo
debet locupletari alienâ jacturâ*. This leads the mind
to the interest of the *locus contractús;* and I incline
to be of opinion that that interest is due.

Under the head of covenants, marriage comes celebrated abroad. The municipal law of Scotland,
regulating the solemnities of marriage, respects no
marriage but what is made in Scotland: and as
foreign laws have no coercive authority here, such a
marriage must be regulated by the law of nature.
According to that law, the matrimonial connection is
founded upon consent solely; the various solemnities
required by the laws of different nations, having no
view but to testify consent in the most complete manner. In that view, the solemnities of the country
where a marriage is celebrated, ought with us to have
great weight; because they show the deliberate will
and purpose of the parties. Justice, however, requires, that a marriage be held good here, though not

490 FOREIGN MATTERS. B. III.

formal according to the law of the country where it was made, provided the will and purpose of the parties to unite in marriage clearly appear.

According to the doctrine here laid down, a child ought with us to be held legitimate by a subsequent marriage, provided the marriage-ceremony was performed in a country where such is the law; because marriage in such a country must import the will of the father to legitimate his bastard children. But we cannot justly give the same effect to a marriage celebrated in a country where the marriage, as in England, hath not the effect of legitimation. The reason is, that marriage in that country is not a proof of the father's will to legitimate.

A minor, in the choice he makes of curators, is not confined to his own countrymen; and, therefore, a foreigner chosen curator has the same authority here with a native. Neither is it of importance in what place curators be chosen; and, accordingly, a choice made in England of curators, whether English or Scotch, will be effectual here. The powers of a guardian to a lunatic in England are more limited. The custody of the person of an English lunatic, and the management of his land-estate in England, belong to the Court of Chancery; and the Chancellor names one guardian to the person, another to the estate. But the Chancellor having no power over a lunatic's land in Scotland, cannot appoint a guardian to manage such land.

Having discussed civil matters, I proceed to criminal. A crime committed at sea, may be tried by the Court of Admiralty: but this case excepted, no crime committed in a foreign country can be tried in Scotland. The jurisdiction of the Justiciary Court

CH. VIII. FOREIGN MATTERS. 491

is strictly territorial, being confined within the limits of Scotland; and the extraordinary jurisdiction of the Court of Session, with respect to foreign matters, reaches civil causes only. Nor is it necessary, that it should be extended to crimes. It is of great importance to every nation, that justice have a free course every where; and to this end, it is necessary, that in every country there be an extraordinary jurisdiction for foreign matters as far as justice is concerned. But there is not the same necessity for an extraordinary jurisdiction, to punish foreign delinquencies: the proper place for punishment, is where the crime is committed; and no society takes concern in any crime, but what is hurtful to itself. A claim for reparation, arising from a foreign delinquency, is different: being founded on the rules of common justice, it is a claim that undoubtedly belongs to the jurisdiction under consideration. No man, who injures another, ought to reckon himself secure any where till he make reparation; and if he be obstinate or refractory, justice requires that he be compelled, wherever found, to make reparation.

To secure the effects of the deceased from embezzlement, every person who intermeddles irregularly, is, in Scotland, subjected to the whole debts of the deceased, without limitation. This penal passive title, termed *vitious intromission*, is confined to irregular intermeddling within Scotland. The intermeddling in England with the moveable effects of a Scotchman, who dies there, must be judged by the rules of natural justice; and, therefore, in this country, cannot infer any conclusion beyond restitution or damages.

492   FOREIGN MATTERS.   B. III.

SECT. II.

Foreign Covenants and Deeds respecting Land.

IN order to have a distinct conception of this branch, the extent of our own municipal law with respect to land in Scotland, must be ascertained ; for we are not at liberty to apply the *jus gentium*, or the principles of natural justice, to any case that comes under our own law. As to this preliminary point, things, it is certain, as well as persons, are governed by municipal law. Land in particular, next to persons, is the greatest object of law ; and in every country, the acquisition and transmission of land, are regulated by municipal law. Our law, for example, with respect to the transmission of land-property, requires writing in a certain form. Such a writing is held a good title of property, whether executed at home or abroad. A writing, on the other hand, in a form different from that prescribed by our law, will be disregarded wherever executed : for our law regards the solemnities only, not the place. Thus, a testament made in England, bequeathing land in Scotland, is not sustained by the Court of Session ; because, by our law, no man can dispose of his land by testament : nor will it be regarded that land is testable in England ; because every thing concerning land in Scotland is regulated by our law. In general, the connection of a land-estate with the territory where situated, is of the most intimate kind : it bears the relation of a part to the whole. Thus, every legal act concerning land, the conveying it *inter vivos*, the transmitting it from the dead to the living, the security granted on

Ch. VIII.   FOREIGN MATTERS.   498

it for debt, are ascertained by the municipal law of every country : and with respect to every particular of that kind, our courts are tied down to their own law.

Are we then to hold, that a conveyance of land, in a form different from what is required by us, can have no effect? Suppose a man sells in England his land-estate in Scotland, executes a deed of conveyance in the English form, and perhaps receives payment of the price: such conveyance, not being in the form required by the law of Scotland, will not have the effect to transfer the property. But has the purchaser any claim in Scotland against the vender? None at common law; because a court of common law hath not authority to transform an actual disposition into an obligation to dispone. But such claim is supported in equity : because where a man, in order to transfer his land to a purchaser, executes a disposition, which is afterward discovered to be imperfect, it is his duty to execute a perfect one; and if he be refractory, it is the duty of a court of equity to compel him, or to supply his place. If the action be laid within the territory where the land is situated, the judge, in default of the disponer, may adjudge the land to the plaintiff : if in any other territory, all that can ensue is damage for not performance. I illustrate this doctrine by a similar case. A disposition of land, within Scotland, without procuratory or precept, will not be regarded at common law : but a court of equity, attentive to justice, will interpose in behalf of the purchaser, by adjudging the land to him. Thus, with respect to an informal conveyance of land within Scotland, the session acts as a court of equity ; and it acts as an extraordinary court for foreign matters, where a conveyance is executed abroad according to the law of the place.

A covenant was executed in England between two brothers, agreeing, that failing the children, the estate of the deceased should go to the survivor. The brother, who first deceased, had a land-estate in Scotland, a part of which he had gratuitously aliened in defraud of the covenant. A reduction was brought of this gratuitous deed by the surviving brother, and the covenant was sustained as a good title in the reduction. The covenant, though it had not the formalities of the law of Scotland, was, however, good evidence of the agreement; and as the deceased brother had done a moral wrong in transgressing the agreement, justice required that the wrong should be redressed, which was done, by voiding the gratuitous deed.* But in a later case, the court deviated from the foregoing principle of justice. A disposition of an heritable jurisdiction in Scotland, executed in England according to the English form, was not sustained even against the granter, to compel him to execute a more formal disposition.† This was acting as a court of common law. And it must not pass unobserved, that the accumulating different jurisdictions in the same court, occasions frequently mistakes of this nature; which are avoided in countries, where different jurisdictions are preserved distinct in different courts.

* Forbes, July 5, 1706, Cuningham *contra* Lady Sempill.
† February 1729, Earl of Dalkeith *contra* Book.

SECT. III.

Moveables, Domestic and Foreign, and their legal Effects.

LOCAL situation is essential to a moveable no less than to land: we cannot even conceive a horse or a ship, but as existing in a certain place. In a legal view, a moveable situated within a certain territory, is subjected to the judge of that territory; and every action, claiming the property or possession of it, must be brought before that judge. Warrant for execution must be granted by the same judge, as no other judge has authority over it.

It is a different question, by what law the judge ought to regulate his proceedings, whether by the law of his own country, or by what other law. About this question writers have differed widely. Some are of opinion, that moveables *non habent sequelam*, meaning, that without regard to their local situation, they are to be held as belonging to the country of the proprietor, and to be subjected to the law of that country. Others, averse to fiction, are of opinion, that moveables, like land, ought to be governed by the law of the country where actually situated. Opinions, so different, are an incitement to trace this subject to its fountain-head, if it can be traced. That each of these opinions may be right in particular cases, is probable ; for otherwise they would not be adopted : but I suspect, that neither of them will hold in general, and in every case. I take first under consideration moveables accessory to an immove-

496   FOREIGN MATTERS.   B. III.

able subject, the furniture of a dwelling-house, the stocking of a farm, goods in a shop for sale, the implements of a manufacture, which may be termed *permanent moveables.* These are naturally considered as belonging to the same country with the principal subject, and to be governed by the same law. This view may be enlarged, by comprehending under permanent moveables, every moveable that, like those above mentioned, have, beside local situation, some connection with a country. So far the latter opinion appears the best founded. And that this way of thinking has long prevailed in Scotland, is made evident by the act 88, parl. 1426, enacting, " That " when a Scotchman dies abroad *non animo rema-* " *nendi,* his Scotch effects must be confirmed in Scot- " land." Nor will it alter the rule, that the proprietor happens to be a foreigner. The succession to an immoveable subject is not affected by that circumstance : and it is natural that an accessory should go along with its principal : the thinking mind cannot readily yield to a separation of things intimately connected, to regulate the succession of the immoveable part by the law of the country to which it belongs, and of the moveable part by the law of the proprietor's country. This argument must appear in a strong light where both parts belong to a foreigner ; and it can make no solid difference that the moveable part only belongs to him. We adhere to this doctrine in practice. Letters of administration from the Prerogative Court of Canterbury will not be sustained as a title to effects in Scotland that belonged to the deceased, even though granted to those who are next in kin by the Scotch law. The powers of that court are confined within its own territory ;

CH..VIII. FOREIGN MATTERS. 497

and Scotch effects must be confirmed in Scotland. In England, a bastard enjoys the privilege of making a testament, which obtains not here. And, accordingly, notwithstanding a testament made by an English bastard, his moveables here were escheated to the crown.* A nuncupative will is sustained in England; but it will not carry Scotch moveables, writ with us being necessary to convey moveables from the dead to the living.† But the nomination of an executor by the proprietor in his testament, being effectual all the world over *jure gentium,* will be sustained here.

Moveables that are not connected with an immoveable subject, nor in any way connected with a country or territory, but merely by local situation, may be termed *transient moveables;* moveables, for example, that a proprietor carries about with him, his watch, his jewels, his garments, the money in his pocket, his horses, his coach, and such like. These so far coincide with permanent moveables, as that every question concerning them must be determined by the judge of the territory where they actually are. But it follows not that the law of that territory ought to be the rule. By their intimate connection with the proprietor, the law of his country ought to prevail. A gentleman, in the course of travelling, traverses many foreign territories.; and happens to die suddenly within one of them. What a strange law would it be that his succession should depend on such an accident? The nature of man is averse to chance: we love to rest on general principles and permanent facts, rejecting circumstances daily and

* Haddington, 1st Feb. 1611, Purves *contra* Chisholm.
† Stair, 19th Jan. 1665, Shaw *contra* Lewins.

hourly varying. A Scotchman crosses the border, purposing to return home in a week; but dies suddenly in the English side by a fall from his horse. His transient effects, by this accident, remain in England; but it would derogate from the dignity of law to lay any weight on that circumstance; and laying it aside, what other rule is there to follow but to regulate the succession by the law of Scotland? These effects were carried by the proprietor from Scotland: he purposed to carry them back to the same country; and it is no wide stretch of thought to consider them as still continuing there. The English judges, accordingly, considering them to be Scotch effects, will prefer those who are by the Scotch law next in kin to the deceased.(a) Here the opinion, making the law of the proprietor's country the rule of succession, appears the best founded. This case demands peculiar attention: here judges are led to found their decisions, not on their own law, nor on the *jus gentium*, but on the municipal law of another country. A ship is another example of transient moveables. While it is abroad on a trading voyage, the proprietor dies at home. The ship is under a foreign jurisdiction; but when claimed there, the judge, rejecting the casual circumstance of local situation, will consider it as belonging to the country of the proprietor, and will adjudge it to those who have right by the law of that country. A

(a) It may create at first some backwardness of opinion to find a rule of succession founded upon an obscure mental operation; but the argument will acquire weight, on consulting the Essays on British Antiquities, essay 4, where will be found many rules of succession built upon foundations still more slender than that mentioned above.

Frenchman consigns goods in Edinburgh, to be disposed of for his behoof; but dies before the commission is executed. The succession to these goods ought to be governed by the law of France; and the Court of Session, as having jurisdiction in foreign matters, will decree accordingly. In general, such moveables are held to be foreign moveables, conveyable *inter vivos*, and from the dead to the living, according to the law of the proprietor's country. An assignment by the foreign proprietor, formal, according to the *lex loci*, will be sustained here to carry such moveables. And if they belonged to an Englishman, letters of administration after his death will be here a valid title, without necessity of confirmation.

Upon the whole, comparing permanent and transient moveables, the local situation of the former points out the judge, without regarding the proprietor's country. But as to the latter, the proprietor's country points out the judge, without regarding the local situation.

Where a Scotchman, occasionally in England, dies there intestate, the Court of Session, acting as a court of common law, will adjudge his moveables, situated in Scotland, of whatever kind, to those who are next in kin, according to our law. But his transient moveables, locally in England, must be claimed from the English judges; who, acting as a court for foreign matters, ought to govern themselves by the law of Scotland; which brings in the relict for her share. But what if he have made a will, dividing his moveables among his blood-relations, leaving nothing to his wife? Her contract of marriage affords an effectual claim against him, which he cannot evade by any

500 FOREIGN MATTERS. B. III.

voluntary deed. And even without a contract, as the *jus relictæ* is established by the law of Scotland beyond the power of the husband to alter, she ought to have her proportion of these transient moveables, as the English judges are in this case bound by the law of Scotland, not by their own. To fortify this doctrine, I urge the following argument. Where two persons, joining in marriage, are satisfied with the legal provisions, there is no occasion for a contract; and the parties may be held as agreeing, that the law of the land shall be the rule. It is in effect the same as if the parties had subscribed a short minute, bearing, that the *jus relictæ* and every other particular between them should be regulated by the law of their country; and such an agreement, expressed or implied, must be binding all the world over, to support the relict's claim against the testament of a deceased husband.

· It may, however, happen, that two persons carelessly join in marriage, having an object in view very distant from a legal provision. Law does not admit of a presumption against rational conduct. But though it should be admitted, it will not avail. As every man is bound, in conscience, to obey the laws of his country, the husband, when disposed to think, will find his wife entitled by that law to the *jus relictæ:* and will see that an attempt to disappoint her would be against conscience. This must be evident to him, when at home; and it must be equally evident, that change of place cannot relieve him. At any rate, the *jus relictæ* must have its effect as to his moveables in Scotland; and it would not be a little heteroclete that his transient effects should be withdrawn, for no better reason than that they happen accidentally to be in a foreign country where the *jus relictæ* does not obtain.

SECT. IV.

Debts, whether regulated by the Law of the Creditor's Country, or that of the Debtor.

DEBTS due by people of this country to foreigners, make another branch of the extraordinary jurisdiction of the Court of Session concerning foreign matters. The form of conveying such debts *inter vivos*, of transmitting them from the dead to the living, of attaching them by execution, &c. have not hitherto been brought under general rules; and our judges are ever at a loss by what law these particulars ought to be governed, whether by our law, by that of the country where the creditor resides, or by the *jus gentium*. In order to remove this doubt, authors and lawyers are strongly disposed to assimilate debts to land, by bestowing upon them a local situation: and yet this fiction, bold as it is, removes not the doubt; for still the question recurs, Where is the debt supposed to exist, whether in the territory of the creditor, or in that of the debtor. Considering a debt as a *subject* belonging to the creditor, it seems the more natural fiction to place it with the creditor as in his possession; and hence the maxim, *Mobilia non habent sequelam*. Others are more disposed to place it with the debtor; a thought suggested from considering, that the money must be demanded from the debtor, and that upon his failure the suit for payment must be in his *forum*.

FOREIGN MATTERS. B. III.

It is unnecessary to bestow words upon proving, that a debt is not a *corpus* to be capable of locoposition, but purely a *jus incorporale*. Rejecting then fictions, which never tend to sound knowledge, let us take things as they are, and endeavour to draw light from the nature of the subject. As here there are two persons connected, a debtor and a creditor, living in different countries, and subjected to different laws, it at first sight may appear a puzzling question, What law ought to govern, whether that of the debtor or of the creditor? One thing is evident, that every question concerning a subject, moveable or immoveable, must be determined by the judge, whose legal powers extend over that subject ; and that execution must be awarded by him only. The same rule applies to debts, according to the maxim, *Actor sequitur forum rei ;* whence it necessarily follows, that the form of the action, the method of procedure, and the manner of execution, must all be regulated by the law of the country where the action is brought. But though there can be no doubt about the judge, it may be a doubt what ought to be his rule in determining questions concerning the subject. With respect to that question, I submit the following hints. When the creditor makes a voluntary conveyance, it is to be expected that he should speak in the style and form of his own country ; and consequently, that the law of his own country should be the rule here. It would indeed be strangely heteroclete to subject him to the forms of the debtor's country, of which he is ignorant, especially if the debtor have a wandering disposition. In a word, the will of a proprietor or of a creditor, is a good title *jure gentium*, that ought to be effectual every where. Thus, an assign-

CH. VIII. FOREIGN MATTERS. 503

ment made by a creditor in Scotland, according to our form, of a debt due to him by a person in a foreign country, ought to be sustained in that country as a good title for demanding payment : and a foreign assignment of a debt due here, regular according to the law of the country, ought to be sustained by our judges. A foreign assignment cannot at any rate be subjected to the regulations of our act 1681, for preventing forgery, nor to any other of our regulations ; because these regard no deeds but what are executed in Scotland.

A judicial conveyance, or legal execution, will fall more naturally to be explained in the last section. The only remaining point is to examine by what law the creditor's succession is to be governed. Debts are part of the creditor's funds, and at his disposal. His alienations for a valuable consideration must be every where effectual, and even his donations. It is in his power alone to regulate his succession ; and if he make a will, it must be effectual. But what if he die intestate ; whether must the law of his country be the rule, or that of the debtor? The former undoubtedly. A man who dies intestate, is understood to adhere to the legal succession ; for otherwise he would make a will. Therefore those who are heirs by the law of his own country ought to be preferred, according to his implied will. The express will of the deceased creditor must have that effect ; and his implied will ought to have the same effect. The debtor has no concern but to pay safely ; the law of his domicil will secure him as to that point : with regard to the creditor's succession, it can have no authority. Thus, in a competition between the brother and the nephew of Captain William Brown, who died

504   FOREIGN MATTERS.   **B. III.**

in Scotland, his native country, intestate and without children, concerning moveable debts due to the Captain in Ireland, the brother was preferred as next in kin by the law of Scotland; though by the laws of England and Ireland, which admit the *jus repræsentationis* in the succession of moveables, a nephew and niece have the same right with a brother and sister.*

From what is said it will appear, that debts differ widely from land and from moveables. It is in vain to claim the property of any subject, unless the title of property be complete and strictly formal. An equitable title, in opposition to one that is legal, can never found a real action: it cannot have a stronger effect than to found an action against the proprietor to grant a more formal right; or in his default, that the court shall grant it. But in the case of a debt, where the question is not about property, but about payment, an equitable title coincides in a good measure with a legal title. An assignment made by a foreign creditor, according to the formalities of his country, will be sustained here as a good title for demanding payment from the debtor: and it will be sustained even though informal, provided it be good *jure gentium;* that is, provided it appear that the creditor really granted the assignment. Such effect hath an equitable title; and a legal title can have no stronger effect.

It must, however, be admitted, that an equitable title hath not so complete an effect in a competition. Suppose an English creditor grants an assignment in the English form, of a debt due to

* Nov. 28, 1744, Brown of Baird *contra* John Brown, merchant in Edinburgh.

CH. VIII.   FOREIGN MATTERS.   505

him in Scotland : this assignment, though it transfer not the *jus crediti* to the assignee, is, however, an
order upon the debtor to pay to the assignee. But
such assignment, even though the first in order of
time, will not avail against a more formal assignment
taken *bonâ fide*, and regularly intimated to the debt-
or. An equitable title may be good against the granter; but can never be sustained in a competition with
a legal title, where both parties are *in pari casu*.

I conclude this section with applying to debts
what is observed with respect to moveables in the
section immediately foregoing. The nomination of
an executor in a testament, is an universal title which
ought to be sustained every where; and is always
sustained in the Court of Session to oblige debtors in
this country to make payment.* But an executor-
dative, with letters of administration, hath not a title
to sue for payment *extra territorium.* And the same
is the case of a guardian to a lunatic's estate named
in England by the Chancellor : he has no title to sue
for payment of the lunatic's debts in Scotland.†

SECT. V.

Foreign Evidence.

UNDER this head come properly foreign writs; because no writ, where there is wanting any solemnity
of the law of Scotland, can be effectual here to any
purpose but as evidence merely. And as, among
civilized nations, the solemnities required to make a

* Durie, Feb. 1627, Lawson *contra* Kello.
† June 21, 1749, Morison, &c. *contra* Earl of Sutherland.

506 FOREIGN MATTERS. B. III.

writ effectual, are such as give sufficient evidence of will, it is established as a rule with us, That contracts, bonds, dispositions, and other writs, executed according to the law of the place, are probative in this country. Thus, action is always sustained upon a foreign bond having the formalities of the place where it was granted :* and an extract of a bond from Bourdeaux, subscribed by the tabellion only, and bearing, that the bond itself, subscribed by the granter, was inserted in his register, was sustained, being *secundum consuetudinem loci.*† Depositions of witnesses taken abroad upon a commission from the Court of Session, were sustained here, though subscribed by the commissioners and clerk only, not by the witnesses, such being the form in the country where the depositions were taken.‡

' The same rule obtains even though the foreign bond bear a clause for registering in Scotland. This circumstance shows, indeed, that the creditor had it in view to make his claim effectual in Scotland ; but it weakens not the evidence of the bond, which, therefore, will be a good instruction of the claim.§

By the law of England, payment of money may be proved by witnesses ; and, therefore, the same proof will be admitted here with respect to payment said to be made in England. For our act of sederunt confining the evidence to writ,‖ regards no payment but what is made in Scotland ; and it would be un-

---

* Haddington, Jan. 19, 1610, Fortune *contra* Shewan.

† Home, Feb. 1682, Davidson *contra* Town of Edinburgh.

‡ Fountainhall, March 19, 1707, Cummin *contra* Kennedy.

§ Home, Feb. 14, 1721, Junquet la Pine *contra* Creditors of Lord Sempill.

‖ Historical Law-tracts, tract 2.

CH. VIII.   FOREIGN MATTERS.   507

just to deprive a man of that evidence which the law of his own country made him rely on. Accordingly, in every suit here upon an English bond, the defence of payment alleged made in England, is admitted to be proved by witnesses.* Yet, where a bond granted in England contained a clause for registering in Scotland, the defence of payment made in England was not permitted to be proved by witnesses.† This appears to me a wrong judgment; for, as observed above, the clause of registration imported only, that the creditor had it in view to make his debt effectual in Scotland. It certainly did not bar the debtor from making payment in England; nor, consequently, from proving by witnesses that payment had been so made.

In Scotland, the cedent's oath is not good evidence against the assignee; because it is the oath, not of a party, but of a single witness. In England, an assignment being only a procuratory *in rem suam*, the cedent's oath is an oath of party, and, therefore, good evidence against the assignee. For that reason, an English bond being assigned in England, and a suit for payment being raised here by the assignee, a relevant defence against payment was admitted to be proved by the oath of the cedent.‡

* Durie, Nov. 16, 1626, Galbraith *contra* Cuningham.
† Stair, Dec. 8, 1664, Scot *contra* Henderson.
‡ Stair, June 28, 1666, Macmorland *contra* Melvine.

SECT. VI.

*Effect of a statute, of a decree, of a judicial convey-
ance, or legal execution,* extra territorium.

THOUGH a statute, as observed above, hath no authority as such *extra territorium*, it becomes however necessary upon many occasions to lay weight
upon foreign statutes, in order to fulfil the rules of
justice. Many examples occur of indirect effects
given thus to foreign statutes. One of these effects
I shall mention at present for the sake of illustration ; reserving others to be handled where particular
statutes are taken under consideration. Obedience
is due to the laws of our country, and disobedience is
a moral wrong.* This moral wrong ought to weigh
with judges in every country ; because it is an act of
injustice to support any moral wrong, by making it
the foundation either of an action or of an exception.
I give for an example the statute prohibiting any
member of a court of law to buy land about which
there is a process depending.† Such a purchase being
made notwithstanding, the purchaser follows the
vender into a foreign country, in order to compel
him, by a process, to make the bargain effectual. A
bargain unlawful where made, becomes not lawful
by change of place ; and, therefore, the foreign judge
ought not to support such unlawful bargain by sustaining action upon it. Courts were instituted to repress,

---

* See *supra*, p. 307, 308.
† 13. Edward I, cap. 49 ; Act 216, parl. 1594.

CH. VIII.   FOREIGN MATTERS.   509

not enforce, wrong ; and the judge who enforces any unlawful paction, becomes accessory to the wrong.

Several questions arise from the different prescriptions established in different countries. In our decisions upon that head, the case is commonly stated as if the question were, Whether a foreign prescription, or that of our own country, ought to be the rule? This never ought to be made a question ; for our own prescription must be the rule in every case that falls under it, and not the prescription of any other country. The question handled in these decisions is, What effect ought to be given to a foreign prescription in cases that fall not under any of our own prescriptions ? Questions of that sort may sometimes be nice and doubtful. By the English act of limitations,* " All actions of account and upon the case, " all actions of debt grounded upon any lending or " contract without speciality, all actions of debt for " arrearages of rent, &c. shall be sued within six " years after the cause of action." The purpose of this statute is to guard against a second demand for payment of temporary debts, such as generally are paid regularly : and to make that purpose effectual, action is denied upon such debts after six years. As statutes have no coercive authority *extra territorium*, this statute can have effect with us, but to infer a presumption of payment from the six years' delay of bringing an action. And, accordingly, when a process is brought in Scotland for payment of an English debt after the English prescription has taken place, it cannot be pleaded here, that the action is cut off by the statute of limitations : but it can be pleaded here, and will be sustained, that the debt is pre-

* 21. James I, cap. 16, § 3.

510 · FOREIGN MATTERS. **B. III.**

sumed to have been paid. Considering that the statute can have no authority here, except to infer a presumption of payment, it follows, that the plaintiff must be permitted to defeat the presumption by positive evidence, or to overbalance it by contrary presumptions, or to show from the circumstances of his case, that payment cannot be presumed. As to positive evidence, the pursuer has access to the oath of the defendant; and an acknowledgment that the debt is still existing, defeats the presumption of payment.* The presumptive payment may also be counterbalanced by contrary presumptions. A case of this nature is reported by Gilmour :† " A bond " prescribed by the law of England, while the par- " ties resided there, was afterwards made the found- " ation of a process in Scotland. The court re- " fused to sustain the English prescription, because " the bond was drawn in the Scotch form betwixt " Scotchmen, and bore a clause of registration for " execution in Scotland." The circumstances of this case show, that the creditor's view was to receive payment in Scotland, or to raise his action there; and, as a bond bearing a clause of registration prescribes not in Scotland till forty years elapse, the court justly thought, that to preserve the claim alive, the creditor had no occasion to guard against any prescription but that of Scotland. To proceed, there are circumstances where the statute of limitations cannot infer any presumption of payment. What, if the debtor, within the six years, did retire beyond sea? The forbearance in that case to bring an action against a man who cannot easily be reached, and

* Feb. 9, 1738, Rutherford *contra* Sir James Campbell.
† Nov. 1664, Garden *contra* Ramsay.

CH. VIII. FOREIGN MATTERS. 511

whose residence, perhaps, is not known, cannot infer the slightest presumption against the creditor. The statute, however, which makes no exception, must in England have been obeyed, till the defect was supplied by another statute. But the Court of Session is not so fettered: a presumption of payment will not be sustained when the circumstances of the case admit it not.

The foregoing defect of the statute of limitations, is supplied by the English statute, 4to *Annæ*, *cap.* 16, declaring, " That where the person against whom " a claim lies is beyond seas, the statute of limitation " shall not run against the creditor." This statute is also defective, because it includes not Scotland; for a presumption of payment cannot justly be urged against an English creditor, who forbears to sue while his debtor is out of England, though not beyond sea. Action, however, must be denied in England by force of the statute, though the debtor has been all along in Scotland. But this is no rule to us: we are at liberty to judge of the weight of the presumption from circumstances; and, accordingly, the Court of Session sustained action after the six years, against a man who resided most of the time in Scotland.*

Though the act of limitations of James I, makes no provision for the case where the debtor happens to be in a different country, it is more circumspect as to the creditor's residence. For, in the 7th section, it is provided, " That the prescription shall not run " against the creditor while he is beyond seas:" and justly, because in that situation, his delaying to bring an action infers not against him any presumption of

* March 4, 1755, Trustees for the creditors of Renton *contra* Baillie.

payment. The case is parallel where the creditor happens to reside in Scotland, and, therefore, his residence there must also bar a presumption of payment. Hence, it appears, that the decision, July 1717, Rae *contra* Wright, is erroneous. James Rae, a Scotch pedlar, having died in England, his brother Richard intermeddled with his effects there at short-hand without any warrant. Richard, during the running of the six years, returned to Dumfries, and died there. After the six years were elapsed, a process was brought against his executor by William Rae, a third brother, to account to him for the half of the effects thus irregularly intermeddled with. The court sustained the defence, That the action was cut off by the English statute of limitations. This was unjust. While Richard remained in England, the circumstance, that William living in Scotland, forbore to raise a suit in England, afforded not the slightest suspicion that he had received payment from Richard. And suppose he had lived in England, payment could not be presumed against him, when his debtor left England before the lapse of the six years.

By established practice in England, action is not sustained upon a double bond after twenty years. The interest, at the rate of 5 *per cent.* equals the principal in twenty years, which, therefore, exhausts the whole penal part of the bond, and makes the double sum due in equity as well as at common law. After this period, the sum must remain barren, because interest is not stipulated in the bond : and in that view, it is justly inferred from the delay of demanding payment after the twenty years, that payment must already have been made. This in effect, is an English prescription, inferring from long delay

Ch. VIII.   FOREIGN MATTERS.   513

a presumption of payment. It follows, therefore, if the parties have lived all along in England, that the presumptive payment from prescription ought to be sustained here.

In the English bankrupt-statute, 13th Elizabeth, cap. 7, § 2, it is enacted, " That the commissioners " shall have power to sell all the goods of the bankrupt, " real and personal, which he had before his bankrupt- " cy, and to divide the produce among the creditors " in proportion to the extent of their debts ;" and § 12, it is declared, " That this act shall not extend to land " aliened *bonâ fide* before the bankruptcy." Hence it appears to be the intention and effect of the sta- tute, to bar all deeds by the bankrupt, and all execu- tion by the creditors, after the first act of bankrupt- cy. And the English writers accordingly invent a cause to support these statutory effects. They hold, that the effects are vested in the commissioners *retró* from the first act of bankruptcy. " Creditors, upon " whatsoever security they be, come in all equal, un- " less such as have obtained actual execution before " the bankruptcy, or had taken pledges for their just " debts ; and the reason is, because, from the act of " bankruptcy, all the bankrupt's estate is vested in " the commissioners :"* which is to suppose the ef- fects of the bankrupt vested in commissioners before they have an existence ; a strange bias in some writ- ers, that they will have recourse to absurd fictions for explaining what is obviously reducible to rational principles ! The statute has a more solid foundation than a fiction : it is founded on equity, as is demon- strated above. † But to confine our observations

* New abridgment of the law, vol. i, p. 258.

† See *suprà*, p. 177

2 K

upon the statute to what more peculiarly concerns this country, I must observe, that the great circulation of trade through the two kingdoms since the Union, makes it frequently necessary for the Court of Session to take the English bankrupt estates under consideration ; and it has puzzled the Court mightily, what effect should be given to them here. That a foreign statute cannot have any coercive authority *extra territorium*, is clear : but at first view it is not so clear, that the statutory transference of property above mentioned, from the bankrupt to the commissioners, may not comprehend effects real or personal in Scotland, or in any other foreign country ; for why may not a legal conveyance be equivalent to a voluntary conveyance by the proprietor ? I have had occasion to observe above*, that law cannot force the will, nor compel any man to make a conveyance. In place of a voluntary conveyance, when justice requires it to be granted, all that a court can do, or the legislature can do, is to be themselves the disponers ; and it is evident that their deed of conveyance cannot reach any subject, real or personal, but what is within their territory. This makes a solid difference between a voluntary and a legal conveyance. The former has no relation to a place : a deed of alienation, whether of land or of moveables, is good wherever granted : an Englishman, for example, has in China the same power to alien his land in England, that he had before he left his native country ; and the power he has to dispose of his moveables will reach them in the most distant corner of the earth: The latter, on the contrary, has the strictest relation to place : the power of a court, and even of the legislature, be-

* Sect. 4. of the present chapter.

CH. VIII.   FOREIGN MATTERS.   515

ing merely territorial, reacheth not lands nor moveables *extra territorium.* We may then with certainty conclude, that the statutory transference of property from the bankrupt to the commissioners, cannot carry any effects in Scotland : these are subjected to our own laws and our own judges ; and cannot be conveyed from one person to another by the authority of any foreign court, or of any foreign statute. The English bankrupt-statutes, however, are not disregarded by us. One effect may and ought to be given them according to the rules of justice : it is the duty of the debtor to sell his effects for satisfying his creditors, if he cannot otherwise procure money; and it is in particular, the duty of an English bankrupt, to convey all his effects to the commissioners named by the Chancellor, or to the assignees named by the creditors, in order to be sold for payment of his debts. The English statute, by conveying to the commissioners all the English funds, does for the bankrupt what he himself ought to do : but as the English statute has no authority over funds belonging to the bankrupt in Scotland, it becomes necessary for the commissioners or assignees to apply to the Court of Session, " specifying the debtor's bankruptcy, and " his failure to make a conveyance ; and, therefore, " praying that the Court will adjudge to the plaintiffs, " the debtor's effects in Scotland ; or rather, that they " will order the same to be sold, and the price to be " paid to the plaintiffs." For that purpose, the proper action, in my apprehension, is a process of sale of the debtor's moveables, as well as of his land. Debts due here to the bankrupt, may also be sold ; but as against solvent debtors, a process for payment is better management, it appears, that in the case of

2 K 2

516　FOREIGN MATTERS.　B. III.

bankruptcy, this process is competent to the assignees without necessity of an arrestment.* The assignees being trustees for behoof of the whole creditors, have a just claim to the bankrupt's whole effects, to be converted into money for payment of the creditors; and in the forms of the law of Scotland, there appears nothing to bar the assignees from bringing a direct action for payment against the bankrupt's debtors here, as he himself could have done before his bankruptcy. In thus appointing the bankrupt's debtors to make payment to the assignees, the Court of Session exerts no power but what is the foundation of all legal execution, namely, the making that conveyance for the bankrupt, which he himself ought to have made. By this expeditious method, justice is satisfied, and no person is hurt.

Whether the price of the bankrupt's moveable funds, and the sum arising from the debts due to him, ought to be distributed here among his creditors, or be remitted to England for that purpose, is a matter purely of expediency. The rule of distribution seems to be the same in both countries; and the creditors, therefore, have no interest in the question, but what arises from receiving payment in one place rather than in another. But if the bankrupt's lands in Scotland have been attached by execution, which is almost always the case, the price of it upon a sale must be distributed here; for the purchaser is not bound to pay the price till the real debts be conveyed to him, and the real creditors are not bound to convey till they get payment.

In the last place come foreign decrees; which are of two kinds, one sustaining the claim, and one dis-

See supra, p. 155.

missing it. A foreign decree, sustaining the claim, is not one of those universal titles which ought to be made effectual every where. It is a title that depends on the authority of the court whence it issued, and therefore has no coercive authority *extra territorium*. And yet as it would be hard to oblige the person who claims on a decree, to bring a new action against his party in every country to which he may retire, therefore common utility, as well as regard to a sister-court, have established a rule among all civilized nations, That a foreign decree shall be put in execution, unless some good exception be opposed to it in law or in equity: which is making no wider step in favour of the decree, than to presume it just, till the contrary be proved. But this includes not a decree, decerning for a penalty; because no court reckons itself bound to punish, or to concur in punishing, any delict committed *extra territorium*.

A foreign decree, which, by dismissing the claim, affords an *exceptio rei judicatæ* against it, enjoys a more extensive privilege. We not only presume it to be just, but will not admit any evidence of its being unjust. The reasons follow. A decreet-arbitral is final by mutual consent. A judgment-condemnator ought not to be final against the defendant, because he gave no consent. But a decreet-absolvitor ought to be final against the plaintiff, because the judge was chosen by himself: with respect to him at least, it is equivalent to a decreet-arbitral. Public utility affords another argument extremely cogent: There is nothing more hurtful to society than that law-suits be perpetual. In every law-suit there ought to be a *ne plus ultra*, some step that ought to be ul-

518   FOREIGN MATTERS.   **B. III.**

timate; and a decree, dismissing a claim, is in its nature ultimate. Add a consideration, that regards the nature and constitution of a court of justice. A decree, dismissing a claim, may, it is true, be unjust, as well as a decree sustaining it. But they differ widely in one capital point: in declining to give redress against a decree dismissing a claim, the court is not guilty of authorising injustice, even supposing the decree to be unjust: the utmost that can be said is, that the court forbears to interpose in behalf of justice; but such forbearance, instead of being faulty, is highly meritorious in every case where private justice clashes with public utility.* The case is very different with respect to a decree of the other kind; for to award execution upon a foreign decree, without admitting any objection against it, would be, for aught the court can know, to support and promote injustice. A court, as well as an individual, may, in certain circumstances, have reason to forbear acting, or executing their office: but the doing injustice, or the supporting it, cannot be justified in any circumstances.†

To illustrate the practice of Scotland with respect to a foreign decree, sustaining a claim, I give a remarkable case. By statute 12*mo Annæ, cap.* 18, made perpetual 4*to Geo. I, cap.* 12, it is enacted, " That the collector of the customs, or any other " person who shall be employed in preserving any " vessel in distress, shall, within thirty days after " the service performed, be paid a reasonable re- " ward for the same; and in default thereof, that " the ship or goods so saved shall remain in the " custody of the collector, till such time as he and

* See Conclusion of Book 2.   † Ibid.

CH. VIII.   FOREIGN MATTERS.   519

" those employed by him shall be reasonably gra-
" tified for their assistance and trouble, or good
" security given for that purpose." This is where
the merchant claims his ship or cargo. But in case
no person appear to claim, there is the following
proviso :—" That goods, which are in their nature
" perishable, shall be forthwith sold by the collector ;
" and that, after deducting all charges, the residue of
" the price, with a fair and just account of the whole,
" shall be transmitted to the Exchequer, there to re-
" main for the benefit of the rightful owner ; and that
" the same shall be delivered to him, so soon as he
" appears, and makes a claim." Brunton and Chalmers, owners of a vessel called *The Serpent's Prize*,
loaded the same with 100 quarters of wheat for Zealand. In her voyage she was stranded at a place
called *Redscar*, near the town of Stocktown. Chalmers having got notice of the accident, repaired immediately to Redscar ; and found his wheat in the hands
of John Wilson, collector of the customs at Stocktown, part of it laid up in lofts, and part in the open
field ; the whole greatly damaged by sea-water. Finding it necessary to dispose of the wheat instantly, he
applied to the collector for liberty to sell ; offering to
put the price in his hand as security for the salvage.
This being obstinately refused, he took a protest a-
gainst the collector, and brought against him an action of trespass upon the case before the King's
Bench. And the defendant having put himself upon
his country, the cause came to a trial at Newcastle ;
where a special verdict was returned, in substance,
finding, " That all reasonable care was taken of the
" wheat by the collector and others by his order :
" That on the 3d of October then next following,

530 FOREIGN MATTERS. B. III.

"James Chalmers applied to the collector, desiring
"that the wheat, being much damaged, might be
"forthwith sold; and that the money produced by
"such sale might be left in the hand of the collector
"to answer all charges; but did not then offer to
"pay to the collector any money for salvage; neither
"did the collector then make any demand on that ac-
"count, he not knowing at that time what the salv-
"age amounted to; but then refused to deliver the
"said wheat, or permit the same to be sold, he hav-
"ing an order from the commissioners of his Ma-
"jesty's customs for that purpose." And the verdict concludes thus :—" But whether, upon the whole
"matter aforesaid, by the said jurors, in form afore-
"said, found the within-named John Wilson be
"guilty of the premises within written or not, the
"said jurors are altogether ignorant, and pray ad-
"vice from the court thereupon." The judge at that
circuit having referred the cause to the Court of
King's Bench at Westminster, judgment was at last
there given on the 18th July 1751, after several con-
tinuations, " Finding, That the said John Wilson is
"not guilty of the premises; that the said Brunton
"and Chalmers shall take nothing by their said bill;
"but that they be in mercy, &c. for their false claim;
"and that the said John Wilson go thereof without
"day, &c. And it is further considered, That the
"said John recover against the said Brunton and
"Chalmers sixty pounds, for his costs and charges
"laid out by him about his defence on this behalf;
"and that the said John have execution thereof,"
&c.

For this sum of £60 awarded to the collector for
costs, he brought an action against Brunton and

CH. VIII.   FOREIGN MATTERS.   521

Chalmers, before the Court of Session; and, in support of his claim set forth, That it is founded on the presumption, *Quod res judicata pro veritate habetur.* The defendants insisted, That this presumption must yield to direct evidence of injustice, which would clearly appear upon comparing the decree with the statute. And the following circumstances were urged. First, That though the wheat was in a perishing condition, the collector refused to permit the same to be sold, even contrary to his own interest, as the price to him was a better security for the salvage than the damaged wheat. Secondly, When the application for sale was made, the collector was not ready to make his claim for salvage, not knowing at that time the amount thereof; in which circumstances, to forbid the sale, was not only rigorous, but unjust: it was, to abandon the wheat to destruction, without permitting the defendants to interpose. Even the offer of ready money to pay the salvage would not have availed them, seeing the collector was not in a condition to make any demand. This case being reported by the Lord Ordinary, it occurred at advising, that the statute provides nothing about selling perishable goods, except in the case that the merchant does not appear to claim the wrecked goods. Therefore the present case is not provided for by the statute. It is a *casus omissus*, which in equity must be supplied agreeably to the intendment and purpose of the statute. Viewing the matter in this light, it appeared, in the first place, that the defendants, being proprietors of the wheat, were entitled to dispose of it, provided the collector suffered no prejudice as to his claim of salvage, which he certainly did not, if the price were put in his hand. Nay, his security

522   FOREIGN MATTERS.   B. III.

would be improved by the sale, which would afford him current coin, instead of perishing wheat. It was considered, in the second place, that this is agreeable to the intendment of the statute; for if the custom-house-officer must dispose of perishable goods, where there is none to claim, much more where the owner appears, and insists for a sale. Thirdly, The statute, entitling the officer to retain the goods for security of the salvage, undoubtedly supposes that the officer can instruct his claim, in order that the merchant may have instant possession of the goods, upon paying the salvage. In this view the conduct of the collector was altogether unjustifiable: the statute gives no authority for retaining the goods as a security for the salvage, unless as a *succedaneum* when satisfaction is not offered in money; and as the collector here was not ready to receive satisfaction, it was a trespass to retain the goods in a perishing condition. With regard to this matter in general, one observation had great weight, That it never could be the intention of the legislature, to force merchants first to pay salvage, and thereafter to undergo the risk of perishable and damnified goods, the price of which possibly might not amount to the salvage. The collector, therefore, could not in common justice demand more than the value of the goods for his salvage; and *a fortiori* could not demand any security beyond that value. The court, accordingly, unanimously refused to interpose their authority for execution upon this judgment.*

The judgment of the King's Bench may possibly

* January 6, 1756, John Wilson, collector of the customs at Stocktown *contra* Robert Brunton and James Chalmers, merchants in Edinburgh.

CH. VIII. FOREIGN MATTERS. 523

be justified as pronounced by a court of common law, which, in interpreting statutes, must adhere to the letter, without regarding the intention of the legislature. If so, the proprietors of the wheat ought to have applied to the Chancery, or have removed their cause there by a *Certiorari*. If courts of common law in England be so confined, their constitution is extremely imperfect. But supposing the Court of King's Bench to have acted properly according to its constitution, it was notwithstanding right in the Court of Session to refuse execution upon a foreign decree that is materially unjust, or contrary to equity.

An appeal entered by Collector Wilson was heard *ex parte*, and the decree of the Court of Session reversed; by which the £60 of costs decerned in the Court of King's Bench was made effectual against Chalmers and Brunton. The decree, if I have been rightly informed, was reversed for the following reason; that in England the decree of a foreign supreme court has such credence, that judgment is immediately given, without entering into the merits, provided the matter have been litigated; that in all countries the decrees of the Court of Admiralty are, for the sake of commerce, entitled to immediate execution; and that the same credence ought to have been given by the Court of Session to the judgment of the King's Bench. It would seem then, that in England greater authority is given to foreign decrees than in any other civilized country; and, indeed, greater than can be justified from the nature and constitution of any court. A foreign decree has no legal authority in England; and for the courts of Westminster blindly to authorise execution upon a foreign decree, without admitting any objection against it, is a practice that cannot be approved, because it must frequently lead them to authorise injustice. But admitting the practice of England, it ought to have been considered, that the practice of England is no authority in Scotland. In reviewing the decrees of the Court of Session, the law of Scotland is the rule. And if the decree in question was agreeable to the law of *Scotland*, it ought to have been affirmed ; especially as the law of Scotland with respect to foreign decrees, is not only in itself rational, but agreeable to the laws of all other civilized nations, England excepted. The House of Lords, we may rest assured, could not intend to try the merits of a Scotch decree by the law or practice of England. But as the appeal was heard *ex parte*, the reversal has certainly been founded upon the erroneous supposition, That, with respect to foreign decrees, the practice of Scotland is the same with that of England.

With respect to a judicial conveyance, or legal execution, the nature of it is sufficiently explained in a former part of this chapter, that it can carry no effects but what are subjected to the authority of the court from which execution issues. In our poinding, for example, the goods of the debtor are conveyed to his creditor, not by the will of the debtor, but by the will of the sheriff ; and his will can operate no farther than to convey effects within his territory. In England, debts, like other moveables, are attached by the legal execution of *Fieri facias*, similar to our poinding. But a *Fieri facias* can carry no debts but what are due by persons within the territory of the court from which the execution issues. It is not a title to force payment from a debtor in Scotland : the

CH. VIII.   FOREIGN MATTERS.   525

court must be applied to within whose territory he resides; and that court will authorise the execution that is customary in Scotland, namely, an arrestment and decree of forthcoming. The same holds as to other moveables. And the titles necessary to a foreigner for attaching moveables or debts in Scotland, are set forth in the third and fourth sections of the present chapter.

INDEX.

A

ABSOLUTE Warrandice. See Warrandice.
Acceptance defined, p. 127.
Accessory. *Accessorium sequitur principale,* 156, 157.
Actions or causes of an extraordinary nature were originally appropriated to the King and council, 3.
Action on a foreign covenant, 487.
Action denied, unless the pursuer can shew an interest, 42, 319.
Action upon the case, 96.
Action, penal, in what time it prescribes, 239.
Action of mails and duties, 390
Actio negotiorum gestorum, its equal foundation, 7, 117. Inferior courts competent to this action, 21.
Actio in factum, 96.
Actio de in rem verso, 97, 372.
Actio redhibitoria, 175.
Actio quanti minoris, ib.
Acts *contra bonos mores,* 331.
—— *contra utilitatem publicam,* 336.
—— repressed, because of their bad tendency, 332.
—— of parliament explained. That concerning conditions in bonds of borrowed money, 48.
—— enacting an irritancy *ob non solutum canonem,* 235.
—— concerning cautioners, 237.
—— for making effectual the debts of heirs who die in apparency, ib.
—— Regulations 1695, concerning decreets-arbitral, ib.
—— authorising an apparent heir to sell the estate of his predecessor, 240.
—— concerning the creditors of the predecessor, ib.
—— for preventing the frauds of heirs-apparent, 242.
—— concerning gaming, 237.
—— concerning executions of a summons, 250, 251.
—— concerning the triennial prescription, 254.
—— concerning expences of process, 380.
—— concerning bankruptcy, 416, 423.
—— ranking apprisers *pari passu,* 426.
—— about salvage, 516.

INDEX.

Acts of sederunt explained. Concerning irritant clauses, 49.
—— concerning the creditors of a defunct doing diligence within six months, 428.
—— ranking arresters *pari passu* in the case of bankruptcy, 429.
—— Power of the Court of Session to make acts of sederunt, 417.
Adjudication, during the legal, is a *pignus prætorium*, 245, 297, 390. Its nature and effect after expiry of the legal, 244. Adjudication of a moveable debt, 282. Adjudication in implement, 286. Adjudication declaratory, ib. What effect has *pluris petitio* upon an adjudication, 296. It renders the subject litigious, 399. Forms dispensed with, in order to give an adjudication the benefit of the act 1661 ranking apprisings *pari passu*, 430.
Adultery. Does it deprive a wife of her legal provisions, 312.
Æmulatio vicini, 36, 89.
Alien incapable to inherit land in Scotland, 351.
Alii per alium non acquiritur obligatio, 319.
Alii per alium non acquiritur exceptio, 329.
Ambiguity in the words of a deed or covenant, 133. In the words of a statute, 235.
Apprising. See Adjudication.
Approbate and reprobate, 205.
Arbiter. Arbiters named, without bearing *jointly*, 466.
Arbitrium boni viri, 134, 154.
Arrestee, 391.
Arrestment, what remedy where the debtor is dead, and no person in whose hands to arrest, 282. What claims are preferred before an arrestment, 290. Different kinds of arrestment, 391. Arrestments of debts or moveables, its nature and effect, ib. Arrestment bars not poinding, 394. Arrestment makes a *nexus realis*: this proposition explained, ib. Competition between an arrester and assignee, 396. Intimation of an arrestment, 397. How far arrestment makes the subject litigious, 398. Ranking of arrestments in the case of bankruptcy, 429. Arrestment *jurisdictionis fundandæ gratia*, 286. Arrestment of a delinquent, 475.
Assignment, what right it confers, without intimation, 38. The cautioner paying the debt is entitled to an assignment, 74. Secondary creditor entitled to an assignment from the catholic creditor, 78. An assignment of a debt implies a conveyance of what execution is done upon it, 156. Effect of an assignment intimated, 262. Assignment originally but a procuratory *in rem suam*, now a *cessio in jure*, 263. Assignment by a foreign creditor, 504. Cedent's oath not good against the assignee, 507.

B

Bankrupt. An insolvent person, purchasing goods, without having a prospect of making payment, 290. Powers of a court of equity with relation to bankrupts, 406. *Curator bonis*, in the case of bankruptcy, 414. Disposition *omnium bonorum* by a

INDEX.

bankrupt to trustees for his creditors, 359. Statutes of bankruptcy in England, what effect they have here, 513. A reduction upon the head of bankruptcy, whether good against purchasers, 446. Bankrupt-statute 1772, 451.

Barbarius Philippus, 353.

Bargain of hazard with a young heir, 53. Inequality not regarded *inter majores, scientes, et prudentes*, 66. But redressed where made with one weak or facile, ib.

Bastard, has not the privilege of making a testament, 497.

Beneficium competentiæ, 295.

Benevolence as a virtue distinguished from benevolence as a duty, 71. In the progress of society, benevolence becomes a duty in many cases formerly disregarded, 6. Duty of benevolence, how limited, 71. Duty of benevolence to children, ib. Connections that make benevolence a duty, when not prejudicial to our interest, 74. Connections that make benevolence a duty even against our interest, 89.

Bona fide purchaser, 306.

Bona fide possessor *rei alienæ*, has a claim for meliorations, 94, 378. Is not accountable for the rents levied and consumed by him, 350, 368; unless he be *locupletior*, 372. Will rents levied by the *bona fide* possessor impute in payment of a debt due to him, 373.

Bona fides. How far *bona fide* transactions with a putative proprietor are supported in equity, 349. How far the acts of a purative judge or magistrate are supported in equity, ib.

Bona fides contractûs, 219.

Bona fide payment, 347.

Bond secluding executors, by what legal execution it is attachable, 281. Bond of provision, cannot be claimed if the child die before the term of payment, 384. Rigorous and oppressive conditions in a bond of borrowed money, 45.

Bonos mores. Acts *contra bonos moros* repressed by equity, 12, 331.

Book. Exclusive privilege of printing books given to their authors and their assigns, 228.

Bribery in elections, 311.

Brieve, 94.

Burden. A sum with which a disposition of land is burdened, by what legal execution it is attachable, 281.

C

Catholic creditor, his duty with respect to the secondary creditors, 80. Catholic creditor purchasing one of the secondary debts, 82.

Cautioner, making payment, is entitled to have an assignment, from the creditor, 74. In what terms ought this assignment to be granted, 77. Mutual relief between co-cautioners, 76. How far is a cautioner bound to communicate eases, 106.

2 L

INDEX.

Cess, is *debitum fructuum*, 86.

Cessio bonorum, 296.

Chance disgustful, 94.

Charity, why it is not supported by law, 15.

Children. Duty of parents to children, how far extended, 71.

Citation, at the market-cross of Edinburgh, pier and shore of Leith, 284. Citation at the head borough, when the debtor cannot be found, 286.

College of justice, its members prohibited to purchase law-suits, under a penalty, 228.

Combinations, unlawful, 336.

Common law, 1. Common law farther extended in Scotland than in England, 5. Whether common law and equity ought to be committed to the same court, 18. A court of common law cannot decree specific performance of a covenant, 208. Limited nature of a court of common law, 220, 284. Powers of a court of common law with respect to statutes, 224, 231. Limitation of common law with respect to covenants, 317. Common law strictly territorial, 482.

Commissioners of bankruptcy, 416.

Compensation, its equitable foundation, 7. Injustice of common law with respect to compensation, 258. Equitable rules with respect to compensation, ib. Whether compensation be good against an assignee, 262.

Competition between two assignees to the same debt, 103, 504. Between a reduction upon the head of fraud and an arrestment, 289. Between a purchaser by a minute of sale and an adjudger, 291. Between an arrester and an assignee, 396. Competition among powers and faculties. See the chapter, Powers and Faculties.

Condictio ob injustam causam, 53.

Condictio indebiti, 200.

Condictio causa data, causa non secuta, 131.

Condictio ex pœnitentia, ib.

Condition. Conditional bonds and grants, 149. Conditions distinguished into suspensive and resolutive, ib. Implied condition. See Implied.

Connections that make benevolence a duty, when not prejudicial to our interest, 74. Connections that make benevolence a duty even against our interest, 89. Connections that entitle a man to have his loss made up out of my gain, 90. Connections that entitle a man who is not a loser to partake of my gain, 109. Connections that entitle one, who is a loser to a recompence from one who is not a gainer, 116. What connections ought to be disinterested, 334,

Consensual penalty in a bond of borrowed money, 381.

Consequential damage, 63. Who liable for consequential damage, 64.

Constable and Marischal Court, instituted for foreign matters, 483.

Contracts *bona fide* and *stricti juris*, defined, 129. See Covenant.

INDEX.

Conveyance. Difference between a voluntary and legal conveyance, 513.

Correctory statutes, whether they can be extended by the Court of Session, 356.

Correi debendi, 78.

Costs of suit, upon what principle founded, 382.

Court of equity distinguished from a court of common law, 2. Jurisdiction of courts of common law, ib. Court of equity must be governed by general rules, 12, 48, 73, 364. Whether the same court ought to judge both of equity and of common law, 17. Powers of a court of equity with respect to a deed or covenant, where writing is an essential solemnity, 141. A court of equity cannot overturn law, 142. Powers of a court of equity with respect to statutes, 220. Its powers with respect to matters of utility, 333. A court of equity cannot overturn a statute; but is not bound by any argument drawn from a statute, 246. Has power to extend statutes that are preventive of wrong, 355. Has power to prevent harm even to a single person, 353.

Court of Chancery, 3.

Court of Justiciary, its jurisdiction, 491.

Court of law. To make effectual an unlawful act is inconsistent with the nature of a court of law, 229, 282, 330. Courts of law were originally confined to pecuniary matters, 315. Promises and covenants were not regarded originally in courts of law, 318. Jurisdiction of courts of law, 482.

Court of Session is a court of equity as well as of common law, 21, 49. Was originally considered as a court of common law only, 419. Various executions, unknown in common law, introduced by the Court of Session, 281. Is the proper court for matters that are not pecuniary, 314. Trust-rights appropriated to the Court of Session, 324. Is a court of review with respect to matters of police, 341. By what power doth this court name factors for infants who are destitute of tutors; and give authority for selling the land-estate of a person under age, 353. Privilege of this court to make acts of sederunt, 420. Cannot alter a writ of the common law, 401. Jurisdiction of the Court of Session with respect to foreign matters, 480. Its different jurisdictions, 485.

Courtesy. A tenant by courtesy is bound to extinguish the current burdens, 86.

Covenant defined, 126. Words in a covenant how interpreted. See Words. Was not enforced by an action in our law, 3, 319. Equity with respect to covenants, 9. Use of covenants, 126. A covenant implies two persons, ib. Is a mean employed to bring about some end or event, 128. Where a covenant tends not to bring about the purposed end, 168. Equity with respect to a deed providing for an event that now can never happen, 177. Where there is a failure in performance, 208. Specific performance, ib. Where the failure is partial, 214. Indirect means employed to evade performance, 219. In what cove-

INDEX.

nants is repentance permitted, 131. A covenant occasioned by error, 178. *Lesio ultra duplum*, 183. Covenant in favour of third person, 316.

Creditor taking benefit beyond the interest of the money lent, 63. Creditor obtaining payment from the cautioner must assign, 74. In what terms ought this assignment to be granted, ib. Mutual duties between creditors secured upon the same subject, 80. See Catholic creditor. Creditors of the predecessor preferred before those of the heir, 241. Creditors ought to have the benefit of every privilege competent to their debtor, in order to make their claims effectual, ib. 282. Creditor ought to abstain from attaching by legal execution a subject that the debtor stands bound to make over to another, 290. In England, the heir is not liable to the personal creditors, nor the executor to the real creditors, 285.

Crime committed abroad, 491.

Cujus commodum ejus debet esse incommodum, 188, 210.

Curators, what if some refuse to accept, or die after acceptance, 467. A foreigner may be a curator, 490.

Curator bonis, in the case of bankruptcy, 414.

Curator bonorum, 12.

Curtesy. See Courtesy.

D

Damage occasioned by a fault without intention to do mischief, 41. How far a man is liable for damage done by his servants and cattle, ib. Damage distinguished into direct and consequential, 62. In estimating damage arising from a culpable act, power of a court of equity, 63. Is there room for *pretium affectionis*, 65. *Loco facti impraxtabilis succedit damnum et interesse*, 211. Whether in awarding damages from breach of contract there be any difference between a court of equity and of common law, ib. What damage is a creditor entitled to upon the escape of his debtor from prison, 212. Damage against a messenger who neglects to put a caption in execution, ib. Damage from failing to obey a statute, 224. Damage from transgressing a prohibitory statute, ib.

Deathbed. Reduction upon that head, in what manner attachable by creditors, 282. In what cases can a reserved power of faculty be exercised on deathbed, 462.

Debitor non præsumitur donare, 137.

Debts, by what law regulated, 320.

Deceit, 56. Deceit distinguished from fraud, 57. Examples of deceit, ib.

Declarator of expiry of the legal, its nature and effect, 246.

Declaratory Adjudication, 286.

Decreet-arbitral, how far supported in equity against legal objections, 202. Decreet-arbitral *ultra vires*, 203. Objections against a decreet-arbitral, 238.

Decreet of mails and duties, 390.

INDEX.

Deed, is of two kinds, 123. A deed is a mean employed to bring about some end or event, ib. Implied will in a deed, 154. Where a deed tends not to bring about the purposed end, 168. Where an event happens, which, had it been foreseen, would have prevented the deed from being made, 177. Where the intendment of the granter is clear, the deed will be supported in equity against defects in form, 165. Deed *ultra vires*, 201. A deed occasioned by error, 179.

Delivery. Subjects are transferred from the dead to the living without delivery, 325, 387.

Dies cedit etsi non venerit, 387.

Dies incertus conditionem in testamento facit, 388.

Dies nec cedit nec venit, ib.

Discharge. In a discharge of a debt, accessories are understood to be comprehended, 157.

Disposition *omnium bonorum* to trustees for behoof of creditors. See Bankrupt.

Donatio inter virum et uxorem, 108.

Donatio mortis causâ, 177.

E

Ease. Who are bound to communicate eases, 103, 104.

Electio est debitoris, 265.

Elegit, resembles an adjudication, 286.

Entail. A tenant in tail bound to extinguish the annual burdens arising during his possession, 85. The rents of an entailed estate are the property of the heir in possession, no less than if it were a fee-simple, 86. Irritancies in an entail, 148. Notwithstanding clauses irritant and resolutive, the full property is in the tenant in tail, 235. An entail is of the nature of a fidei-commissary settlement, ib. Whether an entail, after being completed by infeftment, can be altered or annulled, ib. What right is acquired to the substitutes in an entail, ib.

Equity. Difference between law and equity, 1, 4. No precise boundaries between common law and equity, 5, 324. Progress of equity, 5, 10. Acts *contra bones mores* repressed by equity, 11, 330. A court of equity ought to be governed by general rules, 13. He who demands equity must give equity, 48. One cannot claim equity who suffers by his own fault, 101. Equity with respect to a deed or covenant, where writing is an essential solemnity, 141. Equity yields to utility, 361. Equity with respect to compensation, 260. Equity with respect to indefinite payment, 265. Equity with respect to indefinite intromission, 272. Equity with respect to legal execution, 280, 290. Equitable title, 504.

Equity of redemption with respect to wadset, 46. Why there is not the same equity with respect to an adjudication after the legal is expired, 244. No equity of redemption with respect to a poinding, ib.

Erroneous payment, 197, 317.

INDEX.

Error. How far one is permitted to take advantage of another's error, 92, 181, 296. A deed occasioned by error, 179. Error in a contract of sale, 182. Error *in-substantialibus*, 188.

Eviction, 116, 183.

Evidence. Equity with regard to evidence, 255. Evidence of fraud in the case of bankruptcy, 420, 433.

Exceptio doli mali, 277.

Exceptio rei judicatæ, 516.

Exceptions, intrinsic and extrinsic, 297.

Execution. Imperfections of common law with respect to legal execution, 280. Injustice of common law with respect to legal execution, 289. Legal execution is of three kinds, 389. The creditor's privilege to attach any particular subject for his payment, and the debtor's obligation to surrender that subject to his creditor, make the foundation of execution, 394. No subject ought to be attached by execution that the debtor is bound to convey to another, 289.

Executor may pay himself at short hand, without a decreet, 273. Next of kin preferred before the creditors of the executor, 293. Nomination of executor by will sustained in every country, 497, 502. In England, the executor not liable for real debts, 285.

Expence, laid out by one upon a common subject, 112. Liquidate expences in case of failzie, 380. Expences of process, who liable for them, 382.

Extortion, in a bond of borrowed money, 45. In a contract of marriage, 49. In other matters, 53.

Extract of a decree implies a passing from any claim for costs of suit, 157.

Extrinsic exception or objection, 297.

F.

Facility and lesion, 67.

Factor. Constituent preferred before the creditors of the factor, 291. Factor applying his constituent's money to purchase goods in his own name, 291. Factors prohibited from purchasing their constituent's debts, 335.

Factum infectum fieri nequit, 62.

Faculty. Powers and faculties, 451.

Feu-duties, are *debita fructuum*, 85.

Fideicommissum. Nature of fideicommissary settlements among the Romans, 322.

Fieri facias. Is not a good title for demanding payment of a debt in Scotland, 524.

Foreign. The King and council originally was the only court for foreign matters, 482. In Scotland foreign matters are appropriated to the Court of Session ; in England, to the courts of common law, 483. Personal actions founded on foreign covenants, deeds, or facts, 487. In a pursuit upon a foreign bond, what interest ought to be awarded, 488. A foreigner may be

INDEX.

chosen a curator, 490. A crime committed in a foreign country cannot be tried in Scotland, ib. Reparation arising from a foreign delinquency, 491. Foreign covenants and deeds respecting land, ib. Moveables domestic and foreign, 301. Foreign covenants and deeds respecting debts, 500. Foreign evidence, 505. Foreign writs, how far a good title to sue in this country, 508. Foreign bond, with a clause for registration in Scotland, ib. Foreign statutes, 508. Foreign prescription, ib. Statutes of bankruptcy in England, 513. Foreign decrees, 516.

Formulæ actionum, 95.

Forthcoming. Process for making moveables forthcoming, its nature and effect, 389. Decreet of forthcoming is a security only, not payment, 390.

Fraud, 56. A covenant procured by fraud will be set aside, 57. Fraud distinguished from deceit, 58. How far the maxim obtains, *Quod nemo debet locupletari aliena jactura*, in the case of a fraud, 107. *Fraus facta contractui*, 219. Fraudulent purchase of goods where the purchaser has no prospect of making payment, 290.

Freight due *pro rata itineris*, 215.

Fructus percepti et pendentes, 370.

Frustra petis quod mox es restituturus, 348.

Furnishers, have they any preference upon the house they contributed to raise, 99.

· G

Gaming, laws prohibiting, extended by a court of equity, 354

Guardian, not entitled to any recompence for his labour, 331.

Gift of marriage or of ward taken for the superior's behoof, 115.

Glebe. Is the present minister liable for the expence of meliorations laid out by his predecessor, 112.

Government. Duty of submitting to a regular government, upon what founded, 221.

Gratitude, is a duty in the *actio negotiorum gestorum*, 118. Punishment of ingratitude, 284, 302.

H

Harmony between our internal and external constitution, 94.

Harm done in exercising a right or privilege, 29.

Hazard, bargain of, 54.

Heir, bound to communicate eases, 104. An heir who serves while there is a nearer heir in possibility, is only a conditional proprietor, 352. An heir *cum beneficio* entitled to sell the estate, 241. Heir-apparent acquiring right to debts due by his predecessor, 243. What privileges descend to heirs, 327. Is an heir liable for the debts of the interjected apparent heir, when he possesses only without infeftment, 356. What obligations transmit to heirs, 384. Every obligation transmits to the heir when his predecessor survives the term of payment, 385. The heir

INDEX.

liable to fulfil the will and purpose of his predecessor, 454. The heir in England not liable to the personal creditors, 285.

Horning, charge of, makes not the subject litigious, 396.

I

Jailor, how far liable when he suffers a prisoner to escape, 212.

Imbecility, 66.

Implied will explained, 154.

Indefinite intromission, injustice of common law with respect to it, 272.

Indefinite payment, injustice of common law with respect to it, 265.

Inferior courts, confined to common law, 21. Competent to an action for recompence, and to the *actio negotiorum gestorum*, 22.

Ingratitude. See Gratitude.

Inhibition, its nature and effect, 400.

Insurance. Policy of insurance affords not an action at common law, 213.

Intention is what determines an action to be right or wrong, 36, 108.

Interdiction, 399.

Interest. The pursuer must show an interest, otherwise his process will not be sustained, 37.

Interest, in a pursuit upon a foreign bond, what interest ought to be awarded, 488.

Intimation of an assignment, 38. Of an arrestment, 488.

Intrinsic exception or objection, 297.

Irritancy in a bond of borrowed money, 45. Irritancies in entails voiding the contravener's right *ipso facto*, 148. Irritancy *ob non solutum canonem*, 150, 235.

Jurisdiction with respect to foreign matters, 480. A crime committed in a foreign country cannot be tried in Scotland, 490. Jurisdiction of the Court of Justiciary, ib. Jurisdiction of the Court of Session; see *Court of Session*. Jurisdiction of courts of law, 491.

Jus quæsitum tertio, 321. What right is acquired to the substitute in an entail, 327.

K

King and council originally the supreme court, 2.

L

Latent insufficiency of goods purchased, 147. What if the goods be delivered and the property transferred, 175.

Latter-will defined, 126.

Laws. Every voluntary transgression of municipal law is a moral wrong, 220, 508. Laws originally personal without regard to place, became territorial without regard to persons, 480.

INDEX.

Laws have no authority *extra territorium*, 481. What matters are regulated by municipal law, 480.

Lease. A lease of land must imply a power to remove tenants, 154. How far sterility will relieve against the tack duty, 216.

Lectus ægritudinis, 69.

Legacy. A verbal legacy may be proved by witnesses to the extent of £100, 203. Different kinds of legacies, 324. What action competent for making them effectual, ib. In what cases legacies transmit to heirs, 388.

Legal execution. See *Execution*.

Legatum rei alienæ, 168.

Legitimation, 489.

Lesion, 66. *Læsio ultra duplum*, 167, 182, 363.

Lessee, what claim he has for meliorations, 113.

Letters of administration in England, not a good title here, 496.

Levari facies, 390.

Lex Aquilia, 39.

Lex commissaria in pignoribus 45, 248.

Lex Rhodia de jactu, its equitable foundation, 6, 119. Whether the goods saved ought to contribute according to their weight, or according to their value, 120.

Liberty of the subject, 337.

Liquidate expences in case of failzie. See *Expence*.

Litigious. Inchoated execution renders the subject litigious, 307, 395, 397. A subject is not rendered litigious with respect to third parties, unless there be a public notification, 398.

Locus pœnitentiæ, 132.

Lunatic. Guardian to a lunatic, 490. Named by the Chancellor in England, is not entitled to sue for debts in Scotland, 506.

Lyon Court, 316.

M

Magisterial powers of the Court of Session, 353.

Magistrate acting *extra territorium* 474.

Malevolence, 36.

Man. His internal constitution adapted to his external circumstances, 92.

Mails and duties, process of, its nature and tendency, 390.

March-fence, a neighbour who takes the benefit of it not liable for a recompence, 114.

Marriage, celebrated according to the *lex loci*, 490.

Meditatio fugæ, 289.

Meliorations. What claim a lessee has for meliorations, 111.

Members of the College of Justice discharged to purchase a subject controverted in a law-suit, 229.

Messenger, how far liable, when he neglects to put a caption in execution, 212.

Minority, is excepted from the prescription of forty years, 252.

Minority and lesion, 67. Reduction upon this head, how attachable by creditors, 282.

2 M

INDEX.

Minute of sale of land, in what manner attachable by creditors, 283.

Missio in possessionem, in the case of bankruptcy, 414.

Mobilia non habent sequelam, 430.

Monopoly of printing certain books, 229. Monopoly repugnant to the public interest, 341. Statutes introducing monopolies, cannot be extended by the Court of Session, 361.

Mora in performing a covenant, 208.

Moveables have a local situation, 495. Moveables permanent and transient, 497. Moveables domestic and foreign, 495.

Municipal law. See *Law.* What matters are regulated by municipal law, 492, 494.

N

Negative prescription. See *Prescription.*

Ne immittas in alienum, 32.

Neighbourhood, how far it bars a man from exercising his property, ib.

Nemo debet locupletari alienâ jacturâ, analyzed, 92, 215, 372, 411, 412, 440.

Nexus realis. See *Arrestment.*

Notary signing for a party, 202.

Nuisance, 32.

Noncupative testament or legacy, may be proved by witnesses, to the extent of £100, 203.

O

Objection, extrinsic and intrinsic, 296.

Obligation *ad factum praestandum*, 214. What obligations transmit to heirs, 384. What if the creditor survive the term of payment, 385.

Objection personal. See *Personal objection.*

Obligor and obligee, defined, 127. Obligor may be bound without an obligee, 317.

Occasional benefit affords not any claim against the person benefited, 113.

Offer defined, 127.

Officer. Power that officers of the law have to act *extra territorium*, 473.

P

Pactum contra bonos mores, 11. *Contra utilitatem publicam*, 335. *Pactum contra fidem tabularum nuptialum*, 50. *Pactum liberatorium*, 329. Must be effectual even in a court of common law, 330. *Pacta illicita*, 331, 334. *Pactum de quota litis*, for what reason prohibited, 12, 335.

Parent. Duty of parents to children, how far extended, 71.

Payment. A debtor, who knows privately of an assignment, making payment to the cedent, 37. Erroneous payment, 197.

INDEX.

Indefinate payment, 265. Payment made by a third person, without a mandate from the debtor, 329. *Boná fide* payment, 405. Payment analyzed, 375. Payment of money in England, how proved, 507.

Penalty. Penal clauses in a bond of borrowed money, 45. A court can order a thing to be done under a penalty, 226, 316. Statutory prohibitions under a penalty, 227. Whether it be in the power of a judge to inflict any penalty beyond what is enacted, 228. A penalty cannot be extended beyond the words, but it may be limited within the words, 313. *Bona fides* with respect to penalties, ib. A penal statute cannot be extended by the Court of Session, 361. Powers of a court of equity with respect to conventional penalties, 378.

Personal objection, 227, 303, 306, 309.

Pignus prætorium, 297.

Pleas of the Crown, 2.

Pluris petitio, what effect it has with respect to legal execution, 296.

Poinding, nature of this execution, 389, 390. Whether barred by an arrestment, 392, 396. Competition of a poinder with an assignee, 403. Admits not an equity of redemption, 244. Effects *extra territorium* not carried by a poinding, 524.

Police, 341.

Policy of Insurance, affords not an action at common law, 212. Where fraudulent, is set aside by a court of equity, 57.

Popular action, 237.

Positive prescription. See Prescription.

Positus in conditione non censetur positus in institutione, 157.

Possession, retention of, till debts due to the possessor be paid, 345.

Potior est conditio possidentis, 231.

Powers and faculties, 450. Powers given to a plurality, 465. Power to act jointly, 466. To act *extra territorium,* 473.

Pretium affectionis, 65.

Prescription. Positive prescription protects not against burdens that naturally affect property, 35. Prescription of penal actions, 237. Runs not against persons under age, 252. Triennial prescription, 254. English prescription of six years, 252. What effect it has in this country, 510. The statute 1617, introducing the positive prescription, explained, 355. Extended to similar cases by the Court of Session, 356. The statutes introducing the negative prescription of forty years extended, ib.

Prior tempore potior jure, ib.

Privileges, how attachable by creditors, 281.

Process, for payment before the term of payment, 282. Of forthcoming before the term of payment, 284. Of poinding the ground before the term of payment, ib. Process of forthcoming. See Forthcoming.

Procuratory *in rem suam,* 263.

Promise defined, 127. How far binding by the law of nature, 316. A promise to give a man a sum not to rob me, is not

INDEX.

binding, 58. Advantage of promises, 126. A promise implies two persons, an obligar and obligee, 127. Promise in favour of a third person, 317. Imperfection of common law with respect to promises, 318.

Property. A man ought not to exercise his property *in aemulationem vicini*, 36, 89. He may fence his bank against the encroachments of a river, 29. Must not throw any thing into a neighbouring field that may do mischief, 30. How far the use of a river may be intercepted from inferior proprietors, ib. Mutual duties between conterminous land proprietors, 87. In what cases law permits me to act within my neighbour's property, ib. No man can be deprived of his property, who is guilty of no fault, 294, 308, 398, 403, 410, 425. Though the transference of property be ruled by the will of the vender, it depends on the will of the purchaser, whether to accept delivery for his own behoof, or for behoof of another, 292. Property transferred from the dead to the living, without delivery, 326, 887.

Proprietor. Transactions with a putative proprietor, how far good in equity, 350.

Punishment. An act without intention to do mischief, is not the subject of punishment, 40. The transgression of a prohibitory statute may be punished by a court of common law, 227. Powers of a court of equity with respect to punishment, 302. The proper place of punishment is where the crime was committed, 491.

Pupil. The sale of a pupil's lands for payment of debt, 12, 353.

Purchase. It is fraudulent to purchase without a prospect of making payment, 58. Purchaser not bound to receive the subject if insufficient, 174. But after it is delivered to him he has no remedy, 175. Effect of a purchase made *bona fide*, 307. Effect of a purchase made with the knowledge of a prior right, 306. Effect of a purchase made with the knowlege of execution inchoated upon the subject purchased, 308. A creditor accepting a security upon a subject which he knows was formerly disponed to another, 308.

Putative proprietor, 353.

Q

Quæstio voluntatis, 138.
Quasi contracts explained, 118, 221.
Quorum of curators, 468. Of tutors, 470.

R

Ransom. Where a ship is ransomed, who are liable for the ransom, 99, 120. What if the cargo be lost after it is ransomed, ib.

Reasons. Instances of inept reasoning, 311.

Recompence, 117. A person who benefits another without hurt-

INDEX.

ing himself has no claim for a recompence, 113. A person is not liable who takes the benefit of a march-fence made by his neighbour, 114.

Redemption. Equity of redemption with respect to a wadset, 243. Whether there ought not to be the same equity with respect to an adjudication after the legal is expired, 248.

Relief. Mutual relief between co-cautioners, 76.

Rem versum, 96, 372.

Rent-charge, 455.

Reparation to those who are hurt in their rights or privileges. 62. There can be no claim for reparation if the action was innocent, whatever be the mischief, 371, 381. In what cases a man is liable for reparation where he acts in prosecuting a right or privilege, 29. In what cases when he acts without having in view to prosecute a right or privilege, 39. How far is reparation extended at common law, 40. Who are liable to repair consequential damage, 63.

Repentance, in what covenants permitted, 131.

Representation in moveables, 505.

Resignation, made by one who hath no right, but having the proprietor's consent, 452.

Res judicata pro veritate habetur, 517.

Retention, its equitable foundation, 344, 363. Retention of possession till every debt due to the possessor be satisfied, 346.

Reversion, by what legal execution it is attachable, 281.

Right. Why equitable rights are reckoned less steady and permanent than those of common law, 16. In exercising a right the harming others must be avoided, 29. A right exercised intentionally to hurt others, 37.

Rigorous conditions in a bond of borrowed money, 45, 48.

River, how far the use of it can be intercepted from inferior proprietors, 33.

S

Sale. A power of redemption in a bargain of sale within a limited time cannot be extended in equity, 47. Sale of an infant's estate, *sine decreto*, 354.

Salvage. The foundation of this claim, 4. Who liable for salvage, 112, 418.

Satum solo cedit solo, 371.

Sequestration, 391.

Sine qua non in a nomination of tutors and curators, 460.

Smuggling prohibited goods, a crime against the law of nature, 223, 231.

Society. Unlawful societies, 335.

Solatium. Reparation *in solatium*, 305.

Solutio indebiti, 197.

Specific performance of a covenant, 208.

Sponsio ludicra, 22.

Statute. Statutes are binding in conscience, 220, &c. Statutes

INDEX.

distinguished into different kinds, 224. Statutes prohibitory without being enforced by a penalty, 225. Neglect in obeying a compulsory statute how redressed, ib. A statute that gives remedy for a wrong shall be taken by equity, 235. What is the remedy where the will of the legislature is not rightly expressed in the statute, 236. Where the means enacted fall short of the end purposed by the legislature, 239. Where the means enacted reach unwarily beyond the end purposed by the legislature, 250. Statute of limitation in England, 253. Statutes preventive of wrong extended by a court of equity, 355.

Stellionate, 305.

Sterility, how far it will relieve from paying tack-duty, 216.

Subjects that cannot be attached by execution at common law, 281.

Submission, 218.

Substitute in an entail. See Entail.

Superior, acquiring right to the gift of his own ward, is bound to communicate the same to his vassals, 115. The same as to a gift of marriage, 116.

Surrogatum, 293.

Suspension. In what cases is compensation a ground of suspension, 260.

T

Tack. See Lease.

Teinds are *debita fructuum*, 85.

Tenant in tail, bound to extinguish the annual burdens arising during his possession, ib.

Territorium, power to act *extra territorium*, 473.

Testament, 127.

Title. It is *pars judicis* to deny action where the title is imperfect, 279. What effect an equitable title has in a competition, 595.

Town. How far neighbourhood in a town bars a man from exercising his property, 32.

Transaction. Error in a transaction, 181. Inequality not regarded in a transaction, 182, 365.

Transient moveables, 498.

Triennial prescription, 254.

Trust-right, nature and effect of, 286, 325. Trustee prohibited to make profit, 334.

Turpis causa, 170. *In turpi causa potior est conditio possidentis*, 305.

Tutor, how far, by converting moveable debts into heritable, or, *è contra*, he can regulate his pupil's possession, 108. In what cases death or non-acceptance voids a nomination of tutors, 467. A tutor barred from making any profit to himself in managing his pupil's affairs, 334. Selling his pupil's land *sine decreto*, 353.

INDEX.

U.

Usucapio. The Roman *usucapio* differs from our positive prescription of forty years, 355.
Usury prohibited under a penalty, 228. The most lucrative wadset is not usury, 49. Laws prohibiting usury may be extended by a court of equity, 355.
Utility, 11. Equity yields to it, 362. Matters of utility belong to the court of equity, 333. Acts and covenants repressed as *contra utilitatem publicam*, &c. 336. Opposed to equity, 363.
Utilis actio, 323.

V

Vassal, may claim the benefit of a gift of the superior's ward, when taken for the superior's behoof, 114. The same as to a gift of marriage, 115.
Vergens ad inopiam, 284.
Vicious intromission, 524.
Vigilantibus non dormientibus jura subveniunt, 408.
Violent profits, 64.

W

Wadset, where the power of redemption is limited within a certain time, 45. Even the most lucrative wadset is not usury, 49. Nor can it be reformed by equity, ib.
Wager. Whether a wager ought to be enforced by an action at law, 21.
Wages. Mariners' wages due *pro rata itineris*, 215.
Ward. See Gift of Ward.
Warrandice, how far extended, 116. Warrandice in a sale of land, 185. In the conveyance of claims or debts, 190.
Will. In what cases will has the effect to transfer property without delivery, 325, 387. A man's will ought to bind his heir, 453. Implied will. See Implied.
Witness. Payment of money may in England be proved by witnesses, 507.
Words. Where the words of a deed or covenant are imperfect, what remedy there is in equity, 132. Words cannot bind without consent, 143. Defective words cannot be supplied where the writing is an essential solemnity, ib. Where the words of a statute are imperfect, 235. Words the best evidence of will, but not the only evidence, 133.
Writ, defective as not being duly signed by notaries, supported to the extent of £100, 202. Cases where writ is an essential solemnity, 141.

CPSIA information can be obtained
at www.ICGtesting.com
Printed in the USA
BVOW06*1251021117
499360BV00011B/196/P